Michael Polanyi

Michael Polanyi

Scientist and Philosopher

WILLIAM TAUSSIG SCOTT

AND MARTIN X. MOLESKI, S.J.

OXFORD

UNIVERSITY PRESS

2005

OXFORD
UNIVERSITY PRESS

Oxford University Press, Inc., publishes works that further
Oxford University's objective of excellence
in research, scholarship, and education.

Oxford   New York
Auckland   Cape Town   Dar es Salaam   Hong Kong   Karachi
Kuala Lumpur   Madrid   Melbourne   Mexico City   Nairobi
New Delhi   Shanghai   Taipei   Toronto

With offices in
Argentina   Austria   Brazil   Chile   Czech Republic   France   Greece
Guatemala   Hungary   Italy   Japan   Poland   Portugal   Singapore
South Korea   Switzerland   Thailand   Turkey   Ukraine   Vietnam

Published by Oxford University Press, Inc.
198 Madison Avenue, New York, New York 10016

www.oup.com

Oxford is a registered trademark of Oxford University Press

Library of Congress Cataloging-in-Publication Data
Scott, William T. (William Taussig), 1916–1999
Michael Polanyi : scientist and philosopher / William Taussig Scott
and Martin X. Moleski.
p. cm.
Includes bibliographical references and index.
ISBN-13 978-0-19-517433-5
ISBN 0-19-517433-X
1. Polanyi, Michael, 1891– I. Moleski, Martin X., 1952–
II. Title.
B945.P584S365 2004
192—dc22 2004010795

9 8 7 6 5 4 3 2 1

Printed in the United States of America
on acid-free paper

To Bill's wife, Ann Herbert Scott,
and the Scott children,
Jennifer, Stephanie, Melanie,
Pete, Kate,
and to Christopher and his widow,
Carol

Preface

Martin X. Moleski, S.J.

Michael Polanyi was a restless man. His determination to grasp the basic processes of life drove him from the study of medicine to research in physical chemistry, economics, social and political analysis, philosophy, theology, and aesthetics. Born to a family of non-observant Jews, he was baptized Catholic as a young adult, but was married in a civil ceremony and later endorsed Protestantism. When he moved from Hungary to Germany, he did so as an Austrian citizen; driven out of Germany by the rise of the National Socialists, he took England as his new home, then spent his last years traveling the world to share his prophetic vision of the strengths and weaknesses of Western civilization.

Polanyi saw the corruption of European civilization stemming from a loss of faith. He hoped his work in philosophy would "restore to us once more the power for the deliberate holding of unproven beliefs" (PK, 268). After a fruitful career in physical chemistry, he dedicated the last three decades of his life to a defense of faith. In every field to which he turned his attention, he was "guided by a sense of obligation towards the truth: by an effort to submit to reality" (63). Even as his intellectual powers faded late in life, Polanyi kept struggling to clarify and communicate his conviction that the liberal tradition had become poisoned by a false ideal of reason and that the antidote lay in understanding and affirming the tacit dimension of personal knowledge.

Bill Scott was a theoretical physicist with a profound interest in philosophy; one of his special interests was the study of how water coalesces to form droplets within clouds. He authored a textbook on electromagnetism[1] and an intellectual biography of Erwin Schrödinger.[2] Scott made Polanyi's acquaintance in 1959 and stayed in close contact for the last seventeen years of Polanyi's life. They communicated both by letter and in person, spending time together on both sides of the Atlantic. In 1969–1970, Scott took a full year to study science and philosophy at Oxford under Rom Harré, supported by a grant from the National Science Foundation. During that year, he and his wife, Ann, were able to visit regularly with the Polanyis. In 1977, a year after Polanyi's death, Scott began to work on this biography.

Scott worked on the story of Polanyi's life from 1977 to 1994, aided by Ann and by his research assistant, Monika Tobin. His first draft ran to 293,000 words and included detailed summaries of Polanyi's contributions to epistemology, economics, patent law, social and political theory, aesthetics, theology, and six areas of physical chemistry. Because of failing health, he was unable to make the substantial revisions recommended by those who read the manuscript.

My interest in Polanyi dates from my studies in English literature at Boston College in 1971–1973 under the direction of Professor Alan Weinblatt. I came back to Polanyi's writings repeatedly as I continued studies in philosophy at Fordham University and in systematic theology at The Catholic University of America; in my doctoral dissertation, I compared Polanyi's theory of personal knowledge to John Henry Newman's understanding of "the grammar of assent."[3] I made the acquaintance of the Scotts through the Polanyi Society and, in 1991, I was privileged to hear Scott present a synopsis of this book at the Kent State conference honoring the centennial of Polanyi's birth.[4] It was an impressive and memorable performance, but even then Scott was succumbing to the complex of illnesses that prevented him from finishing the story of his friend's life and work. Scott died on February 22, 1999, the twenty-third anniversary of Polanyi's death.

In 1997, Ann Scott, acting on behalf of her husband, named me coauthor so that I might have a free hand to revise the manuscript. The book placed before you is not the book that Bill wrote, nor is it the book that I would have written if I had started fresh and worked alone, nor is it the book that would have emerged from a true collaboration between two authors who could fight fairly with each other to achieve a true union of thought. Nevertheless, I hope it will provide a solid foundation for future investigations of Polanyi's life and work.

Bill Scott's acknowledgments detail the extensive research that forms the foundation of this biography. I would like to echo his thanks to all who have contributed to the work, especially to Richard Gelwick, Phil Mullins, Charles McCoy, Robin Hodgkin, Joan Crewdson, Thomas Torrance, Norman Wetherick, Richard Allen, John Puddefoot, Thomas Nickles, Ronald A. Phaneuf, and Mary Kliwer. Monika Tobin worked tirelessly with Bill for seventeen years; she and her husband, Frank, were most gracious to me in my visits to Reno. Ann Scott was a companion to Bill in all of his labors, editing, proof-reading, and shepherding the first draft to completion. The Department of Physics at the University of Nevada at Reno graciously maintained an office to house Bill Scott's research materials for many years after his retirement from the faculty. I am deeply indebted to those who have supported my work on this project: my rectors, James P. Higgins, S.J. and Patrick Lynch, S.J., the Canisius Jesuit Community, the Jesuit community of Campion Hall, Wood-lawn Jesuit Community, Dan and Dale Warner, and Regina Lea Utz. My most substantial revisions were guided in large measure by the criticisms of Robin Hodgkin and Mary Jo Nye. At the 1998 *Appraisal* Conference in Sheffield, England, I had the good fortune to make the acquaintance of Professor Norman Sheppard, FRS, who knew Polanyi personally and who himself is a physical chemist; his very generous, detailed comments have greatly improved our treatment of Polanyi's scientific career. Special thanks to our editors at Oxford University Press, Cynthia Read, Theo Calderara, and Robert Milks.

Michael Polanyi embodied in himself the full scope of the Western liberal tradition. He moved freely from the world of medicine and science to the domain of art and literature. In a single day, he might return from the la-boratory to care for his family, then turn his thoughts to poetry, art, literature, philosophy, politics, or prayer. We cannot trace all of the influence he has had on those who have mined his thought and found inspiration for their own work. We hope that we have been faithful to the richness and complexity of his vision of reality. For those who have read some of Polanyi's work, this book should deepen their understanding of how his work grew out of his personal concerns. For those who have not yet read Polanyi himself, we hope that this book will inspire them to do so. Lao Tzu said that the tao that can be put into words is not the real tao. So, too, the Polanyi we can put into words is not the real Polanyi. He still speaks for himself in what he has written, sharing a vision that words can never completely express.

Acknowledgments

William T. Scott

I am indebted to many persons, libraries, archival collections, and institutions for the resources that have made this book possible.

At the start of my project the American Philosophical Society gave me an immediate grant that enabled me to spend May and June 1978 in Oxford with Magda Polanyi, Michael Polanyi's widow; she, in turn, introduced me to Polanyi's family and friends. Soon afterwards the National Endowment for the Humanities provided me with a major grant (1978–1981), not only to travel and interview but also to hire a research assistant.

After my retirement in 1981, the National Endowment for the Humanities offered a new matching grant award that called for third-party contributions and which extended to August 1985. Of the many individuals and institutions that contributed matching funds I want to especially thank the Max Planck Society for the Advancement of Science of Germany, which enabled me to visit important sites in Berlin and Karlsruhe, the Max Planck Gesellschaft Archives, the Manchester City Library, the John Rylands University Library of Manchester, and the Rockefeller Foundation Archive Center of New York.

The Joseph Regenstein Library of the University of Chicago is the repository of the Polanyi Collection, the most extensive collection of Polanyi's correspondence, notes, manuscripts, and memorabilia. John M. Cash of the Regenstein devised an invaluable guide to these papers which I have consulted throughout my work. The box and folder numbers given in the references refer to Cash's arrangement of the Polanyi papers.

Polanyi's niece, Eva Zeisel, provided hospitality for two of my three sojourns in Chicago and former Regenstein staff member Michael Ryan served as a helpful host to the Collection.

I am also indebted to a number of other archives and libraries: Akademie der Wissenschaft (Göttingen), Center for History of Physics (American Institute of Physics), Bentley Historical Library (University of Michigan), Bodleian Library (Oxford), Butler Library (Columbia University Library), Robert A. Millikan Memorial Library (California Institute of Technology), Duke University Archives, Edinburgh University Library, Imperial College of Science and Technology Archives, Keele University Library, Museum of Modern Art, National Film Archive, Olin Library (Wesleyan University), Österreichisches Staatsarchiv-Kriegsarchiv, Universität Karlsruhe, University of Leeds, Richmond-Manchester University, Seeley G. Mudd Manuscript Library (Princeton University Library), Staatsbibliothek Preussischer Kulturbesitz, University College London, the Weizmann Archives (Rehovot), Zentrales Staatsarchiv (Merseburg), and especially the University of Nevada Library whose staff have often assisted me.

I have received information, reminiscences, and correspondence from a great many people. Crucial to my research was a series of taped interviews, first with Magda Polanyi, then with many of Polanyi's co-workers, family, and friends. I am grateful to each one of the more than 150 people who found time to speak with me on behalf of the project. In addition I consulted approximately the same number of other persons by letter. My appreciation goes to each of them. Polanyi's son, Professor John Polanyi of the University of Toronto, has provided the important bibliography of his father's scientific work. Professor Richard Gelwick of the University of New England, for many years the coordinator of the Polanyi Society, drew up the original bibliography of Polanyi's nonscientific writings with the assistance of a grant from the Pacific School of Religion Library. My own bibliography is based on these two earlier works with some later additions from Professor Thomas Torrance of the University of Edinburgh; I have also made a few additions of my own.

I am grateful to have received collections of Polanyi family correspondence from many individuals. Of these the most encompassing was in the hands of Eva Zeisel; her collection included invaluable early letters that her mother had managed to shepherd through frequent moves during a period when she was keeping one step ahead of the Nazis. This vast collection was put in order by Ersébet Vezér of Budapest and taken to the archives of the National Széchényi Library in that city. Miss Vézer also sorted the collection of correspondence in the hands of another Polanyi niece, Professor Kari Levitt Polanyi of McGill University, putting on microfilm for me 150 pieces of correspondence between her parents, Karl and Ilona Polanyi, and Michael Polanyi. I have also received copies of correspondence from John R. Baker, Angela Blackburn, Olive Davies, Gretl Dentay, Kathleen Farrar, Brian Glover

Gowenlock, Silvia Kind, S. J. Knox, John D. Lewis, Leah Martins, Peter H. Plesch, Erich Schmid, G. M. Schwab, Sir Mark Richmond, Lady Drusilla Scott, Bela Szilard, Ian Stevenson, George Striker, Veronica Wedgwood, and Norman Wetherick.

I intend to donate the collection of taped interviews and their transcriptions, as well as the Polanyi correspondence from individuals, to the Polanyi Collection at the Regenstein Library. It should be noted that much of the earlier correspondence was conducted in Hungarian and German. The late Professor Andrew Halacsy of the University of Nevada did all the translations from the Hungarian, and my research assistant, Monika Tobin, did the translations from the German. One of the many gifts Monika Tobin has brought to the project is her ability to read the almost illegible scrawl in the mass of undated handwritten letters written in German by Polanyi's mother, Cecile Polanyi.

Throughout the long years of my project I have received generous and consistent support from the University of Nevada, Reno. Not only has the university given me two sabbatical leaves, but the Physics Department has provided office space for both me, my research assistant, and our files and, perhaps most precious of all, the assistance of the departmental secretary, Mary Kliwer, who has typed all my correspondence and every last word of my manuscript from the first draft to the final version. For her cheerful dealing with my own terrible handwriting and for her thoughtful and accurate work on innumerable revisions it is difficult to thank Mary Kliwer enough.

Professor Hyung K. Shin, Professor James Hulse, and Professor Tom Nickles, colleagues from the University of Nevada, Reno, have read and helpfully criticized large sections of the manuscript. I have also received detailed and beneficial criticism from my old friend and former editor Leone Stein of Carlsbad, California, who has painstakingly read the entire manuscript. My daughters, Jennifer Scott Lawson, of East Grinstead, England, and Melanie Scott of Reno, have also helped me in numerous ways.

In the last three years, as my own health has diminished, I have received significant assistance from an advisory committee of Polanyi scholars: Professor Richard Gelwick, Professor Walter Gulick of Eastern Montana University, Professor Emeritus Charles McCoy of the Pacific School of Religion, and Professor Phil Mullins of Missouri Western State College. Together they have provided the support in both critical energy and kindly personal concern that has moved the manuscript through the last stages of completion.

Contents

PART IV   Scholar at Large: 1959–1976

A Note on Names

For the sake of simplicity, in telling the story of the Polanyi family, we have tried to use the final English versions of each person's name throughout the narrative. Michael Polanyi was born Mihály Lazar Pollacsek and was nicknamed Misi. The Hungarian spelling of the new surname given to the Pollacsek children includes an accent, Polányi, but the accent is customarily dropped in English; for his Hungarian colleagues, we have kept their accents intact, even though they did not appear in the credits to the scientific articles they wrote in German. Polanyi's mother's name may have been Cecilia or Cecilie; she is also called variously Cecil, Cecile, or Cecil-Mama. His brother Karl was born Karoly. Polanyi's two sons were originally called Georg and Hans rather than George and John. Polanyi's sister Laura is called by her nickname, Mausi, throughout the text. Mausi and Sandor Striker and their children sometimes spelled their name "Stricker." Marika Striker became "Maria" in the United States.

When describing dialogue or correspondence between members of the Polanyi family, we use first names only, for example, "Michael to Mausi" or "Karl to Michael."

Abbreviations

EZC   Eva Zeisel's collection of Polanyi family correspondence and memorabilia.

HON   Letters collected by Hugh O'Neill.

KB   *Knowing and Being*. Edited by Marjorie Grene. Chicago: University of Chicago Press, 1969.

KLP   Letters collected by Kari Levitt-Polanyi.

LL   *The Logic of Liberty: Reflections and Rejoinders*. London: Routledge and Kegan Paul, 1951.

MNG   *Meaning*, coauthored by Harry Prosch. Chicago: University of Chicago Press, 1975.

MPG   Correspondence from the archives of the Max Planck Gesellschaft.

NZL   Correspondence from the archives of the National Szechenyi Library, Budapest.

PK   *Personal Knowledge: Towards a Post-Critical Philosophy*. Chicago: University of Chicago Press, [1958] 1962. "Torchbook Edition," with unique preface—New York: Harper and Row, [1962] 1974.

RFA   Rockefeller Foundation Archive Collection, New York.

RGL   Letters and papers collected by Richard Gelwick.

RPC   Regenstein Library, University of Chicago, Polanyi Collection. Where box and folder numbers are known for materials cited from the Regenstein Archives, they are cited with a colon; for example, box 1, folder 7 is noted as 1:7.

SEP   *Society, Economics and Philosophy: Selected Papers*, edited and introd-
      uced by R. T. Allen. London: Transaction Publishers, 1997.
SFS   *Science, Faith and Society*. Chicago: University of Chicago Press, 1946.
SKL   Letters collected by Sylvia Kind.
SM   *The Study of Man*. Chicago: University of Chicago Press, 1959.
TD   *The Tacit Dimension*. New York: Doubleday and Company, 1966.

PART I

Hungary: 1891–1919

I

Early Years: 1891–1914

Michael Polanyi was born and raised in the middle of the last golden age of European civilization, the great peace that preceded the Great War of 1914. His family and intellectual life were rooted in the Austro-Hungarian Empire. Although he maintained ties with Hungary throughout his life, his career shows that he saw himself above all as a citizen of Europe much more than as a citizen of one nation or another.

Little is known of Polanyi's great-grandfather, Mihály Pollacsek, except that he was born in 1785 in the Carpathian Mountains of Slovakia (part of "greater" Hungary) and was probably descended from Enoch Pollacsek, reputedly the richest man in Slovakia. Mihály Pollacsek and his wife were one of the first Jewish families in Hungary to obtain permission to lease forest lands from the crown, setting up lumber mills in several places late in the eighteenth century. Family legend has it that Pollacsek's wife was asked by the people of their town to bathe on the day the Jewish women used the bath and not when the Christian women bathed. Pollacsek retorted that if they felt that way, he would personally close the bath one day a week and only his wife would use it then.

Polanyi's grandparents, Adolf Pollacsek (b. 1820 in Trsztena in Slovakia) and Sophie Schlesinger (b. 1826 in Dluha), married in about 1846. Adolf was a construction engineer. Sophie's family possessed a large textile mill. She and Adolf inherited control of the Pollacseks' lumber mills. About the year 1860, the couple also took over the management of a flour mill in the northeastern Hungarian provincial capital city of Ungvar, Ruthenia. They negotiated and signed a lease in 1868 that provided for modernizing the mill, including the use of steam for driving power. The enterprise included a distillery for hard liquor, a brewery, and the exclusive franchise for the local sale of beer. The total number of employees was said to have reached a hundred. The lease also included a part of the agricultural land that Adolf's brother Wilhelm had earlier leased in 1864. The combination was a moneymaking enterprise, but Adolf died in 1871, and it was not easy for Sophie to manage the business. In the next twenty years the family fortunes declined from riches to near poverty.

Adolf and Sophie Pollacsek had at least six children. Polanyi's father, Mihály Pollacsek, was born to them on March 21, 1848, in the town of Dluha, in county Arva of Slovakia. Besides Mihály, there were Clementine, Vilma, Therese, Luiza, and Karl (one source lists also Bela, Gisella, and Mathilde), a list of names borrowed from the Habsburgs rather than from the Israelites and Jews of the Hebrew scriptures. The Pollacseks thus produced a plentiful supply of aunts, uncles, and cousins, some of whom intermarried—Therese Pollacsek married her cousin Emil Pollacsek (son of Wilhelm), who spent some time in the United States as an inventor in the field of chemical engineering. Luiza married Gyula Schlesinger, a collateral descendant of Sophie Schlesinger. Particular relatives important to Polanyi were Therese's granddaughter, Eva Carocci; Ervin Szabó, the influential syndicalist and library modernizer, son of Gyula and Luiza Schlesinger; and Karl Pollacsek, the lawyer, and his wife, Irma, who were a constant source of encouragement and help to all of the Polanyi family. Eva Carocci remembers hearing that her great-grandparents had twelve children, who lived in Maramarossziget (now Sighet, Romania) in northeast Hungary when they were young. Most of Adolf and Sophie's brothers and sisters migrated to Budapest as they grew up. About the year 1893, Laura wrote from Budapest to her maternal grandfather, Andreas Wohl, that the whole family, including the small "Misike," had gone to visit Grandmother Sophie and the aunts and uncles and cousins, and had had a glorious four days in the country; there were games for the children, many festivities, and even a formal ball one evening.

Mihály Pollacsek had his early education in Kassa (now Kovice, Slovakia) between Dluha and Ungvar, and his secondary training at the Catholic Theresianum boarding school in Vienna.[1] He was obviously somebody special, for in those days that school was a most unusual place for a Jewish boy. After graduation, he had a year of private studies in Zürich while he did practical office work for an architect. In 1866 he enrolled in the Swiss Federal Institute of Technology in Zürich (Eidgenossische Technische Hochschule). He passed his first year of study, but during his second he began to cut classes and avoid work. He was warned in March 1868, and was discharged in May for lack of diligence, a lack which he more than made up in his later engineering work. The certificate of discharge and his records were sent to the

Technische Hochschule in Stuttgart, Germany. Alumni records show him as having studied at Dresden as well as at Stuttgart.[2]

There are no archives extant in Stuttgart or Dresden, but a poem written for Mihály and Cecile's fifteenth wedding anniversary by their children suggests that Pollacsek may not have gone directly to Germany for study. According to this set of eight verses, he sold possessions to get a ticket home and then joined an acting troupe with which he lived by "taking to the road and posting notices." He studied acting but had "too many problems."[3] It was said in the family that he mumbled his words.

Pollacsek finished his work at Stuttgart and Dresden in 1870 and for the next three years held positions as hydraulic engineer in Ungvar, as section engineer for Danube River control in Pest, an independent city before the 1873 unification with Buda, and as construction engineer with a Vienna building company.[4] In November 1873, he entered the employ of the Swiss National Railway and started work on the design and construction of several railway lines, including the Winterthur-to-Sofungen line, as well as the Seebach-Oerlikon-Zürich line and its extension to Eisenbach. According to unconfirmed family stories, in 1875 he designed the first cog railway up the Rigi peak near Lucerne, the Rigibahn. In 1878, an official of the Swiss railways wrote a testimonial to his creative work, telling of his promotion to the position of independent section chief, and of his being sent on a trip to London and Edinburgh to study British railway practices.[5] He thoroughly enjoyed life in Britain. On return to Zürich he worked out a plan, never realized, for a multilevel, central railroad station in that city.

It was a time of rapid expansion of railroads in Central Europe, two or three decades after the peak of development in England. About fifty privately owned mountain and feeder lines were chartered in Austria between 1880 and 1883. Pollacsek formulated a design for the municipal Stadtbahn in Vienna; although these plans were never carried out, they were consulted by the designers of the Stadtbahn in Berlin. He also was engaged in building collieries and other railroad-related plants. In 1885, Pollacsek held the title of Assistant of the Vienna and City Railway Company.

Sometime in 1889 or 1890, Pollacsek moved from Vienna to Budapest, the capital of Hungary and the largest of the nation's cities; it was one of the great social, industrial, and intellectual centers of the Austro-Hungarian Empire. In the years before the Great War, the artistic, literary, and intellectual life of Budapest was comparable to that of Berlin and Vienna. Pollacsek opened an engineering office in which the largest part of his work was devoted to local Hungarian railroad lines.[6] His last major contract was for the construction of a long railroad line northward from the Danube Valley into what is now Slovakia and Poland. Rising nationalism and social pressure led Pollacsek in 1904 to have his children's surname changed to Polanyi. After her husband's death in 1905, Cecile also used the new surname sporadically. The

Hungarian name "Mihály" is "Michael" in German and English. Until 1904, father and son had the same first and last names, but the younger was distinguished by having been given the middle name Lazar, after Cecile's brother. Once his surname was changed to Polanyi, Michael used his middle name only rarely, and, after World War I, dropped it completely.

Polanyi's maternal grandfather, Andreas Wohl, was a scholar and reformer. He had run away from his orthodox Jewish home at 13 in order to learn Russian, which was forbidden in Orthodox Jewish communities. He soon became immersed in the forward-looking, Enlightenment-inspired modernism that was one of the major trends of thought in Vilna, Lithuania, then a Russian city that was an important center of Jewish culture. He was superintendent of Jewish religious education in a large part of European Russia and directed a teachers' institute in Vilna, one of the two allowed after young men's rabbinical schools had been closed in 1873. In his later years, he was offered the position of chief rabbi of Vilna. The salary was substantial, but he did not like formal Jewish ritual and much preferred doing historical and philosophical research. Wohl's two extant essays are entitled "The Postbiblical History of the Hebrews from the Babylonian Captivity into the Time of Mahomed" and "The Significance of the Talmud for Christianity." Wohl also translated portions of the Bible and other sacred texts. At the request of the czarist government, he made the first translation of the Hebrew prayer book into Russian. For his efforts he was given a medal (Ehrenkreuz des Stanislaus Ordens) from the government and a decoration from the Catholic Church (Annenorden).

Cecile Wohl was a talented and lively woman. She and her twin brother, Lazar, were born in 1862. She graduated at 17 with an excellent record from the Titov Gymnasium in Vilna; Lazar became a doctor. Cecile developed an active interest in the socialist and anarchist student movements that grew up among Jewish revolutionary circles in Vilna in the 1870s. After her graduation in 1879, when the police had started tracking down revolutionaries, her father sent her off to Vienna, where she worked in a jewelry shop.

Mihály Pollacsek was drawn to the same social circle that Cecile participated in when he moved to set himself up in business in Vienna. They were married on February 21, 1881, choosing a place near Warsaw as a halfway point between Vilna and Vienna. Karl Polanyi felt that the greatest formative influence on his life was having a father who was very much a westerner and a mother who was very much a Russian revolutionary.[7] Karl's widow, Ilona, writing in 1971, remarked on the contrast in the natures of Mihály and Cecile: "The parents were strong characters and completely different in their mental structures, in their views, and in their background. In Karl there was a...combination of...the strong honesty in his father with his uncompromising puritanism, and his mother's mental beauty, overwhelming wit, vitality, and anarchic lifestyle—everything that made Cecil-Mama in her later years a focal point of the avant-garde literary and political life of Budapest."[8]

Cecile inherited from her mother's side some Tatar or Mongolian characteristics, probably coming from either the Lithuanian Tatars or the Jewish Khazars. She and Michael were short in stature and had a dark complexion. Like her father, Cecil-Mama was a person of strong mind and spirit. She gave an impassioned, hour-long speech in 1906 to a workers' education society in Budapest on "The Prehistory of the [1905] Russian Revolution."[9] For her, the "Red fire in the East" marked the dawn of freedom for workers everywhere. Clever and amusing in conversation, she loved being with people, drawing out their interests and opinions, as well as discussing what she learned from her extensive reading in literature and social theory.

Because Cecil-Mama expected her children to share her own appreciation for the life of the mind, she was critical of her younger daughter, Sofie, who had no taste for long debates about social issues. Sofie's daughter, Maria, remembers Cecile as a hard, matriarchal woman who admired intellectual eminence and nothing else. On the other hand, George Polya (a distinguished mathematician) and Jeannette Odier Chambaud (Polanyi's first love) recalled an understanding, sympathetic person, "vivante et gaie."[10] Cecile evidently dressed casually—"the opposite of a fashion model" as Laura's daughter, Eva Zeisel, put it—even though she wrote articles on fashions for the German-language Budapest paper, *Neues Pester Journal*.

Housekeeping was apparently not one of Cecile's strong points.[11] Karl's wife, Ilona, reported that in the family constellation, "the figure of the mother is much paler ... than that of the father whose strong personality dominated everything. Taking care of the large bourgeois household did not suit Cecile's Bohemian temperament. Things may have been simplified by the conversion to poverty, but there was hardly any order in either one or the other lifestyle."[12] Bela Szilard described a visit of his parents to Cecile.[13] Whether ill or indolent, she was not up and had had a meal in bed. When she heard the visitors coming, she hid the dishes under the bedding.

For three decades, Cecile's talents were mainly channeled into her weekly literary salons. These had started after her marriage in 1881 with "jours," gatherings of a group of women friends, and expanded to include the bright young men and women of the avant garde. Cecile would pick up some challenging thought as a starting point for the conversation. Every new idea from the West was discussed. Here, right at home, was a model for Polanyi's later idea of a society of explorers, a community passionately seeking to discover new truths and testing them against the highest standards of inquiry. These salons were first held in the family's spacious apartment on the Andrássy ut. After 1900 when the family was impoverished and reduced to living in cramped quarters, Cecile continued to invite a few friends at a time for visits,[14] but also found opportunity for group discussions in the literary cafes. That was where the intellectual life of Budapest was carried on—even the theater directors held "office hours" there.[15] These cafes were the sources of news for all the novelists, playwrights, poets, and short-story writers as well as journalists. After World War I, Cecile organized salons in large hotel conference rooms, sharing expenses with the participants.

For Cecile's children, her father was a warm and inspiring grandfather. Polanyi noted that Rabbi Wohl was the only scholar to be found among his ancestors. Although Wohl was full of concern for the children's education, he did not put the slightest pressure on them to take up his own religious views. He wrote one December to ask the children if the Christmas tree was up yet. When the eldest, Laura, was in her early teens, he encouraged her to write often and gave her some instructions on how to compose her letters. She wrote both in German and French; he replied in German, and generally added a short message in Russian for Cecile—no one else in the family but Cecile seems to have learned Russian. In one letter he asked Sofie and Karl to keep on writing in French. He was especially concerned for Laura's education: "Papa would not be able to build railroads and to equip coal mines and such, if he had not at your age learned geography, drawn maps, drawn geometric lines and circles.... Hundreds of your girlfriends will envy you your knowledge of Latin and not even ten your jewelry."[16]

In 1898 and 1900, Wohl wrote about the debilitating effects of Parkinson's disease, which made it necessary for him to give up teaching. Since the cost of a hospital specializing in nervous diseases was prohibitive, he came to live with Cecile and Mihály and their family. Wohl remained with his daughter's family from around 1900 until his condition required hospital care. He died in 1905 in the Budapest hospital of a Catholic monastic order.[17]

When the family was still well-to-do, they built up an extensive establishment. Pollacsek liked to spend his money and was especially generous to his family and relatives. They all loved to travel, often in a private railroad car. In Budapest, the family's apartment on Andressy ut was in a fashionable part of town. Besides the housekeepers, there were English and French tutors and German governesses. Polanyi's parents spoke German at home and the children learned it early and well; it was said that Cecile disliked Hungarian and never mastered it.

There were many amenities and symbols of affluence in that household, such as fine clothes, Persian rugs, and a silver table service for 24. The riding instructor apparently lived at the family's stable, and each child had a horse. Ilona wrote that Mihály Pollacsek "brought back from Edinburgh a Protestant ethic for his whole life which suited his being.... The education of the children was a Spartan one.... In the morning a cold shower, an hour of gymnastics, hot cocoa with a roll, Schiller and Goethe, Corneille and Racine—all this with private teachers." When Pollacsek had to travel, he would point to one of the older children and say, "You can come with me." It might be on horseback to a construction site at Esztergom, 40 miles north of Budapest, or overnight in a sleeping car for a journey to one of the European capitals.[18]

For the cousins who came to study in Budapest, Pollacsek rented a second apartment, complete with maid service. His engineering office next door to their residence was a rendezvous for employees, their relatives, and young radicals. There was usually a large salami hanging from the ceiling from which they could cut slices for dinner.

The first child of Cecile and Mihály was Laura, nicknamed "Mausi." She was born in 1882 and was to be Polanyi's lifelong friend, although, as with his mother, he often yearned for more contact than she did. After early schooling at home, Mausi attended the Lutheran Boys' Gymnasium for the first four years of secondary school. When the National Women's Educational Association Gymnasium opened in October 1896—the first gymnasium in Budapest for girls—she became part of the initial student body, graduating in 1900. From 1900 to 1904, she was enrolled at the University of Budapest, but she did not receive her doctorate in history until 1909, when she completed her thesis on the topic "The Economic Policy of Emperor Charles VI." Her secondary subject was English literature. She was not only a scholar but an orator, capable of a graceful, flowing delivery in Hungarian, German, or English. She cared deeply for the liberating ideas of socialism, but was put off by the way the Communists mishandled these concepts in the Russian Bolshevik Revolution. Although Mausi still found time for radical and pacifist politics after she married, she set aside her studies in order to care for the family.

Adolf was born a year after Mausi (1883) and was in many ways distant from the others. According to Elsa Hollo, the wife of Polanyi's lifelong friend Gyula Hollo, Adolf was thought by his contemporaries to be the most brilliant of the Polanyis. He was an excellent linguist, but was not inclined to take part in the family debates. During his last school year Adolf translated a novel, *The Career of a Nihilist*, written in English by the Russian revolutionist Stepniak, and had it published in installments in the daily paper *Budapesti Naplo* (Budapest Diary). Adolf wanted to go into engineering, but his father, who hoped he would become a merchant, was against it. Karl spoke of Adolf as "the thin-skinned, shy boy who always seemed to get the worst of it; the lean, stubble-chinned youngster, so feminine, so brilliant and yet a failure; beloved by his friends, adored by the women who mothered him; disliked by most men, but extolled by some of his teachers whose admiration and confidence in him was boundless; I think that he loved nobody more than Mother."[19]

Karl (or Karli), born in 1886, was a charming, sensitive, and complex person. His humor was infectious. His second cousin Eva Carocci reported, "As a child I remember Karli because he was the only one from the family who came to our room and made fun with us and . . . he laughed in a beautiful way."[20] In contrast to Michael, he was not a person for sharp, definitive opinions—he was described as "relativist" and Michael as "absolutist."

Sofie (or Sophie, born 1888), the homemaker, may have been more scholarly than the rest of the family would admit. She helped to keep order in the household ("as pedantic as Karli," Michael wrote to Mausi). How much of the omnipresent flow of ideas she took in is hard to guess because she did not enter the debates as Cecile, Karl, Mausi, and Michael did. During a summer holiday, she translated from the German poet Heine with a friend named Viola. Polanyi had a special affection for her.[21]

Michael came fifth, born in Budapest on March 11, 1891. By that time family life was hectic enough so that his birth was not recorded until the next day, so that he celebrated March 12 as his birthday. Polanyi's early life involved a fair amount of vigorous physical activity. Apart from suffering from scarlet fever at age 5, he was a healthy child. He bicycled with other children, joined his father for Sunday rides on horseback or in carriages, and learned some fencing. The fencing lessons served Polanyi well years later in a duel with a student at the University of Budapest—Polanyi carried the day by wounding the other's ear, which bled sufficiently to satisfy the demands of honor.[22] As he got older, he enjoyed walking and mountain climbing. He was also a vigorous swimmer, and, while a not particularly good skier in his younger days, he later became the best skier in the Hungarian student circle in Karlsruhe.

Polanyi recalled in 1974 that he first learned to read and write at the knee of his cousin, Ervin Szabó.[23] The language was probably Hungarian because Ervin used that language exclusively in his writing. The household servants also spoke only Hungarian. Little as Polanyi used Hungarian in later life, it is interesting that even when he was living in Germany, he wrote to his brother Karl and his sister Mausi, then both in Austria, in Hungarian, and that near the end of his life, when English had become his dominant language, he kept lapsing into the Magyar tongue of his childhood.

At any rate, Polanyi was multilingual by the age of 6. The earliest extant letter from him may have been an exercise assigned by his tutor and is addressed to his father in careful French—the father spoke French fluently. The letter gives the Hungarian words for the end-of-the-year school festival the older children were about to attend.[24] There was also an undated draft of a letter by Polanyi that is obscure in meaning but written in old-fashioned Gothic German script, and in Hungarian and French versions, with mistakes in all three, but mostly in the French version.[25]

As time went on, Polanyi learned enough English at home to have a magazine subscription to the "Boys' Own Annual" from England and later to read Shakespeare. His French studies enabled him to appreciate the poetry of the modern French romantics Musset, Vigny, and Verlaine. Hölderlin was one of his favorite German poets. Polanyi memorized poetry in each of the four languages he knew.

Although poetry was important to Polanyi, it was clearly in science that he found his principal satisfaction in his early years. "The popular scientific books which I used to read as a child were mainly concerned with displaying the wonders of nature and the glorious achievements of science in astronomy, biology, Darwinian evolution and the like" (LL, 68). He also read the novels of H. G. Wells as they came out around 1900 and 1902, and was impressed with the idea that science could solve all problems and alleviate all misery; Polanyi's work in economics and social analysis seems, in part, to have been inspired by the hope that scientific methods might help to clarify social mechanisms.

When Cecile gave the young Michael her attention, he responded with delight. Once, when he was 12 and they were living in a fourth-floor flat in Ferencziek Square, he ran half-a-dozen errands for her, running up and down the stairs "like a willing lamb."[26] In later years, Polanyi was often burdened by his mother's health and money problems. The family correspondence has many references to her numerous ailments and efforts at cures, especially by trips to spas with their hot baths and by frequent consultations with their family doctor, Gyula Hollo. Her hypochondria and appeals for money became yet another means of dominating family life. Some time in 1910, after Cecile had received some psychoanalysis and seemed to be entering a period of steady good health, Polanyi wrote,

> Your sickness was for years the frame of my imagination; it absorbed everything that flowed over from my ordinary life. I am like one who . . . cannot find his new frame, now that I see that you are going to be healed, truly and without regression. Do you remember when at the beginning of the psychoanalysis you couldn't write a line and you complained that your world had disappeared; you had no more acquaintances to whom you could write? Had I not been your Virgil in your trip to hell, I wouldn't know how to recognize you myself now that you are supposed to descend from heaven soon. . . . now your person is reality for me, it flows through me. My imagination is stretching its limbs.[27]

Polanyi also had his own ailments. He suffered migraine headaches in the summer of 1907. He sometimes found travel stressful: "When I was young, I often had tears in my eyes when I thought that I would never see the people again with whom I was accidentally together in the waiting room of a railroad station. It was the suffering because of transitoriness which had already tormented me as a child."[28] In the winter of 1913, he had to take a period of complete rest, trying as best he could to forget about his studies.

Throughout his life he was troubled by insomnia, which he lamented in diary entries and correspondence.

The sixth child, Paul or "Pali," was born about 1893 and was said to be mentally retarded. He must have been institutionalized at an early age, since there is hardly any reference to him in family correspondence, except for a mention in 1907 of the good quality of the institution where he was living in western Budapest and of a visit to him by Michael. According to Polanyi's nephew, George Striker, "Paul's fate was never discussed in the family—it was just not a matter of conversation."[29] Paul apparently died in late adolescence.

Before the end of the nineteenth century the family's period of good fortune came to an unexpected end. First, they lost the lease to the Ungvar steam flour mill. Polanyi's father, aunts, and uncles covered the expenses of their aging mother, Sophie, who continued to live in her large apartment in Budapest as if her income had not disappeared. The expenses could have lasted only a year or two, as Sophie died in 1898.

The much more serious economic catastrophe was the result of three months of steady rain in the region where Pollacsek was constructing a long rail line from the Danube Valley into Slovakia and Poland. Although the rails were washed out in the flood, the government refused to recognize the "Act of God" clause in the contract, possibly because Pollacsek was a Jew. If the 2,000 or so workers who were extending the line were to be paid, the money had to come from Pollacsek's capital. Although his firm finally went bankrupt on April 16, 1900, he used all his resources, including the family silver, to repay his creditors. The certificate of bankruptcy issued by the court in Vienna suggests that he had paid all his debts. The family was forced to move into a considerably smaller, fourth-floor apartment at number 9 on Ferencziek Square (now Felszabadulas Ter).

The family managed to survive surprisingly well in spite of the fact that Pollacsek was unable to revive his railroad firm. He obtained a position traveling for the widely known and popular Frankfurt Fair. Letters to his wife and children tell of long trips in uncomfortable and unpleasant third-class railroad coaches. He endured hard benches in crowded compartments—quite a change for a man used to the first-class comforts of his own railroad car!—but his letters show him bearing it cheerfully.

The loss of income brought out Cecile's neurotic side. Mausi later remembered her as lying around on lace pillows while others were busy taking care of things. Cecile also spent time with relatives, including the Szabó family in Dömosh, a small town frequented by summer visitors about 25 miles north of Budapest on the Danube. Mausi was just finishing her secondary schooling and, with her father's enthusiastic support, was ready to enter the university in the fall. The whole burden of caring for the household fell on her because her father was absent and her mother was incapacitated. She later thanked Michael for helping her endure the strain: "The pitying condolences with which you followed my life always felt good. It is true that I imagined more behind them because I thought you understood my torture from the time I was 17 years old, with all the causes effective then and since.... Of course I always forgot that you were then just the same age as your [son] George is now [8 years old], when my Calvary started."[30]

In the midst of the hard times, Mihály wrote a tender birthday letter to Cecile from Frankfurt: "This love...must give us the strength to bear the many blows of fate without losing our resilience and our faith in the future.... I am happy when I think about my dear children that in the end all will work out for the better and only the memory of what we have lived through will remain."[31]

Mausi took on a three-year term as editor-by-correspondence of the *Bibliographia Economica Universalis*, which had its main office in Brussels, and a year later she started a three-year term of development work with her cousin Ervin Szabó in the library of the Central Statistical Institute of the Hungarian government. In both jobs she introduced the Dewey Decimal system, so the work was by no means routine.

In spite of the troubles, all the children were able to finish their schooling. There were also good times at home. In 1903, Mausi wrote to "Dear, good Papa" that there was a lot to do, and that Adolf was busy, but (as was their custom), they had performed skits for each other at home: "Karli sang the Empress's part, I the doll's, and Misi laughed at all of us." She also said that under Karli's supervision, Sofie went to her first dance looking very pretty.[32]

Mausi was thoroughly worn out by 1904: "So I had to get sick for years from the troubles from conflicting ideologies, from self-denying feelings, and from so many other things."[33] At age 23, she addressed a group of matrons on how to choose a proper father for one's child and how to raise the child, quoting from French and German philosophers, painters, and artisans.[34] Although Ervin Szabó fell in love with her and courted her, she decided that she should marry a non-intellectual, a businessman with a stable character, secure in himself, and especially "not carrying any genes of a super-intellectual family." Such a man she found in Alexander ("Sandor") Striker,[35] co-owner and manager of a textile mill in Königinhof, in Austrian Bohemia (now Hradec Kralove, Czech Republic). Mausi and Sandor were engaged in August 1904, and they married the following October. They set up house at Andrássy ut 83. Striker became a mainstay for the Polanyi family. The Strikers' children were Michael ("Misi," b. 1905), Eva (b. 1906), and Otto (later George, b. 1913).

In 1901, Adolf was studying Japanese at the Oriental Trading Academy and law at the University of Budapest. He was successful at the academy, but not at the university. After a year or so at the university, he, his new union-organizer friend Frida Szecsi (whom he later married), and his cousin Ödön

Pór took part in "anti-capitalist activities." They sought to develop social consciousness among intellectuals and to help in the battle of workers for improvement in wages and living conditions. While still a gymnasium student, Karl also took part in this short-lived, Marxist-oriented group. Adolf and Ödön posted a notice seeking members for a Socialist Students Club and received a much bigger response than they expected. A physical clash of the new club with the gentry's organization, "A Thousand Christian Youth," led to police interference, a demonstration with Adolf as main speaker, and a call for a strike. Three days later Adolf was suspended from the university, shortly before his successful graduation from the Oriental Academy and his departure for the Far East.

Karl graduated from the *Minta Gymnasium* ("Model School") in 1904 and then entered the School of Law at the University of Budapest. He gained some notoriety for responding to a challenge to a duel with the riposte, "I am always pleased to fight you with intellectual arms."[36] Karl went on to finish his education at the University of Koloszvar in Transylvania because he wanted to study with a man he admired, the well-known professor of law and disciple of Herbert Spencer Bódog (Felix) Somló. Karl earned some money tutoring rich schoolboys and caring for children in the summers. In due course, Michael also turned to tutoring. Gyula Hollo reported that "Misi gave lessons when he was still a boy and was wonderful." One of the boys Polanyi tutored was Ervin von Gomperz, destined to become one of his graduate students, then his colleague in Berlin, and a lifelong friend.

Polanyi's uncle and aunt, Karl and Irma Pollacsek, had a particular fondness for him and provided considerable material and emotional support for him in those years. Although the whole family got along reasonably well with help from these and other close relatives, everyone must have thought that Mihály Pollacsek's persistence would eventually restore the family fortunes. Their hopes were destroyed in January 1905, when Pollacsek came down with a serious bout of pneumonia after a hot-and-cold cycle at a Budapest sauna bath and died three days later. The family was devastated.

In Tokyo, Adolf learned of his father's death through a condolence card and returned home via the Trans-Siberian Railway. During the two weeks en route, he became quite ill. A search was made on the train for a medical doctor, and one was found—his own uncle, Lazar Wohl. On his return to Budapest, he was allowed to return to the part-time study of law at the university, which he completed ten years later. He supported himself by working in the steam laundry owned by Frida Szecsi's family—a huge affair, the first of its kind in Eastern Europe. It had 200 workers doing the laundry for hospitals and hotels. Adolf rapidly developed both technical and managerial expertise in relation to the laundry's equipment. Thus he entered, without a formal diploma, into the field of combustion engineering that was becoming his main professional interest and livelihood. His marriage to Frida in 1907 secured his job and his finances, at least through World War I. Their first child was Vera (b. 1909), and then came Esther (b. 1911), Michael Lajos (b. 1913), and Thomas (b. 1917), with a third boy lost in infancy in the 1916 diphtheria epidemic.

After their father's death, 19-year-old Karl saw himself as the head of the family: "Last night I was alone with our father's memory. Until my marriage 17 years later, his memory was the strongest force in my life.... for the next 10 years I was head of the family and earned our keep."[37] Michael was like a son to him: "In my memories you are still the 14-year-old boy who talked with me, sitting in my lap and hugging my neck when I returned home tired from the business." Karl's efforts to act like a father toward Michael were not welcome after the younger brother reached maturity; Michael often kept his distance from his elder brother, much to Karl's dismay.

Karl's doctorate in law was awarded at Koloszvar in 1909, but he had already returned to Budapest in 1908 more interested in taking part in intellectual activities and reform movements than in taking a job. In a letter written before Karl's return, Michael reported that "Mother is not happy about your future plans, which are financially insupportable.... You should have taken a job for the moment." In due course Karl did go to work in their Uncle Karl's law office. But he did not have the temperament to be a lawyer. Ilona wrote: "His attorney training in the office of his uncle can only be called bizarre. The usually conscientious man is late to the court sessions; he feels a disgust for legal work. After all he is not only the man who cannot lie but also the one who finds his real vocation in the pronouncing of unpleasant truths."[38] Nevertheless, Karl was admitted to the bar in 1912, and until the war had a reasonably successful practice as a law partner. It must have been during this time that he "earned the family's keep."

Of Sofie's reaction to their father's death or her activities outside the family we know little, except that in 1911 she married Frida's brother, the lawyer Egon Szecsi, who had been a member of Adolf's socialist student organization. Egon was shortly called up to serve in the Balkan Wars, a service which shattered both his health and his peace of mind, so that life was not easy for them from that time on. Their children were Edith (b. 1912), Maria ("Maria," b. 1914), and Karl ("Bubi," b. 1919).

Polanyi had an excellent high school and university education. Polanyi started at the Minta Gymnasium ("Model School") in 1900 with the assistance of a Brill Armin Foundation scholarship for poor Jewish students.[39] The Minta was organized in 1872 by Mor Karman, one of the early educational innovators of modern Hungary. Designed as a practice teaching school for the training of future professors, it was conceived as a working example of Karman's progressive educational theory—a model for future expansion of the state educational system.[40] Classes were based on lively informal interchange between teachers and students, and the learning was achieved through practicing and reasoning, rather than by rote memory of the material given in formal lectures. Polanyi entered grade 1 in 1900; grade 8, which he completed in 1908, was roughly the equivalent of the sophomore year in an American college. Attendance at the school was expensive, and only about thirty boys were admitted to each grade.

The Minta was the leading "Humanistic Gymnasium" in Budapest and was considered superior to the "Realiskola," the type of school which stressed the sciences.[41] Among the subjects Polanyi studied were Hungarian and German language and literature, Latin and Greek, religion and ethics, philosophy, geography, natural history, representative geometry, mathematics, and physics. Geza Schay, who attended the Minta from 1913 to 1918 and later became a colleague of Polanyi in chemistry, viewed that school as the first one where a student did not simply learn subject matter, but learned to think. Among its graduates were luminaries like Georg von Hevesy, Edward Teller, Eugene Wigner, Leo Szilard, and John von Neumann.

The Minta stimulated Polanyi's interest in literature, philosophy, natural sciences, and sociology. Physics and the history of art were his favorite subjects.[42] When he was about 16 years old, he and a friend decided in school to read Latin poetry together: "We went through the whole text of a great poetic masterpiece."[43] He also remembered that he received "journals representing novel scientific accounts" and found their views of the universe and of scientific explanations "mechanical." He made notes in the margins and was sharply reproached at school "for such views." It is not clear whether the reproach was for his interest in the mechanical view or for his criticism of it.

Polanyi later wrote that at school he "started to produce scientific theories and literary essays" (1975a, 1151). In the fall of his fourth year at the Minta, when he was 12 (1903), he sent Mausi an account of money he had spent, and he included a list of the books he wished to read. The seven titles were all in German and included two books on physics, one on technology, and four works of literature. At about the age of 16, he read William James's famous book *The Principles of Psychology* and wrote an essay that he called "The Fringe," which made reference to James's book.[44]

In October of 1907, Polanyi tried his hand at writing a scientific paper. It was written in German because he had a correspondent at the University of Vienna who offered to discuss it with him. The subject was the molecular specific heats of gases, that is, the amount of energy needed to raise the temperature of a given volume of gas by one degree. Polanyi thought he had found a simple relation between the ratio of these heats to the number of atoms per molecule and the molecular weights of the gases. The graph showed approximately a relation of proportionality, out of which he got a simple formula. He wrote later to his friend Dodo (András Györgyey) the honest truth: "actually it was nonsensical."[45] However, this first paper showed Polanyi's early comprehension of the spirit of scientific investigation. The question of the underlying cause of difference in specific heats of gases is a good question, even though the young man lacked the resources to find the answer, which involves a calculation of the various forms of motion both within and between molecules of the gases.

Polanyi had no appreciation for music until much later in life, but poetry and drama had deep appeal for him. He studied both of these at the Minta, and at times went with his mother to the avant-garde Thalia theater. Mausi's daughter, Eva Zeisel (born in 1906), as well as her contemporary, Eva Carocci, recalled Cecile's great delight in theatrical improvisation. She would put everyone of the family or members of a small get-together into a play and invent the plot as they went along. "She developed the story and, as she directed it, she became more and more dramatic and wild."[46] Polanyi predicted lightheartedly: "You'll yet be in an Ibsen drama,—you'll see."[47]

Polanyi's most noteworthy adventure with poetry was his lecture on Endre Ady for the literary association at the Minta. The talk was given on March 15, the anniversary of the revolution of 1848. He found the "main excitements" of the new cultural life flowing through Ady's poetry. The poet had started his career as a libertine, simply reacting against restrictive Catholic schooling, but his love of wine and women awoke something deeper and more primitive within him. He felt called to devote his poetic skills to a movement of national regeneration governed by moral principles. From the materials provided by Hungary's past, he wrought fresh symbols that reflected his desire to rework the foundations of European civilization.

Polanyi responded to Ady's poetic emphasis on the universal human experience over against the poet's own personal feelings. The student-critic was already developing a concern for the general human situation and showed strong opposition to subjectivism. He later lamented the "legacy of subjectivism in the family."[48] Ady sought to deepen the Hungarian sense of nationhood and to move it away from the stultifying traditional culture of military glory toward a wider sense of morality and affirmation of life. In later years, Polanyi found these same ideals in the English national spirit with its deep commitment to truth, justice, charity, and tolerance.

At the time of Polanyi's speech at school, Ady had been condemned by the Hungarian Academy of Science. The teacher of Hungarian literature became furious with Polanyi because he thought a quotation in which the poet expresses contempt for himself was being used to mock him. It was a memorable event. Imre Gorog, who was the teacher-chairman at the time, called the presentation "pioneering." Years later Gorog wrote Polanyi that he still kept a volume of Ady on the shelf above his bed.[49]

Another literary and political influence on Polanyi's education was the Russian emigré Samuel Klatschko, the husband of Cecile's friend, Nyunja. Cecile had first taken Adolf to visit Klatschko (who exerted a strong influence on the boy), and later on took Sofie and the younger boys. Klatschko's life was a stormy one. As a 14-year-old revolutionary, he left his Vilna home in 1861 and got to America, where he joined a short-lived Utopian community, and then became a cowboy. He earned enough to return to Europe, first working in Paris as a photographer, and then in Vienna as a translator in the patent office, which he later administered. He became acquainted with the literature of Marxism and with the leading Russian Marxists—Leon Trotsky even became a close friend. A great part of Klatschko's income was used to support refugees from Russia, of whatever party or faction. Passports were somehow provided, and many were sent on to the Szecsis' laundry in Budapest with stamps positioned to indicate to those who knew the code that the bearer was politically reliable.

It was no wonder that the Polanyis' visits with the Klatschkos were filled with exciting stories. They would see him in the summer on the Semmering Pass, in the resort area where both families spent vacations, and at other times at his house on the Belvedergasse in Vienna. They were introduced to the works of Bakunin, Tchaikowsky, Chekhov, Plekhanov, Axelrod, Dostoyevsky, and Tolstoy. Karl became, like Adolf, a special friend of Klatschko and recorded some of his life story. Cecile became aware of Freud's ideas through his early disciples, Carl Furtmuller and Alfred Adler, who were good friends of the Klatschkos. She herself underwent a short period of Freudian analysis in Zürich at the Bircher-Benner sanatorium and then practiced some analysis for summer visitors.[50]

Along with modern literature, modern painting became important to Polanyi. He became absorbed in the artists' visions of the world and the spirit of the times represented in their works. First, the Impressionists attracted him, then the post-Impressionist founders of modern art, Van Gogh, Gauguin, and Cezanne. He was especially influenced by two art circles that followed the new Parisian styles, "The Hungarian Impressionists and Naturalists" and "The Eight." Polanyi shared George Lukács's complaint that the art of the Impressionists no longer had a moral and social commitment. Although it represented a new burst of creativity, Impressionism may have contained the seeds of the nihilism that Polanyi later recognized at work in modernity. Like Franz Alexander, he believed that nihilism came out of "the rationalistic and materialistic orientation" spreading through the culture.[51]

Because of the Minta's emphasis on classics, English was not in the curriculum, but Polanyi and others were drawn to the English tradition: "When I was a little boy Podmaniczky [a theatrical producer] was about, aping the English. My father was full of the English. . . . The leading nation in the greatest century in modern history. Mother of Parliaments."[52]

In his youth, Polanyi was sent to one or another resort for summer vacations. He wrote occasional letters home. Eight letters have survived from the summer of 1907, before Polanyi's last year at the Minta.[53] The letters are imaginative and self-aware. Polanyi sometimes appears boyishly theatrical as he tries out various emotional as well as rational attitudes. Mausi replied as often as Michael wrote, but Cecile's correspondence seems to have been restricted to only two picture postcards, each with a poem of her own.

Polanyi expressed genuine affection at the end of his July 17 letter—"I am, you know, very fond of you, Mother, and you are a very dear woman." He lamented that he did not know just what to say. In the previous letter he had said it was not in his nature to "write himself out," as he believed was Karli's habit. Polanyi wrote that his own letters were parasitic on the thoughts and activities of the recipient. If he did not know about his mother's comings and goings, he could say almost nothing. While she was in full swing with her friends in Stuttgart, he wrote in his letter of July 11 in self-deprecation "At any rate, you are swimming in impressions and it is simply ludicrous that I, grey green numbskull, should call on you with the idyllic boredom of my writing you at the great center of 'Grand Garnie.'"

Polanyi's most thoughtful letter to Cecile, written in Sexten on August 15 and 16, describes the parade for the feast of the Virgin Mary that he, as a removed observer, watched from his second-story window—noticing all the different kinds and costumes of people, the common people who did all the ordinary jobs. The parade was a flowing stream in which everyone seemed at home. It called forth in Polanyi a vision of the well-oiled machine of the "workers of the world." They seemed to be the real source of progress, uninfluenced by the multi-colored fireworks sent up by the intellectuals. Switching images, he portrayed the intellectuals as seated on a black cloth that kept them from seeing the machinery of the world that they so vainly hoped to save. When the machine lurched unexpectedly, it would jar the intellectuals and cause a new stream of ideas just as hopelessly inaccurate as the old. "The T.T.O. [Tarsadalomtudomanyi Tarsasag (T.T.), the Sociological Society?] knew nothing." On the 19th of August, he gently criticized his mother's commitment to social concerns: "I beg little mother to let somebody take your place at the wheel of the world for a few minutes and write a letter to your Misi because he loves you a lot."[54]

In this same letter, Polanyi writes of shifting his view from the Heraclitean ever-changing flux below to the Eleatic realm above, the realm of abiding ideals, symbolized by the blue sky and the mountains. He preferred this perspective and wrote that he dreamt of successes for this older realm, while his mother dreamt of successes in the other, newer one. He closed with the admission that he was aware of exerting a bad influence on his mother, but "que faire?"—"this is the century of the child, my century therefore and not yours." That century was to be one of profound change, but his commitment to unchanging ideals foreshadowed his later insistence that genuinely creative change must be rooted in tradition.

On a practical matter, he presented the evidence that his mother had made off with the landlady's alcohol-operated flat-iron. Inquiries among the Sternbergers (and therefore "among 50% of the local population") had made clear that "it must have traveled in the direction München-Stuttgart." He also asked if she had "stolen books" from Mrs. Diosy. If so, he said, he needed to tell her that the lady was aware of it. Finally, in spite of the snowfall in the mountains on the night of August 15, he planned to be out climbing for three or four hours. Mother should stay calm; he would put on two pairs of socks, three pairs of underpants, six hats, and eight jackets.

In the letter to Mausi on July 3, Polanyi referred to keeping up his personal appearance, and then shifted to a discussion of the philosophical meaning of the term "appearance," using the English word in that otherwise Hungarian letter. He referred to Kant's concept of the *Ding an sich* (the thing in and of itself) and noted that scientists properly judge by appearances. They do not know what the underlying *Ding an sich* is—it may be movement, energy, aether, molecules, but, in any case, some substance that has an effect. It is true that the underlying reality determines why blotting paper is red or a person is honest, but he felt that it was sufficient that we can see the one and observe the behavior of the other.

Another letter to Mausi reports that he has been enjoying good rest and relaxation, and that he had been advised by another guest, Professor Cremer, a psychopathologist, to make a habit of being in bed by 10 P.M.[55] Polanyi did not take this prescription seriously, but told Mausi he would consider 11 P.M. as his bedtime. At age 16, he was already beginning to suffer from the insomnia that was to plague him most of his life.

In this time of peace, the life of the family seemed healthier than it had been for some time:

> I guess a great evolution is taking place in you now...such a stabilization as I went through recently. I would like to sit together with you at Andrássy ut 83....I feel a great change has happened in all of us. When we parted in spring the whole horizon was a chaotic one about which there rose...a damp nervous atmosphere. Now it seems to have evaporated and a clear blue sky shines on us.
>
> Adolf's difficulties are just difficulties—no more the big mountains, the peaks of which are shrouded in fog ...
>
> Sofie is so quiet, so innocent, so simple.
>
> Karli is not so horrible anymore, as if his rage in this family has come to an end.... This will give him a great internal peace. Usually we feel similarly in such cases. Don't you think that something is changing? It could be merely that all this is because of the many years this was

the first summer which we could spend objectively and fairly . . . safe
from elementary troubles. All of us, from you, the oldest, down to me,
become human again after getting through so many things.[56]

Polanyi graduated from the Minta in 1908 and took his maturation examinations in Hungarian, Latin, and mathematics with physics. In each area,
he was graded *vorzüglich* (excellent), although his friend and classmate Paul
Mangold suggested that Polanyi had not been a very good student of mathematics.[57] Josephine Ferencz, the widow of another classmate, Stephen Ferencz,
remembered her husband saying that although Polanyi was the first in his class,
he was so nervous about his mathematics examination that he forgot how to do
an important calculation and asked a fellow student, Stephen Cserna, to slip
him the result during the test.

In the fall of 1908, Polanyi entered the University of Budapest to study
medicine. In later years, he told his younger son, John, that he had really been
more interested in physical chemistry, but that the mathematics in Nernst's
Treatise on Physical Chemistry seemed beyond him. Cecile apparently advised
him that a career in law or medicine would provide reasonable income for
him and for the family. But law had little appeal for him; as to a scientific
career, he may have feared he would be shut out because of anti-Semitism.
Paul Mangold suggested two other factors that may have influenced Polanyi's
choice. One was the popularity of the medical profession (seven out of his
twenty-eight classmates became doctors). The other was that there were a
limited number of places in some of the university's departments, and it was
the custom for a student to find a professor who had space in his department.
Polanyi also believed that the medical faculty provided the best science education at the University of Budapest.

While in Medical School, Polanyi had long conversations with a fellow
student, Gyula Hollo, who had come to Budapest from his native Temesvar to
study medicine and lived at the Polanyis' apartment. An increasingly close
relationship developed between the two young men. Another lifelong friend
made at the medical school was Elsa, Gyula Hollo's wife-to-be. Gyula and Elsa
were to become physicians to five generations of Polanyis.

Polanyi's schoolmate George Polya said that from the time of Polanyi's
enrollment in the university, it was clear his vocation was in science, not
medicine. Polya's own interests lay originally in Hungarian and Latin literature, then shifted to physics before his final choice of mathematics. He
remembered that he and Polanyi talked almost exclusively about physics.
Although Polanyi was to develop a reputation for pontificating on many
subjects, he did not expound at length on medical matters to his friend Polya.

In 1908, Polya, Karl Polanyi, and others founded the Galileo Circle
(Galilei Kör) for "the defense and propagation of unbiased science."[58] Some

of the members were drawn from the remnants of Adolf's Socialist Students Club. Karl was elected by the 256 members to be the first president. In 1961, he recalled the first session: "It was well over half a century ago—you sat with Gyula [Hollo] just left of center, fairly close to the front—attending the first meeting of the 'Galilei,' with myself explaining the epistemology of Ernst Mach. And I remember distinctly expecting some spectacular effect, maybe a manifestation in the audience, a mild form of transfiguration. Nothing happened. I was grateful to you and Gyula, you had both come out of sheer goodwill, to help me."[59]

The Circle was advised by Professor Gyula Pikler, a philosopher of law, economist, and physiologist, who held that "Scientific research and speculation must never give way to religious, social or political considerations."[60] Nevertheless, the group was highly moralistic, concerned with the good of society even while trying to avoid preconceptions about it—an attitude that Polanyi followed throughout his life. According to Paul Ignotus, "sound judgment was not, on the whole, the strength of the Galileo Circle, but it was a place able and ready to appreciate all sound ideas."

The Circle sponsored a series of lectures, opened reading rooms, published scholarly studies, and established a periodical for younger scholars, *Szabadgondolat* ("Free Thought"). Endre Ady, the poet whom Polanyi had praised in his address to the Minta, spoke at the yearly anniversaries of their founding. Mausi and other members of the Galileo Circle also taught courses to various unions.

Although the members of the Circle identified with socialism, they expected that their ideas would prevail by persuasion, not by use of force. They planned no revolutions. Polya found their meetings innocuous and rather dull, with perhaps fifteen or twenty in attendance most of the time. Adolf later characterized the mindset of the group as that of an "apolitical free thinker."[61] Karl Polanyi, who held strong socialist views, looked back on the Galileo Circle as "pioneers in a Europe exploring the world of values."[62] According to Lee Congdon, Polanyi gradually became disaffected with the direction that the Circle took:

> Polanyi played an active role in the Circle's life, serving for a time as a member of the "Committee on Natural Science." Yet, while he was enthusiastic about the pursuit of scientific truth and certainly possessed the moral sensibility that was the animating force behind the Circle's scientific activity, he objected to the ever-increasing tendency on the part of his comrades to view scientific (especially social scientific) research as a weapon in the battle for social and political reform. Hence, while continuing to support the Circle's stated purposes, Polanyi seems to have drifted further and further away from its leaders, including his own brother.[63]

Polanyi objected to rationalism taken to an irrational extreme, an extreme which he was later to repudiate in detail in *Personal Knowledge*. Nevertheless, Polanyi's lifelong efforts at social and economic analysis may be seen as inspired, at least in part, by his participation in the Galileo Circle.

The Marxist thought that played an important role in the Galileo Circle was quite different from the 1848 Liberalism that informed the life of the Polanyis. The working class had suffered from economic depression in 1846, and under the rule of the middle class had their privileges reduced rather than improved. Karl Marx himself took some part in some of the 1848 revolutions, being chiefly concerned to see where revolutionary class-consciousness might be developed among workers and peasants. While the liberal middle-class revolutions involved little violence and almost no vandalism, Marx held that the workers could never achieve a status of equality and dignity without a violent overthrow of the ruling classes. On the other hand, Marx viewed nationalism and the concomitant enthusiasm for military glory as mythology that was used to regiment peoples without solving their problems. He claimed that loyalty to class instead of nation would prevent international wars.

In the sixty years following the revolutions of 1848, liberals were disillusioned by the difficulty of resolving the conflicts between the social classes. Many Hungarian liberals turned to proletarian rather than middle-class socialism and abandoned their 1848 "fancies." They hoped instead to act as the "conscience" of the workers' movement. In Hungary, the Social Democratic Party was organized after the 1890 Marxist "Second Internationale" socialist conclave. In 1903, these Social Democrats developed a political program, and in 1905, they took a stand, together with the prime minister Baron Fejervary, against the "gentry-controlled" political coalition. Between 1902 and 1908 the number of trade-union members in Hungary grew from 10,000 to 100,000, mostly in the textile industry—Frida Szecsi was one of the organizers. A call for a general strike in 1907 was partly successful and the strike of 1912, which led to the shooting of civilians outside the Parliament on Bloody Thursday, May 23, was largely inspired by the Social Democratic Party.

Although the Polanyis and their friends took a relatively small part in the workers' movement, they discussed Marxism at length and in depth. A contemporary noted that "Everyone is talking about Marx or Spencer; the class struggle, historical materialism, evolution, the organic and inorganic view of the world are on everyone's lips."[64] H. G. Wells's scientific conception of progress lost its appeal for Polanyi when he saw it to be too materialistic and depersonalized, especially when taken along with the Marxist version of the scientific approach to society. Paul Ignotus refers to Polanyi as a "dissenter from the dissenters," in the Galileo Circle, almost "a white sheep among the black."[65] He had a horror of the destructiveness of revolution and clearly chose the heritage of 1848 Liberalism over Marx's violent class struggle. The financial difficulties of his family never led him to identify with the working class, in spite of his long-standing support for reforms to improve the condition of impoverished and oppressed peoples.

Early in his medical studies—probably in his third semester—Polanyi worked in the laboratory of the Institute of Pathology and Physiological Chemistry as an unpaid assistant to Berczeller and Cserna. The professor, Ferenc Tangl, soon got to know the talented young man and arranged for him to get a three-year scholarship—he "took care of me from that moment on."[66] Franz Alexander also became an assistant in the laboratory about a year later. Alexander recalls Tangl's belief that work in physiology must be based on a sound foundation of physical chemistry. It was his rule that all his assistants have a thorough training in both physics and chemistry. Tangl opened the school year in September 1909, with a lecture that aroused the ire of the members of the philosophical, judicial, and theological faculties; he suggested that the sciences were of greater value and criticized the insufficiency of Gymnasium education in these areas. Polanyi wrote his mother that "The Gallery applauded for five minutes."[67]

Tangl strongly influenced Polanyi. Polanyi's interest in physical chemistry grew steadily more intense during the period of his medical studies, especially through his work in Tangl's laboratory. His appetite for theory had been whetted by an introduction to thermodynamics from Peter Szabó and Miklos Szíjártó at the Minta. The medical curriculum at the University of Budapest deepened his knowledge of thermodynamics, theoretical chemistry, and physics. Polanyi also studied the work of Nernst and Planck, reading on his own the same books that had seemed too difficult in 1908.

Polanyi's work on adsorption in Tangl's laboratory laid the groundwork for his Ph.D. dissertation and for the first phase of his scientific career. Within the interior of a solid or a liquid, attractive and repulsive forces between molecules generally balance each other out by causing the constitutive molecules to move until the forces are more or less in balance. The molecules at a surface, however, may experience unbalanced forces acting on them due to the differences between the molecules of the solid or liquid on one side of them and the molecules of another substance that are in contact with the surface. When a gas, liquid, or a dissolved substance contacts a surface, the uncompensated attractive forces of the surface cause a layer of the adsorbate to adhere to the absorber. The phenomenon was first noticed by Scala in 1773. In 1881, Crappies and Caster coined the term "adsorption" and observed that the volume of gas that collected on the surface of a solid varied with the pressure of the gas—the higher the pressure, the more the gas collected on the surface, until, under some conditions, it might even condense into a liquid. Scientists use "isotherms" to graph the relationship between the volume of gas adsorbed at various pressures. As the term "isotherm" implies, measurements of the relationship between the volume adsorbed and a particular pressure are taken "at the same temperature."

Polanyi first encountered the phenomenon of adsorption while studying colloidal gels in Tangl's laboratory at the University of Budapest. Colloidal gels are amorphous (shapeless) and flexible solids, like jello or rubber, which allow the relatively free motion of charged particles that are held in suspension within them. This means that the colloid interacts readily at its surface with other substances; much of cellular biochemistry deals with reactions that take place because of the concentration of chemicals at the surface of cell membranes. The jelly-like colloidal substances Polanyi used in his studies had enough resemblance to some of the tissues in the human body that the study of adsorption on colloids served as a model for processes in living tissue. Polanyi's first scientific publications covered the topics of changes in the blood serum of a starving dog; electrical conductivity and adsorption in colloidal suspensions; conductivity in casein suspensions; the second law of thermodynamics in animal processes; and adsorption, swelling, and osmotic pressure of colloids.[68]

Under Tangl's direction, Polanyi applied some thermodynamic arguments to the relation between adsorption and colloidal swelling, osmotic pressure, and surface tension. From his well-worn copy of Nernst's *Theoretical Chemistry*, he picked up a suggestion of Lagergren that adsorbed layers of gases were several molecules thick and highly compressed. Polanyi saw that insofar as the condensed layer of adsorbed gas molecules was an ordered array of molecules, it would have low entropy—very little disorder—approaching the zero value required by the Nernst Heat Theorem when thermal motions cease in ordered crystalline solids at the absolute zero of temperature. The main idea of the Nernst heat theorem is that the entropy of any piece of solid or liquid matter approaches zero as its temperature approaches absolute zero at $-273°$C. Entropy in solids or liquids is the measure of the degree of random disorder, in position or motion, of the constituent molecules, and so the theorem proposes that the closer a substance is to absolute zero, the closer its molecules come to perfect order. If absolute zero could be achieved, the substance would have zero entropy (no disorder) because all of the molecules in it would be sitting perfectly still.

Polanyi's attempts to apply the laws of thermodynamics to adsorption quickened his interest in a career in physical chemistry. He decided to spend the summer of 1912 at the Technische Hochschule in Karlsruhe, Germany. Professor Ignatz Pfeifer of the University of Budapest arranged for Polanyi to be a companion to a wealthy young man in Karlsruhe, so that he could earn his keep while enrolled as a student.[69] By the beginning of the summer semester in April 1912, Polanyi had rented a room from a congenial landlady in Parkstrasse 7. For the first time in his studies, Polanyi could look forward to learning his favorite subject from authorities in the field.

Fritz Haber entered the Karlsruhe Technische Hochschule in 1894 as a student and by 1896 had published a book on the decomposition and combustion of hydrocarbons, a feat which led to a faculty appointment as Privatdozent. In 1900, the school set up an institute for electrochemistry and physical chemistry, which soon became the foremost in Europe. Haber was named director of the institute in 1906, and under his guidance the physical chemistry laboratory became one of the best equipped in the world. The Technische Hochschule also had a well-established program in industrial chemistry and a distinguished faculty. Besides Hans Bunte, who had originally accepted Haber as a student, there were Georg Bredig, Carl Engler, Wilhelm Staudinger, and Paul Askenazy. In 1911, Haber was called to Berlin to set up the Kaiser Wilhelm Institute for Physical Chemistry, the second in what became by the early 1930s a group of thirty-four institutes. A rousing farewell party was given Haber by his staff early in 1912, just a few months before Polanyi arrived; eight years later, Haber would hire Polanyi to work in the Kaiser Wilhelm Institute for Fiber Chemistry.

One of Polanyi's colleagues in Karlsruhe was Kasimir Fajans, a young man from Poland and an assistant in physical chemistry; he became a Privatdozent in 1913. Four years older than Polanyi, he had obtained his doctorate in Heidelberg in 1909. He was a pioneer in the study of radioactivity and had an illustrious career in physical chemistry. Elizabeth Rona, a Hungarian with a doctorate from Budapest who became acquainted with nuclear physics through her studies with Fajans, recalled that he had "all the qualities of a real scientist and teacher. He inspired his students in such a way that they regarded their work more as an adventure instead of as a chore. The students liked him and felt at home with him."[70] Polanyi's relationship with Fajans was almost entirely professional. Fajans's wife, Salomea, remembered only a few times Polanyi was at their home[71] and the two dozen or so letters between him and her husband, all in German, never progressed to the familiar "Du." Nevertheless, the friendship was a great support for Polanyi during the early part of the war, and he was in turn able to help mediate a controversy about isotopes in which Fajans became embroiled as the war went on.

Along with foreign students from Great Britain, Norway, the United States, and Japan, the Technische Hochschule in Karlsruhe had a sizable group of Hungarian students, a further advantage for the young man from Budapest.[72] The record shows that he attended only three courses that summer term: a beginner's course in physical chemistry and electrochemistry, lectures on contact chemistry (now known as surface chemistry) and catalysis, and the first part of the regular physical chemistry course. In addition to taking these courses, Polanyi talked with Bredig about an extension of Nernst's Heat Theorem. Bredig encouraged Polanyi to pursue his ideas. As a result, when Polanyi returned to Budapest in the fall, his priorities had shifted to the new theory: "I set aside my medical studies and worked frantically for six months in developing this theory" (1975a, 1151–1153). Polanyi returned to his medical studies only after sending two papers to Bredig for his advice. The work in thermodynamics also delayed completion of two Seenger prize papers and a pathology paper on the application of thermodynamics in biology.

Polanyi's proposal to Bredig came out of a careful study of Planck's treatise on thermodynamics and of the work of Einstein in establishing the concept of the quantum of energy. His creative contribution was to see, by an act of the imagination, a joint consequence that was not separately obvious in either piece of work. Plank had explained Nernst's theorem that the entropy (the disorder of the component molecules) of a substance would approach zero as the temperature approached absolute zero. Polanyi's new idea was that the same would be true if, instead of lowering the temperature in order to decrease the random motion of the gas molecules, pressure were increased instead. The closer the pressure came to infinity, the more the motion of the molecules would be restricted, thus decreasing entropy to zero at infinite pressure. He drew on Einstein's quantum theory to show that it also predicted that molecular vibration would be impossible under infinite pressure.

Polanyi wrote a short paper with the essence of his theory and also a longer article with more details and sent them both to Bredig sometime in early January. Bredig replied that he did not feel competent to judge them and at Polanyi's request sent them to Einstein in Zürich, who replied:

> The papers of your Mr. Polanyi please me a lot. I have checked over the essentials in them and found them fundamentally correct. The thought that the entropy would behave at $p = 8$ as at $T = 0$ is a happy one. The safest way of supporting the matter is to assume a finite volume in the limit of $p = 8$, and therefore unlimited increase in the elastic coefficients. Then this proposition follows directly from Debye's lovely derivation of the law of specific heat. If I were to suggest one improvement in the papers, it is for greater brevity. That would only increase their power of persuasion.[73]

Bredig's accompanying letter advised Polanyi to send the brief version to Professor Karl Scheel of the German Physical Society in Berlin, to be published in their *Proceedings*. The manuscript was sent off within two weeks and was received for publication on February 20 (1913a). It was five pages long in published form. The longer, thirty-page article was submitted a month later (1913b).

The usual application of Nernst's heat theorem is based on the fact that the approach of entropy to zero as temperature goes to zero is sufficient for the formula to provide relations among observable qualities, such as specific heats, reaction heats, and coefficients of expansion, all at low but still accessible temperatures. Data taken on one quantity thus may be used to improve knowledge about another. In a similar fashion, Polanyi collected what data he could on the changes in entropy and other variables at high pressure. Polanyi realized that data collected on the expansion coefficient would provide evidence for his thesis. As temperature rises or falls, materials expand or contract in a manner quantified by the coefficient of expansion for each material. Polanyi collected data on this coefficient and related quantities from published literature and standard tables, covering 80 solid and 100 liquid materials. The evidence was not very convincing because of the difficulty of making observations under high pressure—for some substances the predicted effects would not show up until truly enormous pressure ranges were reached. Modern theory shows that observing the expected decrease of specific heats would require far greater pressures than are now obtained in the laboratory. It is largely because of this difficulty that Polanyi's idea was never pursued.

On the other hand, recent research in stellar astronomy may provide a corroborating example. In the center of stars, the pressure is so high that the entropy is essentially zero for atomic electron states, yet there is still activity among the nuclei, which interact to release fusion energy. In black holes, however, where the theories suggest that pressure and density increase without limit as the center is approached, it is possible that Polanyi's proposition applies. If entropy can be defined in such singular circumstances, it probably has to be treated as zero.

The pressure-to-infinity papers were an immediate success for Polanyi's own sense of self-worth, as well as for his reputation. He wrote to Mausi, "Finally this campaign in which I try to achieve some permanent results comes to an end. Yesterday I received a copy of Einstein's letter in which he writes to Bredig that he likes my discussions very much and he finds the idea to be a happy one with the development everywhere essentially correct." He noted Bredig's advice and continued, "all this is naturally a subordinate question. The important thing is that I had enough conviction to settle on one thing and declare it. I gambled and I won. The winning has in itself also some value. How much will be clear only after some years or decades. For the time being I am in the nice position of being able again to speculate freely on what I am here for in this world."[74] When Einstein approved Polanyi's ideas, "Bang! I was created a scientist" (1975a).

After the excitement of finishing the pressure-to-infinity papers, Polanyi felt depressed about his place in the world. In a letter to Mausi written after his twenty-second birthday, but before the April examinations for his medical degree, he confessed:

> I am very upset by this perverse state in which I who am forced to a long and difficult profession must spend months with completely unnecessary inactivity.... Eleven months ago I went to Karlsruhe— why did I not stay there? This is a mystery for me. I wonder often why God did not make me a little bigger if he wanted to make me a big man at all.... The achievement of a man is ... dependent on his

weakest characteristic. It seems I was not checked carefully by God
before I was born to this world. At every step are small shortcomings
which make everything useless.[75]

At about the same time, he wrote to Karl asking him on his return home to
bring the monthly allowance from his mother, adding:

> for the moment I need complete rest and those asking-for-money
> discussions are not agreeable. . . . I am under a cure which has been
> prescribed by a Dr. Benedikt and I am putting on lots of weight. . . . I
> guard myself severely from yearning for scientific work. . . . I have to
> force myself [to be] a completely different man. . . . I should forget the
> [scientific] types whom Tangl mentioned. I want to forget the things I
> was interested in. I would love when I get my degree . . . to go on a
> ship's voyage as a doctor, I would think 6 to 12 months.[76]

The depression probably did not last long, for it was not much later that he fell
in love.

Jeannette Odier came from Geneva to Budapest to teach Jaques Dalcroze's
eurhythmics to the pupils of Mausi's fashionable kindergarten, which she had
founded in 1911 to put her educational theories into practice. The ten or twelve
5- and 6-year-olds were introduced to choral singing, modeling in clay, and
speaking German and French, and English.[77] When they put on their tights,
boys and girls changed together to learn to view each other's bodies without
embarrassment. Classes were held at the Strikers' apartment at Andrássy ut
83. Jeannette arrived in January 1913, to finish the school year because the
former eurhythmics teacher had left prematurely. Photographs taken in 1913
show Jeannette leading a procession that included 6-year-old Arthur Koestler
and Mausi's daughter, Eva.[78]

Jeannette's earliest memory of Polanyi was of his excitement at the receipt of the news in February 1913 that Einstein approved of his new idea in
thermodynamics. Jeannette took part in family meals at Cecile's home and
listened to the intense debates in Hungarian and German, all carried on in the
context of mutual affection. "Exhausted by what seemed to be a true circus
spectacle, I retired in amusement to walk along the magnificent Danube, or in
the old city of Buda on the hill. Michael often accompanied me. Since I found
thermodynamics to be completely foreign, he would speak with me in French
on literature and painting. He liked to recite during these walks all the
verses he had in his head: Shakespeare, Goethe, Musset, Vigny and especially
Hölderlin. . . . I never heard him talk of medicine." She suggested that Polanyi
sought in poetry something that science could not offer him.[79] Their friendship flourished during the spring of 1913 and continued when she returned to
Budapest after a summer visit home.

Mausi and her own family moved to Vienna in the summer of 1913 so that Sandor could be nearer to his factory in Bohemia. Jeannette then took part in the second year of an educational enterprise that Cecile had started in Budapest in 1912. This was a feminist-oriented Lyceum for Women, a much more ambitious project than Mausi's little school had been. Classes were held on the top floor of a large apartment building with a lecture hall next to the rooms that Cecile, Michael, and Karl inhabited on Váczi körut 31.[80]

Although Mausi's school had been a success, Jeannette remembered Cecile's school as a financial failure and the state of Cecile's finances as gloomy. In fact, Karl had a conference with Adolf and Uncle Karl about handling her debts and giving the school one more year to break even. Adolf's wife, Frida, analyzed the books to get a clearer picture of income and expenses. Karl asked Michael to endorse the need for radical improvement in letters he intended to write to Adolf, Egon, Sofie, Uncle Karl, and Aunt Irma.[81]

Cecile maintained her poise in the midst of difficulties: "Mama enjoys the calm before the storm. The Lyceum may collapse, but she lets the events come to her."[82] The school did not weather another year, for there is no record of further financial planning by family members, and five months into the war, her address was Akos utca 16, where there was no space for a lecture room.[83]

Polanyi was awarded his doctorate in medicine on April 7, 1913. The two papers he had done early in the year on Nernst's heat theorem led him to wonder about its logical basis. In his two infinite-pressure papers, he had referred to the theorem as coming out of Einstein's theory of the vanishing of the specific heat at constant volume of crystals at absolute zero. Nernst had made the argument more precise in 1912.[84] On August 20, 1913, Polanyi initiated correspondence with Nernst and sent a draft of a paper disputing the latter's derivation.[85]

Nernst took Polanyi considerably to task for errors in the history of his (Nernst's) work, claimed that Polanyi was wrong in interpreting the quantum hypothesis in relation to the properties of specific heats near absolute zero, and urged Polanyi not to publish something that would only bring severe criticism. He suggested that these kinds of questions were not easily put to rest by correspondence—he would rather discuss them thoroughly with Polanyi in person. Polanyi did not foresee being able to meet with Nernst in the next two or three months, and therefore he tried once again to persuade Nernst of the value of his approach in a letter dated September 3, 1913.

The Nernst–Polanyi correspondence was concerned with Polanyi's weaknesses in mathematics and the approach of thermodynamic variables to the zero temperature point, as well as the experimental significance of possible observations near this point. Polanyi reasoned that if Nernst's theorem were not true, certain idealized thermodynamic cycles that one could imagine carrying out between absolute zero and any higher temperature would be inconsistent with the Second Law of Thermodynamics. Agreement on this point was not reached.

Nernst concluded by saying they could agree on caring more about end results (namely, recognizing that his theorem was true) than the method of arriving at them.

Polanyi was not satisfied with the appeal to idealized thermodynamic cycles that were far removed from the ordinary images of molecular activity derived from observation. He preferred to focus on a cooling process based on steps that became progressively smaller as the process approached absolute zero. His steps were sets of pairs, alternating a volume increase and/or heat transfer. Ultimately, such successive changes would become too small to observe.

Polanyi's argument cleverly avoided the mathematical question of whether the temperature and entropy both get to zero at the same step, and required no speculation on what happens at the mathematical limit. The approach has considerable appeal to the experimentally minded, but the lack of rigor is unsatisfying to those for whom the logic of thermodynamics has a fundamental, irresistible attraction. Within a few months, Polanyi had finished an article claiming to have an improved proof of the Heat Theorem (1914a). The paper met Nernst's principal objections: both the mathematical errors and the mistaken historical references were removed.

In the fall of 1913, Polanyi returned to Karlsruhe and enrolled as a full-time student, again earning his keep by tutoring his young companion. In each of the semesters of 1913–1914, Polanyi took a full set of courses.[86] Not only was there more theoretical material, but there was considerable laboratory and technical work of experimental nature. Later in his career (especially in his last years in Manchester) Polanyi did little of the experimental work himself, but he designed some clever pieces of apparatus for others to fabricate and showed a sound practical knowledge of experimental method.

Polanyi returned to Budapest at the end of the summer term in Karlsruhe in June 1914. In July, he finished a five-page paper using Nernst's theorem to correlate the internal energy in an adsorbed layer of molecules to the work that had been done by the attractive forces of the surface in drawing the molecules toward the surface (1914c). In looking for some substantive understanding of the adsorption process, he tried out the assumption that the molecules in the adsorbed layer would obey the ideal gas law, a special case of Boyle's Law, which says that the volume and pressure of a gas vary inversely with respect to each other at constant temperature and vary in proportion to the absolute temperature and a constant associated with that particular gas ($PV = nRT$). Boyle's Law does not hold for all gases at all temperatures. Polanyi was therefore making a simplifying assumption when he tried to fit the ideal gas law to the data. This was not a very realistic conception for a quasi-solid layer of adsorbate, nor for use of the Heat Theorem, which does not apply to ideal gases. He used an adsorption isotherm formula from Freundlich, chosen for its mathematical simplicity rather than from any evidence for its validity. The results, like the earlier ones, did not provide any reliable way to investigate the existence and property of such a compressed layer. In spite of these limitations, Polanyi's work did provide a theory to explain the shape of the adsorption isotherms for differing substances at a variety of temperatures in terms of physical and chemical principles. It was a solid accomplishment on which he could continue to build over the next two decades.

2

Coming of Age in the Great War: 1914–1919

After the Austro-Hungarian declaration of war on July 28, 1914, Polanyi volunteered on August 14 for service as a medical officer in the Austro-Hungarian Army. Two weeks later, he was given permission to practice medicine without having had the requisite year of internship; however, it took a while for Polanyi to get a military assignment. His brother Karl, who was not ready to volunteer himself because of unfinished court cases, spent some time trying to arrange a hospital appointment for Michael in Budapest. Despite Karl's efforts to keep him at home, Polanyi was sent in September to serve as an assistant surgeon in the epidemic hospital at Zombor about 200 kilometers south of Budapest.[1] The Austro-Hungarians met defeat in the Serbian campaign of early August and by September 10 had lost the Battle of Lemberg to the Russians, so Polanyi was immediately confronted with many wounded in need of his attention.

Until the outbreak of war, Polanyi had heard of only one person who had received a military scar, from a wound inflicted in the Caucasus. Now he saw many hundreds of men horribly mutilated and watched others die from wounds the doctors could not heal. Contagious diseases were rampant. The lack of sanitary conditions in the Slavic countries led to a succession of epidemics, particularly of cholera, dysentery, typhus, and diphtheria.

In his first month in Zombor, Polanyi was so taken up by the events of the war and his strenuous duties that he lived as if in another world: "My state of mind became so hardened that I did not recognize myself anymore."[2] In October, Polanyi was scheduled to go to the front, but he fell ill with diphtheria. By October 20, he had returned to Budapest, where he spent several weeks convalescing in the Children's Hospital. That same month, Jeannette took a position teaching rhythm and dance at Miss Baldwin's School in Bryn Mawr, Pennsylvania, so she and Polanyi were forced to rely on letters to keep in touch. They had decided to get married only when he had finished his Ph.D. in chemistry, obtained an academic post at a university, and could afford to support a family.

While he was bedridden, Polanyi decided to put the time to good use. He sent for his notes and began to work on the Nernst Heat Theorem and a theory of the adsorption of gases. Polanyi wanted to find a derivation of the Nernst theorem more suited to his physical intuition. Einstein had published an article in July 1914 in which he called "hopeless" all efforts to use reduction of volume to zero as a means to prove the Nernst Heat Theorem.[3] Einstein's own approach was to show that at absolute zero, all states must have the same value of entropy, which can conventionally be taken to be zero.

Polanyi's interest lay between those of his two mentors—the unpersuasive logic of Nernst and the abstract conception of Einstein, which did not deal with experimentally possible approaches to the absolute zero point. In November or early December 1914, while still convalescing, Polanyi wrote to Einstein asking for advice about a further development of the former's March publication. The two corresponded over the next seven months; four handwritten letters and two postcards survive from Einstein to Polanyi.[4] Polanyi's first letter departed from his March article by considering possible processes that could actually approach absolute zero without ever getting there. Einstein replied promptly with a letter in which he drew a diagram of Polanyi's ideas. He was unwilling to go along with one of Polanyi's basic assumptions. The correspondence continued from December 1914 to July 1915. By the June letter, Einstein felt they had exhausted the subject, but Polanyi sent him a draft of an intended article. On July 7, Einstein remarked abruptly that Polanyi's article contained all that he still found doubtful and again made some arguments against the succession of stages, regardless of whether they were finite or infinite in number. Einstein preferred another type of logical derivation of the Heat Theorem.

Polanyi's short article, obviously revised on the basis of Einstein's advice, was received July 31, 1915. He summarized his correspondence with Einstein and quoted the last postcard almost verbatim, saying that if the series of steps is infinite in number, the theorem is proved; if the series is finite, special assumptions must be made about the last steps of the process. He stressed that the essential matter for such changes is equilibrium with the environment so that the processes are reversible—difficulties arise for many expanded systems that may not readily be able to get into equilibrium at low temperatures.[5] A major part of the article is a careful discussion of the evidence for his position from a number of kinds of systems and changes within them that are problematic for the Nernst Theorem. The discussion ended with Polanyi's statement in his summary that he differs from Einstein only in taking as evident the equilibrium with all surrounding systems.

The other line of research that Polanyi undertook from his sick bed in Children's Hospital was on the adsorption of gases. An article by Arnold Eucken on adsorption in layers appeared in the same volume of the *Proceedings of the German Physical Society* as Polanyi's first article on the Nernst Heat Theorem.[6] Eucken's work was based on the idea of compressed layers of adsorbed material with three additional hypotheses: he assumed that (1) the adsorption forces are independent of the temperature, (2) the force of adherence acting on any one gas molecule was independent of the presence of other adsorbed molecules in the neighborhood, and (3) the molecules in the adsorbed layer obey the same non-ideal equation of state as they do when not adsorbed. Eucken made an additional, less fundamental assumption of a power-law expression for the adsorption force with two undetermined constants. There was no physical justification for this expression—it was merely convenient.

Because of hospital requirements on fumigation, Polanyi had very little to read. He spent a lot of time pondering Eucken's theory. Although Eucken's three basic assumptions were a significant addition to Lagergren's sketchy layer idea, Polanyi found Eucken's results unreliable and unattractive, primarily because he used an artificial formula for the adsorption force, which could not be trusted to reflect reality. In fact, Polanyi realized, at that stage of scientific knowledge, there was no way of finding a correct formula for the forces or for the adsorption isotherm. Polanyi also felt that Eucken's laborious use of series expansions and other abstract calculations blocked the development of any helpful images of the forces at work.

Remembering the kind of thermodynamic relation-between-variables he had used in Tangl's laboratory, Polanyi sought to relate any two isotherms, even if one has to be taken as a given. An isotherm is a graph that shows the relationship between two temperature-dependent quantities, the mass adsorbed and the pressure of the gas. A relation between two such isotherms would require a pair of temperature-independent variables with which to describe the adsorbed layers. Polanyi adopted Eucken's hypotheses that the adsorption forces did not vary with temperature and that it made no difference whether a given molecule adhered with other molecules or in isolation. Polanyi's thesis was that at each point in the adsorbing region outside the adsorbent surface there is a potential energy capable of causing molecules to adsorb. At a given distance outside the surface, no matter whether the surface is flat or convoluted and regardless of the temperature, there is a definite value of this potential energy, so geometrical surfaces representing the force of the potential energy could be constructed. Polanyi described the attractive energy as a "physical" rather than a "chemical" force.

In his article, Polanyi quoted the only available experimental results he knew that could test the theory, those of Titoff for carbon dioxide adsorbed on charcoal.[7] Polanyi was able to show an impressive degree of agreement between the ratios predicted by his theory and those determined by experiment, with allowances made both for the probable degree of experimental error and the approximations used in the calculation. The descriptive model used appeared to have some resemblance to reality.[8]

Polanyi was very pleased with the work he was able to accomplish on his theory of adsorption while he was hospitalized. Mausi, living in Vienna, wrote tender letters to her younger brother and found some help for him. Cecile, full of complaints about lack of money and attention, was the only family member able to visit him in the hospital. Her visits only increased his cares. She had given away all his civilian clothes, even his shoes and underwear, so when he went home on leave, he had nothing to change into.[9] When he was released from the hospital, Polanyi was surprised to find life back home going on the same as before. In fact, once the Hungarian prime minister, Istvan Tisza, had closed the borders, a plentiful food supply was assured, and the general atmosphere of opposition to the war was allowed expression in the Parliament.[10]

Polanyi returned to Zombor on December 11, 1914. One of the first pieces of mail he received there was an offer from Otto Warburg at the Kaiser Wilhelm Institute for Biology in Berlin. The appointment to the physical chemistry section was to start in October 1915, but Polanyi could not get out of his military commitment and so, reluctantly, he had to refuse the offer.

Mausi sent Michael a Christmas package of sweets and books. He jested that the sweets posed serious danger for his stomach and noted that he enjoyed the *Tales of Hoffman* and a romantic piece by Chateaubriand. He felt that the edition of Tacitus' *Roman History* was too precious to carry about in the field, so he sent it back to Mausi to be saved for peacetime.[11]

Work in Zombor in December was monotonous and uninteresting. But Polanyi could study physics and mathematics in the evening—thanks to books sent by his brother Adolf—and sometimes he joined a group of friends in the coffee house. The mending kit that Mausi sent with multicolored threads reminded him of the clothes they were meant to repair instead of the standard Army uniform—he told her that because of its uselessness, he would bring it back unspoiled from the war. He added that many of the troops were not getting shoes or clothing and had to remain in rear camp. Polanyi lamented, "I am very tired of the war because it is senseless and completely unnecessary—it cannot be of interest in the long run. It makes me angry."[12] In a deeper vein, Polanyi told his sister he had gained no wisdom about the war but hoped it would lead to fundamental clarification of social problems and renewal of Europe: "The question is whether one can think of social problems systematically or not. I believe this is possible and later there will be appropriate men who will decide to do it. Up until now, all good minds have been pulled into natural science."

Polanyi's medical duties became more strenuous in January 1915 due to outbreaks of cholera and typhoid fever. His time in Zombor concluded with preparations for moving toward the front. He asked Cecile to thank Sofie for the fur socks she had made for him. On February 15, 1915, he was shifted to the field at a post somewhere in the mountainous country where wounded from the defeats by the Russians arrived in large numbers.[13] No supplies were coming through, and Polanyi remembered hearing the starving horses gnawing on the wood of their empty hay ricks.[14] By February 25, he had already had a rest day in the field, which he used for writing to Einstein and Nernst.

Polanyi's service in the field continued until March 15, 1915, when he was sent back to Budapest for a six weeks' stay in the First Medical Hospital on account of inflammation of the kidneys. He was then given a furlough of another six weeks. He found himself longing "for some scientific life after such a long time" away from the company of his fellow scientists, but he found himself too exhausted at first to do the kind of work he had done during his first medical furlough. Instead, he made some "notes of a general nature in which I try to clarify for myself the whole chaotic moral and social jumble" of recent events.[15] These notes later formed the basis of his essay, "To the Peacemakers" (1917b).

The normality of life in Budapest encouraged Polanyi to resume his study and research in physical chemistry and his correspondence with his scientific colleagues. He was able to squeeze in some scientific research in his spare time: "Here I am busy until 6 P.M. daily. Thereafter I work in the laboratory."[16] That summer, Polanyi wrote Fajans that the lengthy article on adsorption was nearing completion (1916a). The finishing touches must have been made in the fall while he was assigned to light duty at a military office. Fajans wrote encouragingly to Polanyi in March 1916: "Your point of view seems to me very original and substantially deeper than the theories up to now." Although more experimental work was needed, Fajans could not help personally because the laboratory at Karlsruhe could not be counted on during the war—"the number of co-workers is not much different from zero."[17]

With the international exchange of scientific journals interrupted by war, Polanyi had no way of knowing that Irving Langmuir in the United States had constructed what was to become the chief competing theory of adsorption.[18] Unlike Polanyi, Langmuir assumed that only one layer of molecules could be adsorbed. He theorized that the molecules are all held in place by specific chemical forces (this kind of adsorption is now called chemisorption— Polanyi's theory was directed toward what is now called physisorption). He

completely neglected any interaction between adsorbed molecules and calculated the amount of gas that would adsorb at a particular pressure from the
rate at which molecules would condense on the surface, then evaporate, so
that the amount of material sticking to the surface would be a function of the
average time lag between adhering and being released. This gave him a fairly
simple method for calculating the amount of material that would stick to a
surface at any given pressure. Langmuir's approach has proven extremely
useful in industrial and technical applications.

Langmuir collected a large amount of data for adsorption on mica, glass,
and platinum, but did not treat charcoal (a form of carbon) because the effective surface of this rough substance could not be estimated. In any case, the
coefficients required by his formula could not be calculated theoretically because of all the unknowns about chemical forces and surface structures, so
they had to be estimated by examination of experimental data, and there was
no way of relating one isotherm to another.

Langmuir also did experiments on monomolecular layers of oily substances on water, experiments so beautiful and fruitful that he acquired much
fame and later received the 1932 Nobel Prize in chemistry. His early success,
along with all his data and his vast work on chemical forces, lent general
credence to his adsorption theory and made it a formidable obstacle for
Polanyi once the war was over and international communication was reestablished. It was fortunate for Polanyi that he did not know of Langmuir's
theory before he had done enough on his own so that he could avoid being
discouraged by the opposition. At the end of his major adsorption article,
Polanyi suggested that his theory could be applied to adsorbed chemically
reacting mixtures for which the adsorbent acts as a reaction promoter, that is,
as a heterogeneous (solid) catalyst (1916a). He obviously had learned the elementary theory of chemical reactions from his classes in Karlsruhe and
Nernst's text.

During 1915, Polanyi became drawn into a controversy about the chemical
nature of isotopes. The story illustrates principles that Polanyi would later
elucidate in *Personal Knowledge*: intellectual passions are grounded in interpretative frameworks; scientists must make personal commitments in the
course of their investigations; consequently, controversies about objective questions tend to take on an intensely personal tone. Ever since the discovery
of radioactivity, there had been a puzzle over the relations among substances with different radioactive emissions and different atomic weights that
appeared to be experimentally identical in all their chemical properties.
Nineteenth-century chemists had made great strides in recognizing and organizing the chemical elements in the Periodic Table, and the rule seemed to be
that differences in atomic weight were associated with differences in chemical
properties. Once the nucleus of the atom was discovered by Rutherford and
his co-workers in 1911, it became clear that it is the number of elementary

charges, represented by the atomic number of an element, that determines the chemical behavior, rather than the mass or weight of the atom; the atomic number discloses the number of positively charged protons in the nucleus which keep the same number of negatively charged electrons in orbit around the nucleus, and it is primarily the behavior of the electrons in the outer shells which determine the chemical properties of the element. Differing values of the mass for atoms of a given element are caused by a different number of neutrons in the nucleus and are associated with different physical and radioactive properties.

In December 1913, Frederick Soddy had coined the word "isotope" for the various species of atom having the same atomic number but differing in atomic mass.[19] Soddy assumed in his article that the isotopes would have the same chemical properties because they all shared the same external structure, that is, the array of electrons and orbitals capable of forming bonds with other atoms in chemical reactions. By the time of Polanyi's period of creative hospitalization in November 1914, Kasimir Fajans, on the one hand, and Georg von Hevesy and Fritz Paneth, on the other, were in serious conflict with each other on the question of whether different isotopes of the same atomic number were in fact identical in their chemical properties. Polanyi was drawn into the dispute on behalf of his friend Fajans because in an unpublished and now lost manuscript he had argued on the basis of the change in gravitational energy on mixing two substances of different atomic weight that the two substances should have different free energies and therefore different chemical properties. Fajans assumed on this basis that there would be other differences in chemical behavior, especially in respect to electrochemical potential differences. Hevesy and Paneth, on the other hand, assumed that these chemical differences were so small that for all practical purposes, the various chemical species of the same atomic number should be treated as instances of the same element. Einstein entered the argument with a query to Polanyi about whether the entropy difference between two isotopes would go to zero at the absolute zero of temperature, but, in the absence of either experimental data or definitive logic, nothing came of this query.

A good part of the dispute was terminological: Hevesy and Paneth used "element" for any of the isotopes of the same atomic number, whereas Fajans used "element" for any single variety and "pleiad" for the collection of substances sharing the same atomic number but differing in atomic weight. The dispute deepened when Fajans claimed that use of Hevesy and Paneth's terminology would lead to substantial errors. Early in December, Fajans forwarded Polanyi a proof sheet of his article using Polanyi's thermodynamic argument.[20] Polanyi agreed with Fajan's comments on Hevesy and Paneth. He did, however, have a correction and a complaint. An important detail was left out, which Fajans corrected in proof. Polanyi declared, "I like my train of thought and want to have it appear clear and in the form I intended."[21]

Polanyi gave little attention to the controversy until the next fall. He became aware of the "deplorable state" of the controversy in November, when Hevesy showed him his intended reply to Fajan's note.[22] What Hevesy had said revealed to Polanyi the "sad course of the correspondence between you [Fajans] and these two men."[23] Hevesy and Paneth had felt severely attacked, and concluded that because of Fajan's reputation, they had to make an answer. Polanyi expressed his embarrassment and distress over the situation and declared his intention to remain at peace with both parties. He urged Fajans to forego personal defense and to accept what he termed a "very loyal proposition" that Hevesy and Paneth had offered, presumably by letter, for a final, objective clarification. The two positions in Polanyi's view were completely identical—he refrained from comments on Fajan's overestimation of some of the possible chemical differences, some of which may have come from Polanyi's own speculation on the chemical consequences of differing gravitational energies. "Believe me," he wrote Fajans, "your authority is based on a much stronger foundation than one that would require you to be so anxious to beat back any shadow from it."

In a telegram and letter in December 1915, Polanyi again urged Fajans to make peace, suggesting a common conclusive publication with Hevesy and Paneth. It was too late, for two separate but successive articles of January 1916 were already in press, which were intended to lay the controversy to rest.[24] Each party appreciated the concessions of the other, but stuck to their own position, so that the matter was not ended with these articles. On February 2, 1916, Polanyi thanked Fajans for "an objective report," and Fajans replied on the 13th, asking Polanyi to "intervene with Hevesy and Paneth only if you notice they are truly anxious for reconciliation."

Paneth and Fajans each proposed a long review article, and Fajans asked Polanyi on March 22 about using the latter's thermodynamic arguments. Polanyi freely gave his consent on April 7; rather than worry about the presentation of his own ideas, he merely requested that Hevesy and Paneth be given some credit for bringing up the thermodynamic distinction between isotopes. Both articles gave a fair treatment of the opposing view.[25] Hevesy and Paneth won the argument in the court of scientific opinion. It is very likely that Polanyi favored their outlook—he was to work under Hevesy for a short time in 1919—but his friendship for Fajans probably led him to express his disagreement very delicately. In looking back on the controversy, with his understanding deepened and enriched by decades of scientific development, Polanyi was sharply critical of the position Fajans had defended: "For to retain the original conception of isotopy, by which the chemical differences between light and heavy hydrogen would be classed with the chemical differences between two elements filling different places in the periodic system, would have been misleading to the point of absurdity" (PK, 111).

Late in 1914, Polanyi wrote to Fajans that he had been deeply impressed by H. G. Wells's new novel, *The World Set Free*. Although Wells's concepts of freedom and creativity appealed to Polanyi, the writer's nonpolitical conception of society as capable of being run on purely rational principles struck Polanyi as too idealistic: "Without a word, people bear death and devastation, everything terrible. But when the order comes to have their lice-filled hair shorn, they revolt."[26] Again, a year later, when he was at his uncle's home with Oscar Jászi and his wife Anna Lesznai, they "talked a lot about the soul in war among other things. These people drift without rudder or direction through the storm of emotions."[27] Nevertheless, the dream of finding rational principles for the conduct of social life and, equally important, persuading society to adopt such principles, remained with Polanyi throughout his life.

In December 1915, Polanyi made the acquaintance of the "Sunday Afternooners," a group of friends who met weekly at the home of the poet and dramatist, Bela Balazs. Balazs's diary entry of December 23 listed the members as Anna Lesznai, Lajos Fulep, Karl Mannheim, Arnold Hauser, Frederick Antal, Bela Fogarasi, Michael Polanyi, and George Lukács.[28] How regularly Polanyi attended is not known. He was in Budapest during all but six weeks in 1916 and probably was active in the group that year. Lukács was the leader and always chose the subject for the discussion—almost always an ethical one— that might go on for twelve hours, starting at three o'clock each Sunday. In 1915, Lukács was a revolutionary, but he sought a moral, not a violent revolution. He was opposed not only to the orthodox Hungarian culture but also to what he saw as the detachment of the social scientists, the artists, and the literati of the counterculture. Under the inspiration of Dostoyevsky and Kierkegaard, he had become an existentialist and individualist. The authenticity of the soul was his central concern. In place of ethical relations between people, Lukács sought a direct bridge from soul to soul.

Since forms, whether in the older or newer social structures, put limits on individuals, in Lukács's view, life with its restrictions was essentially tragic. Even more, he held that life was determined by self-interest, and he took the concepts of free will and of humanity's unlimited possibilities to be illusions. When he later became a Communist theoretician, he asserted that the effort at ethical purity was essentially a selfish personal one, to be sacrificed for the "purposeful and ephemeral violence of the revolution" over the "meaningless and never-ceasing violence of the old, corrupt world."[29] A person's highest duty then becomes the necessity of acting wickedly, in the hope of establishing the real community of authentic soul-to-soul interactions. Here is the nihilism that denies moral values on the basis of moral passion, which Polanyi later was to denounce as a "moral inversion" (PK, 233–235). By 1917, the Sunday Afternooners had set up their own school, the Free School of Humanistic Sciences, which the following year entered into relationship with the Tarsadalomtudomanyi Tarsasag (T.T., the Sociological Society). But Polanyi was not on the faculty and evidently had left the group by that time.

Like Michael, Karl Polanyi had a strong interest in problems of social progress and reform, ranging from Fabian Socialism to a synthesis of conservatism and democracy. He briefly aligned himself with the Bolsheviks, but his communism lasted only "a single day."[30] Georg Lukács's sudden switch to the Communist Party fascinated him, and on May 2, 1919, when the Bela Kun regime was at its height, he sent a message to Lukács that he was also joining the party. However, he never did take action and was never certain whether his note had been received.

Karl's bride-to-be, Ilona Duczynska, a young woman of the Hungarian gentry, "was born a revolutionary."[31] She rebelled first against her parents and then against the war. She brought "The Zimmerwald Manifesto," an antiwar leaflet, to Budapest from Zürich; the Galileo Circle distributed it to soldiers. In January 1918, the government dissolved the Galileo Circle and brought Ilona and other members to trial. She was sentenced to two-and-a-half years and was imprisoned in June 1918, but was released by the Karolyi revolution in October. Under Bela Kun she served in the Hungarian Diplomatic Corps in Switzerland. After his fall, when the Whites came into power in Hungary, she spent some time in Soviet Russia and then joined other Hungarian refugees in the Helmstreitmühle, the pension in the Viennese suburb of Hinterbrühl where she and Karl became engaged. She was at the time a member of the Hungarian Communist Party, but, faced with its factional strife, she criticized both sides in her characteristically uninhibited way, whereupon the party expelled her.

Bela Balazs was one of Lukács's closest friends. Like Lukács, Balazs held a high view of metaphysics and its expression in drama. He had been influenced by Greek philosophy and theater, both imbued with a sense of the tragic. He felt that transgressions against the social order—even murder—were less sinful than the sin of untruth, which is a sin against consciousness itself, against life. Early in his career, he resolved to "struggle against everything that exists"[32] and hoped to gather the small group of Hungarian intellectuals to form a "moral aristocracy" (68) and a "different breed of men" (65). Polanyi's first cousin, Irma Seidler, was a victim of the Sunday Afternooners' nihilism. She committed suicide after the termination of her affairs with Balazs and with Lukács, who was her real love. Polanyi characteristically did not disclose his feelings about her death, but his mature philosophy countered Balazs's assumption that a new breed of men could simply eradicate the old order and plant another of their own making.

Polanyi's time in Budapest allowed him to make good progress in physical chemistry. After he sent his article on the adsorption of gases to the German Physical Society, he prepared it as a thesis for the Ph.D. degree. He translated the article into Hungarian and matriculated at the University of Budapest in January 1916. After talking to many professors, he found that Dr. Gustav Buchböck would accept the Hungarian article as a dissertation and would proceed to assess it. Buchböck, an experimental chemist, knew little of the topic. The professor of mathematical physics on whom he relied for help reported that Polanyi's conclusions seemed to be correct, but there was a mistake in the mathematical argument. When Buchböck asked Polanyi how this could be, he replied that one often reaches a correct conclusion and only later constructs an argument that leads up to it; the professor scowled in disbelief. Polanyi later saw this incident as a foreshadowing of his theory that discovery depends upon the tacit, intuitive integration of unspecifiable clues (1975a, 1151). It was far from the last time in his life that he would find professors grimacing at his speculations about the tacit dimension of personal knowledge.

Polanyi made the necessary corrections in his mathematics, and the thesis was accepted and published the following year. He passed the written examination for his doctorate in the spring of 1916; his major subject was physical chemistry and his minors were experimental and theoretical physics. He naturally wanted to have his oral when the dissertation was accepted and prepared a defense of his theory in Hungarian. Although the oral was postponed, he published his defense as his second article on the potential theory (1917a).

Now that his studies were nearly complete, Polanyi took up what became a rather steady sideline, consulting with and working for the chemical industry. His only article in the field of chemical engineering describes work done in the summer of 1916 with his brother, Adolf, and Arthur Renyi. The subject was a method for recycling laundry materials in a large commercial steam laundry (1916b). Polanyi did not describe details of the chemistry, which were already known at the time, but gave a diagram of the arrangement and discussed the operations. In particular, he gave amounts for the flows, the losses, and the recoveries at each stage, and then accounted for each element of cost reduction. The results seem to indicate a substantial savings, but peacetime laundries apparently did not find it profitable to recycle washing materials. The article certainly shows Polanyi's competence in process design and evaluation, and his habit of taking up a new kind of work and then dropping it when he felt that his own contribution had been sufficient. Later that fall, Polanyi and Renyi signed a memorandum concerning profits from Renyi's proposed engineering office, for which Polanyi was to be a consultant, and from Polanyi's patents.

The supposed inflammation of the kidneys that had given Polanyi his second period of bed rest later turned out to have been an infection of the bladder, a chronic illness brought on by his exposure to diphtheria. The army medical authorities spent much time and effort examining him and formally reviewing his condition. They characterized him as "small, in delicate health, frail."[33] Polanyi chafed a bit at one period of confinement: "I have spent the whole week in my lonely room.... only yesterday Mama visited me bringing with her her most sympathetic self."[34]

Between medical reviews, Polanyi had several light-duty military assignments in Budapest, including medical duties at garrison hospital No. 17, a desk job at a military command headquarters, and physician's duties at the Infantry Cadet School at the Augusta Barracks at Vasareti ut 27 and at the University Medical School. There were also two six-week periods of furlough. Polanyi used Cecile's address at Akos utca 16 for his mail and shared her apartment most of the time, upstairs from the apartment occupied by Adolf and his family. Polanyi also served as internist for more than 150 sick people.[35] The work kept Polanyi so busy that he agreed with a comment of Fajans, that "one probably has to renounce scientific work during the war," and said he was "not planning anything at all in this respect before the conclusion of peace." Polanyi hoped that peace would transcend old nationalities: "It seems that we all, Poles, Germans, Hungarians, will be in a sense fellow countrymen. If only we were there already!"[36]

The contract with Renyi in the fall of 1916 and the progress that he had made on his Ph.D. allowed Polanyi to contemplate marriage. Jeannette had come back to her home in Geneva in the summers of 1915 and 1916, providing them the opportunity to firm up their engagement. Michael wrote Cecile on October 8 that they intended to marry in May of 1917.[37] He enumerated their resources, including the income from his industrial contract. He discussed sharing a household with Cecile—which undoubtedly would have been better for the mother than for the newlyweds—but came to the conclusion that they would live in a Pension for the first year. Cecile objected:

> My dearest Misi—you are awaiting my answer and I give it with hesitation...you love Jeanette, Jeanette loves you, but she doesn't want to marry you before you have fulfilled certain life-tasks. Nobody pressed these life-tasks on you—it was your inner call that you felt. *You* wanted to become Ph.D. in chem., 'docent' and materially independent....then came the damn war and tore everything apart....I love and value you in your noble detachment—but your wishful thinking has falsified the situation...the mother who loves her wonderful child trembles for it...Whatever is or comes, you remain my dear, good, beloved child whom I embrace.[38]

Whether or not Polanyi was persuaded by his mother's argument against marrying before becoming established in his career, the marriage was not to be. Michael wrote Karl that "there will be nothing of my marriage. From Jeannette no news since the submarine warfare."[39] In retrospect, Jeannette felt the decision was just as well: "Michael had the wisdom and the good sense to break it all off because we had become strangers to each other during those four years of separation and of war."[40] Nevertheless it shocked and hurt her that Polanyi wrote to her parents rather than to her directly to break the engagement.

Polanyi was now free to court other women. He had "two years of real youth" with Durst Margit, nicknamed Manci.[41] He also had a brief romance with Nini Hajos, sister of Edith Hajos. Polanyi also made the acquaintance of pretty, blonde, identical twins, Magda and Ancsi Kemeny, who with their older brother, Bandi, and sister, Elizabeth, were members of a family known in the same social circles as the Polanyis. Handsome and dashing in his uniform, he had met the twins at a picnic and made a lasting impression on Magda.

Mausi, now married to Alexander Striker, was active in a Viennese women's peace movement, and in 1917 formed a delegation of Austrian women with a Mrs. Luzatoto to attend the conference in Stockholm. She was under instructions to report back to the Austro-Hungarian minister of war. Eva remembers that before her mother's trip, the whole family cut up little white ribbons printed in green and affixed them to safety pins. The message read *Für einen Verständigungsfrieden* (for a negotiated peace). It was in opposition to those seeking *einen Sieg-Frieden* (a victory peace).[42]

Through the course of the war, Polanyi had been collecting material for an essay on the origin and significance of the conflict. His impassioned plea, "To the Peacemakers," written in Hungarian, was published in late 1917 in Oscar Jászi's journal (1917b). It was, as he wrote to Karl Mannheim in 1944, "an attack on the materialist conception of history."[43] Polanyi complained that the peacemakers then in conference in Stockholm were facing the catastrophe of modern war with such minor considerations as which countries should possess Alsace and Trentino, what reparations should be paid to Belgium and Serbia, and what arrangements should be made for international courts and arms limitations. These activities failed to get at the true cause of war, which, in his view, was the insistence on sovereignty by the six large states of Europe (Russia, Germany, Austria-Hungary, France, Italy, and Great Britain).[44] These states were in an unstable condition of mutual fear as each continued its own military development, spurred by the fanatic quasi-religious cult of nationalism calling for bloody sacrifices by the populace.

The peacemakers should be aware, said Polanyi, that "our age did not get rid of all prejudices by denying all prejudices. They have their roots in silent assumptions subconsciously directing our reasoning. . . . Only by clarifying our concepts thoroughly can we find them and only so can we get rid of them." (In his mature philosophy, Polanyi realized that "silent assumptions subconsciously directing our reasoning" are the basis of knowledge as well as of prejudice, and he came to see that no amount of clarification or articulation could ever eliminate the tacit dimension of thought.) If the pacifists "should, as good materialists, fail to grasp how European civilization can perish as the sacrifice to a great false idea today or tomorrow, then I speak to them as politicians: midnight is at hand." An even greater threat, he said, is revolution, which is being talked about everywhere. "The sufferings of this war will be dwarfed in our memory if this materializes."

Polanyi's conclusion was that a sound peace could only arise from the creation of a supranational community in which the rights of sovereignty were to take second place to international cooperation toward a new age of wealth and well-being. Only then would the sufferings of the people of Europe come to an end. However, Polanyi did not indicate how to identify, assemble, and empower the sages, saints, and superheroes who would be required to uproot the nationalist institutions nonviolently and supplant them with effective international structures.

Although Karl had at first accepted his role in the military, he later suffered from periods of hypochondria, depression, and suicidal thoughts. In an undated letter to Aunt Irma, Karl says, "in our childhood we were trained to take everything without complaining, but I have forgotten what great misunderstandings exist in great wars, so I don't write. . . . I consider an idiot everybody who can think of anything else than the war, and the greatest idiot the one who understands it. . . . Humanity is a Golem which stares with horror on its own frozen mask, the tortured soul at the terrible machine."[45] Although Michael and Karl would argue passionately about the correct way to describe and correct the flaws in European civilization, both of them hoped to discover what had gone wrong and how to set things right.

Polanyi's last medical review on April 29, 1917, reported for the first time a "general weakness of the nerves." For a man who had experienced the suffering of the wounded and the dying, but who followed his father's stoic discipline in not talking about it, there may have been a strong psychosomatic component to this chronic "weakness of the nerves." Although he was not as debilitated by depression as Karl was, Polanyi does seem to have suffered at times from a similar kind of moodiness and anguish. The military reviewers recommended that Polanyi be retired from all duties save that of being on call for local medical duty in case of a general mobilization.

Polanyi's retirement from active military duty on August 1, 1917, allowed him return to his work in chemistry. In May or June of 1918, Polanyi made reference to doing some experimental work on adsorption. Polanyi worked with László [Ludwig] Berényi in the University of Budapest chemistry laboratory, and their initial tests corresponded well with theory, but no publishable results could be obtained under the wartime conditions. More importantly, Polanyi pursued his theoretical bent on the question of attractive adsorption forces and the adsorption of mixtures.

The appointment of Fajans to Munich as professor of physical chemistry in September 1917 opened a new way for Polanyi to seek employment in a scientific capacity. The very thought of a position in Munich raised his spirits. The main problem was that his reserve status in the military might still prevent his getting permission.[46] Polanyi put forward the best case he could make for himself—his university training, his progress toward the Ph.D. (his orals were slated for September), the offer made to him in 1913 by the Kaiser Wilhelm Institute for Biology, his status as a retired Oberarzt, his Hungarian citizenship, and his loyal pro-German attitude. With respect to religion, he said he had formerly been a Jew, but was at the moment without a church connection and would be inclined to join any Christian denomination Fajans might suggest. In the conclusion of the letter, Polanyi indicated that the appointment would make him feel whole again after the series of setbacks he had suffered physically, emotionally, and professionally over the last year. In the end, the military would not let Polanyi leave Budapest to move to Munich. Polanyi was understandably disheartened by missing this chance to further his scientific career.

Remaining in Hungary kept Polanyi in touch with the vigorous debates about how to rebuild the nation. In spite of his desire for a transformation of the social order, for most of his life Polanyi took no part in politics. He often visited his Minta classmate, Paul Mangold, whose father was an official of the Independent Party, and members of the government of various political persuasions were frequently there. Polanyi was particularly interested in the rights of ethnic minorities, especially the Croats. During the war, he became friends with Oscar Jászi, a moralist and social thinker who combined a kind of Lutheran puritanism with an appreciation of the accomplishments of science.

Jászi issued a call for the development of a scientific Weltanschauung—cosmopolitan, rational, and critical. The topics in his journal, Huszadik Század ("Twentieth Century"), dealt with the failures of political democracy, the plight of peasants and workers, and the question of competing nationalities in Greater Hungary and the cultural backwardness of the Magyars. To further the scientific study of these and other questions, he had helped to found the Tarsadalomtudomanyi Tarsasag (Sociological Society) in 1901. Unlike Polanyi, he was not satisfied just to think about fundamental questions; he moved into action by writing tracts and essays designed to influence attitudes and policies toward land reform, workers, and ethnic minorities. Rules of property ownership, taxation, profession, and ancestry restricted the vote to 6 percent of the population, with complete exclusion of workers and peasants. Many huge estates were held by the church and the aristocracy, and the landless peasants were held in economic bondage on the estates. Jászi was strongly against socialist collective farms. He favored forming small holdings out of the estates, compensating the former owners for the confiscation of their land. Polanyi shared Jászi's reform views on suffrage, land reform, education, administration, justice, and language freedom for nationalities. Jászi formed the

National Citizens' Radical Party in June 1914, a party that he hoped would act without slogans or dogmas, making progress by persuasion rather than by coercion. His vision of a new, westernized Hungary freed from its feudal chains did not materialize, however, until at least temporarily in 1945–1948 when land reform and free elections were instituted just before the Communists consolidated their power. For a few months in the fall of 1956, it seemed that Jászi's dream might be realized before that revolution, too, was suppressed.

On September 29, 1918, the German general Erich von Ludendorff admitted the defeat of the Central Powers. On October 17, Premier Tisza declared in Parliament that the war was over, and the people celebrated in the streets. Nine days later a National Council composed of self-appointed delegates from Karolyi's Independent Party, from Jászi's Radical Party, and from the Social Democrats took authority upon themselves in a bloodless coup and formed a government under Count Mihály Karolyi on the 31st. On November 13, Charles I was forced to abdicate because of overwhelming opposition inside and outside of Hungary to further Habsburg rule, and three days later, the National Council declared Hungary a republic.

Karolyi's regime had wide middle-class support and took its liberal ideology from Jászi. The reformers desired an independent state in which the whole citizenry would enjoy the fruits of science, culture, and enlightenment. While universal franchise and land reform were basic to the National Council's agenda, the leaders did not envision a government based on proletarian power. They thought government should be run by the intellectuals in the three parties in response to the wishes of the democratically elected majority. Former Premier Tisza sent a message of support for Karolyi, but his help was not welcomed. Almost the only blood shed in the "bloodless revolution" was Tisza's, who was assassinated on the night of October 31 by a group of soldiers who blamed him for Hungary's involvement in the war.

The new government attempted to restore Hungarian civil life as best it could. Unfortunately, the anti-political bias of most intellectuals left them unprepared for the intense political efforts needed to force through their two main agenda items. The Karolyi coalition was not able to compete effectively with the example of the Russian Revolution, which called for pulling everything down and rebuilding from the bottom up. This approach, which Polanyi had emphatically rejected in his article "To the Peacemakers" (1917b), appealed to syndicalists, workers' councils, and some of the engineers, technicians, and white-collar workers. They had little sympathy for the new middle-class government, headed by the second richest man in all Hungary. As Minister of National Minorities, Jászi offered equality to the ethnic minorities within the nation, but the Allies had fostered dreams of complete independence for each group, and they were not satisfied with Jászi's proposals.

Three of the Polanyis participated in the new liberal government. Karl served as general secretary of Jászi's Radical Party; Laura stood as a candidate for Parliament; and Michael was appointed secretary to Dr. Max H. Goldzieher in the Ministry of Health. Polanyi's assignment came about through Colonel Béla Linder, the new Minister of War, who had the job of demobilizing and disarming the remainder of the Hungarian army. Linder wanted "to see no more soldiers," but his plans for total disarmament neglected the need to defend the frontiers and maintain order.[47] Although it did not fall under his duties as secretary to the Ministry of Health, the task Goldzieher set for Polanyi was to draft plans for demobilization. Goldzieher was pleased with the draft and submitted it to the cabinet unchanged.[48]

While working in the Ministry of Health, Polanyi published his second article on social issues, which appeared in the journal *Szabadgondolat* (Free Thought) that had been started by the Galileo Circle. Entitled "New Scepticism," it criticized the political ineptitude of the government. Polanyi addressed artists and scientists, calling for them not to get caught in the "fallacies of politics," but to take on the job of truth-seeking in the political milieu. They should analyze unclear political ideas, determine how they originate, and develop a sociology that is based on the actual experience of the people. Then reformers will be able to "build a community less dangerous to itself... in which the people will... show self-discipline and circumspection in handling public matters, just as they do in their private affairs" (1919d, 56). Until then, Polanyi thought, politics would continue to be blind, as much a source of terror and as of hope, and worthy only of skepticism.

The worst problem faced by the new government was the attitude of the victorious Allies, who took steps to dismember Hungary in the name of "self-determination" before the peoples concerned were given a chance to determine anything. Hungary suffered a cutoff of coal supplies in the cold winter and was filled with trainloads of miserable refugees from territories occupied by Romanians, Serbs, and Czechs. Karolyi's government failed to act decisively on land reform and political equality for ethnic groups. An election for Parliament was eventually scheduled under the new democratic rules and a start was made on land reform, but the political ineptness with which it was handled vindicated Polanyi's doubt that Hungary would be renewed by the government in which he served.

Before Parliament could be elected and Jászi's reforms could be put through, the pressure for more revolutionary measures increased. Bela Kun, who had been educated in Communist subversion while a prisoner of war in Russia and who had then been imprisoned in Hungary for provoking disorder, became head of the Hungarian Communist Party. Although Karolyi and his government made arrangements to unite the Social Democrats with the Communists, Kun's Soviet connections and persuasive powers enabled him to take control on March 21, 1919. To counter hoarding, black-market operations, and general chaos, he introduced a reign of terror—a priest was executed for not standing when the Internationale was sung at an opera performance.[49]

When the Communists came to power, Polanyi resigned his post and transferred to the university. He was the only person in the university who refused to join the Red Army.[50] Polanyi's wartime friend, Georg von Hevesy, had just been appointed as professor in physical chemistry and intended to continue his research in radioactivity.[51] He hired Polanyi to teach some physics courses for him; the rest of the time would be free for his own research. His position under von Hevesy gave him his first opportunity to consolidate some of his research on adsorption and to begin studying reaction rates.

Polanyi's oral defense of his dissertation had been delayed for two years due to the war. He defended his thesis in September 1918 and was awarded a Ph.D. in physical chemistry on July 7, 1919. By this time, the political situation in Hungary had deteriorated. Bela Kun's Communist regime was overturned by an "order-restoring national government" headed by Nicolas Horthy, a rear admiral in the former Austro-Hungarian Navy. A White terror of mass killings of workers, peasants, and Jews ensued, even worse from the point of view of Polanyi and his family than the Red terror it had replaced. On March 1, 1920, the National Assembly was forced to elect Horthy the Regent of the Hungarian Kingdom, a post he held until 1944.

Polanyi and his brothers and sisters all coped differently with the political upheavals. As the war came to an end, Sandor Striker, worried that the territory would be taken away from Hungary after the war, sold out his interest in the textile factory in Bohemia. He and Mausi moved their family from Vienna back to Budapest, probably just before the three children needed to start school in the fall of 1918. In spite of the children's previous immersion in the German language, Misi, Eva, and Otto learned Hungarian rapidly. Sandor invested in a comfortable, old, English-style house with plenty of garden space and vineyards, at number 11 on Isten-hegyi ut, a road winding up toward a hill (Szechenyi-hegy) in Buda to the northwest of the castle. Polanyi lived with them there until he left for Karlsruhe in November 1919.

The revolutions in Hungary beyond the first one involved considerable violence and danger and much economic disruption, making life precarious, especially for people out of sympathy with Reds or Whites. It was a great advantage for the family to grow their own food. At one point Sandor brought home two cows, several pigs, sheep, ducks, geese, and guinea hens. The animals lived in the hot house and started to multiply. Eva remembers a scene of the piglets racing through the vineyards eating the grapes, followed by the French governess, who in turn was followed by the children. The ducks ate the goldfish in the little pond, the sheep ate the pomegranates, the dogs hunted the poultry, the neighbors stole some of the chickens and ducks, and every-thing was "absolutely crazy." While the family were having coffee under the linden tree with a damask table cloth, a servant called "Onkel" Knapp came and asked Sandor to help the new calf get born. No one knew how much milk should go to the calf and how much to the family. The milk was kept in the unrefrigerated basement, and no one was skilled in making butter. "It was a time of high household comedy," but the family managed to produce meat, vegetables, and potatoes for itself.[52] Only coffee, tea, cocoa, and flour had to be purchased.

At one time, a Red army officer was quartered in Sandor's study down-stairs, while Polanyi had his room on the second floor. At any suspicious noises during the night both were likely to come out onto the landing, revolver in hand. When a couple of Communist government officials were sent to arrest the senior Strikers, no shots were fired. One of the commissars had been in the Galileo Circle with the Polanyis, and Mausi and Sandor were left in peace.

During each of the revolutions, the city water was temporarily turned off. The family knew the third revolution was over when water started to come down the stairs in their home—the tap had been left open in the bathtub while the water was off. The family had considerable money invested in tex-tiles. When the Rumanians were marching on Budapest, Polanyi took bun-dles of cloth and silver off to a nearby hillside, and simply sat on the pile until it was safe to bring it back. It was not so easy to defend themselves against the aggressive anti-Semitism of the new regime. Because their portraits hanging in the entry hall showed them in Hungarian costumes, Sandor and Mausi were able to escape being thrown into the Danube along with other Jews.

All but Mausi, Sandor, and Cecile decided to emigrate. Adolf, who had represented the Bela Kun government in Vienna, left there for Italy after the government fell. His family stayed in Vienna until March 1920. Karl, who was hospitalized in Budapest with war injuries, moved to Eugenie Schwarzwald's rest home in Vienna in June 1919 and became a freelance social critic. Sofie, Egon, and their children also moved from Budapest that year, first to Hin-terbrühl, a suburb of Vienna, and later into the city.

Polanyi was the last to leave. He was removed from his university post in September 1919, while Hevesy was visiting Bohr in Copenhagen. With the anti-Semitism of the Horthy regime, there was no possibility of his obtaining a permanent post anywhere in Hungary. The combination of terror and bu-reaucratic feudalism destroyed any hope of finding a supportive scientific atmosphere in his own country.

PART II

Germany: 1919–1933

3

Karlsruhe: 1919–1920

When Polanyi recognized that he had to leave Hungary, Karlsruhe drew him back. The Technische Hochschule appeared to be the place to continue his research in physical chemistry and to pursue the personal connections that might lead to a permanent position. Polanyi laid his plans carefully. As a sign of his conversion to Christianity, he was baptized in the Roman Catholic Church on October 18, 1919, though he never participated in any other Catholic sacraments; it is likely that his decision to be baptized was motivated in part by the anti-Semitism that was driving him out of Hungary and that he might expect to find in Germany as well as by a personal desire to identify with Christianity. A few months later, Polanyi also adopted a new national allegiance. Austro-Hungarian citizens who had lived in the old Hungary were given the option of choosing Austrian or Hungarian citizenship; with Karl's help, Polanyi obtained an Austrian passport in May 1920.

Polanyi had no prospect of earning a living in Karlsruhe, but he received some income from the business with Renyi and was subsidized by Mausi's husband, Sandor.[1] Polanyi asked Bandi Kemeny, a fellow student in Karlsruhe and the older brother of Magda and Ancsi, to help him find lodging. Bandi found a place for him with the same landlady who had housed Polanyi in 1913–14.

Polanyi departed for Karlsruhe in early December. The trains were crowded, scarce, and late because of the coal shortage, and his Austrian passport had not yet come through. Polanyi arrived on December 10 and found everything as he expected: "complete peace, orderly, simple living conditions, a small, warm, science-loving circle."[2] Reis, Koenig, and Antropoff were all back. It was an ideal environment for work. In a letter to Fajans he outlined his plans for study of statistical mechanics as an aid to his work on reaction rates.

Polanyi's landlady provided room, board, heating, lights, laundry, and a hot water bottle every evening, but coal for heating was short. In his first month in Karlsruhe, there was no electricity for lights and the gas lamp went off at 9 P.M. Food was scarce and often dreary. Clothing was so expensive that Polanyi immediately asked his mother to send him three dozen collars via Sofie in Vienna. Nevertheless, the German economy seemed relatively stable in contrast to Hungary, so Polanyi was able to make good progress in his studies.[3] He became part of a group of twenty to thirty Hungarian undergraduate students who socialized together in the cafés. Magda Kemeny was part of the same circle. She had left her parents and her sisters behind in Budapest a few months before to complete the fourth year of her education in chemical engineering at the Technische Hochschule. As one of the few women among the several hundred chemistry students, Magda enjoyed a great deal of attention. At Christmastime, Polanyi hosted a party for the Hungarian students at his landlady's place and honored Magda with a single Lily of the Valley in a wine glass at her place.

That first winter in Karlsruhe, Polanyi immersed himself in the work on reaction kinetics that he had begun at the University of Budapest the previous spring during the frantic months of the Bela Kun regime. This study of the conditions under which chemical reactions take place stands at the boundary between physics and chemistry. A chemist is interested in the special properties of particular chemical compounds, and the energies required or released by chemical reactions are interesting to him only insofar as they affect how these compounds are formed or transformed. By contrast, a molecular physicist cares about the general principles that govern atomic and molecular behavior apart from specific chemical properties. Chemistry, of course, is important for selecting suitable substances for the physicist to perform experiments and develop theories, but the aim of the physicist is to discover principles that are independent of the materials used in the research. To determine the energy transactions that broke old bonds and formed new ones among atoms and molecules would require the skills of both physics and chemistry.

Polanyi began his research in the quiet of the department's library, studying chemical literature, making calculations, and writing papers. In January, electricity was restored and he was once again able to work late at night. The food situation deteriorated as the months went by. Dutch margarine and a few other staples remained available, but were of poor quality. Polanyi lamented, "You can get food—as long as it is not fit for human consumption."

Compared to the other Hungarian students, Polanyi had a decent supply of pocket money, so he often picked up the tab for refreshments or excursions.

His friend, Imre Brody, who had also just received his doctorate in chemistry from the University of Budapest, arranged trips to the countryside. On one trip to the mountains near Freiburg, the group skied all night because they could not afford rooms in a hotel.

Polanyi delighted in the expeditions. He was a passionate skier and an energetic hiker. Along with the sport, he enjoyed the opportunities to become better acquainted with Magda. He found her attractive, lively, and full of wit, altogether enchanting. They explored the surrounding hills or walked together in the pleasant park of the Schloss, right between his place at Parkstrasse 7 and the home of Baron von Rothberg at Bismarckstrasse 7, where she lived along with other women attending the Technische Hochschule.

As they walked, they shared their memories and their dreams. Magda told Polanyi of the day she first caught a glimpse of him in Budapest. She had gone into a shop with her mother. He was there in his military uniform with a grey cape and a sword, clicking his heels at the clerk. She had found him "devastatingly handsome."[4]

Magda's interest in chemical engineering had developed with the encouragement of a gifted cousin who had lost his life in the war. She had begun her studies at the Technische Hochschule in Budapest, but women could not get technical degrees there, so she convinced her family to allow her to transfer to Karlsruhe, where her brother could act as her guardian. She dreamed of going to Russia, where she could use her technical skills to help establish Soviet chemical industries.

The Kemeny family, like the Polanyis, were involved in technical business and finance. Magda's mother, Josefine, was from a family of bankers who had moved from a small town in Hungary to a spacious apartment overlooking the city of Pest. Magda's father, Reno Kemeny, had met Josefine when he came to work in a business run by her mother's brother, himself a civil engineer and financier. Kemeny was self-taught. He had learned German from the newspapers and became the financial organizer for a number of steam-operated grain mills in the northeast of Hungary.

Magda and Michael found more and more time to spend together. On one walk in the hills, with the Hungarian student group, someone saw a particularly beautiful flower down the slope. Polanyi hurt his ankle racing downhill to win the prize. He leaned on Magda's shoulder on the long way home. She was somewhat puzzled by his behavior on other occasions, when he would just tip his hat to her. Like her mother, Polanyi could not tell Magda apart from her twin; consequently he acted more formally until he was sure it was Magda to whom he was speaking, not Ancsi. For Magda, Polanyi's courtesy "added to the attraction."[5]

In the laboratory, Polanyi's thoughts were focused on unraveling the physical mechanisms underlying chemical reactions. When Polanyi began his work on this question with Hevesy in Budapest, it was clear that gas reactions were the simplest kind of chemical reactions to study. Tracing the energy exchanges in other types of chemical reactions would require extensive analysis of interactions with liquid solvents, other solutes, solid surfaces, and catalytic agents; when two gases react, it is primarily a question of understanding what happens when molecules from the gases hit each other. From his reading, Polanyi was familiar with the theory that colliding molecules needed excess energy of at least a minimum amount, the "activation energy," if they were to react with each other. But little had been done to formulate a theory of reaction rates that would parallel in its profundity the well-established statistical mechanics of a non-reacting gas by which the physical properties of the gas (pressure, temperature, heat conductivity, viscosity, and the like) could be described and predicted. Different reactions take place at different speeds. Some happen very quickly, some very slowly, some vary with the presence of catalysts (which speed the rate of reaction without entering into the final product), some require energy to fuel the process, and some release energy. Polanyi knew that there had to be physical mechanisms explaining these differences in reaction rates.

Just as in his work on adsorption, Polanyi began by thinking theoretically about data provided by others' experimental work. He was intrigued by an unsolved puzzle reported in an article on the formation of hydrogen bromide from hydrogen and bromine gases.[6] In their ordinary states, most gases consist of molecules formed by two atoms of an element. So, for example, two atoms of oxygen combine to form O_2, two atoms of hydrogen form H_2, two atoms of bromine Br_2, and so on. The careful experiments of Max Bodenstein and Samuel C. Lind seemed to indicate that hydrogen bromide (HBr) is formed from one separated bromine atom combining with one hydrogen atom from a pair of H_2, leaving one hydrogen atom free at the end of the reaction. The assumption was that the bromine atom was broken free from a bromine pair (Br_2) by a particularly energetic collision with another bromine pair—the energy of the collision would activate the breakup of the molecule into its constituent atoms and therefore make it possible for each atom to become attached to a hydrogen atom. The puzzle arose because the addition of hydrogen bromide to the mixture of hydrogen and bromine slows down the reaction; the amount of this retardation and its dependence on the concentration of bromine seemed inexplicable.

As the hydrogen and bromine gases are mixed, collisions take place at random between all of the molecules in the reaction chamber. Some collisions would favor the dissociation of the bromine molecule and the subsequent formation of hydrogen bromide, but—because the environment is filled with random collisions—some would instead break a molecule of hydrogen bromide back into its component parts, freeing them to pair up again with similar atoms to produce H_2 and Br_2. In his first article, Polanyi's analysis was based on two variables of importance in gas reactions: the equilibrium constant and the rate constant (1920a). The equilibrium constant gives the ratio of concentrations of hydrogen and bromine needed to produce a reaction that comes to equilibrium, the point at which the rate of formation of hydrogen bromide just matches the rate of breakdown of hydrogen bromide into hydrogen and bromine. The rate constant, when multiplied by the concentrations of each of the reactants, gives the number of molecules per unit volume and per unit time that react in one particular direction, say in the direction of forming hydrogen bromide. If the rate constant is also known for the opposite reaction (the breakdown of hydrogen bromide), then, at equilibrium, the equilibrium constant would be the ratio of one rate constant to the other.

It had already been established that, if volume is held constant, the rate of a chemical reaction would vary with changes in temperature and pressure. Just as a graph or equation describing the rate of adsorption at a given temperature is called an isotherm, so a graph or equation describing the changes that take place at constant volume is called an isochor. Polanyi found a simple way of extending the theory of statistical mechanics in its new quantized form to describe the state of equilibrium between unreacted initial-state molecules and reacted final-state molecules. Drawing on an article by Einstein,[7] Polanyi derived a formula containing the ratio of proportions of the before-and-after concentrations which is just the equilibrium constant, so that its temperature variation is easily found. Although Einstein relied on a partition function, which was a sum over all the possible distributions of energy among quantity of molecules of the same type, Polanyi's formula required no calculus.

To obtain an estimate of the two reaction rate constants, one for each direction in which the reaction could proceed, Polanyi assumed that the chance was 50–50 whether on collision two molecules would react or return to their original states. This concept was a natural first step toward the theory he wanted to develop. When the article was in proof, he added an appendix showing that if the energy needed to bring about a reaction was large, then there would be a less than equal chance of reaction when the molecules collided.

Polanyi made an important simplification, known as the quasi-static hypothesis, by treating the concentration of the intermediate atomic species such as H and Br as constant during the reaction, whether or not the initial and final species have reached their equilibrium values. This is a highly artificial assumption, since the random nature of the molecular collisions may produce varying amounts of dissociated atoms, but this approximation has turned out to be a valid and most useful one for the large proportion of chemical reactions. Without such an assumption, the variation of intermediates would each enter at least two equations and only a complex coupled set of differential equations could handle them.

By thinking in terms of the concentrations required to produce a balance between the rate of formation of hydrogen bromide and the rate of its breakdown into hydrogen and bromine molecules, Polanyi was able to explain why the addition of hydrogen bromide slowed down the reaction of the hydrogen and bromine gases: after two bromine molecules had collided with sufficient energy to dissociate one into two atoms of bromine, one of those free bromine atoms might collide with a molecule of hydrogen bromide, causing it to release the hydrogen atom and allow the two bromine atoms to form a molecule of bromine gas (Br_2). When the concentration of hydrogen bromide (HBr) equaled that of bromine gas, the two processes of hydrogen bromine association and dissociation would go on at the same rate, and the concentration of hydrogen bromine would not rise any further, even though there was still plenty of unreacted hydrogen and bromine gas available in the mixture.

This article initiated a thoroughly fundamental approach to the use of statistical and probabilistic methods for the treatment of reaction rates (1920a). Polanyi had pretty well completed it in Budapest before he went to Karlsruhe.

In Polanyi's second article on reaction kinetics, which he wrote entirely in Karlsruhe, he gave an account of three difficulties that he perceived in the theory of reaction velocity (1920c). Two of these were misperceptions caused by his ignorance of reaction mechanisms and by mistakes in his assessment of the probabilities involved. The third difficulty was the question of where the energy came from to cause a molecule of bromine gas (Br_2) to break down into two bromine atoms. Polanyi followed Trautz's notion, introduced in 1906, that radiant energy from heat and light drove chemical reactions.[8] But endothermic reactions (such as the dissociation of a bromine molecule into two atoms) consume more energy than they release, and it seemed that these reactions needed more energy than the thermal energy in the gas could provide, creating a crucial problem for chemical theory. In 1920, Langmuir said the theory that radiant heat activated reactions "had all the earmarks of an unsuccessful theory,"[9] but Polanyi was excited by the thought that there might be a new source of radiation in the "aether" analogous to the electromagnetic radiation produced by electrons moving from one quantum state to another. Although the term "aether" had already been discredited by Einstein, Polanyi used it as a symbol of an as yet undiscovered reality, the existence of which he believed he was on the way to proving. He used the term "atom jump" for processes such as the dissociation of a molecule, AB, into its atoms, A and B, caused by the absorption of aether energy, or the combination of atoms A and B into molecule AB, causing a corresponding emission of aether energy.

One of the difficulties Polanyi perceived was that the acts of absorption and emission of energy were dissimilar. The absorbed aether energy had to be concentrated on the collisions where molecules were reacting, whereas emission energy could go off anywhere. Polanyi adopted a formulation from a mistaken and little-known article of Arnold Sommerfeld in which the probability of entering or leaving any given quantum state depended on that state alone;[10] we now know that such transitions always depend on energy differences between the states and therefore require a different approach to the correct calculation of the probabilities of the transition taking place. Polanyi knew that his results were only provisional and noted that they were only partially corroborated by experiment.

In his next article, Polanyi attempted to show that chemical reactions are nonmechanical as far as the process of energy transfer is concerned (1920d). The first part of the article involved a mistaken interpretation of how energy is conserved in atomic systems; this is not surprising, given the state of quantum theory in 1920. The second part of the article was groundbreaking. Bodenstein and Lind had found that the overall rate of the formation of hydrogen bromide varied with the square root of the initial amount of bromine, showing that the slowest stage, governing the overall rate, must involve single, dissociated bromine atoms instead of a molecule composed of two bromine atoms. That meant that the breakdown of a bromine molecule into two bromine atoms had to go faster than the reaction of a hydrogen atom and a bromine atom to form a new compound.

Polanyi decided it was time to show directly that this energy could not be obtained from the kinetic energy of colliding Br_2 molecules. He made a careful, correct, and innovative calculation of the maximum rate at which the dissociation of the molecule into two atoms could proceed, using only the kinetic energy of bromine molecules along with their internal rotational and vibrational energy as the source of the heat of dissociation, and he found a result 300,000 times slower than what was actually observed in the laboratory. Polanyi failed to give himself credit for his novel technique of calculating the kinetic energy needed to drive the chemical reactions, possibly because he was so focused on the thought that he had found evidence pointing to the operation of a previously unnoticed form of energy. If the reaction required 300,000 times the amount of energy apparently available from the motion of the molecules, then it seemed that it must come from some other source. In hindsight, Polanyi's supposition that energy was appearing out of nowhere—or, to use his terms, was emerging from the aether—seems bizarre now, but it made sense to him at that time. Bohr's efforts to correlate quantum theory with observed properties produced equally bizarre assaults on logic. There was every expectation that more examples of strange behavior in the atomic realm would be found. In private correspondence, Polanyi called the phenomenon *Zauberei*, "magic," a word that captures both the element of wonder that he felt and, perhaps, too, the element of being tricked by a sleight-of-hand. It was a classic case of a thoughtful person noticing a discrepancy in the data; without a clear and convincing explanation of the discrepancy, Polanyi had every reason to hope he might be on the verge of making a fundamental breakthrough.

In May 1920, Polanyi elaborated his claim that there must be a new form of "aether energy," and made a general suggestion of how it might operate: The aether energy must be absorbed specifically in connection with particular collisions of a "jump-exciting" (*sprungerregend*) type (1920f). In the same article, Polanyi introduced the fundamental idea of the traveling state (*Fahrzustand*) of an atom system, such as a bromine atom and a molecule of hydrogen gas moving toward or away from a collision. While he did not refer to the state of a colliding pair at collision, it later was seen to be a corollary of the traveling state. Another important contribution of this article is Polanyi's explicit discussion of his quasi-static postulate, which assumes that the atoms and molecules in the intermediate stages of an overall reaction are present in small and essentially constant amounts. This article suffered, like the previous one, from inadequate formulations of transition probabilities.

The fifth article was the last Polanyi sent in before his move from Karlsruhe to Berlin (1920h). It undertook to show quite explicitly that the use of electromagnetic radiant energy was totally inadequate to explain chemical reactions. Polanyi analyzed the dissociation of N_2O_4 into two molecules of NO_2. Assuming a balance of absorbed and emitted thermal radiation at equilibrium, and using the known rate at which energy was consumed in one of the two reaction paths, Polanyi calculated that the kinetic energy in the gases was 20,000,000 times too small to account for the experimental data. Langmuir calculated a similar discrepancy in his articles criticizing the radiation theory.

In this article, Polanyi suggested a specific source for the energy, namely that the "aether" couples two mechanical systems—an N_2O_4 molecule in the process of dissociating is coupled through space to an associating pair of NO_2 molecules. The idea turned out not to work, for in the parallel case of bromine, such coupling would steal energy from where it is needed. Polanyi mentioned at the end of his article some analogous cases of coupled quantum jumps that make sense, including a dye-shift absorption with a silver grain sensitization, and a nuclear energy change with energy that goes into an emitted electron.

In spite of the errors he made about aether energy and estimates of probabilities, Polanyi's work in Karlsruhe laid down a number of fundamental principles for reaction kinetics. He used statistical quantum mechanics for the derivation of the reaction isochor; formulated a way to derive the reaction velocity constants in terms of an interaction probability; developed the quasi-static approach to the multi-step reactions; made the first calculation of the rate at which a molecule obtains by collision the necessary energy for activating a reaction; and introduced the conception of initial and final states of reacting molecules. These aspects of his early work provided a firm foundation for later research in Berlin.

While in Karlsruhe, Polanyi also pressed forward with his work on adsorption. Because he had avoided any attempt at formulating the adsorption forces, he had written his dissertation without taking into account the theories of atomic structure then current. Understanding of the atom was then just in its infancy. J. J. Thomson had begun the investigation in 1897, when he calculated the charge-to-mass ratio of the electron, which suggested an extremely small particle. In 1902, Rutherford and Soddy used radioactive decay to demonstrate that one element could change into another through the release of radioactive energy. In 1904, Thomson proposed a model of the atom, which suggested that electrons sat inside the atom like plums in a pudding or like raisins a loaf of raisin bread. Rutherford developed evidence in 1911 that there was a tiny, massive nucleus, orbited by electrons, just five years before Polanyi did his dissertation; in Rutherford's model, there were no constraints on the movement of electrons around the nucleus. Bohr hypothesized in 1913 that atoms could absorb or emit energy only in fixed amounts, known as quanta, and that the stable states of the electron orbits explained the characteristic patterns shown by spectroscopy.

Although Bohr's model placed some restrictions on the motion of electrons, it was not until 1924 that Wolfgang Pauli recognized that no more than two electrons could occupy any orbital. When Polanyi was at work on his dissertation in 1915–16, the prevailing view was that electrons could move relatively freely in response to nearby positive or negative charges and would therefore prohibit the accumulation of forces necessary to form the multiple layers of adsorbed molecules postulated in Polanyi's dissertation. Under the influence of nearby charges, the electrons would simply redistribute themselves until all of the electrostatic forces were back in balance. Any adsorbed layer of molecules would necessarily contain enough freely moving electrons to shield any further layers from the attractions of the underlying solid. More particularly, if two atoms attracted each other and a third, charged atom, came up, it would surely disturb the charge distributions in the first two atoms and change the strength of their attraction. The consequence would be to rule out multilayer adsorption potentials independent of neighboring molecules and of temperature, for there could be no forces that could produce a compressed layer like that postulated by Lagergren and Polanyi. Neither Polanyi nor Buchböck noticed this difficulty in the development and defense of the dissertation.

Polanyi's instinct in avoiding assumptions about forces among electrons and molecules in a condensed state turned out to be sound, but the full elaboration of a theory of quantum mechanics, which restricted electron mobility and provided for his postulated forces, would not emerge until years later. He was not able to work out a complete account until 1930. As Polanyi began to explore the nature of adsorption forces in 1920, he reckoned with the electron mobility difficulty in an essentially correct but incomplete way.

Polanyi started with an atomic point of view, focusing first on the relationship between a solid and a single atom or molecule adhering to the surface; calculating the forces at work between a surface and a whole layer of molecules would be far more complex. Using data from Berényi's 1920 article on adsorption,[11] Polanyi derived the necessary properties of the adsorption forces and directly confronted the problem of electron mobility. He argued that the adsorption forces, the existence of which he believed he had proved, must involve permanent dipoles (molecules with equally strong positive and negative ends) without mobile electrons; such molecules would rotate so as to attract other molecules. In spite of some fallacious electrostatic reasoning, the conception that adsorption forces involve dipole and higher polarities of charge distributions was a physical insight of far-reaching significance.

In his discussion, Polanyi recognized a difficulty with the permanent-dipole idea. Molecular rotations are subject to heat energy and therefore would produce attractive forces that vary with the temperature. This ran counter to his theory, as corroborated by Berényi's interpretation of the data, that the adsorption potential of a particular surface did not vary with temperature. Hence Polanyi replaced the hypothesis of permanent dipoles by the still more important idea of deformations in neighboring molecules that induce temporary dipole–dipole attractions while the molecules are near to each other. He saw this source of attractive forces as a necessary property of all atoms and molecules, and reintroduced an old idea of Haber that the deformations would amount to shifts of nuclei away from the centers of atoms, so that the centers of positive charge are displaced from the centers of negative charge, thus giving the atom a negative and a positive pole.

Polanyi sought an opinion on his induced-dipole hypothesis from Einstein, but on March 1, 1920, Einstein replied with a disappointing one-paragraph answer: "I haven't carried out any reflections on the effect of the deformability of 2-atom molecules, because I do not consider the available Bohr model correct, and because the specific heat at higher temperatures and the optical behavior in the infrared seem sufficient to prove the approximate rigidity. Considerations of the kind you suggest can probably only show the inapplicability of that model. In asking you to pardon my brevity due to overwork, I am with a collegial greeting yours, A. Einstein."[12]

In April 1920, Polanyi presented a brief version of his new adsorption theory without using the dipole conception at a meeting of the Bunsengesellschaft in Halle, Germany.[13] The conference brought together a fine constellation of scientists, including Max Born, Walter Nernst, Fritz Haber, Kasimir Fajans, Georg von Hevesy, Fritz Paneth, and Polanyi's old friend Alfred Reis. Polanyi's full argument that deformation could produce stable charge separation in molecules was published in the fall of that year (1920i).

One evening in May 1920, Polanyi went to visit Magda at her boarding house. Sitting together in the parlor with her house mates and other visitors, Polanyi suddenly turned to her and quietly asked, "Shall we become engaged?" Magda agreed at once. Although she did not announce her engagement to her

Karlsruhe friends, one of her house mates guessed the good news. "Magda Kemeny would not sit like that with a young man, in two chairs close together, unless
they were engaged."[14]

Magda planned to continue her studies toward the doctorate. She saw
herself more as a woman about to embark on a professional career than as a
woman preparing to keep house. Although Polanyi was six years older than
Magda and had far higher standing in the academic community, these differences seemed unimportant compared to their common social and national
roots, joint scientific interests, and the love they felt for each other. One of
Magda's friends from Budapest was delighted with the engagement: "Let me
kiss you right and left and congratulate you.... I would like you to be here
now...so I could look in your face and eyes, you little rational, cold icicle, and
see there how happy my Magda is."[15]

4

The Fiber Institute:
1920–1923

Polanyi's presentation on adsorption at the Bunsengesellschaft meeting in Halle helped win him a job in Berlin. Fritz Haber, director of the Kaiser Wilhelm Institute for Physical Chemistry and Electrochemistry, had met Polanyi and was impressed by his talent. Polanyi's application to the institute was backed by references from Bredig, Fajans, Karman, Paneth, Hevesy, and others. In the summer, R. O. Herzog, director of the Kaiser Wilhelm Institute for Fiber Chemistry in Berlin, offered Polanyi a position, starting in the fall.

Polanyi moved to Berlin in September 1920. The staff at the institute in Berlin had found quarters for him, a furnished room at Habsburgerstrasse 3 in the suburb of Schöneberg, five or six stops on the municipal railway from the institute. It was deeply satisfying to be starting out on his profession with a job in the new center of German—and, therefore, of world—research. Magda stayed on at Karlsruhe through the winter semester. She passed her preliminary examination for the doctorate on November 3, thus giving herself the right to be called a "candidate in chemistry."[1]

Herzog had hired Polanyi because of his ability and talent, and trusted him to develop sound physico-chemical underpinnings for the work of the institute. Herzog's letter had said, "I'm not thinking of subjects that are too specific, so that difficulties between us can hardly be foreseen."[2] When Polanyi called on Fritz Haber a few weeks after his arrival in Dahlem, he talked for a while about his articles on reaction mechanisms, hoping to get permission to continue this line of research. Haber replied that the study of reaction velocity was a "world problem" and that what Polanyi really needed to do as a new member of the institute was to "cook a piece of meat" (KB, 98). He assigned Polanyi to join the team investigating the structure of cellulose.

Unfortunately, Polanyi had not studied the chemistry of fibers, and the physical chemistry work in Tangl's laboratory and the courses in Karlsruhe had not prepared him for atomic or molecular studies. He also had no experience with the new techniques of X-ray analysis that were being used in the study of the structure of cellulose. Nevertheless, Polanyi was confident that he could quickly learn what he needed for the assignment. He was never afraid to tackle new fields—he had taught himself enough about thermodynamics to enter into dialogue with Einstein and Nernst, enough about the adsorption of gases to write a successful dissertation, and enough about the kinetics of chemical reactions to have a series of articles accepted for publication; in later years, he would educate himself in economics, social analysis, philosophy, theology, and aesthetics. The great advantage of his willingness to enter new fields was that he saw them with fresh eyes, unencumbered by the prejudices of conventional wisdom; the great weakness of his many career changes was that he lacked maturity of judgment that comes only with long exposure to the field. Changing careers also meant that he sowed more than he reaped. He picked good problems, big enough to spend an entire lifetime on, did some seminal work, then moved on to another field of inquiry equally worthy of a lifetime's devotion. As a self-taught economist and philosopher, Polanyi had no mentor and represented no established school of thought, so he often found himself isolated, for good or for ill, from those who had engaged in an orthodox apprenticeship in those disciplines. Those who had the advantage of such professional development often saw Polanyi as a gifted dilettante at best and a misguided amateur or interloper at worst.

Polanyi joined the Fiber Chemistry group just six months after it was founded. It had been a division of Fritz Haber's Institute of Physical Chemistry and Electrochemistry, and was still located in a few cramped rooms of that building, where Polanyi had a desk in a small office, and his equipment was quite scattered: a microscope was available in the Kaiser Wilhelm Institute for Biology, photographic equipment was located in the Material-prüfungsamt (Materials Testing Laboratory) a few blocks away in the suburb of Lichterfelde, and the vital X-ray apparatus had been set up in the basement of Haber's private mansion around the corner.

Fritz Haber had moved to Berlin from Karlsruhe in 1911 to head the Kaiser Wilhelm Institute for Physical Chemistry and Electrochemistry, one of the first two research institutes to be created by the newly founded Kaiser Wilhelm Gesellschaft zur Förderung der Wissenschaften (Kaiser Wilhelm Society for the Advancement of Science). Adolf von Harnack, a theologian, had persuaded Kaiser Wilhelm to subsidize basic research in science; the Kaiser made von Harnack the president and organizer of the new society, a post he held until 1930. Haber's Institute of Physical Chemistry and Electrochemistry was located with Otto Hahn's Institute of Chemistry in the pleasant, spacious, and wooded suburb of Dahlem in southwestern Berlin. The institute carried on a variety of war research projects based on the work that won Haber the Nobel Prize in 1918, a process for making ammonia out of atmospheric nitrogen and hydrogen; the ammonia, in turn, was useful for making high explosives and fertilizers.

The research on fibers began within Haber's institute in 1919 under the direction of Reginald Herzog. Leaders in the German textile industry were interested in scientific and technical research on the basic properties of textile fibers. As the fiber work expanded, a group of industrialists and the German government provided funds for a separate institute, but there was not to be a separate building for two years. The primary task of the institute was to study the nature of cellulose fibers. Cellulose fibers are the main constituent of cotton, flax, and hemp, and form structural elements in all kinds of plants. Under the microscope, a high degree of complexity and irregularity is visible in a cellulose sample. Fundamental work on the fibers meant grasping the nature of structures that were too small for a microscope to reveal. X-rays could provide some clues about the submicroscopic structure of atoms and molecules, but only indirectly. In an X-ray taken of a broken bone, the radiation is used in a very direct fashion to produce a picture of the bones; the X-ray negative simply records where the rays passed through the body easily and where they were diminished or stopped altogether by more solid structures. In the study of submicroscopic structures, what gets recorded on the photographic plate is not an image of the structure itself, but a picture of what happened to the X-rays as they interacted with the molecules of the sample and with each other; like any waves, X-rays can interfere with other X-rays, producing more intense energy where the crests of the waves add together and less intense energy where the troughs between waves align. If the sample contains molecules that are lined up in a very precise order, the X-rays will be deflected by diffraction in a very orderly fashion, and the photographic plate will show a pattern of light and dark spots that record the interference patterns of the rays that emerged from the sample. Armed with this information, scientists can then reason backwards to infer what kind of structure might have produced the patterns on the X-ray film.

Herzog and Jancke's first X-ray photographs of cellulose used the method developed by Debye and Scherrer. Samples crushed into a fine powder generated a distinctive pattern of concentric rings when exposed to X-rays.[3] They used cotton, ramie, and wood pulp, and obtained rings on a photographic plate set perpendicular to the beam. These rings came about because among the many tiny, randomly-oriented crystals, those that were positioned to reflect an X-ray off the face of the crystal always did so at an angle determined by the way the reflecting molecule fit into the latticework of the crystal.

By the time Polanyi arrived on the scene, Herzog and Jancke knew that the fibers were built up from units containing six carbon atoms ("hexoses") derived from glucose, a form of sugar. Early X-ray observations seemed to indicate an amorphous, non-crystalline jumble of molecules in the material, a result that was inconsistent with the patterns noted when the cellulose was illuminated by polarized light. To resolve the contradiction, Herzog had asked his superb experimental assistant, Willi Jancke, to make improved X-ray experiments. These experiments provided fresh information for the physicists, physical and organic chemists, mathematicians, and technicians who worked together in the institute.

Although Herzog's and Jancke's results were obtained in July, their article was only sent in for publication on September 28, 1920, just before Polanyi joined the group.[4] The two men had also done a different type of experiment in which a bundle of natural, unpulverized fibers were lined up together. A beam directed along the fibers produced a pattern like those generated by the powdered samples, but a beam shot at right angles to the bundle of fibers produced an unfamiliar rectangular pattern. Here was the small, manageable problem that Haber set Polanyi to solve: What properties of the geometry of X-ray beam and crystal alignments could account for the four-spot diagrams? Haber was too busy with administration and Jancke was not trained in mathematics and geometry, so neither was able to tackle the puzzle.

On Friday, October 1, his first day of work, Polanyi was shown the results and was asked to seek an interpretation. He had to learn from scratch, and quickly, about X-ray diffraction, of which "owing to wars and revolutions and my exclusive interest in thermodynamics and kinetics, I had heard little before" (KB, 98). Sir William Henry Bragg and his son, William Lawrence Bragg (just one year older than Polanyi), had developed the technique of X-ray crystallography in 1912 and won the Nobel Prize for Physics in 1915. Despite Polanyi's unfamiliarity with the use of X-rays to determine crystal structure, it took only a week or two for him to find the key to the interpretation. Its finding was a great success, carried out with a rapidity similar to that six years before in November 1914, when he converted Eucken's proposals into the essence of the potential theory of adsorption. Herzog presented Polanyi's interpretation to the October 18 meeting of the Chemical Society.[5] The article included the diagrams of the four-point diffraction pattern. Polanyi argued that a single crystal rotated about the axis of the bundle of fibers would produce a similar pattern; at only four points in its circuit around the axis would the crystal catch and deflect the X-rays toward a focal point on the negative. The fibers must therefore have their constituent crystals lined up at a definite angle to the lengthwise axis of the fiber, but arranged randomly about it, corresponding to the succession of positions taken by the imagined rotating crystal. Geometric calculations gave information about the size of the units that composed the crystal and, combined with diffraction patterns produced by X-rays taken at other angles, helped to determine the positions of the atoms within the molecules. Polanyi's discovery of the rotating-crystal method was thus announced at the very start of his work—almost a full year before its details were spelled out in publication.

Almost immediately after establishing his explanation of the sets of four points, Polanyi saw that the same analysis applies to the case of a single crystal that is steadily rotated about one of its axes. The separate spots will turn into circles in exactly the same way as for the fibers. Since that discovery, the rotating-crystal method, with some later variants, has become of the first importance in the whole field of X-ray structure determination, while fiber analysis remains a small corner of the field.

Herzog wanted Polanyi to investigate the properties of fiber strength and the organic chemistry of cellulose, but Polanyi was eager to get back to the *Zauberei* (the "magical forces"), which he thought were at work in chemical reactions. While his solution of the four-point puzzle helped Herzog and assured the young assistant's bread and butter, it was not a topic that stirred his intellectual passions. Polanyi deliberately took advantage of Herzog's vague job description to fit his own research into his daily schedule. Polanyi had looked forward to discussing the *Zauberei* with his colleagues in the Physical Chemistry Institute. His new friends were cordial enough, but they neither went along with Polanyi's interpretation of the data nor offered well-reasoned criticisms. They reacted with indifference, taking Polanyi's basic statistical approach to gas reactions as uncontroversial and assuming that future developments would clarify the source of the activation energy.

This disappointment, coupled with the stress of moving to new surroundings and the accompanying loneliness, caused Polanyi some anguish. Early in October, he confided his doubts to Alfred Reis, a friend in Karlsruhe. Reis wrote back immediately, sympathizing with his frustrations, but urging Polanyi to set aside his doubts and to trust that he would make discoveries that would satisfy him and his peers; in his view, Polanyi was a "decisive, consequential, and rigorous-thinking man" who would go far in the field of science.[6]

In November, Polanyi initiated some experimental work in crystallography. In accordance with Herzog's policy of allowing staff members in one group to do occasional work in another group, Polanyi got permission to call on two Herzog assistants, Willi Jancke and Karl Becker, to start looking for other ways to find or create the one-dimensional directionality that the new X-ray method utilized. They started on this project shortly after the dust had settled on Polanyi's original success and before the Christmas season was upon them, and the work went on to final publication in February (1921c). The stage was set for experimental and theoretical work that was to develop over the next year.

Besides his work on crystals and reaction kinetics, Polanyi was also continuing his work on adsorption. He received galley proofs to read for his article on the deformation theory of adsorption forces, probably in October (1920i), and set about the writing of a review lecture on the potential theory of adsorption for the tenth birthday celebration of the Kaiser Wilhelm Gesellschaft on January 11 (1921a). Polanyi was especially anxious to combine his adsorption ideas and those of his reaction kinetics. His first article on adsorption catalysis was built on his reaction articles (1921h). In this article, Polanyi was able to contrast the rates of simple chemical reactions in a gaseous state to the rate that the same reactions would take place on a surface. His analysis showed why the presence of the surface would favor some chemical reactions over others due to the different attractive forces experienced by single atoms as compared to diatomic molecules.

Polanyi's demonstration of the effectiveness of a surface merely because of its physical nonspecific and nonchemical attractive properties was an important preliminary step in the development of his transition rate theory. It had taken Polanyi a while to realize that surface catalysis would necessarily lead into the situation like that of Langmuir where the study of reaction rates would have to stick with only a few molecules at a time at separated sites on the surface. This program of research in catalysis was to be an important part of Polanyi's development in reaction kinetics, but he never reached the point he first envisioned, an analysis of reactions carried on in the thick, dense layers posited in his adsorption theory.

By November, Polanyi realized that no one had yet developed a molecular explanation of how solids deform or break. It seemed evident to Polanyi that polycrystalline strength should be related to both the resistance to stretching and the resistance to rupture of single crystals. A chain is as strong as its weakest link; similarly, it seemed that a crystal structure should be as strong as the bonds between its component molecules. Polanyi began to formulate a theory of crystal breaking strength and made an elementary calculation of rupture strength on a simple model of a cubic crystal, sodium chloride, common salt, where the binding forces between the sodium and chlorine atoms were well understood; the molecules were held together by the attraction of positive and negative electrically charged ions. A chlorine atom steals an electron away from a sodium atom, making the chlorine a negatively charged ion and the sodium a positively charged ion. Since the strength of attraction in such bonds followed relatively straightforward laws of electrostatic attraction, it was possible to calculate how much force would have to be applied to separate one plane of a sodium crystal from another plane in contact with it. But the "breaking strength" of sodium chloride—that is, the actual force required to break a sodium chloride crystal—was from 150 to 1,000 times smaller than this theory predicted. This discrepancy was an important puzzle driving Polanyi's research into crystal properties.

For Polanyi, the unexpected weakness in crystals looked like more of the magic he had already identified in chemical reactions. Some extra source of energy might be released by the mechanical pressure, causing the ion bonds to break sooner than expected. Polanyi communicated the results to Bredig, his old friend and mentor in Karlsruhe, who wrote that they were interesting and suggested a test with high-frequency vibrations. Bredig said that it was unlikely that there would be the great dependence on temperature that Polanyi had predicted.[7] Polanyi had not revealed his deeper interest in the strength discrepancy, namely that it might prove to be another case where a new type of quantum jump might be operative—he had already tried to interest Bredig in this subject without success.

Polanyi wanted to have some competent experimenters explore the puzzle and see the new quantum jumps for themselves. Max Born was at that time in the forefront of work on the theory of ionic crystals, and Polanyi had met him at the Bunsengesellschaft meeting in Halle in April. Polanyi persuaded Born to join him in offering a prize for the best study of whether ordinary electrostatic forces can explain the breaking strength of sodium chloride crystals.[8] After Born accepted the professorship of theoretical physics in Göttingen in 1921, the prize in the amount of 2,200 M, was announced in the issue of the *Physikalische Zeitschrift* for August 1, 1921, under the sponsorship of the Göttingen Academy of Sciences. The announcement said nothing of Polanyi's thesis that a new quantum process would be required to explain the cohesive forces at work in the crystal. The deadline for receipt of essays was set at one year later, but no one seems ever to have been awarded the prize, which presumably was wiped out by inflation.

After three and a half months in Berlin, Polanyi returned to Karlsruhe early in December for a month-long Christmas holiday, taking a room in Baron von Rothberg's villa at Bismarckstrasse 7, where Magda lived. Polanyi had originally anticipated carrying on some experimental research in Karlsruhe over the vacation, but shortage of heavy batteries in the laboratory left him free to enjoy a vacation with his fiancée.

Polanyi returned to Berlin two or three days ahead of the date for his adsorption theory lecture, which was presented at a special meeting of the Haber colloquium at the Kaiser Wilhelm Institute for Physical Chemistry and Electrochemistry. Einstein, a frequent visitor, had been specifically invited to attend this session. Polanyi detailed his assumptions of multilayered adsorption under the influence of an as-yet-undetermined potential energy and described how his theory of this attractive energy could be used to get one isotherm from another. In the discussion, Einstein and Haber insisted that according to the current electron theory, such forces simply could not exist; there could be no structure that would prevent charge mobility from shielding one layer from another. They rejected Polanyi's hypothesis that electron orbits could be deformed enough to produce positive and negative poles in molecular structures (dipoles) but not so much as to produce shielding of the electrostatic charges by the first layer of adsorbed molecules.

Polanyi already had, by that time, the burden of countering the theory of Langmuir, the chief authority in the field, even though the scope of Langmuir's theory was quite different from Polanyi's. The suggestion by Einstein and Haber that his opposition to Langmuir was ill founded in principle made his task even harder—after all, Langmuir assumed incomplete, single layers of adsorbed atoms or molecules, and therefore needed no theory to explain multilayer attraction.

The majority of the chemists present were not bothered by the attack. The physicists' argument did not appeal to their own sense of the range of possibilities for the structures of molecules in solids, and Langmuir's theory of monomolecular layers held in place by chemical bonds had not become authoritative for them. The correlation between Polanyi's theory and the data was more important than the objections.[9] Nevertheless, Polanyi felt some disquiet. If he had not already built a reputation in his new, but quite different field, X-ray fiber analysis, his scientific career might have sustained a severe blow. The controversy illustrates the pervasive role of plausibility considerations in evaluating a piece of research (PK, 137–138, 155).

Polanyi had other things to worry about that winter besides the development of his scientific career. He and Magda originally planned to be married in a Catholic church in Budapest because Magda and her family were Catholic. The date was set for a week or so after the end of her term at the Technische Hochschule. Unfortunately, Magda's father, who was to give her away in the ceremony, died just before the wedding day. They attended his funeral in Budapest and were married immediately afterward on February 21, 1921, in a civil ceremony attended by Karel Vermeŝ, a friend of her father. Magda and Michael stayed on in Budapest to help her mother settle the estate. They got away for a brief honeymoon together, then took the train back to Karlsruhe. Polanyi went on to Berlin to find a place to live and to prepare for his presentation on the structure of cellulose; Magda ended her enrollment at the Technische Hochschule, said a few goodbyes—she did not want to spread the news to everyone—and prepared to move.

Magda arrived in Berlin on March 21. She and Michael lived in two furnished rooms without cooking facilities at Dahlemerstrasse 75 in nearby Lichterfelde West, a good walk from the laboratory in Dahlem. The toilet in the hall provided for the use of the tenants often had a notice on the door: "Out of order, do not use." Polanyi always joked about it, calling it *das Sorgenkind* (the problem child). After Michael and Magda were established in their new home, Cecile came for a visit, staying in a nearby Pension. She thought Michael and Magda were very well matched. "Magda is Misi's best woman," she wrote, "simple, selfless, devoted, disciplined, his alter ego.... He is inordinately in love." Cecile was pleased with what she saw in her son: "First the person: husband, son, son-in-law, brother and friend, with a softening goodness, love, and willingness to make sacrifices. Second the deep mystic and thinker who internalizes a coherent image of the world like a mirror of his clear, noble soul. Then there is Misi as a scientist, but you know that."[10] She was also impressed by the way Polanyi helped around the house.

Magda's move to Berlin coincided with Polanyi's presentation of his evidence on the structure of cellulose, which had been gathered five months previously. He was not completely satisfied with the talk. Aside from a general feeling that the results were not up to his standards, he had been held up by a slight deviation from the predicted position of two spots on the equator of the cellulose diagram that impaired his confidence in his interpretation. He never did find the reason for the discrepancy, but came to recognize that the difficulty should not have interfered with his reporting his proposed analysis (KB, 100).

Polanyi's results from the X-ray data were the first to give the dimensions of the periodic unit cell in cellulose. He found a rhombic cell (mutually perpendicular axes) with edges 7.9, 8.45, and 10.2 angstroms, respectively, close to the modern values. Analysis had shown that the cellobiose units each consist of $C_6H_{10}O_5$ and have a molecular weight of 162. From the volume of a cell and the known density of pure cellulose, it was easy to calculate that exactly four 162 molecular-weight units must make up each unit cell.

Polanyi puzzled over the way the groups of cellobiose units could be connected. There were only two possibilities. The first was a set of chain molecules of indefinite length made of hexoses (molecules structured around six carbon atoms) linked by oxygens and bundled in groups of four, and the second was a set of self-contained molecules, one in each cell, either made of two pairs of two hexose rings or of one ring of four units. Any larger but finite hexose rings would show up as a different unit cell size in the X-rays. In either case, weak forces of a postulated but not understood secondary valence type would hold the molecules together sideways. The weak bonds would also act, in the second case, to aggregate the small molecules into long fibers.

Polanyi considered the long chain idea far more likely than the absurdly small cell-sized molecules, but Herzog favored the latter view and insisted that it should be recognized.[11] When Polanyi presented his paper, the chemists in the audience raised a storm of protest. It was not just that the X-ray analyst could not make up his mind but that some of the chemists considered it absurd for Polanyi even to suggest an indefinitely long molecule as the structure of cellulose. Polanyi was amused by the chemists' resistance to a new concept of molecular length, but he overlooked his duty to establish the chain structure definitively. He later admitted that he lacked the necessary chemical sense to pursue his hypothesis (KB, 99). If Polanyi had done a proper apprenticeship in the field under the tutelage of a master, he might have been better prepared to take advantage of his own ground-breaking insight into the structure of cellulose.

Polanyi did not know then that there was a long-standing dispute over the possible existence of large, chained molecules, which are now called polymers. Those who rejected the idea of long structures formed from regularly repeating units argued that the aggregates were a case of matter in a special colloidal state for which the ordinary physical laws used in measurement did not hold. Conventional wisdom held that chemists would eventually be able to isolate the small molecules that made up the complex compounds.[12] A year before Polanyi's presentation, Hermann Staudinger had strongly resisted the idea that complex substances would prove to be simple aggregates of relatively small molecules.[13] Karl Freudenberg had an article either just published or still in press at the time of Polanyi's lecture proposing a chain of glucose or cellobiose units for cellulose.[14] Polanyi remarked to Robert Olby that if he had known about Freudenberg's pioneering suggestion of an indefinitely long chain (polymer) for cellulose, he would never have backed Herzog's position that cellulose was composed of small molecules.[15] While Polanyi was the first to suggest that the chains in cellulose were consistent with X-ray data, the final determination that the molecule was a polymer was left to Hermann Mark, Kurt H. Meyer, and Hermann Staudinger.[16]

Polanyi never submitted a formal article to a journal on his results. All that appeared under his name was a brief note in the April 15 issue of *Naturwissenschaften* that was included in a section entitled "contributions from other areas" and was not set apart from the previous text with a special heading.[17] The note reported that Polanyi had spoken at the Kaiser Wilhelm Institute for Physical Chemistry and Electrochemistry on the chemical constitution of cellulose and summarized the presentation in four paragraphs. Polanyi's signature appeared at the end. More details were included in Herzog's paper on X-ray research on high molecular-weight organic compounds at the May 19–22 meeting of the Union of German Scientists in Stuttgart. The half-page abstract of this talk reported extensive observations by Jancke and Becker, which supported Polanyi's interpretation of the fiber diagram and repeated the conclusions he had stated in *Naturwissenschaften*.[18] On July 26, Herzog and Jancke published a two-page article developing the arguments more fully. Since Polanyi did not appear as a co-author, these articles never became part of his bibliography.

In May, Polanyi published the first account of the new geometric approach to analyzing crystals in three pages of *Naturwissenschaften* (1921e). It included Polanyi's discovery of a relation of great generality and simplicity. All the spots in the diagram turned out to lie on a fourfold series of symmetrical hyperbolas whenever a flat photographic film was used, and on a set of circles when the film was wrapped cylindrically around the fiber bundle or crystal rotation axis. These lines of spots were called "layer lines." In the early, primitive X-ray photographs only a few spots were visible in each quadrant, showing the four-point diagram rectangles but not their layer line connections. The separation between any two successive layer lines gave a direct measure of the size of the unit cell in the fiber axis direction, and other information could also be derived from them.

Polanyi's work on the fiber diagram received a great boost when the mathematician Karl Weissenberg moved to the Institute of Applied Mathematics in Berlin and became an assistant to four of the Kaiser Wilhelm Institutes, Fiber Chemistry, Metallurgical Research, Physical Chemistry and Physics. In the spring of 1921, he was assigned as an aide to Polanyi. Weissenberg was fascinated with the mathematics of the X-ray fiber diagram and was ready to take up some of its applications. Polanyi immediately recognized the benefit of superior mathematical expertise. "I was anything but a mathematician," he told Olby, perhaps underestimating the value of his geometrical and physical intuition. Polanyi had found the key to a clear explanation of the genesis of the four-point fiber diagrams, but he presented his findings in "a very clumsy form, which Ewald [a well-known crystallographer] found despicable."[19]

Weissenberg's assignment was twofold. He was to continue developing the X-ray theory and he was to help with experiments exploring one of the recently discovered applications. Weissenberg's first task was to assist Polanyi in turning his brief May article into a substantial one in the *Zeitschrift für Physik* (1921f). He and Polanyi published two further articles in that journal, with Weissenberg clarifying many details about the rotation of the crystals around the axis of the molecule (1922b, 1922e). Along with his work with Polanyi on straight fibers, Weissenberg published papers on the application of the method to distortions of various kinds, spirals, rings, statistical asymmetries, and so on. In 1923, he developed an extension of the rotating-crystal method by rotating the film with the crystal so that each layer of lines would correspond to a particular setting of the crystal around the axis.[20] The "Weissenberg camera" allowed a complete set of three parameters to be found for each set of lattice planes and is a powerful analytic tool for determining crystal structure.

Weissenberg's other assignment involved the design of an experiment to determine how crystallites lined up in ordinary polycrystalline metal wires, which were hardened by drawing them through holes in diamonds. Becker and Jancke had pioneered this method of generating fiber-like structures. Their work brought metallic fibers into the purview of the Fiber Institute (1921c).

The ongoing project for which Weissenberg's interpretive help was needed was the Ph.D. work of Margarete Ettisch, the first research student employed in Polanyi's group. A student of the organic chemist F. Ullmann at the University of Berlin, she was using Weissenberg's method to determine the crystal arrangements in hard-drawn wires of several metals. Careful results for seven polycrystalline metallic wires that form cubic crystals were reported in a brief article with Weissenberg and Polanyi, sent off in July (1921g), then in a paper given at the *Deutsche Physikertag* conference in Jena, September 18–24 (1921i), and finally in a more extensive article published in October (1921k). The work showed how the particular faces in the cubic crystals tended to line up in the drawing process and how a cross-section of the wire would appear when examined under the microscope. Annealing the wires at high temperature destroyed the alignment of the crystal faces.

At some point in April or May, Polanyi resurrected his manuscript from the previous November on single-crystal breaking strength and added a section attempting to explain the discrepancy between the theory of crystal strength and the experimental results by invoking the *Zauberei*, the energy-collecting quantum jumps. The article was finished in June, and he sent a copy to Born before publication (1921j). Born expressed doubts that the measured strengths were the "true" ones, attributing the discrepancy to "local and thermal fluctuations."[21] In effect, Born was answering the prize question and rejecting Polanyi's quantum theory. However, the announced question was more general and called for detailed analysis, so Born did not make any effort to collect the reward Polanyi had promised.

In July, Polanyi finished an article on the X-ray fiber diagram and another on fibrous structure in metals (1934f, 1934g). Near the end of the month, Michael and Magda left on a three-week holiday, visiting family briefly in Vienna and Budapest. Michael told Mausi he hoped to spend more time in the city on his next visit: "I am attracted to Budapest with a peculiar strength and I want to nourish this attraction."[22] Back home in Berlin, they kept on looking for a better place, but Magda did not really mind too much: "Unfortunately we still have no apartment of our own. Luckily I'm not a good . . . or more honestly not a housewife at all, so that the kitchen, etc. inconvenience doesn't bother me."[23] Polanyi wrote to his mother later that month that Magda was tired and sick, and that he felt the need for more income. After some frustrating delays, Magda was allowed to enroll at the Berlin Technische Hochschule. She carried on some work on a dissertation in the winter of 1921–22 with the help of Polanyi and Ervin von Gomperz, whom he had tutored in Budapest and who had arrived in Berlin in the fall of 1921 to take up scientific studies. Magda abandoned her efforts to finish her Ph.D. after the summer of 1922, when the Technische Hochschule was forced to close due to the surge of inflation.

Sometime before the fall of 1921, Polanyi sent Einstein a carbon copy of a marked-up, preliminary draft of an article entitled "Isolated Collisions and Collisions that Happen in Dilute Equilibrium Systems."[24] In this article, he dealt with the radiation of visible light that sometimes occurs in a very tiny fraction of collisions between certain atoms or ion-electron pairs. He argued that the very rare emissions of light (one out of 10^{13} cases) must demonstrate the transmission of energy from one molecule to another through the aether. Polanyi's concept of coupled quantum jumps turns out to be a case of a second-order transition, like that of two electrons undergoing simultaneous transitions in certain atomic processes, processes into which serious research began only in the 1960s. The atom-jump idea, although wrong for chemistry, had some profound connections with realities yet to be discovered.

Polanyi became convinced of the error of his quantum-jump hypothesis by talking with colleagues who took his ideas seriously, even though they disagreed with him. His most detailed and far-reaching dialogue was in correspondence with Karl Herzfeld, but the influence of Max Born and others was considerable.[25] Herzfeld had received his Ph.D. in Vienna in 1914 and joined Fajans's department at Munich in 1920. After his war service, Herzfeld wrote a lengthy article on reaction velocity in which he argued that a collision between a free hydrogen atom and a molecule of bromine gas (Br_2), producing a molecule of hydrogen bromide and an unbound bromine atom, would accelerate the rate of dissociation of Br_2 without requiring energy from the aether.[26] Polanyi knew of this article and referred to it in the second of his articles, but he considered the side reaction as negligible because he estimated the bromine atoms would very rapidly recombine into molecules of Br_2 (1920b).

Max Born wrote Polanyi on June 13, 1921, to say that he considered the quantum-jump idea neither necessary nor plausible, and added that he and Franck had worked out an explanation of the speed of reactions in ordinary quantum theory using only the kinetic energy available from collisions, and expected to publish it soon.[27] Born told Polanyi that he should not make wild hypotheses about atom jumps because they only serve to cut off reasonable lines of inquiry. Polanyi did not immediately heed Born's advice; he wanted stronger reasons for abandoning his hypothesis.

Born and Polanyi discussed the problem of reaction velocity in some detail at the German Physicists Meeting (Physikertag) in Jena, September 19–24, 1921.[28] Franck, Herzfeld, and Smekal were also there and took some part in the conversation. Born wrote on September 26 that he was happy to have seen Polanyi and that he had learned that reaction velocity is much more complicated than he had thought. Nevertheless, Born was not persuaded that unknown processes of energy transmission were needed for an explanation—he declared that he would steer clear of this topic.

The decisive series of five letters each between Herzfeld and Polanyi on the "magic" began after the September meeting. The main issue the two men needed to discuss was whether bromine atoms released by the collision of a hydrogen atom with a molecule of bromine gas would rapidly combine together, as Polanyi had thought, and remove themselves from further repetition of the first reaction, $Br + H_2 \rightarrow HBr + H$. Herzfeld described his theory of equilibrium in the breakup of Br_2, which means that at whatever rate the molecules dissociate, equilibrium will rapidly set in and maintain a certain concentration of Br atoms in relation to the Br_2. When one bromine atom is used up in the formation of hydrogen bromide, it is replaced almost immediately (a fact beyond dispute) by the dissociation of a bromine molecule into two atoms, maintaining the equilibrium between bromine atoms and molecules so there could not be a rapid disappearance of free bromine atoms.

Polanyi wanted more details, and the two men exchanged thoughts on whether a molecule made by the collision of two bromine atoms would have enough internal energy to dissociate almost immediately. They came close to agreement that it would and quibbled a bit on whether such a fast association-to-dissociation process should even be counted as a collision. The idea of quantum jumps was accepted by Herzfeld in the narrow sense of occurrences on collision, but this only added another mechanism for the energy transfer processes.

Polanyi's second letter of the series bore a scrawled message at the top "Herewith a small communication on *Zauberei*. I would be very thankful to you for your opinion." He wrote that he would be comfortable without the magic if someone could disprove the need for it. In his next letter, he accepted the hypothesis that the concentration of bromine atoms remained constant, but still thought something was wrong with some of Herzfeld's rate calculations.

In November, Polanyi visited Göttingen. Conversation with James Franck, Max Born, Wolfgang Pauli, and others helped him to reconsider his position. On November 29, Born wrote Einstein about Polanyi's *Zauberei*: "I would like to know what you think of Polanyi's papers on rates of reactions; he maintains that these could not be explained without an as yet unknown kind of energy-transmission. . . . Langmuir was here recently; he thinks on similar lines but we (Franck and Born) still do not believe it. P's paper about tensile strength is also quite crazy and yet it contains a grain of truth." Einstein replied on December 30, "Polanyi's ideas make me shudder. But he has discovered difficulties for which I know no remedies as yet."[29]

By the time Einstein expressed his distaste for Polanyi's speculations, Polanyi had already conceded defeat; in his fourth letter to Herzfeld on November 4, he said, "I guess that everything is as obvious to you as to me and that we have arrived at a complete understanding, for which I am very happy." Although a few small points were still to be discussed, the *Zauberei* had vanished. Herzfeld sent Polanyi the manuscript of his own article, which took into account the results of their correspondence and cleared up the whole business. He requested that if Polanyi had no more corrections to suggest, he should deliver the article to H. Scheel, the editor of the *Zeitschrift für Physik*, who was located in Berlin. Polanyi replied on November 18 that "on purely logical grounds I agree with everything you say," but suggested that Herzfeld's definition of "collision" might lead to later difficulties. After the article appeared, Herzfeld thanked Polanyi for his thoughtful remarks.[30]

Polanyi's persistent claim that he had made a new discovery were couched in the objective language of science and did not reflect the great excitement he must have felt. His failure to recognize the answer that lay right before him is a prime example of what he later called his excessive speculations. "Icarus-like, I flew so near the sun that my wings were ever in danger of melting away" (1975a, 1152). Elsewhere he remarked that "ambition is absolutely necessary in a scientist" but "it is almost needless to point out the possible abuse arising from excess ambition."[31]

This episode of misdirected speculation was not wholly fruitless. Polanyi's colleagues never ridiculed him for being wrong. By creating a method to estimate the energy needed for the hydrogen bromide reaction, he made an important contribution to the field, even though his interpretation of the meaning of his calculations proved false. The debate with other scientists broadened his awareness of the current state of scientific knowledge and deepened his personal insights. Instead of being pushed aside or cut off from the community of his peers, he became more fully a part of the scientific enterprise. The loneliness in which he had written his reaction papers of 1919 and 1920 was a thing of the past.

Polanyi never made an explicit retraction or apology, nor was he expected to. Scientists frequently make competent conjectures that are later refuted by superior arguments or new evidence. To make a retraction or an apology would wrongly suggest that the idea was due to flaws in intelligence or character. Many suggestions made in good conscience turn out later to have been mistaken, and research scientists generally allow such mistaken conceptions to drop out of sight without further comment.

As Polanyi's scientific work went on steadily during the winter and spring 1921–22, the main interest on the home front was Magda's pregnancy. The stress of teaching himself a new field of research and establishing his credentials with his peers had diminished considerably. Polanyi was glad that the pressure of work had decreased before the baby's birth. He was less tired than he had been and thought he had overcome his sleeplessness "for a while." He naturally expected changes once the baby was born, but, in spite of some current difficulties, he was very satisfied with what he had accomplished: "In the last one to one and a half years here, I have settled into a profession, a position. I have created an organization, a work-environment.... For me, the task was to make a talented, though not brilliant, somewhat poorly educated, young foreigner, into a useful person. That involved much weariness, but, in the end, contentment."[32]

Magda's mother, Josefine Kemeny, had moved to Berlin in August 1921 and had found a small place at Ehrenbergstrasse 31, quite a change from the large, elegant, and centrally-heated apartment she had been accustomed to in Budapest. She had also reconciled herself to the fact that she could only afford to hire help for just an hour and a half each day.[33] As the time for her daughter to give birth drew near, she realized that her little flat, with a kitchen and private bath, was far superior to the two rooms Michael and Magda were living in, so she moved to a boarding house and let them take over her lease.

Their new home did not have enough room for a cot for the baby. Polanyi hooked a playpen onto the couch so the child could sleep there without falling off.[34] Unfortunately, tensions developed between the owners of the apartment, a mother and daughter, and the Polanyis. Cecile described the hallway where the families had entrances to their own rooms as a place full of "aggressiveness, mistrust and rejection."[35]

In the laboratory, there were frustrations of a different sort. On the basis of his speculation about atom jumps in crystal deformation, Polanyi supposed that a small crystal, a millimeter in size or less, would have proportionately less energy stored up to "jump" and so would require a larger force to break. He enlisted H. Schönborn and J. Peters, two postdoctoral experimentalists in Herzog's group, to test this consequence on single crystals of rock salt. The results convinced Polanyi to announce forthcoming publication at the end of his September article (1921j). However, the problems involved in measurements of force versus change of length on a millimeter-long crystal were exasperatingly difficult. Max Born expressed serious doubts that such tests could be made reliably. Efforts to verify Polanyi's prediction had to be given up, and the results were never published.

What happened instead was that with the help of his assistants, Polanyi made a new discovery: the well-known strengthening of ordinary polycrystalline wires by cold working—being drawn, stretched, or bent at ordinary temperatures—happens also for single-crystal wires. He showed by geometrical calculation that the degree of hardening of drawn polycrystalline wires was too large to be accounted for by the reorientation of the crystallite directions. The explanation had to be that the single crystallites themselves became harder, and this conclusion was verified by experiments on single-crystal tungsten wires and simple rock salt crystals by Schönborn, Peters, and Polanyi's friend and student, Ervin von Gomperz.

The uncomfortable result presented itself that the more nearly ideal the atomic arrangement of a crystal, the weaker it becomes; but the more the crystal gets distorted by cold-working, the more its strength approaches the predicted values. The subject became so interesting that Polanyi gave a paper on his calculations and a sampling of the results of his three collaborators on September 15, 1921, at a meeting of the Bunsengesellschaft at Jena, announcing that Schönborn, von Gomperz, and Peters would each later publish the details of their work (1922a). Tammann, the moderator, was taken back by its novelty and strangeness. Polanyi had reported many particulars but had no overall conceptual explanation to offer for the surprising effect.

At the Bunsengesellschaft meeting, Polanyi heard how Jan Czochralski made single, fiber-shaped crystals of various metals. He promptly assigned von Gomperz the task of adapting this method to the work being done at the Kaiser Wilhelm Institute. The crystals produced by von Gomperz considerably enriched the research work on metals, turning them from a side issue for the laboratory to a matter of central and fruitful activity. Von Gomperz's procedure was to insert a small crystal of the same material into the surface of melted metals and then to pull it out slowly and carefully, so that the melted material would continuously "freeze" onto the crystal and make it grow longer. It worked well, but irregular lumps tended to be generated on the resulting single-crystal wire. A visitor to the laboratory, Hermann Mark (soon to become a member of the group), suggested putting a mica cover with a small hole over the top of the liquid metal and drawing the wire out through the hole. The idea worked and was put to use, first by Schönborn with zinc and then by von Gomperz with tin, the principal metals studied by the laboratory group.

Polanyi added some notes to his Bunsengesellschaft paper about the results of hardening zinc and tin fibers. He also included data obtained by Peters on the work-hardening of rock salt crystals by bending. This article (1922h) and publications by Schönborn and by von Gomperz all appeared early in 1922.[36]

On his return from the Jena conference, Polanyi welcomed Rudolf Brill, a newcomer to the fiber X-ray project. Brill had been a chemistry student at the University of Berlin since 1918 and became a student of Herzog in the fall of 1921, but it was Polanyi who suggested he apply the cellulose method to silk as his Ph.D. research. Herzog and Jancke had published preliminary four-spot pictures of fibrous silk material, known as silk fibroin,[37] and Polanyi had obtained a tentative cell dimension that needed confirmation.

Brill's main problem was to get good X-ray pictures that would determine the precise cell dimensions and the atomic arrangement of the components of the fiber. The tubes were built out of metal and glass with a special vacuum-sealing glue, modeled on an X-ray tube invented in the United States by W. D. Coolidge in 1913. Keeping the tubes tight and the vacuum high was a time-consuming chore, as was maintaining the 40,000 volt power supply, but Brill mastered the techniques and obtained good interference patterns. He applied Polanyi and Weissenberg's method to pictures from nine varieties of silk, measuring sixteen different spot locations. All the varieties of silk had the same crystalline component, and he was able to make a good determination of the size of the elementary cell. He concluded that there were three possible arrangements of the alanine and glycine amino acids within the fibroin molecule.

Brill saw Polanyi very little. Polanyi kept track of the work just enough to know that it was going well. He stayed away from the apparatus, for he had not acquired the skills needed to keep the tubes going and to take the X-ray pictures.[38] Contrary to his approach with other doctoral students, Polanyi let Brill write his thesis and then publish his results with his mentor's name used only in the acknowledgments and not as an author.[39] Polanyi later judged that he had misjudged the implications of Brill's work, just as he had failed to see the significance of his own work with cellulose (1962g, 99). It seems likely that a longer, more orthodox apprenticeship in chemistry might have led Polanyi to make more substantial contributions in both areas.

Polanyi's work during the fall of 1921 was still diversified, but the X-ray research had more focus now that single crystals could be handled. Besides Brill, he also supervised von Gomperz and Schönborn in their work on tin and zinc and in their work with Weissenberg on the X-ray methods. Polanyi's initial success with X-rays was an auspicious beginning to his career at Kaiser Wilhelm. The great power of his new method thoroughly justified Herzog's plan to develop a school of fiber research utilizing X-rays. The consequence was that "Herzog, with kindly enthusiasm, showered me with every facility for experimental work, most precious of which were funds for employing assistants and financing research students. In this I was incredibly lucky. I was joined by Hermann Mark, Erich Schmid, Karl Weissenberg, all three from Vienna, by Ervin von Gomperz and some others; the place was soon humming" (KB, 98–99). By the spring of 1922, Polanyi had six scientific co-workers, five Ph.D. candidates, and one laboratory assistant—the biggest team he ever had in Berlin. They became close friends as well.

Besides the excellent associates he found in his laboratory, there were a host of other world-class scientists in the area. Fritz Haber founded a colloquium in 1920 for the Institute of Physical Chemistry and Electrochemistry, but it soon came to include scientists from Herzog's Institute of Fiber Chemistry and Otto Hahn's Chemistry Institute. Although Haber left it to Freundlich to arrange the program and introduce the speaker, Haber himself was always the leader. It was generally accepted that only he had the privilege of interrupting the speaker before the end of the lecture, often punctuating his comments with a sip of water. The sessions often became quite lively, especially when Haber and Nernst engaged in heated discussions over many controversial aspects of physical chemistry. Haber often seemed to come out ahead, although Nernst often retorted that "It is already in my book."[40] It was said that one did not have to keep up with the literature because the author of a good paper would show up to address a Haber colloquium sooner or later.

The Physics Colloquium organized by von Laue and held at the physics laboratory of the University of Berlin became the most exciting event of Polanyi's week. While many of the topics addressed in the Haber Colloquium dealt with aspects of chemistry that he considered dull, the lectures on the many aspects of modern physics fascinated him, for he never lost his love of fundamental physics nor his awe at the mathematical expertise of the discoverers: "The seminar at the physics laboratory in Berlin, where Planck, Einstein, Schrödinger, Laue, Hahn and Lise Meitner met every Wednesday for informal discussion is still the most glorious intellectual memory of my life."[41]

Besides the physicists from the university, there were colleagues from the Technische Hochschule and the Reichsanstalt (the latter group headed by Walter Nernst for two years) and from the Kaiser Wilhelm Institute, particularly Haber. People were said to be disappointed if there were fewer than three Nobel Prize winners present.[42] The arguments among Nernst, Einstein, and Planck were lively and interesting. As in Haber's colloquium, Nernst frequently managed, with much wit and charm, to direct the discussion into a field in which he himself felt superior, but the effect on the younger listeners was that, as in the Haber sessions, they did not know how to tell who had won.[43]

The physics students all knew Polanyi by sight: the "remarkably good-looking" young physical chemist from Hungary who had the knack of putting difficult things in a simple way.[44] Polanyi also had the gift of expressing criticism without provoking hostility. He exercised an acute physical insight, thinking and speaking in helpful images, rather than arguing by means of calculations. After overcoming his initial shyness, Polanyi earned a reputation in the colloquium for his critical faculties and his ability to clarify disagreements. After listening to a difficult lecture, Polanyi would often take the podium and give a lucid summary and critique of what had been said.

On the first of January 1922, Polanyi was named acting division leader of the newly formed physical chemistry section.[45] The promotion allowed him to fill out his team with Mark and Schmid. Hermann Mark had received his doctorate in Vienna in July under Wilhelm Schlenck and moved to Berlin as Schlenck's assistant when the latter took the position of director of the First Chemical Institute at the University of Berlin. Schlenck and Herzog agreed that Mark would work as an assistant to Polanyi and as Director of the Technical Applications Division of the Fiber Institute. During the previous fall, Mark had made several visits to Dahlem to see the laboratory and talk with Polanyi. In November, Polanyi proposed using the X-ray equipment to study the deformation of metallic single crystals.[46] Mark arrived at the institute early in January 1922 and headed straight for Polanyi's small home in Lichterfelde. Polanyi came to the living room in lounging pajamas, looking to his new colleague like an Asian prince.[47] Mark found rooms to sublet in Lichterfelde, not far from the Polanyis, and enthusiastically set to work on metallic crystals.

Erich Schmid joined the staff a little later in the year. After getting his degree in physics with Ehrenhaft in Vienna, he had worked with Mark in Berlin, developing expertise in metals. Although it was a new experience for

Polanyi to be responsible for the work of a team of co-workers, "he did it with great charm, infinite patience, a resounding success. He was our gentle genius."[48] The spirit in the laboratory was "Communist" in the best sense of the word.[49] The four men played tennis together, often with their wives—both Schmid and Mark married that year—and entertained each other at dinner. Weissenberg remained a bachelor and was often invited home by the others, especially the Marks. The Polanyis also visited frequently with the Herzogs, and on occasion had dinner (served on golden plates!) at the Habers. Another joy for Magda was sitting near the head of the table at dinner parties. When they lived in Karlsruhe, Polanyi had been seated among the scientists and professors while Magda was forced to sit "below the salt" with the students.[50] Polanyi was also happy in his marriage and in his work.

Things were also starting to look up for the rest of the family. Adolf had been confused and miserable in Rome, scraping by through a series of short-term jobs, until he finally found work in a steam laundry in 1922. Sofie, Egon, and their three children eked out an existence in Vienna, made more difficult because of some unwise business decisions. However, at the end of 1922, Egon joined a small, but well-established Viennese film enterprise, which enabled Sofie to retrieve her furniture from Budapest. Karl was hampered a great deal by sickness (or perhaps hypochondria). He had hoped that his cousin Emil Kiss from the United States would find a job for him, either at the newspaper *La Prensa* in Buenos Aires or in the United States. Neither job materialized, and it was not until the fall of 1921 that Karl found regular employment as secretary to Oscar Jászi and later as an assistant in the editorial office of Jászi's Hungarian language paper, *Bécsi Magyar Ujsag* (Viennese Hungarian News).

Mausi and Sandor did their best to help Cecile hold onto her apartment in Budapest. With housing in short supply everywhere, the authorities could requisition an apartment for those whom they judged to be more needy or more worthy than the current occupants. Cecile's trips to spas and her visits with her children, usually Mausi and Sandor, worked against her. To forestall the authorities, she rented one of her two rooms to Dr. Kertesz, a professional chemist and a friend, and began to spend more time in Budapest, which may have been somewhat of a relief to her children. She did prove herself a most welcome guest when Mausi was sick for a month. She tapped "her various power sources" and cared for the whole household "with understanding and tact." Mausi enjoyed her mother's "incredibly good cooking" and was surprised by her many hidden talents, especially "her easiness and grace in management."[51]

Inflation struck Germany in Polanyi's second year at the institute. In 1922, the Mark dropped to one-fortieth of its original value; in the course of the next year, it fell to a billionth of its original value! The Dahlem group worked together to mitigate the difficulties: "The economic crisis hit us all equally. We suffered the hunger lightly and bore it with humor."[52] Herzog had trouble paying everyone and welcomed the efforts of the post-doctoral assistants to find solutions, partly through the mechanism of the Studiengesellschaften, consulting groups which contracted with industrial concerns to conduct specific pieces of research. The Fiber Institute got the nickname of "*Assistenten-Republik*," in contrast to the more hierarchical Haber institute. Salaries were paid daily after the value of the mark for that day was determined, and everyone took off from work after lunch to buy food and anything else available; many things could be bartered. The three wives, Magda Polanyi, Mimi Mark, and Gretl Schmid enjoyed shopping together in the big Wertheim store, making an adventure of the difficulties. Special finds, like a huge ball of cheese, were divided among the four families. Polanyi said of their life together, "We had a glorious time" (1962g, 99).

Polanyi had been offered a good position at Izzo, the United Incandescent Lamp and Electric Corporation in Budapest. Ignaz Pfeifer, his old teacher and friend, was a director of the firm. He invited Polanyi in February 1922 to become his successor as scientific director for the firm's work both in Hungary and in Germany. The offer was appealing. Both the technical problems in manufacturing electric lamps and the increase in salary tempted Polanyi to consider shifting from his occasional consulting work with the firm into this stable full-time position.

Magda considered the opportunity a "fabulous job" and Cecile begged him to take it. But Polanyi was reluctant to leave the stimulating life in Dahlem to work in industry. Instead, on a trip to Hungary early in April, he agreed to act as a consultant, devoting 30 percent of his time in the Fiber Institute to work for Izzo and directing researchers whom the firm sent to study in Berlin. In return, Izzo would underwrite 30 percent of his regular stipend, paying it directly to Uncle Karl in Budapest as a hedge against inflation.

While Weissenberg was pursuing the last of the technical articles with Polanyi on the X-ray method and preparing other articles of his own, the team of Mark, Schmid, and Polanyi took up the investigation of the stretching, deformation, hardening, recovery, and rupture of single zinc wire crystals. Their research was later described by Polanyi as "a rare instance of something supposed to be a common occurrence, namely, of the participation of as many as three scientists as equals in a fairly important piece of work."[53]

The remarkable thing about single wire crystals of zinc is that some of them can be stretched to five or six times their original lengths without breaking. As the crystals stretch, they get harder and need greater force to pull. This lengthening is plastic; in contrast to elastic behavior, the material does not go back to its original shape when the tension is released. Zinc crystal wires formed by methods other than that developed by von Gomperz and Mark are quite brittle and break with almost no stretching, never getting beyond elastic behavior to plasticity. Since all such wires are crystallized from randomly placed crystal seeds, they differ in the orientation of the crystal axes with respect to the length of the wire and therefore the orientation of the principal lattice planes. Certain sets of these planes have the property that adjacent pairs can slip past each other rather easily. When such planes lie diagonally across the wire, pulling on the wire allows them to slip, much as a pile of pennies easily slips one way or the other. If the planes are not at a good angle for slipping, then pulling will cause the wire to break right away. But if the planes lie along the length of the wire, each pair in a stack of planes only needs to slip a little with respect to each other in order to make the whole wire slip considerably, bending over sideways and getting longer and longer in the process. Bending of crystal planes occurs particularly in the transition region between the fixed ends and the sliding planes of the main part of the wire. This bending induces discontinuities between adjacent crystal planes that inhibit slipping, a process that is one of the main factors in work hardening.

The behavior of the crystals was studied by ordinary photography of the changes in shape and by the angle and length of the streaks on the surface that were caused by slipping. The key to success in determining the behavior of the stretched crystals at the atomic level was the use of X-rays to determine the orientation of the slip plane. Since a single crystal has none of the randomness of a fiber, the rotating-crystal method was used and Mark was chosen to run the apparatus.

The team of three found many crystal properties, and they produced their first three articles with remarkable speed. Still more aspects were elucidated in later articles. Sections of the originally circular wires could be visibly seen to stretch into ellipses as they slipped past each other, and to twist around as well as to bend. Some of the hardening could be quantitatively accounted for by the changes of orientation, but some could only be attributed to a change of the friction between the sliding planes. Once breaking occurred, the two new parts were distorted and had enhanced stretching and breaking strengths. Breaking sometimes occurred between the sliding planes, but sometimes other sets of planes were more prone to break.

Once a description was found for the structural changes underlying the hardening of single crystals, a natural next step was to apply the results to the processes involved in the drawing and hardening of polycrystalline metals. These materials consist of microscopic crystallites or grains, each of which has its own lattice planes that are orderly within the crystallite but are random with respect to the other grains of metal. The boundaries between the grains tend to maintain themselves during stretching.

At the end of their series on zinc, the three researchers pointed out that some of the mixed-up grains will have their planes oriented for easy stretching and some will not stretch at all. Furthermore, the stretching process, which widens a single crystal grain, will be inhibited by the pressure of neighboring grains preventing a change in size. This kind of interference produces not just bending of the planes at the boundaries, but crumpling. The grains that do elongate have their crystal planes move toward an axis and become like the planes of a fiber crystal. The combination of hardening by reorientation of some crystals and the crumpling of others is quite sufficient in a general way to account for the overall hardening of the wire, but the complexities and randomness of the grain structure prevents the derivation of any simple quantitative relation between tension and elongation.

The team's study of the stretching properties of fibers and crystals required an improved method of physically stretching them while simultaneously measuring the force applied and the degree of elongation. When the work started, there were some devices available through the Materialprüfungsamt, particularly one designed by Schopper, but these instruments were not originally set up for thin fibers, and extension and force could not be independently measured. Polanyi worked out a new device in the summer of 1922, with help from Schmid, Jancke, and Fräulein Karger, who was working on her Ph.D. in another division of the institute. The device was made with great care by the institute's machinist, R. Starke. It was the first of many useful instruments. According to Mark,

> The Dehnungsapparat (DA) was conceived by Misi early in our work—summer 1922; several models were tried out by Schmid and myself during our work on [zinc] wires. Misi was always very helpful and carried out many measurements himself; he was a very careful and precise experimentalist. Usually he initiated and directed the tests, but, if appropriate, he did also the work with his own hands. He was not an 'ivory tower theoretician.'... Gomperz and I made the wires, Schmid extended them in the DA and measured modulus, strength, and elongation. Then he returned samples to me in different stages of deformation and I made the X-ray diagrams which demonstrated what had happened to the crystal structure during deformation. Misi supervised it all and formulated the conclusions. It was a very pleasant and successful collaboration.[54]

The focus of the work with crystals was to disclose the actual process whereby crystal planes move across each other—why they are able to slide so readily in some cases, why certain planes and directions are preferred, why this preference persists as stretching continues, and what happens in shear hardening, where the resistance increases without bending and twisting. Metallurgists use high temperatures to relieve crystal deformation by annealing. Subjecting part of a stretched crystal to a temperature just below its melting point and then letting it cool often starts a recrystallization process that brings about a restoration of the uniform crystal arrangement. This healing or recovery of uniformity starts from a single part of the crystal and spreads down the wire as each part of it is heat-treated. On the other hand, if the wire is heated as a whole and allowed to cool, recrystallization starts everywhere from small fragments, and a polycrystalline wire of the ordinary type is produced instead. The group found that some degree of recrystalli- zation went on slowly at room temperature so that it counteracted hardening processes that were also relatively slow.

Polanyi began to develop his ideas on recrystallization in the spring of 1922. He needed a reference for the disorientation of the crystal structure prior to the healing process and had found what he needed in Jan Czochralski's lecture at Jena the preceding fall. On April 8, Polanyi wrote Czochralski for a reprint of the lecture and asked to meet him either in Berlin or in Czo- chralski's metallurgical institute in Frankfurt.[55] The lecture does not seem to have been published, and what Polanyi did get was a reprint of a 1914 pub- lication that described highly disoriented crystal structure in worked metals.[56]

Polanyi's study involved less severe disorientation than that studied by Czochralski. Polanyi presented his theory to a meeting of the Recrystallization Committee of the German Society for the Investigation of Metals on October 4, 1922, where he used the reference given by Czochralski and a related one of 1916 (1924c). Czochralski was at the meeting; on October 9, he wrote Polanyi that he regretted that they had spent so little time together. It was evident to Polanyi that the experiments described by Czochralski, if valid, would contradict the whole basis of gliding with hardening, the "translation hy- pothesis." Czochralski responded that the motion of the elements of the lattice in stretching and twisting had little or nothing to do with crystal directions.

Polanyi postponed his publication of the October talk for three years (1925f). At the First International Congress on Applied Mechanics, held in Delft (Holland) in April 1924, Czochralski gave a long paper on "The Relation of Metallography to Physical Research." He presented the results of extensive studies done on the stretching, twisting, and bending of aluminum crystals, using mainly the reflection of light from cut and etched surfaces. The nu- merous photographs in the published article showed none of the slip-plane phenomena that Polanyi and his co-workers found for zinc.[57] Czochralski asserted that Polanyi's group was quite mistaken, having failed to notice the facts brought out in the aluminum studies. In fact, the bending and distortion of the crystal structure had been noticed by Polanyi's group, as well as the fact that cubic crystals such as aluminum would slip on such a wide variety of glide planes that no one mode of slippage would show readily, in contrast to the hexagonal zinc crystals. Czochralski referred to an overall dislocation of the crystal lattice (*Verlagerung*) in a way that presaged the later discovery by Polanyi and others of the atomic-level dislocation (*Versetzung*) that—in con- junction with gliding—has proven to be the key to a proper understanding of the phenomena. Gliding on preferred planes and in preferred directions in those planes remains an important part of the modern account of plastic behavior in crystals.

The article that Polanyi delayed publishing (1925f) contained a diagram that held a clue to the crystal strength problem that neither Polanyi nor anyone else recognized when the article appeared. Polanyi chose to represent the effect of discontinuities in a hardened crystal in terms of two adjacent planes with n atoms on one side and $n + 1$ on the other. He concluded that extra potential energy caused by the asymmetry must pile up and increase the tearing strength. The fact that the $n{:}n + 1$ arrangement could appear in naturally grown crystals and would make the gliding of the two planes past each other easier was not noticed until seven years after the article appeared. In part, this substantiates Polanyi's later theory that when we establish contact with reality, it continues to manifest itself in surprising fashion; at the same time, the failure to recognize the implications of his own discovery may also show the limitations of Polanyi's self-instruction in the field.

On October 1, 1922, George Michael Polanyi was born. All went well in the hospital. Magda was the darling of the nurses there, and mother and child were able to come home to a decent—if cramped—apartment. George was a small, good-natured infant, with black hair, dark eyes, and a beautiful, smooth, Tatar complexion inherited from his father. Polanyi's letter to Cecile about the birth was generally optimistic. Mother and child were healthy, and he was grateful for the wonders of nature: "Its gifts are of full value." The birth of his son lifted his spirits. "The end of all times" seemed further away than he had supposed.[58] Sofie was anxious to hear of the baby, and wrote about how at age 6, Michael had dreamed of having a son: "He didn't want to trust even this to the women. I still remember how he pondered on the big problems of life in his little bed for hours."[59]

The next spring, Polanyi received an appointment as Privatdozent to the Berlin Technische Hochschule in the suburb of Charlottenburg; he belonged to the Faculty of Materials Technology, division of Chemistry and Smelting, with the particular subject matter Physical Chemistry. Polanyi had to present a Habilitation lecture, for which he chose the title, "On Stretching and Hardening Against Stretching."[60] Although there was no stipend attached to this position, he was authorized to lecture and guide students as he wished. In late March, he asked the Technische Hochschule to announce his topic of X-rays and crystal structure for the summer semester, but found that the models of atoms that he wished to use were unavailable, so in mid-April he canceled the series.

On May 15, 1923, the governing board of the Fiber Institute made Polanyi the "official" rather than "acting" head of the physical chemistry division—after all, the division's work was entirely his creation. The board also named him to a position as Mitglied (Scientific Member) of the Fiber Institute, which also gave him membership in the Kaiser Wilhelm-Gesellschaft. As with the appointment to the faculty of the Technische Hochschule, the promotion brought no added income—the economics of the time simply did not allow it.

5

Institute for Physical Chemistry: 1923–1933

Having established his credentials as a physical chemist by his work with crystals, Polanyi could now focus on the question that interested him the most, the speed of chemical reactions. One might argue that there is no more comprehensive question to be answered in chemistry. Everything a chemist studies comes from or contributes to chemical reactions. To understand why some reactions go slowly and others go quickly and to see why some consume energy and others release energy is to understand the most fundamental principles of the field. The work Polanyi had done at Karlsruhe had established several important principles for a theory of reaction rates; however, further theoretical advances depended on finding a way to determine the rate constant (k) values. In the absence of a theory to calculate these values, Polanyi was eager to try experimental measurement, both to acquire a body of data to compare with a future theory and to seek clues in the experiments for developing such a theory.

Haber was well aware of Polanyi's researches into X-rays, fibers, and metal crystals, and was quite ready to bring this able young scientist into his own institute, the Kaiser Wilhelm Institute for Physical Chemistry and Electrochemistry, where he would have experimental facilities, research assistants, and general support for the reaction velocity work. In April 1923, Haber had urged Polanyi to accept a transfer, but the terms offered were not satisfactory. Polanyi replied that he needed at least "as solid a basis as now,"[1] which included the consulting contract with Izzo and the other improvements in his status at the Fiber Institute.

Although Polanyi expected that Haber would eventually offer him a suitable contract, he did not want to postpone his research. He sought outside funding from the Emergency Organization of German Science (Notgemeinschaft der deutschen Wissenschaft), which was founded in 1920 to assist deserving science projects. In early May, Polanyi described these experiments to both Haber and Hahn in their capacity as members of the Japan subcommittee, which had funds available from a Japanese industrialist. On May 30, he applied for a grant of 100 yen to cover costs of setting up an elaborate experiment. The money was needed for the various parts of the apparatus and associated equipment. No funds were needed for assistants—H. Beutler, a new Ph.D. who had worked with Polanyi on phase diagrams for metal crystals, had sufficient funds to assemble and operate the equipment.

Polanyi's initiative on this proposal inspired Haber to take another step toward Polanyi's transfer to his own institute. Haber found that he had one and a half unused assistantships from which he could shift funds to help with a proper salary for Polanyi. On June 9, 1923, Haber sent a letter to the board of the Kaiser Wilhelm Gesellschaft recommending the transfer and describing the honor Polanyi had brought to the Fiber Institute through his fundamental advancement of the theory of metal crystals.[2] Adolf von Harnack, president of the KWG, approved, and on September 1, the governing board appointed Polanyi as a scientific member of Haber's institute with responsibility for supervising the division of basic research in physical chemistry. Haber had personally directed this division heretofore, but needed more time to do administrative work and to manage the revenue-producing applications that grew out of the research. Polanyi's salary was guaranteed, he was allowed to keep the consulting contract with Izzo, and funds were set aside for his reaction experiments; he was also given a grant from the Notgemeinschaft for the study of the Joffé effect in salt crystals immersed in water (1924c).

The new position suited Polanyi well. Although Fritz Haber was formal in dress and discourse, running his institute more strictly than Herzog, Polanyi had observed that he nevertheless gave his group leaders a great deal of freedom. The young scientists on his staff did their experimental and theoretical work according to their own scientific insight and conscience. This suited Polanyi's temperament and his philosophy of freedom of inquiry within a collegial atmosphere. In September, Polanyi moved from Herzog's building at number 16 Faraday Way to Haber's, next door at number 4, where he was given several laboratory rooms on the third floor. He got everything settled in time to attend the Deutsche Physikertag in Bonn toward the end of the month. On his return, he called in his new assistant, Beutler, and made plans for the new experiment. Beutler was good at putting together gas-handling apparatus with its glass tubing, bulbs, valves, gauges, and pumps, equipment with which Polanyi had little experience. Polanyi established the general principles for the experiments; Beutler made them work.

The simplest type of chemical reaction is called an "atomic reaction." This is very different from nuclear reactions, in which fission or fusion release forms of energy popularly known as "atomic energy." When physical chemists speak of atomic reactions, they are thinking of the simplest chemical reactions in which a single atom, call it A, binds to another atom, B, to make a new molecule, AB, or else the reverse process of dissociation, in which the molecule, AB, breaks down into two atoms, A and B—these are the most elementary chemical reactions imaginable. Complex reactions often involve a series of such simple exchanges. In Karlsruhe, Polanyi had already worked on two examples in connection with the hydrogen bromide formation: one, a reaction in which a hydrogen atom transferred from one molecule to another ($Br + H_2 \rightarrow HBr + H$), and another reaction in which a bromine atom transferred ($H + Br_2 \rightarrow HBr + Br$).

By the 1920s, rates of reactions were represented by the Arrhenius equation $k = Ae^{-Q/RT}$ where k is the rate constant for a given reaction at a given concentration of reagents. Q is an energy that was called the "activation energy," but was assumed to be either the energy taken up in endothermic reaction (a reaction that consumed energy), or zero in the case of an exothermic reaction (a reaction that released energy). The constant A is a large number, called the "pre-exponential factor," and represents the order of magnitude of the rate of collisions. The basic idea expressed in the equation is that the rate of a reaction is a function of the rate of collision between pairs of molecules multiplied by the probability of a reaction occurring in a given collision.

Polanyi wanted to determine which elementary reactions were taking place and then to measure the rate constant, k, for each of those reactions. By measuring the rate of a given reaction at two different temperatures, the value of Q can be found from the ratio k_1/k_2, independently of A. The value of Q and the resulting value of A would be quantities to be explained by an as-yet-to-be-developed theory.

The challenge Polanyi faced in trying to design a meaningful experiment to measure the rate of reactions was that they happened in such a short length of time, since each molecule could collide with other molecules billions of times a second, depending on the gas pressure. Endothermic reactions— reactions that consume more energy than they release—are slower than exothermic reactions, which produce excess energy, but even endothermic reactions take place far too quickly for the unassisted senses to follow. Polanyi needed to find a way to time such extremely fast reactions and to make the intermediate steps in the reaction detectable. Clues to both problems were suggested by the experiment of Haber and Zisch, carried out in Haber's institute.[3] In these experiments, yellow light generated in a controlled sodium gas flame was used to investigate the reactions taking place in the flame. The rate at which molecules move through a steady flame can be calculated by using the same collision rates that are involved in reactions. The patterns in the flame showed the place and time that the sodium atoms had been excited to their second quantum levels; on returning to the ground state, the atoms emit a characteristic yellow light.

Because the Haber–Zisch gas-flame experiment was conducted at more-or-less ordinary pressures, the average distance that molecules traveled between collisions was extremely short. This meant that the precise location of the edge of the flame was not easy to determine, which meant, in turn, that the experiment did not provide a very precise indication of the rate at which the reaction took place. Polanyi decided to conduct a similar experiment in a tube at roughly a hundred-thousandth of ordinary atmospheric pressure. With so few molecules in the tube, each one, on average, would travel a relatively long distance before finding another gas molecule to strike. If the "mean free path" between collisions was about a hundred-thousandth of a centimeter in gases at ordinary atmospheric pressures, reducing the pressure by a factor of a hundred thousand would mean that the molecules would travel a whole centimeter, on average, before striking another molecule. Under ordinary conditions, sodium and chlorine react so quickly that it is impossible to measure the rate at which the reaction takes place. By vastly increasing the distance between molecules and therefore the time between collisions, Polanyi would have a chance to determine more precisely exactly where, and therefore when the key reactions took place.

Polanyi supposed that the yellow light produced by the excitation of sodium atoms would not be generated at these low pressures, but the location and pattern of reaction products deposited on the glass walls of the apparatus would enable him to tell at what rate the reaction products had formed. Polanyi asked Beutler and the glassblower to put together a low-pressure apparatus in which sodium and chlorine vapors would enter at the opposite ends of a tube, mix in the middle, and, if all went well, deposit an observable amount of sodium chloride (NaCl) on the inside of the tube. If the two gases were admitted to the tube at the same rate, the molecules would meet for the first time exactly at the mid-point of the tube. The distance at which the reaction product (in this case, sodium chloride—ordinary table salt) was deposited on the tube from that mid-point would show how long it took for the reaction to reach completion after the mixing of the two gases began at the mid-point.

Polanyi's first design involved a thin glass tube about a meter long. Because the mean free path between collisions in this experiment was roughly equal to the three-centimeter tube diameter, the molecules of each gas made about as many hits on the tube wall as they did on each other or on the molecules of the other gas encountered near the center where the two different gases met. Collisions with the wall created resistance to motion of the two gases toward the middle of the tube, but it was easy to calculate from molecular gas theory for the "Knudsen regime" (a condition of temperature and pressure in which the mean free path—the average distance between collisions—is greater than the size of the gas molecules) how the density of each gas decreased from its point of entry toward the center. Polanyi estimated there would be enough collisions between the two kinds of molecules to make a reaction zone about 10 centimeters long where the salt would be deposited on the sides of the tube.

The results of the experiment surprised Polanyi. The sodium light appeared quite visibly in a round, readily measurable blob. Although no ordinary burning by oxidation was involved, the bright spheres were called "flames," for lack of a better word. Polanyi's first thought was that this light proved the existence of a nonmechanical form of energy exchange—he still had some residual interest in *Zauberei*. He changed his mind after considering more conventional explanations: "I discovered to my disappointment the true mechanism of luminescence, which did not show any anomalies of energy transfer."[4] Although Polanyi's results were disappointing from the point of view of his desire to discover a new quantum process, they vindicated his long-standing ambition to trace the forces and mechanisms underlying reactions between one atom and another.

Polanyi and Beutler designed a second version of the experiment, which allowed the study of unequal mixtures. In this experiment, the chlorine gas was led down the inside of the tube in a thin glass pipe so that it could be released at the center into a cloud of sodium atoms. This method produced considerably more light. In both experiments, the light was "cold," that is, not radiated by a thermal equilibrium process, which would be associated with a temperature of several thousand degrees. The idea of cold light had a popular appeal. In view of the high intensity efficiency of the dilute flames, some lay observers predicted a new, low-cost light source. In a newspaper article entitled "The Light out of the Salt-cellar,"[5] a Berlin reporter drew a not very accurate parallel with Edison's invention of the incandescent lamp. He failed to comprehend the similarity between Polanyi's cold light and the neon lamp invented in 1911 by Georges Claude. The scientists were amused by the publicity. When Haber's research group gathered for a Christmas celebration, Polanyi's colleagues recited:

> Meines Kindes schönster Traum
> Ist kaltes Licht am Weihnachtsbaum.
> (My child's prettiest dream would be
> To see cold light on the Christmas tree.)

Although the reporter's dream was a mere fantasy, the method of highly dilute flames was a fruitful experimental procedure. It came to be used for about forty reactions with sodium and some with potassium, which produced deep red light along with other tints. Sodium, a metallic element, reacts

with a large variety of compounds containing one or more of the halogens—
fluorine, chlorine, bromine, and iodine. Thus many kinds of regularities
among similar elementary reactions can be studied. The method was particularly useful for cases of low activation energy, chemical reactions that require
only a small number of collisions before a reaction occurs and which therefore
proceed quite rapidly under ordinary conditions.

Polanyi and Beutler published the first report on the new method in a
short article in Die Naturwissenschaften in August 1925. They listed thirteen
inorganic substances that produce light when reacted with sodium and six
organics that did not (1925m). It had taken nearly two years for the method to
be developed to the point of a preliminary announcement, and over four years
to develop a detailed analysis. The early tubes were tricky to maintain: "any
one was reliable for only one week per year."[6] After Polanyi's lab assistants
acquired the skill to make and monitor the tubes, the flame work elucidated a
series of new reactions without much change in the basic techniques.[7] No
other laboratory attempted to use this difficult technique.

One of Polanyi's most important colleagues in the early flame experi-
ments was Eugene Wigner. In the fall of 1921, Wigner left his home city of
Budapest to take his university education in chemical engineering at the
Technische Hochschule in Berlin. Early in 1922, he was assigned to work for
Hermann Mark, who himself had just become a half-time assistant to Polanyi.
At Mark's suggestion, Wigner studied the symmetries of the rhombic sulfur
crystal for his diploma, thus taking the first step toward his distinguished
career in symmetry physics.[8]

Wigner's parents hoped that their son's work in the Fiber Institute might
benefit the family's leather-goods plant in Budapest. They were not in sympathy with Wigner giving up his work in chemical engineering and fiber
technology. Polanyi paid a visit to the family and persuaded them that their
son would have a distinguished career in physical science. Wigner began his
doctoral work under Polanyi's guidance in 1925, examining how two-atom
molecules are formed and broken up, a complex subject that had been raised
in Polanyi's correspondence with Herzfeld, and could equally well be called
physics or physical chemistry.

Polanyi had realized that if two atoms collided, for instance two bromine
atoms, they would automatically have enough energy between them to be able
to fly apart on the first bounce, so it was hard to see how they could form a
molecule. The deeper problem that Wigner raised on the basis of the quantum theory of the day was that the existence of quantized energy levels in the
separate atoms and independently in the molecule would make it extremely
unlikely that the sum of the energies of the atoms would fit any of the molecule's possible levels so as to allow even a fleeting existence of the molecule.
The solution lay in Niels Bohr's suggestion that, because of the possibility of
the emission of radiation, atomic and molecular levels would all have finite

energy breadths.[9] Molecules have many energy levels, so it was not as unlikely as it first had seemed that a pair of atoms would fit into one of the possible energy states of the molecule.

The molecule once formed, if it does not somehow lose the energy involved in the collision, will have only a short average time of existence. Polanyi and Wigner found a novel implication in Bohr's work about the average time of the molecule's existence and the breadth of energies that the molecule could accommodate. Their statement of the energy–time relationship also anticipated a form of the uncertainty relation proposed in more general terms by Heisenberg in 1927. However, Heisenberg's considerations dealt with the problem of measurement, as well as that of inherent indeterminism, and observation questions were not raised by Wigner and Polanyi. They also applied Bohr's rule that the angular momentum of a rotating atomic or molecular system would always be a multiple of a constant; a final understanding of how angular momentum was conserved in collisions that did not neatly match the allowed energy states had to wait for further developments in quantum mechanics.

In any case, the authors obtained valid results for the rates of association and dissociation, and also for the ratio between the two, which does not depend on the possible energy states of the molecule. These results inspired Wigner's later formulation of the rate of absorption of neutrons by nuclei.[10] After earning his Ph.D., Wigner obtained a position at the Technische Hochschule that allowed him to continue to work with Mark and Polanyi.

In spite of his new position and the freedom to explore reaction rates, Polanyi's research on single-crystal gliding and deformation continued. His group studied the behavior of crystals at low temperature, mostly at liquid-air temperatures (about $-190°C$ or $80°$ Absolute) and in one set of experiments with liquid helium at about $12°$ Absolute (1929a, 1930d). Plastic flow and extensibility disappeared, as did any recrystallization. However, the rigidity and the brittle type of breaking strength became independent of temperature at these low values, showing their dependence on static structural features and not on the kinetic energy or heat motion of the component atoms. Effects dependent on this motion, such as the strength of disordered, amorphous glass, would be expected to be temperature dependent, and in fact they were found to be so. A number of experiments were done that verified these conclusions, most extensively in 1923 by Masing (1923i, 1924d). As was the case in much of his research, Polanyi contributed insights, inspiration, and the challenge of good questions; his name often appeared on the resulting publications even though he left the experiments and writing largely in others' hands.

The work on tin was parallel to that of zinc, but easier because it could follow the lines already laid out. Polanyi, Mark, and Schmid had found early on that the previously published structure of tin was wrong. A brief four-paragraph letter dated March 10, 1923, was sent to *Naturwissenschaften* by the three, giving the correct structure, which they had found in what was the first extensive application of the Polanyi/Weissenberg rotating crystal method (1923f). This structure was settled by unit cell measurements, symmetry considerations, and the absence of certain reflections; taken together, the data determined that only four of the two hundred thirty possible space groups were possible candidates. Three of these were eliminated by the logic of falsification in terms of cell density, symmetry, and reflecting-power factors, leaving a tetragonal (four-sided) lattice as the answer.

Shortly after this article was published, a visitor from Holland, A. E. van Arkel, came to Berlin to complain that he had also determined the structure of tin, but had different results. It took a lengthy conversation to find out that the Netherlander's structure was the same as that of the Dahlem group, but was described with respect to axes rotated by 45° from those used by Polanyi's group. Polanyi was to remember this case as an example of two apparently contradictory analyses of a common problem carried out from differing perspectives. The later publications, two by Mark and Polanyi (1923e, 1924a) and two by Polanyi and Schmid (1923f, 1925i), gave details of their work, including both ways of looking at the tin structure. Tin was found to behave like zinc. Its preferred glide planes and directions were reported, as well as flow rates for gliding. The rate of recovery was studied and indicated that the reforming of the regular crystal arrangement was always happening, but slowly, imperceptibly whenever the deformation was rapid.

Another priority dispute in the fall of 1923 concerned the rotating-crystal method. Ernst Schiebold of the Materials Testing Laboratory noted that he had developed the technique in 1919 and arranged to have it used in several student dissertations at Leipzig. He avoided publication in order to allow the students some priorities of their own, so that Polanyi's and Weissenberg's publications actually came out first. Polanyi settled the dispute in a joint publication with Schiebold and Weissenberg (1924f). The three authors described the steps each had taken and also gave credit to the advances made by the others.

While he was building a solid career in chemistry, Polanyi's experience of the vicissitudes of the German economy fueled his interest in economics. He recognized that the sufferings of the unemployment associated with each depression in a capitalist economic system helped engender the revolutionary ideologies and passions of the times. Polanyi had experienced the full force of the German inflation, observed the early bungling efforts at stopping it, and witnessed the final success. He had come to recognize both the serious problems of capitalism in practice and the difficulties and cruelties reported by visitors to Russia.

The belief in the possibility of creating a coherent economic and social theory had been bolstered and stimulated by his warm and friendly correspondence with Karl during the early 1920s. Unfortunately Michael's letters to Karl from this period have all been lost. Karl's letters tell about his work on a series of sociological and economic matters and deal with some of the criticism he received.[11] Among the authors Karl mentioned reading were Proudhon, Carey, Duhring, Henry George, Rudolf Steiner, Cole, and Spengler. He responded to Polanyi's comments and critiques, remarking, for instance, that Spengler and Steiner are "preaching your new skepticism" but on the model of Goethe instead of Tolstoy.[12]

Karl suggested the need to look for more particular reasons than capitalism itself for the plight of the proletariat. He laid stress on the urgency of restoring the Christian moral viewpoint, using persuasion rather than force. Karl's concept of a "World Revolution" was based on the ideas of free cooperation as expressed in the rise of the Labour party in Britain in early 1921: "The English socialist practice confirmed the direction of my work. To discuss definite problems from a Christian viewpoint—this is my socialism."[13] Karl hoped that the party's Fabian Socialism, which advocated compromise and partnership between labor and capital in place of the older insistence on class war, would substantially reduce the influence of Bolshevism in England and in Europe.

Michael clearly shared Karl's view of "the undissolvable binding of man to society, the effect and countereffect of all deeds on society."[14] They both now agreed that the Tolstoyan individualism they had earlier espoused was fundamentally inadequate. For Polanyi, the coordinated set of relevant structures and organizing principles in society—public belief systems, social passions, economic elements—would be revealed by investigation rather than derived from one or more sweeping generalizations. Karl held sociology was not yet a "science of human life and human future."[15] Unlike Michael, Karl believed that the essential reality of social relations leads to the necessity of politics and to the presence of considerable amounts of distortion of these realities in the public mind.

Polanyi was also influenced by the economists Gustav and Toni Stolper. In 1924, Karl started to work on the weekly paper edited by Gustav and Walther Federn, *Der österreichische Volkswirt* (*The Austrian Economist*). Toni Stolper recalled "the intellectual and personal kinship" she and her husband had shared with Karl and Ilona, a friendship that "endured as long as any of us lived."[16] The Stolpers found themselves more and more drawn to Germany, and in October 1925, they emigrated to Berlin, where they rented a house in Dahlem. They contacted Michael and Magda that fall and invited them to celebrate Christmas with them. The next year, backed by a group of six men ready to put up 30,000 to 50,000 new German marks for the project, Stolper founded a new journal in Berlin, *Der deutsche Volkswirt* (*The German Economist*).[17] Karl had hoped to join Stolper at that time, but some basic disagreements with Gustav interfered.

Polanyi subscribed to *Der Deutsche Volkswirt* from its inception and took advantage of the opportunity to extend his knowledge of economics and the structure of society. Among the topics discussed in the weekly were problems of the allied occupation, the slow recovery from the 1921 depression, the huge mass of the unemployed, and, in a more positive vein, the widespread order and stability in the German state and successful economic improvements through technical and fiscal rationalization. As time went, the journal addressed the problems of the European capital markets, the increase in total credit and the powerful influence of the world economic crisis. The articles helped Polanyi grasp the complexities of the German capitalist system and laid some of the groundwork for his later work in economics.

Polanyi was initially convinced that natural scientists could ferret out lawlike regularities in social affairs better than the economists themselves. As Erika Cremer remarked, "The scientist always thinks he is in the center of the machine of world affairs."[18] Polanyi began by studying the various national economic policies to see whether he could uncover general principles underlying economic events. He was grateful for Toni Stolper's weekly column in *Der Deutsche Volkswirt*, which summarized factual news from other countries, especially reports from the Soviet Union. He continued to collect a great deal of data even as it became evident that generalizations comparable to those of natural science would be hard to find.

In March 1924, Dr. Hjalmar Schacht ended the German inflation by a simple edict, creating a new Reichsmark equal to a trillion of the old ones. With the new fiscal stability, the Polanyis began to make plans for a home of their own. The two small sublet rooms on Ehrenbergstrasse provided the little family with the absolutely essential kitchen, but not much else. As their social life developed, their cramped quarters made hospitality awkward. When the dining table was extended to accommodate even a few guests, it got in the way of the door to the kitchen, which therefore had to be taken off its hinges. Between household chores and the baby, Magda's hands were full. Since money was tight, they could not afford to send out the laundry, so Magda washed the sheets in the bathtub. Polanyi estimated that the cost of building a wooden house would be roughly equal to the cost of renting a place for several years. In a city of brick and stone dwellings, it was unusual to build a house of wood, but it was much more economical.

Plans were developed for a simple house at No. 15 Waltraudstrasse with two stories and a cellar. The kitchen and a room for live-in help were in the basement. The main floor had a living room, a dining room, and an entrance hall with a wooden bench around the wall. George had a room to himself, and there was space for a piano for Magda. It was a great relief to move into their first real home. For the first time in his life, Polanyi had his own garden. Although the planting was not completed until the next year, he enjoyed sitting in the unfinished garden, chatting with family and friends. He also enjoyed his daily walk to and from work, about a mile and a half each way.

Whereas most scientists in Berlin came from wealthy families and were able to live well in spite of their inadequate salaries, Michael and Magda had to live on what he could earn. In the fall of 1926, when George was 4 and a live-in maid provided more freedom from home responsibilities, Magda embarked on classes in business correspondence, English, and other languages. Her study led to regular work as a translator, providing an appreciable and welcome addition to the family income. Polanyi sent regular contributions to support his mother. Although Cecile had written some short, entertaining pieces for the German language *Neues Pester Journal* in Budapest, the job was short-lived. By 1928, Polanyi was sending his mother 200 marks a month out of his institute salary of 1,200 marks.

Polanyi's work as a consultant and inventor helped make ends meet. He developed several patent claims with Bogdandy,[19] but the patents provided little income—it was easier to invent than to market the invention. Consulting was more lucrative. Although some of the work involved research at the Haber institute, Polanyi's principal clients were the Siemens Electric Works and the Osram Lamp Works in Berlin, the Philips Lamp Works in Eindhoven, and the United Lamp Works in Budapest. In addition to consulting, Polanyi explored job openings in industry, primarily as a device to get a raise in his salary at the institute but also in the hope of finding a commercial opportunity he really would enjoy. One autumn day, he accompanied representatives of a big industrial combine on a trip to the nearby mountains. The businessmen wanted to offer Polanyi a position. Even though Polanyi anticipated that he would refuse their offer, he was curious about it and was pleased to let Haber know of the company's offer.

In the summer of 1926, at the vacation resort of Gastein in the Salzburg province of Austria, Polanyi filled twelve pages of his notebook with ideas about the troubles of his current life and his conception of how to find happiness. In his list of "troubles to fight against" he mentioned, among other things, "worry about position and existence, overwork, bodily deterioration, lack of independence in work with partners, smoking, softness (getting up late), disorderliness (not getting things done, not having a system), feeling sorry for myself, impatience, and longing."[20] His next entry declared his intention to create an excellent, joyful life for himself, a "life that turns out well." Polanyi felt that each person needed to produce a piece of creative work, a magnum opus. His criteria for the good life included independence, consistency with tradition and memory, acceptance of pain and danger, and a sense of permanence derived from channeling that intellectual passion by which "the mind rushes on ahead of the string of events." Even at this early stage in his scientific career, Polanyi seems to have felt the lure of social and philosophical issues that could not be addressed within the confines of physical chemistry. He desired a life between that of the saint and the common person, perhaps that of a knight or an aristocrat disciplined in body and spirit, a description that came to suit him more and more.

A second reflective essay was entitled "Vom Wege zur Wahrheit," "Of the Way to Truth."[21] Polanyi started with questions to himself about whether he would stay on the path and avoid the abyss at the edge of the path. The problem is that there are many ways and many truths, a whole population (*Volk*) of them. The arbitrariness of life troubled Polanyi, for he saw no way to resolve the tensions objectively. He referred to the lack of absolute criteria for values in social action, quoting his brother Karl: "Society is the second Fall of Man." Physical laws are subject to experimental constraint, but moral laws are arbitrary, by which he meant that in moral matters we have to take personal responsibility for our actions.

A few months later, in December 1926, Polanyi was promoted at the Technische Hochschule to associate (extraordinarius) professor. He had already been given a stipend of 500 marks for his work at the Technische Hochschule, and the promotion allowed him to raise his consultation fees. On one of his trips to the Philips plant in Eindhoven, Polanyi celebrated their increasing prosperity by buying Magda a silver vase, but, distracted by his technical work, he left the gift behind in the overhead rack of the train.

Developments in the world of physics allowed Polanyi to refine his understanding of reaction rates. As in his flame experiments, Polanyi had begun to work on the question of reaction rates by considering the simplest possible reaction in which a single atom (A) is joined to another atom (B) which has been broken away from a bond with a third atom (C): $A + BC \rightarrow AB + C$. In order for this reaction to take place, the B atom must be lifted to a sufficiently high energy level for the molecular bond with C to be broken; the energy required for B and C to dissociate is called the activation energy for the reaction. Polanyi graphed the potential energy of the B atom against its various positions with respect to the other two atoms. This representation of potential energy versus position showed that B would have to pass over a hump in the energy landscape, comparable to a mountain pass, on the way to its new position in union with the A atom. (Anyone who has had trouble getting a car to start on a damp morning knows how important activation energy is: without sufficient spark at the right time, the gasoline and oxygen mixture will not ignite and the engine will not run.)

In the chaotic world of chemical reactions, just reaching the top of this pass does not mean that the desired reaction between B and A will take place. After being pushed up the potential energy hill into a position where it might form a new bond with an A atom, B might also slide right back down into its old relationship with the C atom. Nevertheless, when the desired reaction does take place, we may be sure that energy had to be supplied to break the old bond and make the new one possible. If a three-dimensional plaster model

were made of the graph and a ball placed on it and given a push, the New-
tonian dynamics of the motion as it rolls out of one valley, over the top of
the hill, and down into the valley on the other side would be approximately the
same as the motion of the representative point of the reaction under the
influence of the potential energy as modeled. The necessary energy calculation needed for such contour maps called for an assessment of the joint
interaction of three atoms, a difficult task for which several applications of
quantum mechanics developed during 1927 and 1928 were required. Wigner
played a vital role in helping Polanyi grasp the implications of the new
developments.

In the absence of a theory of how to calculate the true forces operating
between the three atoms, the contour map had to be built on an understanding
of the forces of attraction between each pair of atoms. In 1927, Walter Heitler
and Fritz London developed the first significant theory of chemical binding
by applying the new quantum mechanics to the valence binding of two hydrogen atoms into a molecule of hydrogen gas $(H + H \rightarrow H_2)$.[22] Heitler and
London reasoned that the attraction between the two atoms derives to a small
extent from ordinary electrostatic attraction (Coulomb energies) and, to a far
greater degree, from the quantum-mechanical attraction produced by the
exchange of electrons between the atoms (exchange or resonance energies). At
the time there was no way to detect the interaction of two identical hydrogen
atoms in a hydrogen molecule. Even the calculations in this very simple case
were only approximate, since the equations for a single hydrogen atom, composed of a single electron and nucleus, do not directly describe the molecular
state with its two electrons and two nuclei; measurements made for H_2
showed that the value of the binding energy between the two hydrogen atoms
predicted from Heitler and London's theory was only about three-quarters of
the experimental value, demonstrating the error caused by use of single-atom
wave functions and the "best fit" method.

The Heitler–London theory, which was essentially correct in spite of the
unavoidable approximations, was only carried out for the hydrogen molecule,
H_2. To apply it to a case like HBr would require further developments in
the quantum mechanics of chemical binding. In 1928, London took up the
complicated "best fit" problem of three hydrogen atoms, each with a single
electron capable of entering valence binding, and treated the energy of the system in terms of Coulomb and exchange energies between each of the three
pairs.[23] His approximation gave fair results; the final energy values were not
very accurate, but they enabled a qualitatively reasonable set of contours for the
potential hill to be made.

In 1927, Wigner and Polanyi worked on an extension of their first article (1925l), which had focused on the vibrational modes of two atoms. They
now studied the dissociation of multi-atom molecules that had acquired considerable energy through internal vibrations. The idea was that a complex

mechanical system, like a molecule containing a number of atoms, would have several possible patterns of joint oscillation, called "normal modes," each with a different frequency. Any single one of these patterns would lead all the atom-to-atom bonds involved to have more or less the same amplitude of vibration, but if there were two or three superimposed patterns present simultaneously, they would keep shifting their phase relations so that now and then a particular bond would get an unusually large dose of vibratory motion, sometimes big enough to rupture the bond and thus dissociate the molecule. Multi-atom molecules would have many more vibration modes than molecules formed of two atoms.

In this article, Polanyi and Wigner were the first to combine the mechanical theory of normal modes with some statistical considerations on phase distribution to derive a formula consonant with experiment. The joint work must have been finished by the summer of 1927, for Wigner took an assistantship at Göttingen for 1927–1928. The final publication appeared in October 1928 (1928n).

In September 1927, Geza Schay, who had obtained his doctorate at the University of Budapest in 1923, took a leave of absence from a dull job as an analytical chemist in Budapest in order to work with Polanyi in Berlin. Schay was recommended by Georg von Hevesy, and Polanyi gave him charge of the flame experiments, hoping to at last put the work on a sound footing. Schay was asked, in particular, to develop a jet tube that Bogdandy had proposed. Bogdandy was an ingenious experimenter with whose help Schay soon had a good working apparatus built and operating.

Schay met regularly with Polanyi for guidance and supervision, reporting on progress and discussing the theoretical implications of the results. Schay found the discussions inspiring. He appreciated Polanyi's knack of finding the weak point in a proposed analysis and then offering helpful suggestions for improvement. Schay described Polanyi's mind as "most remarkable and admirably intuitive":

> He had an introverted look when deep in thought, then uttered his opinion or new idea, and only afterwards supplied a more or less sketchy explanation of it. Often, when it involved some quantitative relation, he jotted a derivation down on a sheet of paper which, at closer inspection, proved to contain several errors, but the result was almost unfailingly correct.[24]

Polanyi was probably quite capable of making the correct calculations by himself, but he was glad to leave this tedious work to his young assistant. As in his doctoral work, his intuition grasped sound conclusions that outstripped his mathematical expertise.

In January 1928, Schay and Polanyi published work on the reactions of sodium and potassium with tin halides. In these reactions, intense light is produced by the tin compounds (1928e). Five months later Schay's organizing powers were shown in a set of five articles on the highly dilute flames, three written by Polanyi and different collaborators, Beutler (1928h), Bogdandy (1928i), and Schay (1928j), and two by Ootuka and Schay.[25] The five articles reported measurements on fourteen new reactions, described a new microphotometer for measuring the flame intensity, showed that one reaction between sodium and chlorine proceeded at a rate ten times faster than that predicted if the reactants had behaved like single hard spheres, reported greatly improved light output by using the jet tube, and demonstrated the flame versus precipitation curve differences between those reactions that involved individual chlorine atoms and those that did not. Haruo Ootuka reported in late 1929 on a few more reactions.[26]

Polanyi asked Schay to stay on as paid assistant after his leave was up, but he had promised his parents he would return to Budapest. However, he came back to Berlin for six months, starting in the summer of 1930, and carried out experiments with hydrogen chloride, bromide, and iodide.[27] He also wrote an extensive review of all of the flame experiments.[28] After Schay's second stay was over there was one more article on the dilute flame method, which gave results on cadmium and zinc halide compounds (1932c).

A combination of circumstances encouraged Polanyi to make a serious return to adsorption in 1928. An exchange of views with Eucken in 1922 had persuaded Polanyi that adsorption layers in general were probably quite thin and that his theory should be revised to apply to such cases. A. S. Coolidge in 1926 and H. H. Lowry and P. S. Olmsted in 1927 had published data supporting Polanyi's theory.[29] Polanyi had never completed any experimental work on adsorption. Now his laboratory was well equipped with apparatus that could easily be adapted to this type of work, and F. Goldmann, a highly competent young physical chemist destined to go into industrial research, was on hand to take up the work.

Goldmann carried out the experiments with extreme care, using liquid air and pumping techniques to eliminate unwanted vapors and purify the gases being used. Careful measurements were made of volumes, pressures, and temperatures; Goldmann estimated the margin of error at 0.1 percent (1928b).

Polanyi and Goldmann altered the potential theory to be able to consider, in place of a layer on the surface several molecules thick, a two-dimensional liquid in the form of a random set of islands partially covering the surface. The roughness of the carbon surface was important in this conception, and they did not claim that the theory would fit other substances. In Langmuir's approach, the state-determining forces between the adsorbed molecules were neglected, whereas Goldmann and Polanyi treated each molecule as having its own attractive potential at a spot on the surface. Polanyi's original idea of the importance of the intermolecular forces was simply shifted from a three-dimensional analysis to a two-dimensional. Although a radical shift of thought away from Lagergren's layers had occurred, the mathematical changes in the theory were not hard to make.

Like Berényi, Goldmann focused on easily condensible vapors. Under the right conditions of pressure and temperature, the surface layer becomes an ordinary liquid wetting the surface, which readily grows into a substantial body of fluid with only a very slight increase in pressure. From this point on, the concept of adsorption no longer has much meaning. Goldmann was able to take advantage of this fact to substitute information about condensation and wetting for the volume of gas adsorbed at a particular pressure.

Polanyi and his group published three papers in a row in the *Zeitschrift für physikalische Chemie* for January 1928; the respective authors were F. Goldmann (1928b), K. Welke (1928d), and Walter Heyne (1928f). The Welke–Polanyi work used Goldmann's apparatus for long, difficult experiments on the adsorption of sulfur dioxide on carbon at extremely low percentages of surface covering. For the first time, they were able to explore pressures on the order of a thousandth to a millionth of the vapor pressure at 0°C. The results suggested that adsorption took place in three stages. The first stage was very low coverage, with the gas molecules tightly bound to the surface so that they had very small effective volumes to move around in. Polanyi's group conceded that this state, with its very high heat of adsorption and low intermolecular interaction, was a Langmuir phase. In the second stage, the two-dimensional gas covered the remainder of the surface, but had too low a density to be a liquid. In the third stage, the free space was reduced and a compressed liquid appeared.

In that same year, H. Zeise took up the defense of Langmuir, claiming that Langmuir's equation fits the adsorption of gases on carbon better than Polanyi's.[30] Polanyi was clearly annoyed. He replied in a short article that Langmuir's arbitrary constants can always be adjusted to fit the data; but when Zeise made the fit, he set one variable to a value highly dependent on temperature while another was set on an opposite assumption. Zeise defended the temperature variations in a second article. Finally, a further argument by Zeise and a rebuttal by Polanyi, referring to the recent data that Zeise had ignored, were published together the next year.[31] Polanyi granted that he could deal with monolayers, but insisted on using an equation derived from the classical theory of gases. Although Polanyi's molecular conception of adsorption had moved closer to Langmuir's, the two theories were still quite different.

In April 1928, Abram Joffé, who had done studies on the strength of salt crystals immersed in water, invited Polanyi to visit the Soviet Union; the trip gave Polanyi a chance to experience the Soviet system firsthand. Joffé had visited German laboratories as chairman of the Soviet Technical Council, the office that oversaw all building plans for science and technology. In

Leningrad, Polanyi recorded some observations about new technical research facilities, and more importantly, several facts on prices, wages, and over-crowding of apartments.[32] He expressed his disgust: "The economic system functions so badly that one cannot judge from the result what its fundamental and dubious principles are. Everything is permeated by brutal and stupid fanaticism considering all other opinions as devilish nonsense. The tone of voice heard in public is a distasteful, monotonous cursing."[33]

While on vacation in August with Joffé in the Tatra mountains of Czechoslovakia (now Slovakia), Polanyi recorded his impressions of Russia: "Wild, worthy of passionate interest, and completely impossible.... [Yet I see] Russia filled with the ideals of the West." Polanyi seemed to have little grasp of the structure of political power in Russia—he predicted that the Bolsheviks would remain in place for a short time to protect the farmers, but that the farmers would ultimately undermine the Bolshevik military power. The trip deepened Polanyi's belief in the "deep, eternal meaning of our Western World" and intensified his sense that he was being called to defend the liberal tradition.[34]

In the same notebook, Polanyi criticized Mahatma Gandhi's rejection of Western civilization. Gandhi had at first fought for several causes inspired by Western ideals—halting child marriages and cleaning up public places, for instance—causes that Gandhi and the British rulers both supported. However, he aligned himself with anti-Western views in order to consolidate the independence movement. Polanyi lamented that "Gandhi did not suc-ceed in drawing a line through the manifestation of Western life that ex-cludes the evil and lets the good remain" (6). Although Polanyi admired Gandhi's commitment to truth and freedom of thought, to compassion and justice toward all, and to the principle of a free, democratic society, on balance he judged that Gandhi's work was an incomplete model for human community.

In December 1928, Polanyi read the polemical book of Julien Benda, *Le Trahison des Clercs* (*The Treason of the Intellectuals*), which denounced those who put the intellect into the service of racial or political ends instead of devoting it to universal spiritual values. Benda's book showed him "the turn-ing point of the crisis to which the development of the last eight years has brought me: the growing and finally basic conviction that civilization is the most important embodiment of the human mind."[35] Polanyi found no at-traction in the idea of abandoning civilization and "going back to nature." For him, technology and culture were essential works of *homo faber*: "There is no nature-lover who, naked in the jungle, could appreciate nature for just half an hour" (4). The problems of technology come with new inventions to which we are not yet well adapted. There was never a golden age in the past with a better opportunity for the moral life; abandoning the fruits of human creativity would not alter the moral landscape (18).

Polanyi's notes end with a list of three economics books: Landauer's *Nature of Economy*, Henderson's *Supply and Demand*, and Robertson's *Production*. As he was approaching the peak of his scientific career, he was—consciously or unconsciously—assembling the materials that would allow him to take up a new career in the social sciences and the humanities.

Polanyi wrote an article in praise of Fritz Haber on the occasion of the latter's 60th birthday, December 8, 1928. He pointed out that there are two kinds of scientific investigators worthy of honor and identified them with the Hindu gods, Shiva, the destroyer, and Vishnu, the preserver. Scientists like Einstein, Planck, and Rutherford are the "destroyers" of old ways, the radical reformers. Haber and others are the "preservers" who build additional structures on the current scientific outlook and explain the new in terms of the old.

Haber is honored in scientific circles for his researches in physical chemistry, especially for discovering how to synthesize ammonia, which enabled Germany to fight World War I and to resurrect its chemical industry afterward. He played an essential role in the founding of the Kaiser Wilhelm Gesellschaft and its research institutes, and in providing a powerful contact between science and the wider world. Haber upheld the ideal of a new type of scientist who knows that science is called not only to provide enlightenment but also to take decisive action beyond fighting wars and epidemics. Science needs to direct its own life of research and also regulate its relation to the state and the economy, which means that there must be scientists who know how to rule. Fritz Haber, said Polanyi, is a forerunner of the new breed of scientific leaders.

Hans Karl Polanyi, later to be known as John, was born January 23, 1929. At first sight, the wrinkles on the newborn's face made him seem "ugly and degenerate" to Polanyi, but within a day the boy began to look more handsome. At this time, Polanyi was enjoying a "miracle" of harmony with George, who at age 6 was a favorite companion of his father in outdoor activities and who enjoyed having his father read to him. Michael spent many summer evenings in the garden with Magda and the boys, enjoying John's pale face and dark eyes. Polanyi was a tender father who did not believe in corporal punishment. One day John, then about 2 years old, was found on Michael's desk scribbling on his notes. Polanyi calmly lifted him off the desk with the remark that "he doesn't understand."[36]

In January 1929, Wigner returned to Berlin after a year in Göttingen and a visit to his family's factory in Budapest. With Polanyi's help, Wigner had been appointed a Privatdozent at the University of Berlin with Richard Becker, professor of theoretical physics. Although Wigner immediately found his attention taken up in physics with the complex and rewarding subject of symmetries and groups in spectroscopy as predicted by the Schrödinger equation, he kept in touch with Polanyi. In the early part of 1929, the two men had many conversations on quantum mechanics and reaction rates, bringing different kinds of expertise to the discussion;[37] Wigner continued to develop Polanyi's grasp of quantum mechanics, as he had in their collaboration in 1927–1928. Polanyi's interest in reaction rates had started with questions about catalytic reactions taking place in adsorbed layers. In an address to the Réunion Internationale de Chimie et Physique at Paris in October 1928, Polanyi recalled that in his earlier analysis of activation energy (the energy needed to initiate a reaction) he had not considered whether or not it was equal to the heat released by the reaction (1928l). He still maintained that no activation energy was needed for exothermic reactions, which release more heat than they consume. This position seemed to be corroborated by his studies of fast reactions in the gas phase and by observations of chlorine molecules on hot copper surfaces that Leopold Frommer had carried out under Polanyi's direction a few months before. The chlorine reacted so fast that the authors judged that "the activation energy was vanishingly small" (1928m).

In the extensive lecture on activation processes on interfaces that Polanyi gave to the *Bunsengesellschaft* in Berlin on May 10, 1929, he gave a straightforward account of applying the new quantum mechanics to the conception of valence-like forces between an adsorbed atom and the mobile electron cloud in a crystalline surface.[38] His analysis made sense of the saturation effect he had postulated eight years before. He proposed that activation energy and the unstable intermediate state were general properties of chemical reactions. He spoke of the forces that resist reactions as "chemical inertia." Activation energy can then be intuitively understood as the energy needed to overcome chemical inertia or, to speak metaphorically, to push an atom over the hump standing between its present state and a path or paths to alternative chemical states. The height of the potential energy hill would reveal the rate of reaction, both showing the amount of energy required to reach the transition state (moving uphill against inertia) and the velocity at which the subsequent reaction would take place (running downhill to a new state).

In the week between May 19 and 27, 1929, Polanyi retreated from home and laboratory to a guest room in Harnack House. He told his close friend and colleague, Erika Cremer, who had come to work with him in reaction kinetics, that he had to work on his "adsorption paper." He was not able to think at home because "there are the children, and then I must eat, and I must do this and that, and then there is the garden."[39] During this time away, Polanyi only asked once to see his mail from the institute. The success of this retreat set a pattern for other such excursions throughout the rest of his life.

Along with preparing the text of the Bunsen lecture for publication, Polanyi worked on updating his adsorption theory. He sent a 400-word note to the *Zeitschrift für Elektrochemie* on June 1, 1929, addressing the big problem of the range of the adsorption forces (1929c). If the range is large, the key assumption of Polanyi's theory that the adsorbed molecules obey the ordinary equations that describe the behavior of gases is likely to be valid, thus going beyond Eucken and opposing Langmuir. If the range is small, the theory may still be valid, but it would call for monomolecular adsorbed layers, as Langmuir posited, rather than thick ones. With the new evidence from Coolidge and from his own laboratory, Polanyi began to explore this new version of the theory.

At this time Polanyi commented to Erika Cremer: "Whose fate is better, mine or Langmuir's? My theory is absolutely right but not accepted. Langmuir's theory is wrong but he is very famous.... Langmuir is better off!"[40] Time has not proven either man to be simply right or wrong. There are some situations in which very strong bonds form at the surface between an adsorbent and an adsorbate (chemisorption), yielding the kind of monomolecular layer that Langmuir posited; other experiments using different substances and conditions have measured as many as 9,500 layers attracted to the surface by the kind of potential energy field that Polanyi focused on.[41] Langmuir is still more famous than Polanyi—he won the Nobel Prize in 1932, and his method of analyzing adsorption isotherms is routinely used as the best practical method of predicting adsorption in industrial processes and chemical engineering: "A quantitative and nonempirical approach...works best for physical adsorption, where surprisingly simple models frequently turn out to be useful caricatures of reality."[42]

In 1929, Polanyi's friend Karl Bonhoeffer (brother of Dietrich Bonhoeffer, who would give up his career, his freedom, and his life to oppose the Nazi regime) and his assistant, Paul Harteck, set out to test the predictions of David Dennison for the ortho- and para-hydrogen reaction. These are two forms of the hydrogen molecule, which have different alignments of their two nuclear spins. The difference has negligible effects on the chemical reactivity of the molecules—all forms of hydrogen have just one electron in orbit around the nucleus—but physicists are able to discriminate between them. The two forms only interconvert with difficulty. Bonhoeffer and Harteck were able to change para-hydrogen into ortho-hydrogen by bombarding the molecules with halogens. The two scientists broke the news of their discovery on February 26 at the Haber colloquium. In his diary, Polanyi mourned: "Oh, if only I could claim such a solid discovery. My achievements are scattered. I am depressed."[43]

Although he may at times have felt that he had not accomplished as much as others, Polanyi had a good reputation. In 1928, when his flame research was in full swing, Polanyi had been offered a full (ordinarius) professorship at the German University in Prague. As part of his duties, he would have become the director of the Physical Chemistry Institute. On a Sunday morning, Michael and Magda went to see the laboratories and were told they would have to wait two hours because the present director, his wife, and four children were having a bath in the laboratory's temperature-controlled tank—they had no bathtub at home. These were hard times for the university—the institute had cracks in the wall large enough to put a hand in. Disillusioned, the Polanyis returned to Berlin. Although Polanyi turned down the offer, it was evidence of the reputation he was earning through his research at the institute.

Even before the Prague offer was settled, two more came from Hungary. In May 1929, Count Cuno Klebelsberg, the Hungarian minister of education, offered Polanyi a full professorship at Szeged. On a trip to Budapest the following month, Izzo, for whom he had worked for seven years, again tried to persuade him to accept a full-time position with a salary at 65,000 pengö. The offer was very attractive. Polanyi had tried to augment his income by creating a Studiengesellschaft to do consulting work with Joffé for Siemens and Halske, and the Allgemeine Elektrische Gesellschaft. Polanyi had high hopes for this contract, but long discussions and considerable efforts at reorganization throughout 1929 produced very little activity. The two plants had very little need for scientific consultation. Polanyi stayed on call for advice at his usual fee, but was disappointed at the lack of interest in his talents and the small amount of money he earned for the institute.

What Polanyi needed most was a contractual arrangement at the Kaiser Wilhelm Institute that would assure him a permanent position. The offers from Prague and Izzo became bargaining points in his negotiations. Haber's institute had limited funds. The list of budgeted positions for 1929/30 mentioned four assistants for Haber, two for Freundlich, one for Ladenburg, and one for Polanyi. During that period, von Hartel and Frommer both seem to have been assistants to Polanyi, but most likely von Hartel was self-supporting. Schmid worked in connection with the Metal Institute, Eyring was supported from the United States, London collaborated by correspondence and by frequent visits, and Beck and Cremer did not get support until later.

While in Budapest, Polanyi stayed up late on the night of July 1, 1929, to write Haber a report on his contract with Izzo and on his still "extremely uncomfortable financial situation."[44] Back home five days later, feeling somewhat anxious, he met with von Harnack to request a salary of 20,000 marks.[45] Von Harnack was very reserved. After another six days, Haber asked Polanyi if he would consider taking over the Metals Research Institute, saying "among the talents of our time, yours is in the first line."[46] The flattery did not overcome Polanyi's reluctance to change his field of research once again.

Eugene Wigner and Leo Szilard, who were later to play key roles in the development of the atomic bomb, were concerned that Polanyi might succumb to the enticement of increased income, but they need not have worried. Germany had captivated him, and he was delighted with life in Berlin, a center of science and culture. "Should I emigrate into the wasteland of Ujpest, into the horrible sphere of influence, the childish activity of making money?"

he asked himself in his diary. He turned down Izzo's invitation to travel to Budapest in late November for further negotiations about the job offer. When Szilard told him of the celebration of the 50th anniversary of Planck's doctorate, Polanyi commented: "A great mind is at work here and my corner in its temple is assured."[47]

In July 1929, the Council granted Polanyi a new contract, giving him a lifetime membership in the Kaiser Wilhelm Gesellschaft, which included the same provisions that were in use for the Prussian civil servants, a generous retirement plan, and a raise in pay. Though this was far short of the salary Polanyi felt he deserved, this was the best that Haber could do to put Polanyi in "the reserve space of the top story," and Polanyi accepted the contract with good grace and considerable satisfaction.

That same summer, Polanyi made his first visit to the United States to lecture in the second summer session at the University of Minnesota and to speak at the opening ceremony of the Frick Chemistry Laboratory at Princeton University at the end of September. On July 24, he set sail from Bremerhaven on the small liner *SS München*. Karl Bonhoeffer, who was also to speak at Princeton, was his cabin mate. The trip provided a relaxing ten days at sea. The *München* landed in New York early on the fourth of August, and George Kistiakowsky and Henry Stewart were at the pier to meet Polanyi and Bonhoeffer. They introduced the Berlin scientists to the sights of New York, ending with the view from their seventeenth floor room in the Hotel Pennsylvania.

The Minnesota lectures were to start on August 6. The university had scheduled a month-long symposium on chemical kinetics in the second summer-school session, July 29 to August 31. Along with regular classes, each of four invited lecturers took part in one of the weekly seminars. Polanyi's title for his seminar was "The Flow of Energy in Chemical Reactions." His class covered the general field of gas kinetic experiments, focusing especially on his work with dilute flames. His sojourn in Minneapolis was punctuated with social events, excursions into the towns and countryside of nearby Minnesota, fishing trips, and many conversations. On a bus trip to nearby Stillwater, Polanyi admired the new bridge over the St. Croix River. He saw the demolition of the old bridge as a prime example of the American tendency to build afresh rather than to repair or renovate. Polanyi also enjoyed a three-day camping trip to a small logging town called Finland, northeast from Duluth in the wild northern woods near Lake Superior. Moose and bears were about, and he was surprised to learn that a forest fire had been burning for two months. A fire ranger explained that the flickering lights Polanyi had observed in the night sky were not from the fire—they were the northern lights, the Aurora Borealis. One afternoon, Polanyi went for a hike by himself. The forest was not as interesting to him as an article he had just read by the Russian chemical kineticist, Kondrat'ev, and he lost his way in the woods. Luckily, he was on a hill and could see Lake Superior through the trees, which helped him find his way back to camp.

Polanyi thought that the atmosphere of egalitarianism on U.S. campuses fostered a cafeteria attitude toward education. Students picked their courses by whim and fancy. Jászi told him that Americans believed they could learn anything—languages, business, law, playwriting—just by taking the right courses. Polanyi worried that faculty teaching loads in the universities were so heavy that there was little chance for research, and that the research undertaken was motivated by practical applications, so that the men and women of pure science who are "our most precious assets" were being neglected.

During the trip, Polanyi made notes on prices, wages, and labor relations, and on such activities as the wrecking business, advertising, and life insurance. The way large numbers of automobile drivers cooperated with each other impressed him—it was a vivid example of what he later called dynamic order, which arises from constant mutual adjustments, without overall supervision. He noted the importance of friendliness to strangers in merchandising—the "selling of pleasantness." Polanyi pondered the tension inherent in industrial negotiations: fair contracts required full disclosure of information, but bad patent laws made it necessary to keep trade secrets. He expressed the basic argument against untruthfulness that it ultimately cuts off mutually beneficial communication. Henry Ford's views also interested him—he agreed with Ford that "Unemployment is the shame of the world."

By September 25, Polanyi had arrived in Princeton and was preparing for the lecture he was to give to help inaugurate the new chemistry laboratory that had been funded by Henry Clay Frick. He got his flame tube operating in the chemistry building, visited around the department for a while, and "settled down to the last dull work on the lecture—with gritted teeth."[48] On September 26, the University awarded honorary degrees to Irving Langmuir, Max Bodenstein, Jean Baptiste Perrin, Sir James Iwin, and Frederick Donnan. After the degree ceremony, Polanyi took part in a formal tea and a social evening with Stewart, Kistiakowsky, Bonhoeffer, and Conant. Hugh S. Taylor was in charge of the festivities for the chemists. Polanyi commented, "I like Taylor with his quiet, kind nature more and more, even though I perceive his position as chairman of the Department of Chemistry at Princeton as extravagant. He cannot fill it scientifically."[49] Polanyi was very much mistaken in his assessment of Taylor, who subsequently received many honors for his work in science, becoming a knight and a Fellow of the Royal Society.

Part of the celebration was a conference on catalysis and the mechanism of chemical reactions. Following papers by Langmuir, Bodenstein, Francis Perrin, and Cyril Norman Hinshelwood (knighted in 1948 and co-winner of the Nobel Prize in 1956), Polanyi spoke on "Atomic Reactions and Luminescence in Highly Dilute Flames," illustrating his talk with a flame in the tube he had brought along (1929d). He had put the demonstration together himself, using facilities of the new laboratory, and reported that it came off quite successfully.

Polanyi had kept in touch with Bonhoeffer during the summer through letters and telegrams. During their stay in the States, both men had been offered, and both declined, a position at Harvard. They returned home on the elegantly furnished steamship *Bremen*. The decor of the ship was so clearly European in style that it aroused Polanyi's affection for Germany and European culture. He had had enough of America. During his journey, he had felt his original attraction turning into repulsion. "Here in the middle of the old world, you do not have to hold your hand in front of your forehead when you're thinking."[50] But if America fell short of Polanyi's expectations, so did his own career: "I'm dreamily thinking about the reasons for my lack of success." The next day, he outlined an essay on the topic of ethics.[51] He was pleased with the results: "6 October 1929, afternoon, wonderful writing about the basis of ethics."

Magda was at the dock in Cherbourg to greet Michael upon his arrival on October 10. They spent a week in Paris together before returning to Berlin and the routine of laboratory, home, and social life. On October 19, Polanyi wrote of the need to throw everything overboard that could endanger his development and to organize his life purposefully. Although "the mature man always finds joy in his fellow man," Polanyi seems to have felt that he paid too much attention to others' concerns and not enough to his own.

The absence of Polanyi, Bonhoeffer, Harteck, and Bodenstein during the summer of 1929 set the stage for Henry Eyring to make progress on reaction rate theory. After training as a mining engineer, Eyring obtained his Ph.D. in chemistry at the University of California in Berkeley in 1927. He then went to the University of Wisconsin as assistant to Farrington Daniels, who put him to work on the rate of dissociation of nitrogen pentoxide (N_2O_5) in various solvents, the first unimolecular reaction to be studied in detail. Eyring was familiar with the work Polanyi and Wigner had done on reaction kinetics. He obtained a National Research Fellowship to study in Berlin under Bodenstein, the most famous person in the field at that time, but Bodenstein was planning to lecture at Johns Hopkins University for the fall term. Professor Frumkin, visiting Wisconsin from Moscow, advised Eyring to use the grant to study under Polanyi. Eyring sailed for Europe and joined Polanyi's laboratory sometime in August.

Polanyi wrote Eyring from the United States, asking him to work with von Hartel on the diffusion flame experiments until Polanyi returned from America and Paris on October 16. Von Hartel concentrated on the design, construction, and maintenance of the experiment while Eyring took over the problem of graphing the potential-energy surfaces. Eyring had learned to make contour maps during his earlier training in geology and mining; this skill, combined with his interest in the basic problem, made him just the right person for the job.

Eyring and Polanyi were aware that the approximation Fritz London used previously had underestimated the activation energy for the formation of hydrogen gas molecules by 25 percent. They could not find any practical way to use London's three-atom method for reactions with atoms other than hydrogen. Eyring, who had a flair for making useful approximations, latched on to a paper by P. M. Morse, published the previous July, which described a way of approximating the energy levels and wave functions in a two-atom molecule.[52] Eyring used the Morse function to represent the two-body energies as a function of internuclear distance for any given pair of atoms such as Na_2 or NaCl. Eyring called his procedure a "semi-empirical" method. By combining spectroscopic data with the Morse model, Eyring produced graphs of the "resonance mountains" (*Resonanzgebirge*) in the potential energy field of particular reactions. Such graphs could be used to estimate the activation energies for both endothermic and exothermic reactions. Study of possible trajectories out of the valleys and across the hump between them provided information on the exchange of linear and vibrational kinetic energies as well as suggesting the way such exchanges might slow or even prevent the reaction from taking place.

The potential energy summit between the two valleys representing the states of reactants or products was the most useful and crucial part of the diagram. Once the energy diagram is settled to whatever degree of accuracy is practical, the next job is to find the rate at which reacting systems go over the hump. If the reaction were compared to a ball being rolled uphill over the contour map, then descending into the valley on the other side of the hump, the rate of a reaction might be found by studying the variety of all possible trajectories from one valley to the other; this, in turn, would allow a calculation of the relative probabilities of the reaction occurring. In those days before computers, the calculations required by Wigner's theory were too complex to be undertaken, even for the simplest hydrogen–hydrogen reaction. Nevertheless, the theory and the semi-empirical approximations cast light on the fundamental questions of reaction kinetics.

In studying fast reactions, Polanyi and his group learned a great deal from the patterns of light in the dilute flames and from the chemical deposits on the reaction tubes. The values of various rates of reactions were found and reported in terms of the overall number of collisions needed to effect a reaction. At the beginning nothing was said about the activation energy, but after about 1928, they began to calculate this energy in units of kilocalories per mole. Sometimes the values were derived from the ratio of effective collisions to total collisions, that is, the reciprocal of the number of collisions per reaction. At other times the method of measuring two values of reaction rates at two different temperatures was used.

The highly dilute flame technique worked well for fast reactions, those without substantial activation energy. A different technique was required for the study of slow reactions, known as "cases of appreciable inertia," as well as those without spontaneous luminescence. For gas mixtures that required a thousand or ten thousand collisions for each successful reaction, Polanyi could no longer use a design in which the diameter of the tube was roughly the same as the mean free path of molecules between collisions. In order to give the reactants time to collide frequently with each other before reaching the walls of the tube, Polanyi decided to add an inert carrier gas, such as nitrogen, as in the original Haber–Zisch arrangement. The opportunity for the reacting molecules to undergo a great many unreactive collisions with nitrogen in between their collisions with their target molecules meant that their paths were bent back and forth so many times they could only slowly get out of the initial reaction zone, making it highly probable that the desired reactions would take place before the target gases hit the chamber walls. The reactants penetrated slowly into the carrier by diffusion, and Polanyi was able to use a well-known theory of diffusive mixing, although just how to refine it to include an ongoing chemical reaction was not yet known.

The apparatus that solved the problem was made by Hans von Hartel, an ingenious technician, and provided for a jet of sodium vapor to enter the middle of a tube containing the halogen compound of interest mixed with neutral carrier gas.[53] The sodium vapor would then diffuse through the carrier gas and form a sphere containing sodium atoms, molecules of the other reactant, and the two product molecules, the reaction going on to completion in the gaseous sphere before any products reached the walls. As a consequence, deposition and wall collisions had no appreciable effect on the rate of the reaction.

In most of the cases, the reactions did not cause sodium atoms to emit light. To detect the concentration of these atoms in the intermediate stage of the reaction, yellow light from a sodium lamp was focused on the reacting sphere. The sodium atoms in the reaction chamber absorbed the light, raising their electrons to the second quantum level. These atoms would then return to the base level, radiating unfocused yellow light in all directions. This "resonance radiation" made a visible "flame," the size of which showed how far the sodium atoms could move out in a sphere before being converted into a molecular form with different energy levels. The arrangement was a truly clever application of the resonance radiation and allowed a fairly simple formula from diffusion theory to be used to calculate the rate constant for the reaction. Constants expressing the rate of diffusion were derived in a number of ways from existing data. According to Schay, this work of Hartel was decisive for getting reliable results.[54]

Shinjiro Kodama was an industrial chemist who had worked in Tokyo on fairly conventional problems in catalytic chemistry. When he came across

Beutler and Polanyi's article describing the highly dilute flame work (1928c), he was fascinated by the article and resolved to obtain his industrial employer's help in going to Germany for two year's study under Polanyi's direction. On Kodama's arrival in October 1930, Polanyi inquired if he was familiar with quantum mechanics. When Kodama answered no, Polanyi assigned him to learn the subject as a prerequisite for working in the laboratory. Since no textbooks had been written about this relatively new field, Kodama set about reading all the papers of Heisenberg and Schrödinger. However, the use of matrix calculations and partial differential equations was beyond him. At the end of a few months Kodama reported to Polanyi that he had studied quantum mechanics (although he did not say he understood it); he was then allowed to join the laboratory.[55] Kodama was assigned to measure the rates of reaction between sodium atoms and organic halide compounds. He began the tedious work of building the type of instrument that von Hartel had designed.[56]

Of the staff of nine in Polanyi's laboratory, only Polanyi and the two technicians Schmalz (mechanical) and Hauschild (glassblowing) were paid by the KWG. The rest were all from foreign countries; they either paid their own way or had fellowships or other forms of support. The group worked in five small rooms on the third floor. Each room contained only a modest table holding the apparatus on which the occupant was working. The visitor observed none of the usual auxiliary instruments of a typical chemical laboratory. Any measuring apparatus needed was available on short notice from a common store. In addition, the institute had a large machine shop where sophisticated, high precision work could be done, with one section for large articles and one for small. Hauschild's high-quality glassblowing was carried out at the site in each research room where it was needed. Polanyi made frequent visits to each person. Kodama was impressed by his slim, young-looking mentor, always dressed in a well-tailored suit, speaking quietly, slowly, and warmheartedly to each member of the staff. Brilliant ideas seemed to pour out of him, "just like water flowing smoothly from high to low."[57]

As Beutler and Polanyi had reported in their first article on dilute flames, organic halogen compounds do not produce spontaneous luminescence, and therefore needed to be studied by using the sodium resonance lamp (1925m). In the middle of 1932, Hans von Hartel, N. Meer, and Polanyi published an article giving a large amount of data on twenty-seven organic compounds containing one or more halogen atoms (1932f). These were all cases in which the only change was the transfer of the halogen atom from the organic part of the compound, known as the "radical," to a sodium atom. Many regularities were noted among similar compounds, for instance in the increase of reactivity with increasing length of the alkyl chain, or with the degree of branching, or with the presence of more than one halogen. In contrast with earlier experiments, the group found that there were no reactions that occurred on every collision. Their analysis gave the "most complete experimental data on the dependence of the rate of exchange on the structure of the molecule."[58]

Although his work in reaction kinetics could have kept him occupied full-time, Polanyi's interest in social and economic theory continued to grow. In the fall of 1929, Polanyi sent his brother a detailed criticism of a statistical study of the Soviet Union by Arthur Feiler. The ten-page letter started in Hungarian, then shifted to German. The grounds for Polanyi's opposition to the Soviet system and Soviet propaganda lay in his personal impressions from his 1928 trip and in his study of economics. Polanyi criticized Feiler and the Soviets for the misuse of statistics and quantitative measurements. "It is a cause for despair," he wrote, "that there are people who can be led to die or to kill with this kind of scientism."[59] The figures for national income and the production of steel and coal were not too hard to analyze, but the analysis of the relationship between industrial and agricultural production seemed specious. Though Feiler did not draw conclusions, Polanyi did. If the government set prices artificially low, then the affected industries would run at a deficit; if the government provided subsidies to remedy the deficit, the burden of the subsidy would fall on workers and other farmers. He criticized Feiler for giving an error-laden, uncritical, and one-sided representation of the economy. Feiler's book shed no light on what the great experiment was supposed to prove and what there was to be excited about. Instead of removing the burden of poverty from the poor, socialism had covered up its foreseeable failures under the rhetoric of a more noble and just poverty. Feiler's treatment also failed to assess the damage done to human society: "It shocks me to see the indulgent dismissal of the horrors of the Revolution, which rages against life, freedom, and trust, year in and year out" (9).

Polanyi's 1929 diary bears many such signs of discouragement and depression. After a dinner discussing the problem of war with Szilard and Wigner, Polanyi noted that the things which interested him he could not do and the things he could do did not interest him. Throughout his life, Polanyi experienced "creeping depression followed by periods of far-sighted resignation." The dry leaves falling at Freienwalde led him to reflect "that life is the same, the letting go of all desires, the departure of ambition."[60] His diary reveals the wide variety of books that he was accustomed to read: Glaeser's *Jahrgang 1902*, a "dreadful" portrait of his own generation; the *Life of Michelangelo*, who "had less peace but produced after all"; Robert Lynd's *Middletown*, written from the point of view of the working class; Stuart Chase's *Men and Machines*, which helped shape his thoughts about technology; De Kruif's *Mikrobenjäger*; Conrad's *Nigger of the Narcissus* and *Lord Jim*; Alain's *Essays*, dealing with pacifism; Werfel's *Abituriententag*; Haldane's *Possible Worlds*; Tolstoy's *Childhood and Boyhood*; Hauff's *Phantasien*; Ludwig's *Wilhelm der Zweite*; the *Dhammapada*, "delightful verses" drawn from the sayings of the

Buddha; Wilder's *Bridge of San Luis Rey*; Arthur Ponsonby's *Falsehood in Wartime*; Watson-McDougall's *Behaviorism: An Exposition and an Exposure*; Christian Morgenstern's verses; Lewisohn's *Up Stream*; *The Greene Murder Case* and other detective novels that he relied on as antidotes for depression and insomnia. Polanyi experienced kinship with others through his reading: "The belief of the people who read good books flows again together at the moment into a community. Each one knows the same books and is under the influence of the same thoughts."[61]

Early in 1930, Polanyi decided to form a study group to bring natural scientists and economists together to share their mutual expertise. He hoped that solid quantitative data could be obtained on investment, income, and productivity in various countries, in contrast to the vagueness of the daily press. He planned to hold meetings in nearby Harnack House, which served the Kaiser Wilhelm Institutes as a meeting place for many societies and groups and provided daily meals for several hundred scientific workers.

Polanyi struggled to formulate his purpose in sending out invitations to join the group. The draft of his letter to the physicist Erwin Schrödinger shows corrections in almost every sentence. Polanyi hoped that "the interest of scientifically trained people would give all these questions a special character which would make it seem fruitful to national economists to take part in the study group and to take over a great part of the work as well as its supervision."[62] Although Schrödinger declined the invitation, the first meeting of the study group was held on the night of January 17 and included Szilard, Lange, London, Bonhoeffer, Gaviola, Harteck, Reiter, and Forster. Polanyi read an introduction he had written that day in a style that he thought was "freer, less intricate, not at all paradoxical."[63] The discussion focused on a document from the United States National Bureau of Economic Research, "Trends of Philanthropy." Polanyi returned home afterwards feeling happy and peaceful. It was his show, and, although many lively minds took part, Polanyi had been in the spotlight. Karl Söllner, a chemist who also had delved into economics but was not invited to join the group, complained that Polanyi formed the study group in order to be "surrounded by a society of adorers."[64] Söllner also considered this to be "the exact time when Polanyi had begun to be less interested in physical chemistry."

Two weeks later, at the second meeting, Toni Stolper discussed the Russian five-year plan. Twenty-two people gathered for a simple meal from 7 to 7:30, followed by an evening of talk. Polanyi reported to Toni that Joffé and Haber were expected to come, and that he was trying to get in touch with Moellendorf. Toni appreciated his interest. "Michael's keen mind and scientific approach early made him one of the rare factual critics in the face of the great rush of propaganda issuing from Moscow."[65]

The records of Harnack House show nine or ten meetings under Professor Polanyi's name up until the middle of 1931 that were probably gatherings of the study group. We have no records of the subject matter after the first two meetings. Eighteen years later, Polanyi added a note in English to his 1930 diary: "The Arbeitsgemeinschaft [study group] has borne all kinds of fruit. Von Neumann has written a book on Games and Economic Theory. Szilard and I have become Professors of Social Science. I remember others of the circle: F. London, Wigner, Marschak, the Stolpers."

The Polanyis spent Sunday afternoons like many middle-class Berlin families, taking walks in the pleasant surroundings of the Grünewald. Polanyi, Szilard, and other scientists would also set out from Waltraudstrasse, walking and talking for hours on end. On vacations, Polanyi liked to hike and to ride horseback. He once hiked for four or five days near Bolzano in northern Italy before making a visit to Florence, where his aunt and uncle Terez and Emil Pollacsek had settled with their children.

The Wannsee provided a place for canoes, kayaks, and paddle-boats, as well as for swimming and sailing. Polanyi loved a challenge. Once while sailing in a strong wind on the North Sea with Ervin von Gomperz, he climbed up the mast on a rope ladder to untangle the halyard: "I was very happy that I mustered that tiny amount of courage."[66]

As the family became more prosperous, Polanyi enjoyed skiing weekends at Freienwalde, two hours by train northeast of Berlin, and at Zell am See, a ski resort in Austria. Polanyi took many of these trips to get away from the pressures of work and concomitant sleeplessness. But the stress (and the sleeping pills) went with him. Sharing a hotel room on a skiing trip with Erich Schmid, Polanyi demanded that Schmid wrap his watch in a cloth and put it into the drawer of the night table.[67]

At home, Polanyi enjoyed gymnastic exercises and tennis. A middling player, Polanyi found tennis a refreshing break from work. Sometimes during afternoon sessions he would call out, "Let's play tennis!" On some occasions, the exercise helped clear his mind, and he would interrupt the game to discuss a new idea. A slender, vigorous young lady conducted gymnastics and javelin-throwing exercises for men in nearby Zehlendorf and later at Harnack House. The exercises were designed to keep the middle-aged participants in shape. Polanyi relished them and sometimes ran several laps around the gymnasium afterward. His daily schedule was irregular. He often came late to the laboratory and often took an afternoon nap, placing a sign on his door: "Ich möchte schlafen"—"I wish to sleep"[68]—and then worked late into the evening. Unfinished business might be carried over into weekend hikes, where serious conversation settled a point or clarified a disagreement.

The outdoor activities, the new house with space for relaxation, and an expanding circle of friends provided the Polanyis with a satisfying social life. There was a steady round of luncheons, dinner parties, and evening gatherings. Among the friends outside the institute were Franz Alexander, from the Minta and the University of Berlin; Edith Hajos, a playmate from Budapest days and now a fascinating and radical woman; the philosopher Helmut Kuhn; and the Stolpers.[69] There were colleagues and administrators with whom Polanyi worked and also had social contacts: the Berényis, Karl Bonhoeffer, Otto Hahn, Lise Meitner, Abram Joffé and Alexander Frumkin from Russia, Fritz London, Gretl Magnus, Erich Schmid, Erika Cremer, the Meyerhofs, Fritz Paneth, Max Planck, and especially Leo Szilard and Eugene Wigner.[70]

Of course, not all the discussion with colleagues was serious. When Bela Szilard and his wife were on their honeymoon, they took up his brother Leo's invitation to drop in at the institute. Coming in at the afternoon coffee hour, they found Leo, Michael, and others engrossed in conversation. Mrs. Szilard insisted on waiting outside the room so that she and Bela would not interrupt the dialogue. "What have you been discussing so deeply?" asked Bela as Leo and Michael came out. "What to do with a hair brush when it is full," Polanyi replied.[71]

Karl Bonhoeffer became one of Polanyi's closest friends in the later Berlin period. One evening, Magda, George, and Bonhoeffer were sitting around the dinner table. "Upstairs was Hans [John], with his inquisitive, giant eyes." Polanyi reflected on the quiet pleasures of friends and family. "Is this the great achievement in life?" he asked himself.[72] The birth of Bonhoeffer's son touched a chord in Polanyi: "it is a great joy in which I heartily take part. But it also is...a deep shock which renews all of life. That now it shall begin again—from one's own and the beloved other blood and then shall go on incalculably.... People that have sons are closer to each other than others."[73]

In the summer of 1930, before his article with Polanyi was published, Eyring made a few calculations on the role played by vibrational energy in the passage over the hump, but he recognized that a different method was needed; the next year, while teaching at Berkeley, he found the key in statistical mechanics. The new idea was that when all the elements needed to form the products of the reaction are gathered together at the top of the pass, they temporarily form an aggregate, which Eyring called the "activated complex" and Polanyi called the "transition state." Eyring proposed that the activated complex has all the features of a molecule, except that it lacks the full range of degrees of freedom found in normal molecules. By treating the transition state like a molecule in equilibrium with the reagents and products of the reaction, the rules of statistical mechanics can be used to calculate the speed of passage across the pass. Pelzer and Wigner independently conceived of this approach in Berlin and used the method to get a velocity coefficient for the para-to-ortho-hydrogen reaction.[74]

From 1931 on, Eyring and his collaborators took up the activated complex idea and laid the foundations for transition state theory. Polanyi and his friend, Meredith G. Evans, were to take a parallel route in Manchester, following the same statistical principles, but focusing attention on thermodynamic consequences. The initial results of both groups of workers were rough in a quantitative sense, but they provided further insight into the mechanism of chemical reactions. In 1932, Polanyi summed up the results of his research in reaction kinetics and in transition state theory in his first book, *Atomic Reactions* (1932j). This was arguably the pinnacle of his career in physical chemistry: he had developed a comprehensive answer to the question of how to understand the inner workings of reaction rates.

During his last years in Berlin, Polanyi also played a prominent role in the scientific community. In 1930, Polanyi took over the scheduling of the Haber colloquium, which had been Freundlich's job for the previous ten years. His first lecture was "Über die Natur der Festigkeit"—"On the Nature of Solidity." Shortly after this, Polanyi parodied his own presentation in a talk entitled "Über die Natur der Wurstigkeit." "Wurstigkeit" literally means "sausageness"; figuratively, it means "nonsense."[75] Polanyi outlined the goals of his administration. The first was beautification of the colloquium invitations by means of an Academy of Art prize competition. Then he announced a program for rationalizing the order in which authors are listed on publications. The strict observance of alphabetical order purported to be democratic, but alas, gave permanent superiority to the class of Meyers over the class of Schmidts. Polanyi had witnessed this problem on his trip to the United States—Bonhoeffer received far more publicity than Harteck for their joint work on para-hydrogen. Something needed to be done. Because appeals to Haber were unsuccessful, Polanyi proposed to go over the heads of the administrators to the highest authority in the institute, Herr Kuhn, the janitor, to create a system of mathematical formulas that would show the true weight of the contribution made by coauthors. They might be introduced as true partners, "Meyer equals Schmidt." Unhelpful participation could be recorded as "Meyer minus Schmidt." An outstanding contributor would receive exponential honor: "Schmidt to the power of Meyer." For a case of a single author, a split personality might be recognized, as 1 percent para-Polanyi and 99 percent ortho-Polanyi, or 1 percent correct and 99 percent nonsense.

Acting as administrator, Polanyi now introduced the evening's speaker, para-Polanyi, pointing out that the latter had ten years earlier published an idea whose time had not then and never would come, the idea of a nonmechanical basis for the energy of chemical reactions; his topic this evening would be the mechanical properties of *wurstigkeit*. His talk was based on five illustrative slides (probably taken from the studies of metal fibers, where the stretched crystal indeed looks like a sliced sausage). The lesson to be learned was drawn from von Mises: "By pushing this model back and forth all the questions of plastic change of form are solved." A sixth slide was shown with crosses for experimental points and a rather wild curve given by an equation, with the remark that one can always find equations that fail to fit the data.

Polanyi then addressed the implications of Einstein's theory of relativity in which, so to speak, space eats up the aether as well as gravitation and the electromagnetic field, and will surely also eat up both sausages and sausage-ness. Therefore, the essence of *Wurstigkeit* is the structure of space. Polanyi concluded, as was the custom, by thanking the Deutsche Notgemeinschaft, in this case for providing the "steady movement of the sun, moon, and stars and the change of the seasons, without which this paper could not have been written."

In May 1930, Fritz London completed a substantial paper on dipole-dipole interactions of the van der Waals type,[76] building on Wang's work from three years earlier.[77] Van der Waals forces are the electrostatic forces operating between molecules; these forces are relatively weak when compared to the chemical bonds that hold molecules together or the force of attraction that keeps an electron in orbit around a nucleus. London lectured at Haber's colloquium on July 14, which gave Polanyi the opportunity to discuss the dipole-dipole bond he had postulated in 1920 (1920f, 1920i). Polanyi and London had a lengthy conversation and collaborated on a two-page note in *Naturwissen-schaften* in November (1930g). They showed how the quantum-mechanical dipole-dipole interaction provided the long-missing justification of Polanyi's theory of the adsorption potential.

We now understand that the separation of charge into a negative and positive pole is caused by fluctuations of the electron cloud that surrounds the nucleus. The force of these fluctuations varies in direction and in magnitude, but at any instant it produces an electric field in the surroundings, which attracts the positive or negative poles found in neighboring molecules. Quantum mechanics allows the calculation of the average forces brought into play. Van der Walls showed that the attractive component varies inversely as the sixth power of the distance between the molecules. Polanyi proposed the term "dispersion forces" for these because the phenomenon of electron fluctuation also plays a key role in the optical dispersion of light (1932b, 320). In quantum mechanics, electrons in molecules are highly localized. Only in the case of metals, which possess highly mobile electrons, can electrostatic shielding occur. It does not happen in adsorbed gas layers as Einstein and Haber had argued it would ten years earlier.

Taking the inverse sixth power law that van der Waals developed to describe the attractive force between two molecules, London and Polanyi calculated the resultant force on one adsorbed molecule produced by a plane of adsorbing molecules of indefinite thickness and found an inverse third power law.[78] From the fact that the dispersion (attractive!) forces are essentially additive, they showed that the field of potential energy above the adsorbent does not vary with the presence of other molecules and does not affect the interactions of the adsorbed molecules among themselves. They found, too, that the strength of the potential energy varied only slightly with changes in temperature. Thus, to Polanyi's great satisfaction, the principal features of his original theory of adsorption were justified.

When the Faraday Society announced a discussion on the adsorption of gases by solids to be held in Oxford in February 1932, they invited Polanyi to contribute a paper introducing the section on theory, in honor of his pioneering work (1932b). Polanyi, Bonhoeffer, Freundlich, Mark, and Volmer made plans to attend. All thirty-eight papers were to be made available in advance, thus giving priority to the serious business of discussion. Unfortunately, Polanyi and his colleagues were unable to attend the conference, probably due to a lack of funds.

Hugh S. Taylor from Princeton delivered the general introduction. He favored the Langmuir theory, but gave a description of the high rate of mobility of adsorbed molecules that tended to support the Goldmann and Polanyi paper of 1928. Taylor observed that there was evidently a multiplicity of adsorption processes; he also noted that the thick layer initially proposed by Polanyi had gotten thinner over the years.

Polanyi's paper was a general review of the theoretical situation; he interpreted the shape of the isotherms in terms of the three kinds of forces, electrostatic, valence, and dispersion. He used his original diagram of 1920 to show how the displacement of nuclei accounts for the dispersion forces (1920d—the same article in which he had proposed a nonmechanical theory of chemical reactions). He also applied the inverse cube formula he had developed with London to an analysis of the adsorption energies that would be found within a crack in the face of an adsorbing surface. He derived an adsorption curve from this computation that agreed fairly well with observations of CO_2 on charcoal, which has a notoriously uneven surface. Little note was taken of Polanyi's work at the Faraday discussion. Because of his absence, his contribution was restricted to two comments sent in later for publication. Polanyi was disappointed to find virtually no mention of his work in the three dozen advance papers on many aspects of adsorption.

Polanyi's final research paper on metal physics dealt with the phenomenon of crystal weakness for which he had so long sought an explanation. Polanyi had not seen how close he was to a correct interpretation in his 1922 lecture because he was dealing with hardening through bending; it did not occur to him that the defect he described might happen even under ordinary conditions and could also cause weakening. Polanyi was led to his new view by L. Prandtl's suggestion in 1928 that a dislocation between two crystal faces might explain elastic aftereffects;[79] in 1929, U. Dehlinger discussed the idea of dislocation as the basis of recrystallization.[80] When Polanyi was invited to lecture at Joffé's institute in Leningrad in 1932, he proposed a dislocation that would naturally arise in the course of ordinary crystal growth and provide the n versus $n + 1$ atoms described in the 1922 lecture (1934i). This time, however, instead of focusing on extra potential energy, he pointed out that it would be very easy for such planes to glide past each other, because each atom be-longing to one plane would only have to change its net position with respect to the other plane by $1/n$th of a crystal spacing, and the crystal would end up with the same energy after the slippage as before, except at the edges. The net result was that only $1/n$ of the ordinarily calculated force would be needed, and n could quite readily be 1,000 or more. This kind of crystal defect is now called an "edge dislocation." The gliding of one plane against the other allows the dislocation itself to slide, and it could go all the way from the right-hand edge to the left-hand. Polanyi remarked in his article that this process does not explain hardening—that still takes lattice disruption—but tells why the un-hardened crystal is as plastic as it is and gives a hint as to why its breaking strength is so much less than the theoretical value. Temperature had little effect on the breaking strength, as Bredig had originally suggested.

Polanyi delayed publishing his theory of dislocation because Egon Or-owan, a student finishing his doctorate with Richard Becker in Berlin had made the same discovery, and Polanyi wanted to give him due credit. Pola-nyi's article followed Orowan's in the journal. Geoffrey Ingram Taylor also found and published the edge-dislocation idea about the same time. All three publications are listed in the 280-page *Encyclopedia of Physics* article on dis-locations in crystals as representing the first use of this concept. The idea pointed the way to the extensive study of crystal defects and opened up a vast field of crystal science. It was in fact recognized in August 1973 when the three "inventors" of the concept of dislocation were awarded medals by the Dansk Metallurgisk Selskab (Danish Metallurgical Society).

The peaceful, academic village of Dahlem helped to shield Polanyi from the political, artistic, and philosophic turmoil of Weimar Berlin. Occasionally he and Magda enjoyed a play in Berlin at one of the thirty-two professional theaters, a constellation unrivaled anywhere in the world, or attended a movie produced by the nascent film industry. There were approximately six-hundred concerts given each year featuring great artists like Kreisler, Schnabel, and Furtwängler, and modern composers, including Schönberg and Hindemith. Magda enjoyed the music scene more than Michael did. Polanyi kept up with economic and political events primarily through *Der deutsche Volkswirt*. Its weekly accounts documented the rising fear of unemployment. After the mark was stabilized in 1924, there were 120,000 jobless, but a quarter of a million were out of work in 1927, and half a million by the time of the New York stock market crash in 1929. The harsh terms of the Versailles Treaty combined with Germany's economic woes led to extreme proposals for po-litical reform from the left and the right. Athletics was politicized by the formation of the anti-Semitic Wandervögel and the Hitlerjugend. For some German intellectuals, loss of faith in their tradition made the Nietzschean doubt of all belief systems attractive. The twin beacons of the Enlightenment, science and technology, had lost their luster. The nihilistic developments were largely confined to intellectuals and artists, however, as there was in Germany a great gulf between the interests of that small minority and the concerns of the people at large.[81] The cultural foundations on which Germany's scientific edifice was built were being steadily eroded by the rising tide of despair.

By 1931, Cecile felt the situation acutely: "The times in Berlin are beginning to be frightful. Unemployment, privation, disheveled economic, political and emotional life. Riots, brawls . . . in short, from one side, Fascism, from the other Bolshevism! In the middle Democracy, starved, beaten, demolished, . . . behind all [the artistic happenings] the question: how much longer? One says the worst will come in January, the other in February . . . but that it will come they all believe."[82] Novelist Storm Jameson, visiting Berlin in February 1932, noted "the nervous gaiety, the eager abandonment and deriding of morals, the threat of social collapse, the paralysis of all ideals— including the ideal of freedom."[83] Polanyi expressed his concern in "New Morality," an unpublished essay that describes the longing of his contemporaries to find meaning after the devastation of the war. The question of how to address spiritual emptiness of our times and the desire to develop a "new morality" to uphold the work of science remained a leitmotif of Polanyi's social analysis and philosophical reflection.

The life of the institute remained mostly unaffected by the dark currents of the surrounding culture. The staff delighted in costume parties, held each year during Fasching, the period of carnival from New Year's to the beginning of Lent. Harnack House, with its fine dining room and crystal chandeliers, was often the locale for the festivities. Sometimes the refreshments were just a few bottles of beer brought by the guests—they enjoyed each other's company even when money was short. Even after Hitler came to power, carnival was celebrated. The partygoers usually dressed as famous scientists. Otto Hahn always glued on a black beard. Polanyi once came dressed like a Bedouin, announcing, "My name is Polanyi and I'm the nephew of Professor Polanyi," amusing his colleagues with witty remarks about his "uncle."[84] The party of February 11, 1933, was a Würstlabend, a "sausage evening," held at the Schrödingers' house in Cunostrasse. In defiance of Hitler's calls for sobriety, Polanyi expressed his hope that after the party, they might go to the Riemann Ball, "with full sails in the wind of debauchery."[85] Paul Ehrenfest set the theme for the evening by suggesting that the house be renamed "Hotel psi psi star" for the evening, referring to the formula $\psi\psi*$, which represented the density of electrons in Schrödinger's wave-mechanical interpretation of quantum mechanics. The party was a big success. Max Delbrück, wearing a uniform borrowed from the porter at Harnack House, came as a hotel boy "Psi Psi Star." The astronomers came as the sun and moon. Erika Cremer, who was making calculations for Eyring and Polanyi on the resonance mountain in the new theory of reaction rates, came as an alpine shepherd-girl with a pitchfork in the form of a psi.[86]

Although Polanyi was productive in his research, there were times when he felt overwhelmed by his responsibilities and went to the institute late and attacked his duties in a disjointed fashion. He was not alone in his depression. Paul Ehrenfest committed suicide later that year, perhaps partly from professional disappointments as well as grief about his son's retardation. Years later, Polanyi talked with one of his students about what it takes to be a great scientist: extensive knowledge, a critical faculty, and creativity.[87] In Polanyi's view, Ehrenfest had immense knowledge and a great gift for critical reasoning, but was not very original—and could not live with his awareness of his own shortcomings.

Wilfried Heller, who had finished his Ph.D. work at the University of Berlin in 1930, received a two-year Liebig fellowship to work at the Kaiser Wilhelm Institute for Physical Chemistry and Electrochemistry beginning in 1931. He was doing research on colloids in the second floor of the institute, but became intrigued by the work of the reaction kinetics group on the third floor: "I always got an inferiority complex when I saw the complicated vacuum lines and the famous man who worked there."[88] He asked for a chance to work in Polanyi's laboratory. Polanyi was having maintenance problems with the sodium diffusion apparatus designed by von Hartel and was glad to give a part-time appointment to a competent experimenter who could keep the equipment running. One of Heller's duties was to rebuild the sodium lamp when it failed.

The apparatus in Heller's improved form was finally ready in the summer of 1933. Heller knew that, like everyone else, he would have to leave soon, and he worked hard from January to September 1933, both on a series of experiments and on careful analysis of what was needed to make the method reliable. He was not able to write up what he did at the time, so there were two Heller–Polanyi papers published in 1934 and 1936 covering new results in reactions between sodium vapor and inorganic halides. The first was a brief account in French of the method and summary of results in the Paris Academy journal, *Comptes Rendus* (1934p). The second, in English, gave details, including results for thirteen new cases of chemiluminescence (1936b). An important conclusion in this article was that the chemical inertia and hence the activation energy of the halide reactions was larger when the bond holding the halogen atom was longer. A critical discussion of the method and how to make it work reliably came out under Heller's name in 1937.[89]

During their last three years at Waltraudstrasse 15, Michael and Magda were joined in Berlin by several other members of the family. Mausi rented a beautiful roomy atelier apartment at Tauentzienstrasse 8 for her two older children, Eva and Misi. Misi had just finished his doctoral dissertation in national economy in Budapest (1930), a topic suggested by his uncle; he was

looking forward to a career in patent law. Eva, already an accomplished ce-
ramicist, had a job designing porcelain for Carstens. She became famous for
hosting parties with hundreds of guests and, according to Cecile, she spent
her time "inebriated by amusements."[90] Among her friends were three suit-
ors, Alex Weissberg, Hans Zeisel, and Arthur Koestler. Polanyi came to
some of Eva's parties, but the main observer of her amours was Cecile, who
stayed by herself in a rented room when she came to Berlin.

Cecile took part enthusiastically in the life of the city, attending lectures,
social gatherings, and local events like a Communist election meeting in
the sports palace: "25,000 people. What one got to hear was known and flat
but the sight was imposing—they have a sense for decorating the facades."[91]
Polanyi remained the apple of her eye: "Waltraudstr. 15 with Misi is a highly
aristocratic place. How great Misi looked in Irma's suit: like a monarch.
... Without Misi, Waltraudstr. 15 is a nice, small, Berliner household with two
charming little children!"[92] Although Cecile needed regular financial support
from Polanyi, she lived quite independently of her son's household and made
few demands on his time. The two grandmothers understood that they were
to visit only occasionally. Polanyi also felt he had to defend himself against
encroachment on his private life by Mausi's many long visits to her children
in Berlin. He wrote his sister that she should not visit unannounced, give
"urgent, demandlike invitations" to her parties, nor in general presume too
much on their family relationship. His next letter explained that he had just
wanted to clear the air and affirmed that he still loved her.[93]

Clockwise from upper left: Andreas Wohl, Polanyi's maternal grandfather. Mihály Pollacsek, Polanyi's father. Mihály Pollacsek, Polanyi's father. Cecile Pollacsek, Polanyi's mother.

Top: The young Polanyis. Back row: Sofie, Adolf, Laura, and Karl. Foreground: Paul and Michael.

Bottom left: A silhouette from Polanyi's youth.

Bottom right: Laura Polanyi, Polanyi's older sister.

Left: Laura Polanyi.

Below: Jeannette Odier (seated), Michael, Karl, and Cecile.

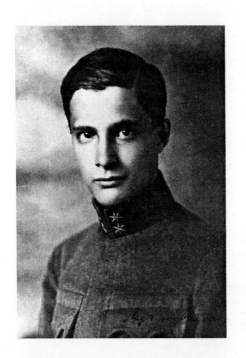

Facing page, clockwise from top left: Polanyi in uniform. Polanyi, 1931. Polanyi in Berlin Magda Polanyi, Polanyi's wife.

This page, top: Polanyi and some colleagues at the Kaiser Wilhelm Institute, 1933.

Right: Magda and son John, 1929.

This page, top: Another group of colleagues at Kaiser Wilhelm, 1933. Left: Polanyi in Manchester.

Facing page: Laboratory equipment used in reaction experiments.

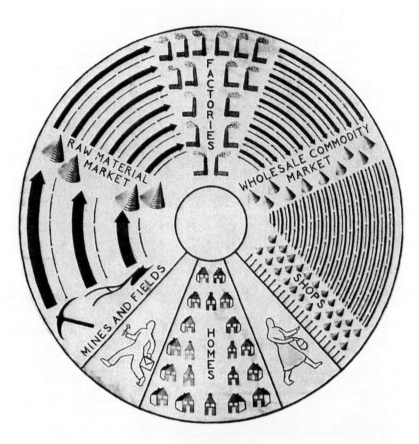

Top: Visual representation of monetary cycle.

Right: Cecile Pollacsek.

Top: The Polanyis in 1948:
Adolf, Karl, Laura, Michael.

Left: Polanyi in 1965.

Top: Polanyi in 1972.
Right: Magda in 1972.

PART III

Manchester: 1933–1959

6

Physical Chemistry and Economics: 1933–1937

The University of Manchester, the oldest and largest of the red brick universities of England, is situated in what has been the leading textile city of England, a center also historically known for liberal reforms and laissez-faire economics. The university had hosted three Nobel laureates in the early part of the century. Ernest Rutherford, who discovered the nucleus of the atom in 1912, held a chair in the Physics Department until 1919. William Lawrence Bragg, famous with his father for their groundbreaking book on X-ray crystallography, taught at Manchester from 1919 until 1937. Robert Robinson took over in organic chemistry from his teacher, Arthur Lapworth; he taught from 1922 to 1928 and won the Nobel Prize in 1947.

At the turn of the century, the laboratory equipment developed by the faculty and students was the finest in England, but it had become dated by 1928 when Robert Robinson left his Manchester professorship. Lapworth went back to handling the work in organic chemistry and decided to create a physical chemistry division with a modern laboratory. In the spring of 1930, Lapworth offered a permanent professorship to Polanyi's friend Hugh S. Taylor, who had invited Polanyi to lecture at Princeton. Taylor was English, but had been at Princeton University since 1914. Taylor lectured at Manchester during the Michaelmas term, from October to December, 1931, but declined the offer of a permanent position.

Polanyi had given three lectures at King's College, London, early in the summer of 1931 (1932b). During Michael and Magda's visit, they became friends with Arthur John Allmand and his wife. Allmand, a professor of chemistry, had close connections with

Manchester and nominated Polanyi for the new position when Taylor turned it down. In the fall of 1931, Nikolai Semenov had offered Polanyi a position in Joffé's institute in Leningrad. Polanyi declined the offer, but indicated that he was willing to visit twice a year for a few weeks at a time.[1] These trips to the Soviet Union were to prove more important for the development of Polanyi's social thought than for his work in physical chemistry.

On February 5, 1932, Lapworth wrote a letter of inquiry to Richard Willstätter at Munich, who was acquainted with Haber's institute, asking about Polanyi's qualifications. Willstätter replied that Polanyi was a person of "so much importance, scientific productivity, and originality" that he would recommend him highly for the Manchester position.[2] He noted that Polanyi was not always easy to deal with, but attributed the friction to crowding too many physical chemists into too small a space, a circumstance that would not be duplicated in Manchester.

Lapworth wrote Polanyi on March 1, 1932, proposing an appointment at a suggested salary of £1,500, the same terms that had been offered to Taylor. It was quite a large sum in those depression years. Lapworth remarked that "the climate is not bad" and told of the good music in the city. Polanyi arranged a visit to Manchester early in May 1932. A pall of smoke hung over the city during the visit, but Polanyi was excited by the thought of building a new division dedicated to the work he had begun in Berlin. At the same time, he was reluctant to leave the heart of Europe. He traveled regularly to Budapest and Vienna to consult at the lamp factory and to visit relatives, especially his ailing mother who by this time had moved into a room in the Carlton Hotel in Budapest because she could hardly walk. Polanyi was also concerned about finding the resources that would be needed in Manchester for the development of physical chemistry. The Manchester administration was taken aback by his request for a new physico-chemical laboratory, an additional £1,000 a year for equipment and maintenance, and a similar amount to provide stipends for eight to ten co-workers.[3]

Fritz Haber had been aware of the Manchester negotiations and had seen all the correspondence between Polanyi and the university. Polanyi asked what kind of future he might have in Berlin. Haber replied that the institute had already done everything possible for him and would continue to do what it could to keep him on the staff. Planck had cut Haber's budget in the 1931– 1932 fiscal year; to make ends meet, Haber had extended the institute's vacation by two weeks and had halved the number of people working at the institute.[4] Polanyi thought that Haber's response to the budget cut was excessive. In spite of Haber's assurances to the contrary, he suspected that Haber and the institute might be happy to get rid of him and his staff.

Besides the attraction of having greater freedom and better funding for his research, Polanyi was also motivated to leave Berlin because of the growing strength of the Nazi movement. Early in November, Polanyi arranged a dinner for a group of prominent scientists, including Haber, Herzog, Bonhoeffer, Hertz, and Wegenstein (a chemist at the University of Berlin). He tried in vain to persuade them to resign en masse if Hitler came to power.[5] That same month, Hitler's party lost two million votes and thirty-four seats in the Reichstag. Although Polanyi was convinced that this election spelled the end of the Nazi threat,[6] he nevertheless continued to search for a way to retire from the KWG.

The University of Manchester deferred its decision on Polanyi's request for a new laboratory and staff to the fall of 1932 because of "the magnitude of the outlay and the uncertainty of the financial situation."[7] In November 1932, Sir Walter Moberly, the vice chancellor of Manchester, asked advice from Robert Robinson, whose resignation from Manchester had created the vacancy in the first place. Robinson replied that Polanyi was "in a different class from most of our physical chemists." Robinson acknowledged that meeting Polanyi's demands might antagonize some people, but "it seems most likely that he is a genius and certainly has been most productive in the past." Although bringing in a foreigner would deprive a British chemist of the position, Robinson suggested that a renewal of the chemistry department would eventually create more jobs for British subjects.[8] Manchester made a commitment to build the new building, but Lapworth asked Polanyi to visit again to continue negotiations about funds for research and other terms of Polanyi's appointment.[9]

When Polanyi visited Manchester in December, he met with the chemistry staff and a committee of the University Senate. G. Norman Burkhardt, at 30 the senior organic chemist with substantial administrative duties, was impressed by Polanyi's first visit to the laboratory: "He was very good-looking, a very live face, very dark—almost Indian—tremendous vitality. Straight away my reaction was, I hope we get him."[10] In his meeting with the Senate committee, Polanyi showed the breadth of his interests. He discussed the strength of metal crystals with F. C. Thompson, a physical metallurgist; the structure of cellulose with W. H. Long, a botanist; and contemporary French literature with John Orr, a French professor. "One of the members of the committee thought this was a bit much," reported Burkhardt. "At lunch he said to Michael, 'I suppose on the Continent they don't have the same interest in detective stories as we do in this country.' Polanyi replied, 'No, not so widespread, but I like your Connington very much' " (J. J. Connington was the penname of the physical and organic chemist Alfred W. Stewart, who taught at University College, London). The effect was tremendous.

Manchester agreed to Polanyi's terms. Polanyi wanted the new laboratory ready on his arrival.[11] Imperial Chemicals promised a grant of £200 to £300 to the research lab if Polanyi took the position. On December 15, the vice chancellor conveyed a warm invitation from the Senate and Council to Polanyi to accept the chair. Polanyi did not say "yes" immediately. On his last visit he had been overwhelmed by the black fog in Manchester—the normal fog of northwest England combined with the thick industrial smoke of the 1930s— and felt a recurrence of his "former rheumatism." He feared the climate would be unhealthy for him, Magda, and the children. Because the position entailed a commitment to hiring personnel, developing new equipment, and establishing new lines of research, the family would have to endure the smog for several years.

Polanyi was also disheartened by the administrative burdens associated with the job offer. Even though Manchester was next in line to Oxford and Cambridge in scientific reputation, Polanyi could not hope to bring its physical chemistry division up to the prominence achieved by Haber and his institute. He would have to become a bureaucrat on the edge of the field instead of a star in the middle of the game. It would also be hard to give up the pleasant home and professional life he had found in Dahlem-Zehlendorf, especially as it now seemed possible that life would continue as usual with the weakening of the Nazi party. Polanyi told his friend Erika Cremer how much he felt at home as he walked along the Van't Hoffstrasse to and from the institute. Sunshine was much more frequent in Germany than in England, and he had a great desire to "live in the sun."[12]

By December 22, Polanyi told Allmand that he felt compelled to refuse the post. Cecile was happy that he had recognized and accepted his dislike of administration. The news was soon all over Manchester and Berlin. Even the chemistry faculty at Stanford University, halfway around the world, had heard by January 4 that Polanyi would probably reject the chair at Manchester; Polanyi had been negotiating with Stanford for appointment as a visiting professor on the assumption that he could get leave from Manchester.

Polanyi wrote the formal letters of regret to Moberly and Lapworth on January 11 and 13, 1933. After profuse apologies, Polanyi described his fear that the wet climate would worsen his rheumatism. He then wrote to Haber, who was on vacation at Cap Ferrat, giving his reasons for declining the appointment at Manchester. Haber replied that he believed a transfer to be in Polanyi's best interest, but that he had no objection to Polanyi's staying.

After Polanyi's refusal, Lapworth had to renew the search, now seeking a younger, less-established scientist from Britain. No suitable candidates were found, so Lapworth decided to return to physical chemistry himself and to offer the chair in organic chemistry to Isidor Morris Heilbron, an excellent chemist from Liverpool.

Things did not turn out as Polanyi had expected after the November elections. Even without a majority in the Reichstag, Adolf Hitler became chancellor on January 30, and the National Socialists staged a highly symbolic torchlight parade through the Brandenburg Gate. A week later, Polanyi was beginning to have second thoughts about turning down the position in England: "[Manchester] is just not for me with its black fog. Will the brown fog that has settled over Germany in the meantime agree any better with me?"[13] The same letter contains Polanyi's impressions of Irving Langmuir, who traveled with him on the train to Budapest. Polanyi remarked on his rival's steady devotion to work and to truth, and his preference for carving things into stone without preliminary sketches. The end of the letter expressed Polanyi's excitement over the news that Blackett from Birkbeck College in London had discovered the positive electron, more familiarly known as the positron.[14]

The burning of the Reichstag on February 27, 1933, dashed the last of Polanyi's hopes for the survival of parliamentary government and civil liberties in Germany. The Nazis blamed the arson on the Communists and used the fire as a pretext to extend their power. A "Decree for the Protection of People and State" was issued the next day, severely restricting civil and personal liberties: freedom of speech and press, freedom from illegal search, the right to assemble in public, and the right to protection of property. On March 5, another election gave the Nazis a bare majority, and on March 23, Hitler was given dictatorial powers. According to the British author Christopher Isherwood, "The whole city lay under an epidemic of discreet, infectious fear."[15]

By early in March, Polanyi felt that the Nazi regime had become intolerable. It was no longer a question of choosing between two equally civilized countries—the choice for Polanyi now was between a civilization he had long admired and one that was descending into barbarism. Schrödinger likened the rise of the National Socialists in Germany to the pouring of black ink over a white damask tablecloth.[16] Polanyi now realized that he and his family had to abandon the sun-filled city and the extraordinary scientific community that they had loved so much. If he did not act soon, a darkness far worse than Manchester's soot would befall them.

About the middle of March, Polanyi met with his friend Frederick Donnan and told him that he was eager to leave Germany. Donnan wrote immediately to Vice Chancellor Moberly at Manchester on Polanyi's behalf. He warned Moberly that the university should communicate through him or Allmand so that the German government would not become aware of Polanyi's efforts to flee the country. On April 7, the Nazis passed a law calling for a "restoration of the career civil service," a euphemism for the removal of Jews from all government jobs. The law applied to Jewish scientists in each of the Kaiser Wilhelm Institutes, but exempted those who, like Polanyi, had served in the military with the Central Powers in World War I. Magda objected to Michael's wish to resign in sympathy with those to be dismissed; she worried about reprisals against their sons. In the end, Polanyi overcame her resistance to his resignation and the move; he expressed his appreciation with a large pot of azaleas.[17]

Three days after the new law took effect, Polanyi wrote Donnan that he would "accept the chair at Manchester on any conditions that are considered fair and reasonable by the university" and that he would not accept any other offers until June. Polanyi had already received one inquiry from a colleague in Hungary, and two others followed from T. S. Baker of Carnegie Institute of Technology and Karl Compton of the Massachusetts Institute of Technology. Polanyi was not eager for an American post because his trip in 1929 had convinced him that American professors were not given enough time for research; he also did not want to lose touch with his family in Europe.

Manchester acted very quickly. On April 7, Moberly told Donnan in confidence that (1) the university had not been satisfied with any of the British physical chemists and had made an offer to an organic chemist; (2) he favored the appointment of a third professor in chemistry for the few remaining years before Lapworth would retire, after which there would be only two professors in the two areas;[18] (3) the salary for Polanyi could not be more than £1,250; and (4) the new building would have to wait for two or three years because of other recent capital commitments. Moberly could not secure final approval from Manchester until after the end of the university's Easter vacation on May 2.

On April 19, Polanyi drafted a letter to Haber, who was Jewish, asking him to take a public stand against the anti-Semitic actions of the government.[19] He praised James Franck, who resigned his chair of experimental physics at Göttingen to protest the way that Germans of Jewish descent were being treated as foreigners, even though at the time Franck, like Polanyi, could have been spared the effects of the new law. "Franck's deed has given back to us part of our honor and brought the other part within reach," wrote Polanyi. He criticized Haber for putting loyalty to his position above the protection of human beings.

> A hundred thousand will breathe easier if Haber stands up against the rising oppression.... For the present we, the thin top layer, are spared, so that we disguise the annihilating campaign directed against the masses of the nameless Jews and against our own children.... When the Jews complain, nobody is interested. An Aryan has to stand up for us. That's the tradition of the *Schutzjudentum* (protection of Jews). "One does not beg for a right, one fights for a right" (A. Hitler).... A right which one permits to be taken away without resistance is lost.... Today's insanity will pass. But what will remain is the damage to their reputation caused by the Jews' own attitude.

It seems that Polanyi never sent this letter to Haber. Three days after he wrote the draft, Polanyi handed Haber his formal retirement application along with a bouquet of flowers and a card that read, "Dear Herr Geheimrat, as I take leave of the institute at this time, I would like you to accept this greeting as a sign of my admiration and gratitude."[20] Haber apparently understood this note as a sign of support for his position. In fact, Polanyi's disagreement with Haber was profound. He disliked Haber's subservience toward authority, and he was disappointed that Haber refused to take a stand against the Nazis.[21] Just four days after Polanyi's resignation, the University of Manchester Senate met and approved the offer to Polanyi. Moberly wrote him at once. Polanyi's friend Leo Szilard telegraphed Moberly that the matter should be kept secret until preparations for the move were finalized. Polanyi's resignation was accepted by Max Planck, the current president of the Kaiser Wilhelm Gesellschaft, on May 15, effective September 30, 1933, thus assuring his pension rights. Polanyi also retired from his position at the Technische Hochschule.[22]

The great days of the Physical Chemistry and Electro-Chemistry Institute were drawing to a close. In May 1933, I. Marcovich reported on a meeting with Max Bodenstein to L. W. Jones of the Rockefeller Foundation: with Freundlich, Polanyi, and Haber all leaving, the entire Physical Chemistry Institute was collapsing. Bodenstein believed that the Nazi attack on spiritual freedom put the future of all German science at stake and urged Jones to make a personal visit to the institute to see what could be rescued. It was particularly urgent to decide what to do with the equipment furnished by the Foundation. It was agreed that Haber would forward recommendations to Planck about whether to keep equipment or give it to departing scientists.[23]

Herzog apparently criticized Polanyi, Franck, and Freundlich for taking the "comfortable" path of resignation instead of resisting the Nazis from within their posts. In a lengthy response, Polanyi reflected on the paradoxical position of the Jews within a Christian society. He thought Jews took on both Christian virtues and Christian vices as a way of concealing Jewishness. Being freed from the ghetto robbed the Jew of the local community that had been central to his religious identity; the emancipated Jew has to find his sense of value in large part in the community where he lives, but the tragedy is that local or national traditions cannot completely satisfy him. To become whole, Jews must invent their own variants of the local mores and maintain their right to exist through the convincing power of their own personalities. This, he said, "is so hard that the Jews have not even tackled it yet."[24]

The social, economic, and political crises that Polanyi experienced strengthened Polanyi's interest in social studies and weakened his attachment to science: "Even though I do not intend to give up science, I feel more distant from it...so that I am more drawn to general thoughts and to our small garden."[25] Nevertheless, when Manchester finalized its offer in May, Polanyi quickly accepted the position. Although Polanyi's Manchester appointment was temporarily kept secret, the news was soon out. *Nature* published an announcement of his resignation on May 13 and reported his appointment at Manchester on June 24; the *Deutsche Arbeiter Zeitung* had the news shortly before July 1. As a gesture of support in response to the news, the Natural

Science section of the Academy of Science of Naples elected Polanyi to membership at their June session.

Meanwhile, work at the lab went on with increased intensity. Because they did not know how long the laboratory could function, Polanyi and his colleagues worked day and night to finish as much research as they could. Polanyi was not sure that he could do any experimental work during the summer term. In the event, except for the loss of staff, the laboratory was not otherwise disturbed until it was occupied by the SS in October.[26]

With Polanyi's official resignation, the dissolution of the family's life in Berlin began. George and John spent Easter vacation in Budapest, 10-year-old George with Magda's mother and sister, and 4-year old John with the Kendes, close family friends. Hard decisions had to be made. Should Magda and the boys stay for a while in Budapest or in Berlin while Michael started his work in Manchester, or should Magda and the children leave for England first? What schooling for George? How soon should he learn English? What nursery school for John in Dahlem? What should they do with their house in Waltraudstrasse? On April 24, the parents still thought about having George come back to Berlin before the start of school on May 2, but by the next day, they changed their minds. George would stay in Budapest and go to school there for the next school term. They hoped to spare the children as much discomfort as possible.

In the following weeks, Magda wrote her older son frequently.[27] Her letters to George show a close, companionable, and easy relationship between mother and son. Using typical German terms of endearment—Georgi, Freundchen (little friend), Gockel (rooster), Affenschwanz (monkey's tail)—she stressed the positive aspects of their past lives in Germany ("In fact it was wonderful for all of us here") and surveyed their future ("We all will have to be a bit patient until we comfortably settle in together in a new country"). She told the children about their Easter presents, a picture book for John and a book by Van Loon for George, which "may be hard to get into for you but will give you much joy when you get over the initial difficulty."

George sent Magda a number of little gifts that he had obtained by sending in coupons, among them a case to hold after-dinner coffee spoons and an Italian aluminum cup. Magda appreciated all of them. When he sent her a festive Mother's Day card, she suggested that there ought to be a Son's Day card. Magda asked George to begin writing in Latin characters, rather than in German script, and arranged for him to take English lessons from a friend's British governess. Magda cleared his savings account and suggested things of his he could leave as gifts for his friends: to Hellmuth his toy electric battery, to Boller his geography lotto, to Helga his copy of Alice in Wonderland. For the last week in Berlin he would stay at the Beckers so he could say all his good-byes in person.

At the beginning of June, Polanyi joined the children, taking along George's bicycle. A few days later he returned to Berlin, taking John but leaving George behind. That evening he wrote his elder son, recalling their beautiful walk the first evening and the excursion to Lake Balaton when George rowed while Michael slept on the floor of the boat. He also asked George to send him the drawing he had made of the villa and the nearby trees.

Back in Berlin, 4-year-old John was sent to nursery school in the mornings and spent the afternoons roaming the neighborhood and dropping in at the houses of friends, just as George used to do. He became more self-reliant in the absence of his brother. After the movers had taken most of their belongings to storage on July 8, John stayed for two days with their former housekeeper, Frau Drechsler, and then went to the sea with a children's group, while Magda spent a week with her brother until the whole family could leave for Budapest on July 18. The family grieved as their possessions were stored or given away and as their house was prepared for its new tenants.

The night before the family left for Hungary, the Kuratorium (Board of Trustees) accepted the final reports of the three administrators retiring from the Kaiser Wilhelm Institutes for Physical Chemistry and Electrochemistry— Haber, Freundlich, and Polanyi. Max Planck presided as president of the Kuratorium. Freundlich reported on colloid chemistry, Haber on work in chain reactions and spectroscopy, and Polanyi on reaction kinetics. *Die Naturwissenschaften* for May 26, 1933, showed how productive the three men and their associates had been in the last year: Haber's group had thirty-six publications by twenty-three co-workers, Freundlich's had twenty-eight publications by seventeen co-workers, and Polanyi's had twelve publications by eleven co-workers.

Max Planck expressed his regret that the work of the three had to end and thanked them for the contributions they had made to German science. Haber expressed his sorrow that he could not remain at his post with honor. E. Telschow gave a report on expenditures and budget, and F. Glum, the general director, reported the decision of the minister that no exceptions were to be made in the employment of non-Aryans, that is, those with a Jewish parent or grandparent, or who practiced the Jewish religion—in other words, most of the staff of the Kaiser Wilhelm Institute would soon be released.

Fritz Haber's health was poor. Shortly after the last meeting with the Kuratorium, he left Berlin for Cambridge, England, "with only his passport," but with no place to continue his work.[28] The following January he died at age 60 in Basel en route to a Swiss resort. Herbert Freundlich, younger and more fortunate, obtained a visiting professorship at University College, London, with Donnan, and in 1938 became a research professor in colloid chemistry at the University of Minnesota. He died three years later. Reginald Oliver Herzog stayed on, true to his conviction, until he was forced to retire on October

10, 1933, when the Institute for Physical Chemistry which he had created and directed was finally disbanded.

The day after the Kuratorium session, the Polanyi family left Berlin for a month in Budapest. While they were there, Michael and the children went with Magda to a service at the Basilica to see the Catholic cathedral where she had worshiped as a child. They visited Cecile, Irma Pollacsek, and Sandor Striker, who was living alone at the time. His wife, Mausi, had left him to join their children, Eva and Misi, in Russia; their other son, Otto (George) was studying in Vienna. The family then joined the families of Karl and Sofie for a vacation at Hotel Edlacherhof in Reichenau, south of Vienna. They did not experience the same grief in leaving Budapest as they had in leaving Berlin, but Michael and Magda did make an effort to say good-bye to all the family before moving to England.

When Polanyi returned from the vacation in Austria, he faced the problem of deciding what apparatus to take to Manchester, some supplied by Rockefeller and some by Polanyi's work with the Studiengesellschaft. Polanyi kept in touch with his colleagues who were continuing their research over the summer and helped obtain passports and permissions for those who were planning to accompany him on the move. It was fortunate that Polanyi had kept his Austrian passport—"That's the best idea I ever had."[29] In those early days of the Nazi regime the proverbial German bureaucratic punctiliousness still persisted. The Polanyis hoped that by complying with the existing laws they would be free to leave without hindrance.

The laboratory staff expected the Polanyis to leave around September 30, the official retirement date. But Polanyi arranged with Fred Fairbrother of the Manchester Chemistry Department to slip away at the end of August. They packed the last of their personal belongings quickly and quietly. Polanyi informed none of the staff of his change in plans—no one knew who might make difficulties with the Nazis. Martin Schmalz, who himself was planning to leave, wrote "we nearly fainted when we heard you had already left" and promised to try to bring along a sack of clothing that the Polanyis had left at a laundry.[30]

Early on the first of September, Michael, Magda, and the boys locked the doors of Waltraudstrasse and left their friendly, sunny neighborhood for the last time. They used German money to buy their railroad tickets at least as far as London, but were not allowed to take any sizeable amounts of money out of the country with them. Fortunately, Ernst Bergmann, a friend and former colleague from the University of Berlin, was on the same train and bought a meal for the four of them.

The Polanyis crossed the channel and arrived in London with no English money in their pockets. Their first destination was the bank where Constance Tipper had opened an account for them by depositing the honorarium from

Polanyi's 1931 Faraday Society Lecture. The cab driver waited while they obtained the money to pay him, then drove them to find cheap lodgings in the Imperial Hotel. The next morning they went to Euston Station to entrain for Manchester.

When the Polanyi family arrived at Piccadilly Station in Manchester early on the afternoon of September 3, 1933, Fred Fairbrother took them straight to the Brookfield Hotel near Victoria Park, not far from the university. Hugh O'Neill, a senior lecturer in Metallurgy, dropped in for a visit and took Polanyi out for a walk. O'Neill had been looking forward to Polanyi's arrival. He was familiar with Polanyi's work with crystals and had made a special point of attending the formal job interview in December. Hugh and his wife, Barbara, had led a tour group to Hungary on their honeymoon several years before, so they were eager to welcome the charming Hungarian and his family.

The two men set out for Withington and Alderly Edge in the southern part of Manchester. As they walked along, O'Neill remarked: "If you throw a stone here, you'll hit three professors"—a saying that Polanyi was to repeat many times. This was the first of many outings led by O'Neill, whom Polanyi came to call "mein Führer."[31] Finding such a good friend so soon was a great help in adjusting to life in England. The two men were temperamentally suited to each other and enjoyed discussing matters that ranged from metallurgy and crystal structure to religion and the social scene. O'Neill was a Roman Catholic who was eager for dialogue on almost any intellectual position or approach to questions of belief and faith.

It did not take Polanyi long to become familiar with the town, the weather, and the general spirit of the people. Writing to Toni Stolper in the middle of the month, he said, "I'm quite content with my own lot. I love the seriousness of this ugly town and the cheerfulness with which the people represent it. Also the horrible climate doesn't bother me—as long as the sun keeps shining."[32]

Michael and Magda decided to place George in a boarding school where he would use English night and day—Magda and Michael still at times conversed in German at home. They chose Bootham, a Quaker school in York. Michael took George on the two-hour train ride to York for the start of school, leaving him to settle into his room and make his first tentative attempts at English with his new classmates. In Manchester a few days later, they received a long letter from George.

John missed his brother very much, and Magda suggested to George that he write a letter just for him. When the letter arrived, John was delighted, carrying it around and repeatedly kissing it. In the first weeks, before John had begun to learn English, Magda sent him for day care to an old "Aunt," but soon sent him to play with another 4-year-old, also called John, whose mother understood a little German. John liked to be there and came home every day very dirty, but happy. For a while, John simply would not say a word to his new English friend while they played together. Polanyi worried at first about his son's slowness in English, but then realized that it was natural for a child to be shy about speaking a new language. Two months later, John suddenly and completely switched to English and was enrolled in a nursery school.

Magda had brushed up on English in Germany to translate correspondence, and she quickly picked up everyday English in her dealings with tradesmen and servants. For a while, she had a German au pair girl who also wanted to learn English. Magda arranged practice sessions for her with the wife of Cecil Bawn, one of Polanyi's new colleagues. Polanyi was already fluent enough to give lectures in English.

George's eleventh birthday came on October 1. In his birthday letter to his son, Michael sympathized with George about being uprooted from their "beloved Germany" and hoped that George would soon feel at home and "safe again as before."[33] Polanyi was undoubtedly thinking of his own losses and loneliness as much as his son's. Magda also sent birthday greetings to George, reporting that Michael was happy in his work and that he was no longer "making such a long face."[34]

The university suggested that the Polanyis rent Kenmore, a beautiful, spacious dwelling at No. 17, Didsbury Park. There were three large reception rooms, five bedrooms, two rooms for servants, and a guest room. Magda wrote George, "Can you imagine us in such a house? Not I!"[35] The housing office recommended hiring four maids to care for the house and the family. Despite some misgivings, Magda relented: "I also agree now that in Manchester it is important to live in a beautiful house. One can't simply go out into the sun as in Zehlendorf."[36] At the end of November, the Polanyis moved into Kenmore—with three maids. Running the house was hard work for Magda, planning the servants' work, settling places for everything, and arranging the purchase of what they needed for the household. In their dining room, they hung a large portrait of all of Polanyi's family, which had been painted long ago during their prosperous times in Budapest.

As they settled into their new home, they began to make new friends. The historian Alan J. P. Taylor, a junior lecturer at Manchester, heard of their arrival through Donald Gray, a faculty member at Bootham, and invited them to his place in nearby Cheshire. There were several invitations to dinner from university people and well-to-do manufacturers who were in the habit of getting acquainted with new professors. One evening they dined with Sir Thomas Barlow, a cotton manufacturer who collected Dürer paintings, and his wife, Lady Esther Barlow, who wrote religious poetry. When Lady Barlow invited them, she explained to Magda that there would only be the four of them at dinner, so no tails would be necessary; a dinner jacket would be fine. Michael shared Magda's amusement at the new dress codes that they would have to learn along with the language. At dinner, Sir Thomas talked about

Dürer to Polanyi and went upstairs in the middle of the meal to bring down a sopping-wet bath mat with a Dürer motif in it. They also spent evenings at the homes of Polanyi's colleagues in physics and chemistry, Robert Robinson, Douglas Hartree, Moelwyn-Hughes, and Rudolf Peierls.

Martin Schmalz, the technician whom Polanyi had brought with him from Berlin, was allowed to work on condition that a British citizen be trained to replace him after six months. The grace period was eventually extended to two years. Schmalz trained an 18-year-old who had already worked for the department for a few years, Ralph Gilson; he became quite competent at laboratory technique and later served as Professor Lord Todd's Laboratory Superintendent in Cambridge.

Schmalz found lodgings in a house whose owner had a large garage with two or three cars, which he hired out. As one of the lucky refugees who had an immediate and regular income, Schmalz often rented one of those cars, and when the Polanyis acquired a car, he became the one who kept it up. Their first car, a used Austin, was a gift from Ervin von Gomperz, Michael's former protegé and Magda's fellow student, who by then had become quite successful in industrial chemistry and wanted to help the Polanyis off to a good start in Manchester. Ralph Gilson called it "quite a jalopy," and Alexander Todd referred to it jokingly as "ten horsepower."[37] Von Gomperz also gave them a beautiful Chippendale table for their living room, with a round, rotating top that could be used for hors d'oeuvres or a few books.

Magda learned to drive first and then taught Michael. When they were going together up to the university, they would race to the car to see who would drive. When Michael won, Magda would ride with her heart in her throat. Michael adored driving, but to Magda, he was "the world's most rotten driver."[38] After the first time Polanyi drove him into Manchester from the university, Ralph Gilson advised people not to accept a lift from Polanyi—it was too nerve-wracking. In November, Polanyi and Aschner, a representative of the Budapest lamp factory, left London for Cambridge in a dense fog. Polanyi was driving very slowly. Suddenly they collided with an oncoming truck. Aschner went through the windshield and suffered a mild concussion while Polanyi cut his nose. Damage to the car was also light.

Even in clear weather, Polanyi had car troubles. On one occasion, he said to Schmalz, "I could do with the car this weekend, will you leave it for me at the laboratory?" Schmalz agreed and left the car in the quadrangle by the chemistry building. When Schmalz came to work on Monday morning Polanyi remarked in irritation: "I asked you particularly to leave the car." "I did," Schmalz responded. "Where did you leave it? I never found it." Schmalz led him to the place where he had left the car. Polanyi had passed the place three or four times and never noticed it standing there.[39] Polanyi seems not to have learned from his mistakes. On another occasion, he forgot that he had parked the car in the University quadrangle and took the bus home, then called the police to report the car missing. In the end, one of the laboratory assistants found the car where Polanyi had left it.

Polanyi's reputation as a driver steadily grew worse. One night the Polanyis were at a party with John and Sylvia Jewkes at the Manchester staff house. When it was time to leave, it started raining hard. John came up to Magda and said, "Magda, drop me on the way two blocks further up. That's where I left our car." But when Polanyi took the wheel, Jewkes refused to get in the car. Instead he pulled his mackintosh over his head and ran through the rain.[40] Cecil (C. E. H.) Bawn also thought Polanyi was a terrible driver, "a disaster on the road," and attributed his carelessness at the wheel to concentration on other things.[41]

Michael and Magda did not "slide to York on the weekends" as often as she had hoped they would, but they did keep up a regular correspondence with George. When he sent a news clipping about the serious troubles in Germany, Magda reiterated the optimism that she and Michael felt for Germany's future. In another letter, she asked if George was attending church, at least on some of the Sundays. She said that there was a beautiful Catholic church in Manchester, but assured him that while he was at school he should do what he felt right. "I think you have gotten quite new concepts about religion from the Friends, probably a much more general idea."[42]

In November, following a visit to York, Michael wrote George in English for the first time, remarking on the shock it had been to use the new language in conversation with him. He was pleased with the school "which gives you such a fine opportunity to become a courteous, able-minded and able-bodied man."[43] Magda, writing in German, told George they felt the school was the right place for him. "You will of course become an Englishman because you are constantly among English boys."[44]

The Manchester Chemistry building was Victorian in style, smog-blackened on the outside like most other public buildings in the city. Even the walls inside were dirty. There was plenty of space, however, and Polanyi immediately went to work setting up laboratories in the area reserved for physical chemistry. Because he was not creating an entirely new department, he was not too burdened by university bureaucracy. From the start he made it clear that his role was primarily that of research director, rather than that of teacher. He did no teaching in his first fall term and in the winter term gave only one set of specialized lectures based on the Bonhoeffer–Harteck book on photochemistry.

Polanyi's last paper on adsorption was prepared after his move to Manchester in 1933. As the newly appointed Professor of Physical Chemistry, he was invited to lecture before the Society of Chemical Industry (1935f). His paper was an extension of his 1929 article in which he had suggested that strong adsorption forces hold atoms too tightly to catalyze reactions (1929b).

The fastest reactions on a surface occur at points where the attraction is just strong enough to hold atoms or molecules for a short while, thus making them far more likely to encounter collisions favorable to forming new bonds.

Polanyi arrived at Manchester with research projects in mind and staff all ready to undertake them: the immigrants from Berlin, the colleagues already established in the department, and two or three students. The Manchester equipment was out-of-date, but glass tubing and bulbs were on hand. High-quality ground-glass joints and stopcocks were coming from Berlin, along with the mercury-vapor vacuum and gas-circulating pumps essential to the various types of flame experiments, a machine lathe and all its attachments, and two hand bellows.[45] Andreas Szabó had spent the summer of 1933 at the laboratory in Dahlem familiarizing himself with Polanyi's high vacuum experimental methods, so that he was ready to begin work as soon as he arrived in Manchester in September. Another student who had started to become acquainted with Polanyi's apparatus in the summer and then moved to Manchester was Lotte Werner. Her area was a continuation of the Walden inversion studies she had done for her Ph.D.

The projects Polanyi had developed in Berlin belonged to several differing lines of research, and he looked ahead to developing at Manchester some of those that still held promise. He had a knack for finding new approaches to old questions. Many of those who worked under him in his new professorial position were to find their own perspectives deepened and their knowledge of research methods strengthened as they followed up on Polanyi's insights.

One of the scientists from Berlin who accompanied Polanyi to Manchester was the Japanese chemist Juro Horiuti (also transliterated as Horiuchi). He had arrived in Dahlem in the early spring of 1933. When he first met Polanyi and learned of his plans at a staff meeting, he objected strongly to them. His negative attitude persisted for two months, but then he had a dramatic change of opinion during a long, solitary walk in the Grünewald. Horiuti promptly joined Polanyi's group and began to work on using heavy water, water that is composed of oxygen and deuterium, an isotope of hydrogen which is approximately twice as heavy as hydrogen. Light hydrogen consists of one proton and one electron; deuterium consists of a proton, a neutron, and an electron. Because of the extra mass, deuterium has some different physical properties from hydrogen—the addition of a neutron makes deuterium about double the weight of hydrogen and therefore changes the kinetics of deuterium reactions—but because of the single electron and single positive charge in both substances, deuterium is capable of entering into the same kinds of chemical bonds as hydrogen. Because of the doubled mass in the deuterium atoms, heavy water weighs about 10 percent more than ordinary water. Polanyi asked Horiuti to study the effect of substituting deuterium for hydrogen in a number of hydrogen catalysis reactions.

In spite of the preparations for the move to Manchester, Horiuti was able to design apparatus that would be useful for the new experiments. He brought the crucial parts of his apparatus with him to Manchester. G. N. Lewis and R. T. MacDonald in Berkeley had used a sensitive method of measuring the density of water by using a small glass float containing enough air for its buoyancy to balance its weight quite closely. At Polanyi's suggestion, Edward S. Gilfillan, an American Ph.D. from Harvard who was visiting the laboratory on a Sheldon Traveling Fellowship, modified the Berkeley approach by constructing a type of float or diver, called a micropycnometer, which varied compression within the float rather than temperature in order to calibrate the instrument. The liquid to be measured—only a small amount was usually available—was put into the bottom of the float, and the glass bulb at the top containing air could be compressed or expanded by applying pressure to the vessel containing the float suspended in standard water. Gilfillan's new design gave the same accuracy as that of Lewis, with much greater convenience (1943h). The equipment was fairly simple, utilizing ordinary devices of electrochemistry. Schmalz taught the art of making these delicate objects to Leslie Robertson, L. K. Parker, and other lab technicians.

Before leaving Berlin, Polanyi had laid plans for obtaining enough heavy hydrogen (deuterium) to carry out experiments. Gustav Hertz and collaborators at the Physics Institute of the Technische Hochschule in Berlin developed a method for separating a variety of isotopes in gaseous form. The method depended on the different rate at which heavier and lighter gases passed through porous ceramic diffusion tubes. The gas had to be recirculated through the apparatus as many as forty-eight times to concentrate enough deuterium for experimental work.

The simplicity of the alternative electrolytic method made it attractive in spite of its costly use of electricity. Meredith Evans had learned the technique from Hugh Taylor, who had followed the lead of Gilbert N. Lewis at the University of California in Berkeley. Evans had hoped to obtain a scholarship to go to work for a year with Taylor in Princeton and before leaving put into operation a battery of electrolytic cells in Manchester so that Polanyi would have some heavy water on his arrival.

When Juro Horiuti joined the group, he started immediately on research in hydrogen catalysis, using the heavy and light isotopes. The importance of catalysts was evident from the fact that hydrogen gas is quite unreactive in the normal containers used for it, even in the presence of oxygen, but with a suitable catalyst in powdered form (and therefore with a great total surface area), hydrogen reactions, such as the combustion reaction to make water, will proceed vigorously with a great deal of heat. Polanyi had learned from Henry Wieland, winner of the Nobel Prize for chemistry in 1927, that biological and chemical oxidation processes are generally matters of "dehydrogenation" (now known as proton transfer reactions because the nucleus of the hydrogen atom is a single proton). Polanyi's interest in the chemistry of biological functions had begun in Budapest with his laboratory work with Tangl and his observations of the human body in his medical training and clinical experience. Wieland's suggestion raised his hopes of finding a biochemical application of his research techniques: "The natural biological oxidation-reductions that have porphyrin as the active groups take place on proteins, and Polanyi speculated that the proteins were simply wires for moving electrons around to match the protons that had ultimately to be removed."[46] Finding out how the active organic compounds stripped electrons from the hydrogen atom or provided an extra electron to attract a hydrogen nucleus thus had promise of opening out into a new area with many basic research problems. The issues surrounding "hydrogen activation" were part of Polanyi's quest to understand reaction kinetics in general.

However, neither Horiuti nor Polanyi had a clear idea of what experiment to do first. The seminal idea for two dozen papers came from Marcus L. E. Oliphant's serendipitous discovery of the uncatalyzed exchange of deuterium gas with water. As reported in *Nature* on October 28, 1933, Oliphant and his co-workers at Cambridge were planning to bombard lithium with deuterium and had stored a helium-hydrogen-deuterium gas mixture in a vessel partly filled with water. After six weeks they found that the deuterium in the gas phase had fallen to one-twentieth of its original value, even though the total gas pressure remained the same. Deuterium atoms from the gas mixture had obviously exchanged places with hydrogen atoms from the water molecules, slowly but surely. Polanyi surmised that this hitherto unknown process could be studied by using a catalyst to accelerate the rate of exchange. Powdered platinum black was chosen and provided good results. For example, hydrogen gas containing about 1 percent deuterium was shaken up with water and catalyst for 10 minutes; only 0.5 percent of deuterium remained in the gas. This was the first observation of the catalyzed gas–liquid exchange of hydrogen.[47]

The basic process of the exchange was easily understood. A small fraction of the molecules in liquid water, H_2O, spontaneously breaks into positive and negative ions, H^+ and OH^-. On the surface of the platinum catalyst, H^+ ions can become neutral H atoms and in a further catalyzed stage join together to form H_2 molecules. These gas molecules, formed at the platinum surface just as they would be if the platinum were the negative electrode of an electrolytic cell, will bubble up and evaporate. Some of the molecules in the gas mixture, H_2, D_2, or HD, will dissolve and go through the reverse process, splitting up, becoming ionized, and joining with OH^- ions to form water molecules, some of which are "deuterated," i.e., formed with a deuterium atom. A net exchange takes place, and the rate of occurrence can give information about what happens at a hydrogen electrode, particularly if measurement is made of the variation of the rate with changes in acidity and with the presence of alcohol. The hydrogen exchange experiments of Polanyi's group were conducted by Horiuti and reported in a series of short notes that provided no details of the stage-by-stage development of the apparatus being used. When Daniel Eley came to Manchester in the fall of 1934, he finished the apparatus design, set out on a series of carefully improved experiments on catalytic hydrogen exchange that lasted eighteen months, and published a detailed diagram of the apparatus (1936g).

The study of another type of hydrogen catalyst began in January 1934 with the arrival at Manchester of Bernard Cavanagh, a senior lecturer from the University of Melbourne, Australia, who came to work with Polanyi for a year. Cavanagh brought with him the idea, following Wieland, that enzymes in certain bacteria exert catalytic action on hydrogen. An experiment was carried out with Horiuti's help, studying the reaction $HD + H_2O \rightarrow H_2 + HDO$ as catalyzed by *bacterium coli* (now known as E. coli in honor of the discoverer, Theodor Escherich) and *bacterim acidi lactii*; some positive results were found, wherein the bacteria acted like metal catalysts. Cavanagh attended the Chemical Society meeting on May 17, 1934, and heard an announcement of a forthcoming article by Hughs, Yudkin, Kemp, and Rideal, which was promised to include the same result. About midnight that night (Thursday) he wrote Polanyi that in London's Euston Station he had written out a short letter on his results and handed it to Mrs. Gale of *Nature* at 5 P.M.—she too was on her way home. Gale promised to publish it as soon as possible, and in particular to have the proofs sent to Polanyi the following Monday or Tuesday. The one-page note appeared in the issue of *Nature* of the following Saturday, May 26 (1934k). Such rapidity has long since vanished from the scientific publishing scene! In this case it seems to have stopped the rival publication, since no record of the latter appears in *Chemical Abstracts*.

There were also many gas reactions waiting to be studied by means of the dilute flame techniques that Polanyi had developed in Berlin. Cecil Bawn and his first graduate student, Alwyn G. Evans (Meredith's brother), joined Polanyi's group. Evans's first assignment was to duplicate a von Hartel reaction tube that was too delicate to survive the trip from Dahlem. Unfortunately, the expert German glass-blower, Kurt Hauschild, had not come over from Berlin. With only a photograph to guide them, it took a while before Martin Schmalz and Ralph Gilson were able to master the techniques needed to fashion the intricate apparatus.

Another research team was led by Fred Fairbrother and Ernest Warhurst. Fairbrother had received his doctorate in science from Manchester in 1925 and had been giving the advanced chemistry III lectures from 1926 onwards. Warhurst, like Alwyn Evans, was a third year student. Under Fairbrother's supervision, Warhurst built the equipment to use sodium resonance in the investigation of gas reactions. Many results were to come out of the Manchester flame experiments, but nearly all were found by these two teams and half-a-dozen other students. Polanyi's name did not appear on any of the papers. Once the equipment was completed and the groups went into action, they published sixteen experimental papers and four theoretical ones, none with Polanyi's name.[48] Polanyi called these efforts "hatching ducklings," relatively routine applications of established methods that did not call for his involvement. He seemed content to work in the background of the research establishment. His personal reading became directed more to social and economic theory rather than to the latest developments in physical chemistry. Even with these distractions, Polanyi paid attention to the work being done in the laboratories and knew what should happen if all went well. He loved to turn a tap that would extinguish a sodium flame and then turn it back on, making the yellow light reappear. Only just the right tap could be used that way, for it was not hard to upset the flow pattern or to lose a carefully prepared compound being brought into reaction, so his colleagues kept careful watch whenever Polanyi approached their equipment.[49]

The laboratory was set up so that each person with an experimental project had a separate room with the apparatus on a table in the middle. Polanyi made the rounds every day he was there and inquired about what was happening and what problems were uppermost in the experimenter's mind. He associated each person with a particular experiment. Returning from a month's absence, he met Frank Perkins in the outer laboratory. "Hallo, Perkins, I have come back," he said, and began to discuss Perkins's work. When Polanyi moved on to another research group, Perkins entered the inner laboratory, which belonged to Gowenlock. Polanyi entered a few minutes later and said to Perkins, "Hallo, Gowenlock, I have come back," then proceeded to speak at length on Gowenlock's research project. It took Perkins a while to break the flow of the monologue; when he indicated that his name was not Gowenlock, but Perkins, Polanyi looked at him closely and replied, "Of course it is."[50]

When things went seriously wrong, as they were bound to with intricate experiments, Polanyi would be upset. It was hard for him to accept the frequent experimental difficulties. He felt that he must have left something out of account in his reasoning, or else that the student doing the work was not competent enough or trained well enough to resolve troubles as they came up. For instance, leaks in the vacuum system were always occurring and were very hard to find. Bawn remembers the flame experiment as being exceptionally tricky: "The sodium flame technique ... became very difficult. You wanted to do chemical analysis on your product gases and because of the enormous variability of results, you had to run one of these flames maybe six or eight hours, sitting up at night nursing the apparatus. In the end it became almost an impossibility."[51]

Although the collection of data might take hours, Bawn remembered how quickly Polanyi could assess the results. "You could give him some measurement you had, and within a matter of minutes he could translate all that in his mind into collision numbers and activation energies, and he would more or less say 'that can't be right,' since he knew exactly what should have happened and the speed it should have gone.... It was almost impossible for me to...understand how he arrived at certain conclusions. I am not at all sure that if you had pressed him that he would have been able to tell you why. It was a sort of intuition; he was usually right, but the logic of arriving there was never clear." Fred Fairbrother, who usually worked independently on his flame experiments, was also impressed by Polanyi's ability to "pick out what was essential and what was not...his experiments were brilliantly designed, with details left for Schmalz."[52]

As conditions in Germany continued to deteriorate, Polanyi wrote many letters trying to help German friends settle in England. Numerous refugees, both friends and family, came to stay with the Polanyis for varying periods of time.[53] Polanyi put Herzog in touch with friends in London, who in turn helped him find a position in a new laboratory in Istanbul. Just before leaving London, Herzog wrote to Polanyi thanking him for his help and noting the bond that had formed between them. He was anxious about the upheavals in his life, but concluded that "My dread is probably not greater than yours was of Manchester."[54] Herzog died two years later at the age of 56.

Polanyi was anxious to become adjusted to the English way of life as rapidly and as completely as possible. Joining the Manchester Literary and Philosophical Society made him part of the high-powered, intellectual group of Manchester businessmen, clergy, and academics. Polanyi was elected to the "Manchester Lit. and Phil." on March 8, 1934, and soon after published two articles on ionogenic reactions in its *Memoirs and Proceedings*. In spite of his criticism of Haber and others for not resisting anti-Semitism in Germany, Polanyi did not join the Jewish community of Manchester, though he was on friendly terms with individual members of this group, such as Lewis Namier,[55] a professor of history at Manchester University. Namier was especially interested in the formation of a Jewish state in Palestine and often tried to enlist Polanyi's support for the cause. Polanyi told Namier that he doubted whether the "noble adventure" would lead to genuine Jewish self-respect rather than to self-righteousness.[56] The creation of a new state would not solve the problem of how to be authentically Jewish in the midst of Gentile civilization. It seemed to him that the Zionist effort would mainly serve to awaken the Jewish national pride associated with the ghetto, a pride that was not supportive of the many great accomplishments of Jews who had made a place for themselves in the Gentile world. Zionists seemed to him to be eager not only to conduct their own national experiment but also to dictate terms to Jews living in other nations as well.

When Hugh O'Neill and his family moved to Derby at the beginning of June 1934, Polanyi gave him Lion Feuchtwanger's *Die Geschwister Oppermann*, a novel that describes the destruction of the life of members of a Jewish family under Hitler. Polanyi and Magda identified with "the conflicts of those who believed in Germany in face of its own professions. . . . It certainly has impressed me and my wife deeply by telling us our own tale."[57] A few weeks later, Hugh and his wife, Barbara, took Polanyi for a vacation in Anglesey, on the northwest coast of Wales; Magda and the boys stayed at home. The O'Neills hoped to provide Polanyi some relief from his months of stress in new surroundings. The day they left for the shore, June 30, coincided with the "Night of the Long Knives," when Hitler ordered the murder of more than a hundred of his own associates and possible opponents within the Nazi ranks, including some generals and other high officials. The news of the atrocity reached England just after Polanyi and the O'Neills had left Manchester. On the way to Wales, Polanyi asked the O'Neills to stop the car several times so that he could buy the latest newspapers. He was "like a man demented, and kept saying 'if they will do this to each other what will they do to the rest of the world?' "[58] Not until then had he realized the full extent of Nazi barbarism. The shock was worse than the trauma of his early World War I experience precisely because it could not be excused as a wartime event.

The next morning, Polanyi was missing from the bungalow. The O'Neills found him wandering on the beach, completely distraught. He decided he could not stay in Wales and returned immediately to Manchester by train. He wrote to Hugh, apologizing for having carried to Anglesey his "chronic cares about a rotten world . . . the lab does me better than the sunny seaside."[59]

Moving to England did not substantially lessen the Polanyis' involvement with Michael's mother and siblings. Karl's vision of a just social system put him at odds with both the Nazis in Germany and the reactionary Austrian government, so his future at *Die österreichische Volkswirt* was not bright. Although Ilona wanted to continue her studies in physics at the University of Vienna, Karl hoped to find employment in England. His long letters and vague plans worried Magda and Michael.[60] They feared that if he came to England, they would be forced to support him. In the event, Karl arranged to move permanently into a spare room that his friends Irene and Donald Grant had in their London house, and *Die öesterreichische Volkswirt* gave him three months leave with pay. He earned some money in occasional lectures, met important people—J. M. Keynes, H. J. Laski, R. H. Tawney, G. D. H. Cole, and R. Gregory—who represented economic journalism and academic scholarship, and began lecturing regularly in Adult Education and Extension courses at Oxford University and the University of London.

More than Ilona's studies kept her in Vienna. She was a member of the Schutzbund, a group of Vienna workers that opposed the fascist Dollfuss regime. She edited their illegal paper and acted as radio-propagandist under the name of Anna Novotny. Mausi's son, Otto (George) Striker, who was a talented radio technician, worked with Ilona on these clandestine radio broadcasts. Hans Zeisel, Eva's future husband, was imprisoned for three weeks because of his participation.

After the uprising of the Vienna workers had been put down by Dollfuss's soldiers, the moral atmosphere in Vienna worsened. Schooling for young Kari became a traumatic experience. A few of her teachers had been chased or taken away; some of her friends had lost their fathers. Ilona and Karl decided that Kari had to join her father in England and go to an English school. She arrived on March 7, 1934, and stayed briefly with another family. Magda then reluctantly agreed to take Kari in while Karl went on a lecture tour. Tensions increased that fall. After spending her vacation in England, Ilona decided to go back to Austria. Karl prevailed upon Michael to pay for her studies. When he wrote to thank Michael for the money, he noted Magda's opposition to the transaction: "Maybe she does not want to be bothered with Ilona and me. But why couldn't we—you and I—try to help each other, to trust each other . . . as man to man . . . we have no reason not to love each other . . . we don't need to agree in all matters . . . I believe in you."[61]

Eight days later on September 26, Karl visited Manchester between lectures at Liverpool. The personal meeting helped to overcome the tension for the moment, but Karl's insistence that Magda take Kari for Christmas vacation—which she finally did—brought more estrangement. Karl's continuing lecture tours, including one in January and February 1935 to Des Moines, Iowa, in the United States, made it necessary for Kari to alternate between living with the Grants and with the Polanyis. Although Magda resented the added burden, Michael seemed content: "Our increased family (both boys at home and a niece living with us) proves to be a success."[62] Cecile was still living in Budapest. She suffered from severe medical problems and needed money regularly. She grieved her isolation and her inability to help her children: "Mausi in Russia, you in England, Sofie in poverty, Karli in complete apocalyptic loneliness."[63]

At Easter time in 1935, Polanyi and Horiuti traveled to Moscow to present their joint paper on proton transfer (1935g). By that time, Polanyi's reputation as a physical chemist was well established in the USSR. He was invited to meet Nikolai Ivanovich Bukharin, a leading Kremlin theoretician, who provided a philosophical, "scientific" rationale for the conduct of the Soviet government. When asked about the Soviet policy on science, Bukharin declared that the concept of pure science, seeking truth without regard to extraneous influences, is an illusion caused by contradictions in the capitalist society "which deprived scientists of the consciousness of their social function." Soviet scientists were supposed to harmonize their personal scientific interests with the needs of socialist society, choosing lines of research to benefit the current Five Year Plan. Governmental planning of science, said Bukharin, would thus not be a matter of central direction but a conscious confirmation of the harmony between individual and communal concerns.[64]

Although Polanyi was at first amused by "this dialectical mystery mongering," he found its consequences staggering. The essential element was the idea that scientists should coordinate their efforts to serve social purposes rather than to discover the truth. Here was a government claiming to run its society on the "strictly scientific" grounds of dialectical materialism, at the same time that it officially denied what Polanyi understood to be the fundamental nature of science. It seemed to him that in the absence a commitment to truth, Soviet research would be dominated by political considerations. He speculated that practical applications might succeed, but only haphazardly or through trial-and-error.

Bukharin's rhetoric suggested that the harmonization of individual and communal interests would be left to the good conscience of the scientists. In fact, the government was very active in seeing that scientists stuck to the party line. Contrary to the tenets of modern genetics, but in keeping with the principles of Marxism, Trofim D. Lysenko, a politically powerful agronomist, claimed to have proven the inheritance of acquired characteristics. Beginning in 1936, he carried on a political persecution of Nikolai I. Vavilov, a world-famous authority on genetics, which led to Vavilov's tragic imprisonment and death. No worthwhile research in genetics took place in Soviet Russia for more than ten years.

While in Moscow, Polanyi looked up his niece, Eva Striker, who took him on a guided tour of the modernized city. At a new high-rise apartment complex built for the proletariat, Polanyi asked if they had running water, to which the guide replied by taking them on a search for the single outdoor tap, hidden in a courtyard, that served an entire block of apartments.[65]

Polanyi's response to the Soviet denial of truth began with a review of the massive, two-volume work of Sidney and Beatrice Webb, *Soviet Communism; A New Civilization?* (1935). Polanyi entitled his review "The Struggle between Truth and Propaganda" (1936k). Although the Webbs admired the extensive political machinery of Soviet "democracy," their account inadvertently revealed many details of the repressive system and its underlying police terror. Polanyi sharply criticized the Webbs' justification of the massive Soviet projects in which dissident voices were ruthlessly repressed. When truth is devalued, there is no hope of reconciling disagreements over social doctrine or practice: "Unless intellectuals make a new departure, inspired by unflinching veracity, truth will remain powerless against propaganda" (118). Over the next two decades, Polanyi devoted more and more time and energy to developing the "new departure" that he hoped would enable truth to stand against propaganda.

After the trip to Moscow, Polanyi found the right person for the hydrogen activation experiments in Melvin Calvin, who had done doctoral work on the surface interactions of atoms at the University of Minnesota. Calvin had written to inquire about a postdoctoral appointment. Polanyi responded that he could support Calvin if he could get to Manchester, for Horiuti was about to leave and a new postdoctoral assistant was needed. Calvin found cheap passage on a cargo ship bound for Manchester, but when he arrived in September, no place had been found for him to live. Since the ship was to stay in port for a week, the captain let his passenger stay on board, in "God-awful" quarters.[66] The university gave Calvin a grant for his first year; Polanyi's Rockefeller grant supported him the next year.

Calvin's first assignment had been to work on the same reaction that Horiuti had studied, but using electrolysis in combination with a platinum sheet to catalyze the reaction.[67] Calvin sidestepped the complexities of both the micropycnometer and the Farkas conductivity method. Instead he used a sensitive quartz microbalance, which had been developed in Cambridge, to measure the density of hydrogen gas and determine the percentage of deuterium.[68]

Polanyi then put Calvin to work on phthalocyanine, sending him to Sir Patrick Linstead at Imperial College to learn how to make the compound as well as its derivative, copper phthalocyanine, and to bring back samples of each in the form of crystals. Polanyi recognized the phthalocyanines as especially adapted for basic experiments in hydrogen activation because of their close relation to many biologically active compounds; unlike the naturally occurring enzymes, the pthalocyanines had an unusual degree of stability. The large central ring of the molecules containing eight carbon and eight nitrogen atoms resembled the structural elements in the chlorophylls (necessary for plant life) and hemins (essential to oxygen transport in animals), as well as the thousands of porphyrin compounds involved in biological processes. Working with E. C. Cockbain and D. D. Eley, Calvin and Polanyi produced two articles in which they described the rates of activation by the phthalocyanine crystals of (1) a self-catalytic interchange between hydrogen gas and the crystal; (2) interchange between gas and water; (3) reaction of hydrogen and oxygen to form water; (4) para-hydrogen conversion.[69] The possibility that small amounts of similar compounds could account for the metabolism of the human body was suggested.

The experiment seemed to work so well that Polanyi was anxious to try another metal-porphyrin compound of much greater biological interest: hemoglobin, the oxygen-carrying substance in blood. Some hemoglobin was put in the vessel of Eley's apparatus with deuterium and water in expectation of catalyzing the transfer. The analysis of the gas after the material was mixed showed a reduction in deuterium, as expected. Following his usual habit, Polanyi promptly wrote out a short note to *Nature* on the assumption that the necessary repetitions of the experiment, including the use of fresh samples of hemoglobin, would bear out the initial results. He went off to London, leaving Eley to fill in the table of results for the subsequent experiments.

After a series of runs, Eley opened the vessel to change the sample of hemoglobin and was met with the "most terrible smell."[70] What had happened was that anaerobic bacteria had grown profusely on the hemoglobin— the bacteria were functioning as catalysts, not the hemoglobin itself. The note to Nature was never sent. Nevertheless, Eley pursued the study of hemoglobin and related compounds and was eventually able to show that in the absence of bacteria, these compounds generally could catalyze the para-hydrogen transformation but not the hydrogen-deuterium reaction. Polanyi gave him the go-ahead to publish his own article, which was written in 1936 but not submitted for publication until after Eley had gone to Cambridge in 1939.[71]

Calvin tried to extend Eley's experiments by the use of dissolved phthalocyanine instead of the solid crystals. The results were negative; probably water molecules blocked the access of hydrogen atoms to the double bonds.[72] Furthermore, the experiments with the crystals were not always reproducible— they, too, were inactivated in some way. In fact, the crystals made in the laboratory of Manchester generally did not work as well as those made by Linstead. Polanyi published a word of warning: the hope for stability and reproducibility was frustratingly disappointing (1938d). When Calvin came to the end of his Rockefeller fellowship, Polanyi helped him obtain a position with Joel Hildebrand at the University of California at Berkeley. Calvin continued to work there on porphyrins, particularly chlorophyll, which ultimately led to the discovery of the mechanism of photosynthesis in 1957, for which he won the Nobel Prize in 1961.

Polanyi's group now focused on experiments designed to distinguish between hydrogen exchange and hydrogenation. Polanyi and his colleagues C. Horrex, R. K. Greenhalgh, J. H. Baxendale, and E. Warhurst developed the experiments and had some success in narrowing down the possibilities.[73] The last piece of work in Polanyi's group on the hydrogen theme was done in 1939 by A. R. Bennett on the "poisoning" of a catalytic surface by impurities in some of original Horiuti–Polanyi work (1940a). The results corroborated the group's earlier article on a catalytic reaction of hydrogen and water (1933l).

Daniel Eley has written several accounts of the work on hydrogen catalysis done at Cambridge after 1935.[74] He shows how the theory of catalysis developed in Cambridge drew on the Polanyi–Eyring conception of the activated complex, Polanyi's description of the role of the mobile electron cloud in a crystalline solid in binding adsorbed molecules, and the research that Polanyi had initiated on deuterium. The hydrogen-deuterium experiments all involved electron switching between neutral atoms and charged ones, that is, ions. So also did the studies initiated by Meer in Berlin on the reaction of ions with simple organic compounds and by Szabó on the Walden inversion. The charge transfers could not be treated by the then available Polanyi–Eyring transition theory with its assumption that the electrons in the interacting atoms stayed in the same states all the time. A new line of research in transition theory was opened up. Richard A. Ogg, Jr., the gifted American postdoctoral fellow from Harvard who had arrived to spend his two fellowship years with Polanyi, took up the challenge.

Ogg's first assignment in the fall of 1933 was to make himself competent in the special field of reactions with charge transfer, including the study of the work of Polanyi's group in the Berlin years. He received an excellent introduction by accompanying Polanyi in late September to the Faraday Society discussion on free radicals (molecules with an unpaired electron, which makes them highly reactive) at the University of Cambridge, where he heard D. W. G. Style read the English version of the article he had published with Horn and Polanyi (1933i).

A number of cases of electron switching and the production of ions occurred in the research Polanyi directed on hydrogen-deuterium reactions. Most of these transfers had the property that an electron departs from one atom, leaving it positive, and moves to another atom, making it negative. A large Coulomb (electrostatic) force between the oppositely charged atoms appears and serves to pull the negative radical toward the position of the positive, a process now called "harpooning" because of the way in which the electron is thrown from one atom to another and subsequently causes the two atoms to be drawn together.[75] The basic way Polanyi and Ogg brought harpooning into the transition-rate theory was to construct separate idealized contours representing the potential energy states before and after an electron transfer had taken place, and then to look to see whether there were places where the two potential energy surfaces touch or cross each other, showing that an electron transfer would be highly probable (1934e). However, constructing energy surfaces according to the London–Eyring method was difficult, and several simplifications had to be made. Ogg's practical task was to construct sets of intersecting curves for a number of conceptually simple reactions and to develop the details of this type of theoretical treatment. Unfortunately, the available experimental evidence was largely from more complex and hard-to-calculate substances, but the values of activation energy and heat of reaction were similar enough to make the treatment seem plausible.

In his spare time outside the laboratory, Polanyi's experience of the upheavals both in Hungary and Germany motivated him to study the economic problems of the unemployed and the poor. He was afraid that efforts to cure these severe problems by socialism in the Soviet Union and by the different forms of fascism in Germany and Italy might cause further destruction of Europe's precious institutions and values. He was convinced that the main difficulties were not matters of morality, for instance capitalist greed or totalitarian love of power, but of mistaken theories of economics and the institutions based on them. Polanyi was determined to carry on, at least for himself, the technical economic studies that he had begun in the Harnack House seminars, paying special attention to production and the business cycle. His scientific outlook and his conviction that each discipline must have its own methods drove him in search of valid economic principles by means of which a planned economy might be run in the Soviet Union, and alternate principles by means of which unemployment and accompanying depressions could be overcome in the economic systems of the West. No such principles had yet been found, but Polanyi was quite confident that he could either discover such principles or else demonstrate that they could not be found. He was also determined to educate the public, at least in the free societies, so that their political processes would have a sound basis for instituting the needed reforms.

Not long after getting settled in Manchester, Polanyi paid the first of many visits to the Department of Economics and Social Studies. He wanted to meet the staff and find out what they were up to. Since the department's main work during those years was on the problem of unemployment, Polanyi found a sympathetic hearing for his own concerns. He found a kindred spirit in the young and gifted economics writer John Jewkes.[76] The Polanyis and the Jewkes became close friends. The Jewkes invited the Polanyi family to their summer place in the Lake District where they talked and hiked and swam, and had great fun flying kites.

Polanyi set himself to reading the existing literature on the business cycle. He also sought information from the Economics Department about the Soviet situation, both its history and the contemporary status of its economy. Two weeks after his arrival in Manchester he wrote Toni Stolper that he had "already had fights with my progressive friends here."[77]

> Manchester at that time was rather like a large Oxford College: Professor John Polanyi, F.R.S., comments in a letter on "the warm and lasting welcome" that the family received in Manchester and on "the vigorous social-cum-intellectual life which enveloped them, not only in the milieu of university professors of many disciplines, but also of remarkable doctors, lawyers, factory and mill owners, people connected with the art galleries, the Northern Service of the B.B.C. . . . the *Manchester Guardian* and the odd (really quite odd) aristocrat—a remarkable village community drawn together by a liveliness of mind through which they triumphed over the . . . nastiness of their environment."[78]

Polanyi regularly had lunch together with chemists, economists, and other researchers at a big round table in the campus restaurant. Their discussions covered nearly every subject.[79] Polanyi soon gained a reputation both for his wide-ranging intellect and also for his absentmindedness. Despite his interest in economics, he frequently forgot to bring money for his lunch and had to borrow from someone. The next day he would have the money to repay but did not remember from whom he had borrowed it, and so asked all around the table until he found out to whom he was indebted.[80]

In August 1934, during Polanyi's early explorations of economics, he went to Vienna to visit Mausi, who was undergoing a gall-bladder operation. Hans Zeisel, who at that time was working for the Austrian shoe firm, Del-Ka, came to see Mausi, too. Zeisel was talking about the problems he faced in designing and marketing shoes. Mausi's son, Misi, who had accompanied her to Austria from the USSR, interrupted Zeisel: "Luckily we don't have such problems in the USSR." Zeisel asked, "How come? After all you have to make shoes that are healthy for the foot and that are pleasing." Striker said, "Well, the shoes I am wearing are made purely in Russia!" Zeisel examined them intently. "What are they—shoes or boots? Such a shoe couldn't be sold in Austria. We don't have people poor enough to buy those."[81] After recording this conversation in his notebook, Polanyi jotted down some economic ideas under the heading "Liberal Theory." He noted that classical economics views the general good as coming from the sum of countless acts of self-interest. The socialist program to eliminate "egoistic individualism"[82] would result in unwanted goods being produced inefficiently—as ugly and shapeless as Striker's shoes.

Polanyi's first publication on economics was a 23-page booklet, *USSR Economics—Fundamental Data, System and Spirit*, which gave one of the earliest accounts, brief as it was, of Soviet production and consumption figures, of government regulation, and of the basis of the Communists' appeal to the public (1935j). Jewkes was impressed with Polanyi's dedication to writing up his economic ideas in vivid English, having observed him regularly filling his wastebasket with rejected versions. Polanyi's interpretation of the Soviet data was shaped by his personal experience on trips to the USSR in 1928, 1931, and 1932. He experienced the weaknesses of the Soviet system firsthand. Polanyi's pamphlet also drew on official data and offered several methods to show what the official data revealed about the state of production. Diet was adequate in calories but consisted mostly of coarse bread, cereal products, and potatoes. Housing was substandard and crowded, four square meters per person. The death rate was twice as high as in Western countries. On the other hand, education was considerably developed, there was less poverty in 1928 than in 1914, and there was substantial improvement in heavy industry, in spite of the fact that poorly organized central control created many inefficiencies. The great "war cry" instilled in the populace was to "overtake and outstrip" the Western countries in terms of housing, transportation, and agricultural efficiency; but the Soviet system failed to reach these goals (1935j, 20).

The government appealed to the population with two contrasting motivations: the hope of personal success—"Every worker feels sure of a job and hopes to get a much better job by working hard and improving his skill"—and the Communist identification of each person as working loyally and enthusiastically for the State, which is made "the fountain of all benefits" (23). In contrast to capitalist mores, only public motives, such as pride in working for the public good, were extolled and subjective ones, such as personal ambitions, were kept to oneself. Even though Polanyi heard monotonous cursing everywhere in 1928, the actual degree of personal satisfaction or dissatisfaction was hard to assess.

Oscar Jászi, who had become professor of political science at Oberlin College in 1925, praised Polanyi's work: "My feeling is that you point out correctly the basic motives and the real causes of the relative achievement of the Russian experiment. The essence is to couple capitalist motives with a collective ideology, and to present this in the form of a new religion saying that all sacrifices are in the interest of the working class. . . . Your picture of the Russian situation is still too optimistic. I don't trust the official Russian statistics when it happens frequently that the unfavorable statistician gets arrested."[83]

Jászi sent a copy of USSR Economics to Walter Lippmann, who in his 1937 book The Good Society complemented Polanyi as "an exceptionally gifted observer."[84] Sir Ernest Simon, chairman of the Association for Education in Citizenship, was also impressed with Polanyi's analysis:

> I should like to congratulate you most warmly on your article on Russia in THE MANCHESTER SCHOOL. It is the first attempt I have seen to estimate quantitatively the achievements of Russian industry and agriculture, which is, of course, vitally important.
>
> After all, the moral achievement in making so many people happy and confident must in the long run depend largely on the economic achievement, and a real attempt to understand and measure that economic achievement is, in view of the whole revolutionary situation, fundamentally important for the future of world civilization. It is astonishing that more economists and sociologists have not attempted to do what you have done.
>
> Anyway, it seems to me, if I may say so, a remarkable achievement for a non-sociologist, on which I should like to congratulate you most sincerely.[85]

In Polanyi's judgment, the few small gains made by the Soviet system were purchased at the cost of destroying the principal institutions of civilized life. In the conclusion of his essay, he touched on the themes that he would develop much more fully decades later: "One of the tragedies of mankind seems to be that the most vivid forms of social consciousness are invariably destructive. If this destruction is to be avoided, the community must be made conscious of purpose in its daily life by some other means than a social revolution. A way has to be found of clearing the sight of the citizens [other] than by the smashing of a mechanism which they fail to comprehend" (1935j, 24).

In the Harnack House discussions, Polanyi had already sought a generally valid and easily comprehensible representation of the economic system. He wanted to embed reliable knowledge of the economic mechanism into the general consciousness. A mere catalog of specific economic facts could easily be made, but would not provide the level of understanding needed for intelligent participation in the economic system. It was the system as a whole, the mechanism, that economists and public alike needed to comprehend.[86] Once the system was understood, Polanyi thought that the proper reforms would follow: "my faith in the moral power of Humanity leads me to assume that if they could be led out of blindness, I mean literal blindness: inability to see their vital surroundings, this moral power would rise to the situation it now must fail to grasp. . . . To find, present and develop truth in social matters is the first revelation we require, a revelation which can be gained by a technique of seeing society and cannot be found without it. This is my obsession."[87] Although others might judge that his optimism was naive, Polanyi dedicated more and more of his energy over the next four decades to "find, present and develop truth in social matters" without worrying overmuch about how his ideals were to be realized in the realm of practical politics.

In 1935, Polanyi had been asked to join the Jewish Medical Society. While he did not accept such invitations to join Jewish groups, he was always willing to give talks and promote his own pro-assimilation views and voice his opposition to Zionism. He accepted the Society's invitation to speak in Liverpool on January 21, 1936, and gave a lecture, "On the Position of Jews," considerably developed from the undelivered letter to Herzog dated May 6, 1933.[88] Polanyi identified himself as a "firmly convinced assimilist" because he found nothing of value in Jewish religion and ritual but much in Christianity.[89] He suggested that those Jews who did not want to give up their heritage should learn to live with incomplete assimilation into a national culture, accepting what they found good in their adopted culture and devoting themselves to the good of society at large. He expressed the hope that internationalism would increase in Europe after the war, offering many opportunities for Jews to serve a great cause with dignity.

Polanyi gave credit to the Jews for the biblical foundation of Western civilization, but did not see any way in which the Judaism of the ghetto affirmed the universal ethical heritage of the Hebrew prophets. He concluded:

The best example for us to follow in this world seems to me that of the Quakers. Politically they are completely detached from national life. Their faith in the works of Christianity fills their lives. The time might soon come when Christianity, fighting against the religions of brutality, will lie in the balance. Jews might remember then that this religion was founded by their ancestors, and that in upholding Christianity they might fulfill their international mission. I think that for Jews who follow such a line there is no need to go to Palestine to become masters of their souls. (16)

Polanyi never identified himself with any Christian denomination, but he clearly saw himself as one who had the kind of "faith in the works of Christianity" that he recommends in this passage as an alternative to a closed Jewish community, whether in the ghettoes of Europe or in Palestine.

The reality of oppression in Russia came home to Polanyi when his niece, Eva, was arrested on May 28, 1936, on false charges of secretly introducing German swastikas in her ceramics designs and owning two pistols for the purpose of assassinating Stalin.[90] An additional charge, which she only overheard by chance, was that she was involved in a conspiracy with Trotskyites. Although the charges were false, the prison authorities were under orders to keep up the appearance of legality, which meant that Eva was protected from physical torture and that she was allowed to defend herself in court, where she showed that the pistols belonged to the old Hungarian revolutionary in whose apartment she was living.[91]

Thanks to special efforts by the Austrian consul, by scientists who signed affidavits on her behalf, and by Mausi, who wore her grandfather's medal from the tsar as a brooch, Eva was released early in September 1937 and put on a train to Vienna. Her brother, Misi, his wife, Hilde, and their mother, Mausi, left the Soviet Union a month later. Eva's husband, Alex Weissberg, had himself been arrested in March 1937. Eva managed to get a message to Alex in prison that she wished to divorce him, and he signed the necessary papers.[92] Hans Zeisel, who had fallen in love with her when they lived in Berlin, was waiting for her in London.

These intense family concerns and his work in the laboratory did not keep Polanyi from making progress in economics. Since 1929, he had been convinced that a motion picture would be the best way to teach people what they needed to know about the realities of the economic system within which they lived. After he had finished the manuscript of *USSR Economics* at the end of July 1935, Polanyi took his family on holiday in Bled, Yugoslavia. In between swimming and playing tennis, he began to sketch his ideas. In October he wrote an overview of the project, "Notes on a Film," and sent a copy to Hugh O'Neill. He argued that the complex structure of a social body or economic system needs a visual presentation if its true nature is to be communicated, and he suggested that the ideal way to provide such a view would be with a working model that would demonstrate the operation of the system and show the effects of possible changes.[93] In 1936, Polanyi created a physical analogue to model the circulation of money. He persuaded Syar, the chemistry department's glassblower, to construct a glass apparatus using water and a vacuum line that illustrated the law of supply and demand.[94] The monetary system was represented by water flowing in and out of flasks and beakers. It allowed Polanyi the pleasure of performing economics experiments in his own office in the intervals between the supervision of chemical research. The technicians came frequently to modify the apparatus; it was the only experiment that the Manchester chemistry staff saw Polanyi conduct all by himself.[95]

Gilson and Syar built a second machine with a conveyor belt and a series of tubes through which colored balls dropped into colored containers on the belt. The belt represented Polanyi's key conception, the circulation of money, and the balls the payments for such things as wages and interest, consumer goods, bank savings and capital expenditures. Another machine with "lots of wheels" was built at the same time that Douglas Hartree was building his clockwork mechanical differential analyzer for atomic physics elsewhere in Manchester. Whether Hartree influenced Polanyi is not known, but his machine influenced the technicians. The shop time taken by the work was a nuisance because the students could not get help with their own scientific apparatus.[96] The final and most successful machine functioned like a modern analog computer in that the effects of increasing the supply of money or of other changes could be explored and a study made of possible cures for economic depressions.

Polanyi was not satisfied with any of the various models and finally decided to shift his efforts back to a motion picture. He thought that hundreds of such films would influence public life in the next twenty years and was concerned that now at the beginning of this development it should be done well.[97] Polanyi's talk, "Visual Presentation of Social Matters" to the Association for Education in Citizenship suggested a symbolic representation of a "community of moneymakers."[98] It utilized a circle around which two sets of arrows pointed in opposite directions. One set represented production of goods and services, with laborers processing raw materials, converting them into salable goods, and supplying wholesalers and retailers. The other set represented householders going out to shop with their money, which entered the circle to pay for costs at each stage and ended up in the pockets of all the workers. As Polanyi said, he had given a simple picture with nothing on foreign trade, no labor exchange, no unemployed, and no banks. The various arrows changed their sizes as goods and money are traded, but the static nature of the diagram made it hard to visualize the circulation of money. In a later document, Polanyi suggested using moving symbols representing people or barrels of goods or stacks of coins.[99]

By tracing the flow of goods and money in the economic system, Polanyi wanted to make evident the reason for the ups and downs of the business cycle that had contributed to the twenty-two years of wars and revolutions since 1914. Polanyi told Toni Stolper that he hoped his audience would join with others in developing a series of ever-better films, building on his own first crude efforts. Although she took his grand aim seriously, to save our threatened civilization and to recover the grounds of freedom, she wondered whether just getting the economic system understood would help—it might not be able to prevent a rejection of the whole system.[100] For instance, Hitler and the Germans had deliberately sacrificed economic well-being for the sake of "higher" social goals. Her principal criticism was that the circular diagram representing the flow of goods and money did not do justice to the troubles with which both ordinary people and the political economist have to struggle. His scheme glossed over changes wrought by technical improvements and changes in the money supply and did not address the key question of whether it is market prices or profit margins that mainly influence economic decisions. Polanyi replied two and a half months later, agreeing in general with her "wonderfully clear-sighted criticism"; however, he did not take the hint that the project should be abandoned.[101]

Polanyi expected to complete the film script over the Christmas holidays and was given considerable help from John Jewkes, Lewis Namier (a historian), J. F. Duff (a professor of education), and other members of the Economics and Social Studies Department. Polanyi hoped that a joint research headquarters would develop to provide a basis for economic education. In his early drafts of the script, he drew especially on Röpke's book, *Crises and Cycles* (1936), which discussed the relation of monetary flow and overall economic activity. He became convinced that the cure for the variations in the trade or business cycle lay in control of the flow of money.

At Christmas time in 1936, Polanyi read Keynes's treatise, *The General Theory of Employment, Interest, and Money* (published the previous February), which gave theoretical grounding to ideas Keynes had promoted since 1929. He reread the book several more times until, during the family's summer holiday in Brittany, he made a breakthrough: "From that second on I could read the whole thing over from the beginning like a novel."[102] Although Polanyi saw Keynes's ideas as similar to his own, he did not follow him in every detail. For Polanyi, the volume of employment is determined by the total amount of money in circulation, which is the sum of money paid out for consumable goods and the investment money spent on new or renewed capital goods. Keynes expressed the employment total at any given time in terms of the number of workers who would provide just that output that would equal the sum of the demands for consumption and for investment. Both men agreed that to smooth out the business cycle and keep employment up, the State should add effective demand by putting more money in circulation through deficit spending.

By this time, Polanyi had become absorbed by the problem of the historical effect of widely held economic fallacies. Melvin Calvin noted that "Toward the end of my stay [in Manchester], in 1937, . . . it became difficult often for me to talk with him because he was thinking in terms of economics and philosophy, and I couldn't understand his language."[103] In February 1937, Polanyi presented an extensive lecture on "Popular Education in Economics" to the Manchester Political Society.[104] The bulk of the lecture was a detailed account of the damage done by liberal, laissez-faire economic policies: (a) the unfair distribution of income; (b) the assumption that everything including public goods and services should be handled by the market; (c) the absence of any remedy or even theory for depressions and unemployment, i.e. of the trade cycle; and (d) overemphasis on blind acquisitiveness without any communal sense of responsibility for economic life. These difficulties were distressing both to liberals, like Polanyi, who sought to reform laissez-faire economics by government regulation, and to Marxist revolutionaries, who sought a completely new system. Polanyi recognized the powerful but disastrous appeal of Communism as based specifically on demands to overcome these capitalist weaknesses by instituting socialized central planning to get rid of exploitative employers, the market, the trade cycle, and the acquisitive system.

Polanyi hoped that his program of economics education would provide a foundation for the reform of the free-market system. "Intellectual power is readily and almost inevitably converted into political power," he said, so that adequate views would "release social forces now entangled in futile issues and would direct them towards reasonable aims.... an enlightened public would have full power to direct its economic life" (11–12). Such optimism! Perhaps he was remembering the truly exceptional influence of the prewar Budapest intellectual elite, although even then the "intellectual power" probably had its greatest effect on the aristocracy rather than on the working class.

On March 8, 1937, the 20th anniversary of the start of the revolution in Russia, Polanyi addressed the Manchester Historical Society on Soviet economic history.[105] Polanyi prefaced his remarks with a comment that the Russian Revolution had been too little and too partisanly studied and warned that the populace had better pay attention to it because the next wave of unemployment might bring about Communist and Fascist action to destroy our liberal economic system and our democratic politics.

Polanyi noted the complete failure in 1919–1921 of Lenin's attempt to found the new state on Communism. Wages, prices, and profits were eliminated, and the use of money was restricted. Workers in the factories were supposed to work according to their abilities. Clothing, drink, cigarettes, medical service, and cinemas were to be provided on a basis of equality, along with food obtained from the peasants. When the system was actually tried, production was so minimal that almost no goods were available to trade for food with the peasants; famine ensued, and the government had to take food from the farmers by force. The entire economy broke down. Agricultural output fell to 50 percent of prewar levels, heavy industry to 14 percent, pig iron production to 3 percent. Essentials for production and for domestic life were lacking, and the hungry population rioted, with outright revolts by workers and sailors.

In March 1921, Lenin announced the end of the experiment in Communism, which he called their "greatest of defeats." He immediately set up plans for the New Economic Policy, which took effect in August, restricting state ownership, restoring money and credit, and allowing buying and selling for profit. From 1921 to 1928 the Soviet Union experienced one of the most brilliant recoveries in European history, which demonstrated the power of commercialism to resurrect an economy largely destroyed by Communism. Stalin's subsequent efforts to restore central control of the economy through the Five-Year Plans of 1929–1932 and 1933–37 provided Polanyi with further evidence that Marx's dream of a pure Communist society could not be achieved in the real world.

Polanyi was impressed by the morale of the people in spite of the hardships they suffered. The challenge for the Liberal State—and for himself— was profound: "The demand for social consciousness in economic life...is a historic force more fundamental for the present century than even the national idea and...the struggle for it will dominate public life until it has found reasonable satisfaction" (32).

Early in 1937, Polanyi finished a 25-page script entitled "Money, Booms and Depressions."[106] His enthusiasm was infectious and led several of his colleagues, along with a well-to-do friend of the university, Sir Samuel Turner of Rochdale, to contribute enough money to get the first part of the film completed by January 1938. The film work inspired Polanyi to plan a course of six lectures on the mechanism of economics, which he gave in the University Extension that spring. The film was finished by the end of February and was first screened at the Manchester Statistical Society on March 9, 1938, under the title, "An Outline of the Working of Money."[107] Polanyi had divided the film into five parts so it would be easier to weave the film into the associated lecture that was intended to accompany the film. He hoped that the discussion could go further than the contents of the film.

The film was shown ten more times before the end of 1938 to different educational and employees' groups as well as to many economists, who generally approved of the film.[108] Professor Henry Clay, economic advisor to the Bank of England, sent a glowing review to the Rockefeller Foundation:

I have been discussing with Polanyi the question of methods of presenting elementary economic facts and theories off and on for some years. If you have met him, you will have recognised the extraordinary brilliance of his mind, and the fact that his interest in economics is not professional enables him to approach the problems of presentation in a way that would be almost impossible for a professional economist. In this film he has taken what one may call the greatest common measure of contemporary theories of the reactions of money upon economic activity, and succeeded in presenting these reactions in a way that is extraordinarily difficult by any purely literary or static presentation. I believe that in his own field of physical chemistry he is outstanding, and that it would be a crime to divert him to another field; but he is a much better economist already than most professional economists, and, if he is able to give a part of his mind to economics, he is much more likely to make an effective contribution than nine out of ten of the people who hold chairs in economics in the Universities.[109]

Other economists, including the outspoken (and non-Keynesian) Friedrich von Hayek, Ludwig von Mises, and Wilhelm Röpke, saw Polanyi's film in Paris at a conference on Walter Lippmann's book, *The Good Society*, at the end of August 1938. The response to the film encouraged Polanyi to work on a more ambitious version.

His work on economics and the production of the movie did not prevent Polanyi from making some progress in the laboratory as well. By 1938, Polanyi and his colleagues had developed the theory of reaction rates in sufficient outline that it was ready for a wide spectrum of applications. The idea that came to him in 1938 was to use his methods of reaction-rate research to seek information on bond energies, the basic physical forces that hold molecules together. Finding out how much energy it takes to break a bond between the component parts of a molecule or, conversely, finding out how much energy is released or consumed by forming a new bond, was directly related to the question of why particular reactions take place at the rate that they do. Polanyi proposed to determine the energies needed to dissociate the molecular bonds of some of the compounds his group had been studying; the energy needed to break the bonds would be roughly equal to the energy released when the bonds were formed.

Polanyi expected that the stronger a bond was in the initial state, the larger should be the activation energy required to break the bond and form a new one, although exchange reactions always involve a shift from one bond to another so that only differences in energy released in the reaction can actually be measured. His interest lay in bonds involving an active carbon atom in organic compounds that are attached to an inorganic atom like iodine or bromine or a group like OH. Polanyi wanted to determine how the bond strength depends on the character of the organic radical, that is, the part of the organic compound that stays unchanged in the series of exchanges being studied, and on the atoms or groups attached to the active carbon atom itself.

The procedure that Polanyi envisioned was first to obtain accurate measure of the energies between carbon and iodine for several organic radicals by the method of pyrolysis, which uses heat to break up the bond in question without forming any new bond, and then to incorporate transition state reactions between iodine and other elements or groups in the final analysis. In 1938, E. T. Butler, a conscientious objector on a fellowship from the University of Wales, undertook an extensive pyrolysis study with an improved flow method, passing the iodide through a tube heated from 300°C to 500°C and measuring the amounts of iodine and hydrogen iodide released. The results for the carbon-iodine bond in thirteen iodide compounds (methyl iodide, ethyl iodide, vinyl iodide, etc.) were published in two articles (1940c, 1943a). The war intervened and Butler was assigned to alternate service. Early in 1941, another student, Erna Mandel, took over the work and added eight more compounds to the list (1945b).

Edward C. Baughan, who had a year at Princeton with Eyring and returned to England in 1939, was too disabled by illness for war work. He joined Polanyi's group as assistant lecturer and carried out several theoretical calculations. He wrote two brief articles on the other various bond strengths (1940i and 1941c). Baughan, M. G. Evans, and Polanyi carried out a theoretical study of the varying bond strength between various atoms or groups attached to the same kind of radical (1941b). Variations in the structures of hydrocarbon groupings attached to a C-X bond (a bond between carbon and some other element such as chlorine, bromine, iodine, sulpher, etc.) are in principle expected to cause changes in the strength of that bond. Hitherto, such variations had been assumed to be small, and it was thought to be adequate to calculate the total heat of formation of organic molecules by the simple addition of constant bond contributions. The new theoretical study much improved on this situation by considering the effects of contributions of the different possible "resonance" forms of molecules, particularly the organic radicals.

A general review of this research on bond energies was given by A. G. Evans in a small book.[110] According to E. C. Baughan, Polanyi had taken the right steps toward understanding organic reactivity, making the "most important move that has been made in the simple theory of organic chemistry.... Polanyi has not received the credit due him. What happened was that [Sir Christopher] Ingold got the better publicity."[111]

7

The Philosophy of Freedom:
1938–1947

In March 1938, Hitler's troops marched into Austria. Karl, Ilona, and
Kari were already safe in England. The day after the invasion,
Polanyi's niece, Eva, fled Vienna with her brother Misi and his wife,
Hilde, on one of the last trains to the West. They headed for England
and spent two weeks with the Polanyis in Manchester; Misi and
Hilde then continued on to the United States. Eva lived with Michael
and Magda for two months. After her divorce from Weissberg was
granted, she and Hans Zeisel were married in London, then sailed to
New York in the fall of 1938. Mausi remained in Vienna with
Michelle, Misi and Hilde's 2-year-old child, living with Sofie and
Egon Szecsi. The Nazis arrested Egon and took him to the
concentration camp at Dachau on March 12. Sofie had no income
other than what she could beg from her relatives and friends. The
only way Polanyi could obtain deutschmarks to help Mausi and Sofie
escape was to sell the house in Berlin, which in turn had to wait until
he obtained British citizenship a year later. However, he offered to
support Egon in England if he were released, and he managed to
send the relatively small monthly amounts in British currency
needed to support Sofie and two of her children, Karl and Edith, in
Vienna; her oldest daughter, Maria, had already left for Chicago. In
December, Sofie took in a boarder, Gyula Hollo's neurotic brother,
Felix, who was a source of both income and exasperation.

Mausi's younger son, Otto George, emigrated to the United
States from Vienna in August 1938, with help from his wife's
American relatives. Even though she already had an English visa,
Mausi remained in Vienna to try to solve Sofie's problems. She made

no progress and finally decided to go to Manchester with Michelle shortly after celebrating Sofie's fiftieth birthday with her on September 18. Although her husband, Sandor, was also in Budapest, Mausi was estranged from him; a few years later, their children helped Sandor emigrate from Hungary to the United States. While waiting for the transit papers to be issued, Mausi helped her son with some of the paperwork for his patent office. During a meeting with one of her son's clients in a coffee shop, the waiter heard her use the word *Zellen*. Thinking it referred to the creation of political cells, he denounced her. She was promptly jailed. In London, Mausi's daughter Eva frantically tried to get Austrian authorities to release her mother from jail. Michael and Magda came from Manchester to London to join their niece's efforts. Mausi and her young granddaughter were soon able to travel directly to England, although she was in such bad shape when she arrived in Manchester, she had to be carried up the steps; after recuperating in Michael and Magda's home, she moved to London.

Only the Szecsis were left in Vienna. Sofie did not want to leave with Egon in the concentration camp, but all efforts to get him released failed. As war approached, Polanyi wrote four to five urgent letters daily concerning family members or friends who found themselves in threatening situations—Alex Weissberg was still in prison in the Soviet Union and Michael's brother Adolf was trying to find a way out of Italy. Karl and Eva had continued negotiating on behalf of Sofie and Egon, but Polanyi's support as a long-time resident of England was urgently needed. At Easter time, Sofie asked him to send a telegram to the concentration camp headquarters at Buchenwald, to which Egon had been transferred, asking for his immediate release and promising to support him in England. In June, Sofie and Egon's passports were confiscated, sealing their fate.

Family anxieties, worry about the coming war, production of the film on economics, and his responsibilities in the laboratory gave Polanyi much to think about in 1938. His limited skills as a driver deteriorated under the stress. When Alexander Todd arrived in Manchester from Scotland late in the summer of 1938 to take up his appointment as professor of organic chemistry, Polanyi picked him up at the Piccadilly Railway Station to take him to lunch. Todd remembered that after leaving the station, Polanyi drove down the steep slope to the London Road, came up behind a tram, and failed to stop when the tram did. The collision led to a friendly argument between Polanyi and the tram driver, who realized Polanyi's absentmindedness and let him go with an exchange of notes. The tram had not been damaged, but the Austin was dented. After lunch, Polanyi found—as often happened—he had not brought his wallet, and Todd had to pay. It was truly a memorable afternoon for the Scotsman.[1]

In February 1939, Polanyi was involved in a much more devastating accident. He collided with a lamp post near the Withington Library at the intersection of Wilmslow Road and Sandileigh Avenue, south of the university.[2] The building and lamp post sat in the corner at a point where Wilmslow Road bends to the right to become the continuation of Palatine Road. Cars approaching on Wilmslow Road face a fork and must turn either right or left. Polanyi missed the turn entirely, plowing straight ahead into the lamp post. The passenger side of the Austin was severely damaged. Although he was thrown against the wheel, a silver cigarette case in a front pocket took the brunt of the force and was cut in two; he also hit his head and sustained a severe concussion.

After regaining consciousness, Michael telephoned Magda to say that he was all right. The call brought her little comfort because he failed to explain that he had been in an accident. The police found him in a state of confusion.[3] Brian Gowenlock relates the story that circulated in the department:

> A telephone call was received by his secretary who was asked, 'Is there a Professor Polanyi who works in your department?' She replied, 'Yes.' 'Is he absentminded?' Again the answer was 'Yes.' The questioner then stated that he was a policeman who had found Polanyi in his car, having hit a tree or a post. He reassured the secretary that the professor was not hurt and explained his questions. 'He told us who he was, and when we asked him how it had happened, he told us he had forgotten that he was driving.'[4]

Polanyi claimed that the left rear tire had burst, but Magda checked with the garage and found this not to be the case. Nevertheless, Polanyi wrote Toni Stolper the following June that the accident had been caused by tire trouble.

The concussion was so severe that he was bedridden for two months.[5] Whenever he tried to get up, he suffered from headaches and dizziness. The doctor diagnosed a general weakness. Michael and Magda spent the month of April in a hotel in Southbourne to give him a chance to recuperate. They were the only guests, so Polanyi did not have to talk to anybody. Magda took over his family correspondence until the end of May. She also, as she put it, successfully fended off the relatives seeking both attention and help.[6] In 1947, Polanyi remarked, "I was glad that my motor accident eight years ago was sufficiently serious to make me lose its recollection."[7]

Polanyi had planned a trip to the United States for the summer of 1939, but canceled the trip after the automobile accident. He needed to supervise the final hydrogenation work and the beginning of the bond energy work in the laboratory, and to help the film team produce a final edition. In December 1939, Polanyi and Jewkes, who had become head of the Economics Research Division, jointly submitted an application to the Rockefeller Foundation, which had been supporting Polanyi's work in physical chemistry and had also given substantial support to Jewkes's Division.[8] Polanyi suggested a budget of

£500 to £600 to revise the film for general educational distribution. He had convinced the Rockefeller people that there should be a series of further economic films and asked them to fund a film on population. Polanyi wanted to show how variations in net reproductive rate affect the age distribution as time goes on and to suggest some of the social and economic repercussions. The onset of war and increased costs for redoing the "Money" film prevented any further consideration of the population film. By June, the new work was moving toward completion and Polanyi expected the enlarged and improved film to be finished by the end of July, and released for general use by the end of September. "Until then there had better be no war."[9] Neither hope was fulfilled; the film was not finished until many months after the war had begun.

Since the early 1930s, a strong movement to promote a Socialist revolution in Great Britain had been growing among a group of English scientists. They believed that the government should organize science and technology to address the whole range of material problems of society.[10] The most prominent member of this movement was J. Desmond Bernal. A crystallographer and Fellow of the Royal Society who played a prominent role in the 1937 Congress, Bernal was responsible for the revival of the floundering Association of Scientific Workers, giving it a decidedly left-wing outlook. He was also prominent in the new, liberal wing of the British Association for the Advancement of Science, its Division for the Social and International Relations of Science. Like Polanyi, Bernal had found himself drawn to explore the social ramifications of the history and philosophy of science.

Bernal's most influential book, *The Social Function of Science*,[11] appeared about the time when Polanyi had recovered enough from the auto accident to give it a serious reading. Polanyi considered Bernal's deceptively attractive position as a serious threat to both basic science and liberal society. In a substantial review entitled "The Rights and Duties of Science," he sympathized with Bernal's desire to achieve "plenitude, health and enlightenment" (1939d, 175). He took issue with the Marxist doctrine that all thought is governed by relations to the mode of production, which in turn suggests that the difference between pure and applied science is not real but a fiction erected in defense of a capitalist ideology.

Polanyi rejected Bernal's view that science should be centrally planned, his conception of a ruling state serving the working class and acting as the arbiter of truth, and his preference for production over the search for truth. In "Truth and Propaganda," the last section of his review, Polanyi pointed out that Bernal agreed with Marxist thinkers who denied the power of truth and rejected the duty to serve it for its own sake. Polanyi noted that Marxism had a more intelligent and complete philosophy of oppression than either Italian or German Fascism. He knew from personal experience the fruits of this oppression for scientists in the Soviet Union: travel difficulties, banning of papers, and imprisonment. Polanyi closed with Lionel Robbins's solemn warning that this generation was "betrayed beyond belief by those who should have been its intellectual leaders" but who instead "opened wide the pass to the barbarians" (193). In later years, Polanyi characterized the mindset of the Marxist intellectuals as "a prophetic idealism spurning all reference to ideals" (PK, 227) and a "moral inversion" (PK, 233–235).

On August 15, 1939, just five days after Polanyi completed the review of Bernal's book, the four Polanyis sailed across the Irish Sea from Liverpool to Cork. Polanyi had rented a small cottage in Kenmare, County Kerry, and to their surprise, the Polanyis quickly felt at home there. As Polanyi wrote his friend O'Neill, the feeling in the little villages was reminiscent of rural Austria: "Catholics, whitewashed houses, tangles of dark hair, poverty, squalor and a ready human interest, much lazy lounging."[12] In the rustic setting they could forget for a moment that war was near.

On the first day of September, the radio broke the news that Hitler had invaded Poland. Overnight the world changed. England declared war two days later. The beginning of the war in Britain meant closer scrutiny of identification for people entering Britain, but no passports were yet needed for English people going to or from Eire. One morning after the announcement of the war, Magda found Michael all packed up in his bedroom, saying he would have to return to his job and would chance it without a passport or his naturalization certificate, which had been granted at the end of August and was awaiting him in England.[13] Looking very English in his trilby hat, Polanyi made it home without difficulty.

On his return, Polanyi learned that every house was required to use blackout curtains at night. He gratefully accepted the Jewkes's invitation to stay with them while the difficulty was corrected. When Magda telephoned from Ireland, there was no answer, and she feared that their home must have been bombed. Confused and upset at having the sole responsibility for George and John in the isolated Irish village, she was also anxious that her accent might cause trouble at the immigration check point. She decided to return home quickly, come what may. When they reached the immigration control, the officer looked at them. "English?" he inquired. Magda nodded and said nothing. They were allowed to pass, looked at each other with relief, and boarded the boat for home.

Shortly after Polanyi had moved in with the Jewkes, he received a telegram from Budapest announcing his mother's death. She was alert to the end. During one hospitalization, she asked her doctor, Imre Horner, to bring her some books. In a few days, she had something pertinent and intelligent to say about each.[14] Her death from heart failure occurred in the hospital on September 4 or 5.[15] The last members of Cecile's immediate family to see her alive in Budapest were Mausi's son George and his wife, Barbara, who managed to visit in August 1938, before emigrating from Austria to the United States. It was sad for all Cecile's children that the outbreak of war prevented their visiting her in her last days, especially for Michael, whom the family perceived to be her favorite child.[16]

The economies of war time and the expense of helping their relatives motivated the Polanyis to move to a more modest home. They found a house that pleased them both in the suburb of Withington, at 30 Sandileigh Avenue, and moved in at the end of September. The new house was nearer to the university, in the area where O'Neill had taken Polanyi for his first walk in Manchester. They appreciated the size of the house—they were able to manage with one part-time charlady—although Polanyi was somewhat dismayed by the small garden. "I hope that after the war a few small houses in big gardens will be built for people of my taste," he wrote O'Neill a few days after the move.[17]

Polanyi volunteered to help in the evenings with fire-watching both at the university and at Sandileigh Avenue. He soon became bored with the lack of action. He was frustrated in not using his talents in a significant way. Waiting for the dawn at the university in his capacity of auxiliary fireman, he wrote: "I am very bad at these things because they give me no sense of adventure and make me resent the waste of my time at every instant." The long, lonely nights on duty gave Polanyi an opportunity to think about the shape of his career. The bond-energy research in the laboratory was going well under the competent management of Butler and Baughan. After his denunciation of Bernalism, Polanyi was convinced that his principal duty during the war was to work out the philosophy by which a free society operates. His specific aim was to mount an intellectual defense of liberty. Polanyi's chemistry colleagues knew he spent a good proportion of his time in his office writing on social matters; as the war progressed, Polanyi's social and philosophical concerns diverted more of his attention from the chemical research being done by his colleagues and students.[18]

Polanyi had already gathered considerable material for his new social philosophy. He did not want to imitate the dogmatism he was attacking, which was based on a few sweeping generalities expressed in polemical rhetoric. Even the non-Marxian schools of philosophy were too specialized and out of touch with the human world to interest him. He preferred to develop his theory step by step, in the spirit of scientific inquiry, rather than by deduction from generalities. Polanyi began with an essay on degrees of sophistication in physics and religion, suggesting that awareness of these stages is a proper basis for tolerance.[19] The efforts of physicists to make the world look tidy have involved a succession of pattern-constructions that work, though only partially; the atomic theories of Bohr, Schrödinger, and Heisenberg successively refined physicists' understanding of the behavior of electrons in atoms. The less sophisticated models contained material that could be further developed: "all honest expression of conviction is...an ore from which [one can]...extract some truth which perhaps is not recognised anywhere else."[20] Polanyi believed that the most elementary level of religious truth could still be found within the church in spite of the "claptrap of Heaven and Hell." He speculated that the "substance of God" might be something like Schrödinger's unobservable waves.[21] Abstract reflection on religious truth might produce something like Heisenberg's imageless, algebraic interpretation of atomic theory.

Polanyi also set himself to write a physiology of a liberal society, including an analysis of the means for producing spiritual wealth.[22] His first effort was entitled "The Struggle of Man in Society" and was intended to counteract the passionate revolutionary intolerance of human values—"for the sake of irresponsible fancies"—that he expected to become dominant after the war.[23] Polanyi tried to trace the principles of a highly diverse, free people dwelling together and forming a coalition against collectivism. The essay initiated in rough form several lines of thought that became of central importance to his later philosophy, but it included just a short portion at the end on the deficiencies of collectivism and only a brief description of science, primarily as a model for liberalism.

Polanyi was so busy during his forty days of working on the manuscript and on his economics film that it had become extremely difficult to attend to anything else, but a letter in *The New Statesman and Nation* by J. B. S. Haldane caused him to compose a reply. Haldane, a geneticist and biochemist at the University of London, had advised against attacking the evils of the Soviet Union for fear that England would be drawn into war with the USSR and Germany. At the same time, he proclaimed his readiness to assist in a new declaration of the "Rights of Man." Polanyi's answer, "Science in the USSR," described the terror he had seen in the eyes of Soviet scientists whom he had met personally and who were fearful of being taken captive by Stalin's secret police (1940b). He challenged Haldane and other politically active Marxist thinkers to acknowledge that scientists were unjustly imprisoned in the Soviet Union in spite of Marxist rhetoric about human rights. Polanyi insisted that "at the present hour of decision truth must be known on this subject" (174).

Polanyi was not satisfied with the first draft of "The Struggle of Man in Society." He returned to the writing desk just after sending off the Haldane letter, and between February 17 and March 9, 1940, his typist turned out 120 pages, which he labeled merely "Chapters," probably intending to put them together with what he had written earlier.[24] These essays updated the historical material covered in the first manuscript. Polanyi feared that because of widespread ignorance about how the economic system operates, the next century would be "marked by history as a modern Dark Age in which the use of rational thought was lost."[25] In these reflections, Polanyi turned to science as a model of a free, unplanned system that nevertheless developed an order of its own based on the common search for truth. He observed that scientists in general are "unsocial people who rarely discuss their plans among themselves" but who coordinate their efforts by keeping track of the results of other researchers.[26] Polanyi's discussion of how scientists select and solve problems foreshadows his later analysis of the tacit dimension of personal knowledge: "Intuitive decisions are always undemocratic, in the sense of not being fully justified by objective reason and ultimately depending on personal judgment.... The most precious element of scientific planning is the inspired guess; the most valuable feature of scientific results [is] their solid reliability."[27]

After the extensive work done for these "Chapters," Polanyi accepted two invitations to lecture. The first, in March 1940, was addressed to the Manchester Chemistry Department Study Group under the title, "Planning and Soviet Science."[28] Polanyi criticized the British proponents of centralized control of science (Bernal, Julian Huxley, Levy, Haldane, Hogben) and showed how counterproductive centralized planning had proven in the Soviet Union. In the second lecture, "Collectivist Planning," given in April to the South Place Ethical Society in Central London, Polanyi ridiculed the notion that a national economy could be organized into a giant factory with a single officer at its head (1940e, 27–60; SEP, 121–143). Using the example of how an army organizes itself for a march, Polanyi distinguished between supervision and direction. Most of the communication in the great system of an army must take place horizontally, with very few questions being referred to the general staff. In arguing for renewal of the liberal tradition, Polanyi drew on his own experience of the freedom he had enjoyed himself and had given to others in his laboratory work in Berlin and Manchester. He continued his reflections on the freedom of inquiry in an address entitled "The Organization of Scientific Life"[29] for the British Association for the Advancement of Science at Reading in June. The life of science depends on performing to self-set standards: "It is only the mind which is sufficiently modest to accept its limitations while steadfastly pursuing its personal intimations, which will attain the rank in which it is of greatest use."[30] At the same time, the results attained by the "personal intimations" of the researcher must then be submitted to the rest of the scientific community: "Objective validity in research is attained," Polanyi said, "when the scientific significance can be borne out by others."[31]

Polanyi's new film, Unemployment and Money, was completed in the spring.[32] The film describes the essentials of the Keynesian theory of labor, monetary circulation, banking, capital investment, and the trade cycle. It ends with a short Epilogue: "Such are the ideas concerning the failures of our economic system, which guide economists and statesmen in their struggle against these barriers. Barriers, which can be overcome only by assured employment."[33] Polanyi adopted Keynes's view, originally proposed in 1936, that full employment could be assured by government control of the money circulation through deficit spending and expansion of the money supply. The alternative, in his view, would be a kind of planned economy set up by business monopolies arranged to provide full employment "on top of an economy ossified by restrictions."[34]

The London premiere on April 25, 1940, was a gala affair. Polanyi sent out several hundred invitations. In addition to the press, he wanted the audience to represent a complete cross-section of society, left-wingers and bankers, women and men, laborers and investors. He asked Karl for help, and—always the democrat—specified that no formal dress should be worn.[35] Although he was somewhat apprehensive about the turnout—"I don't think anyone will take notice of it with the war getting active"[36]—the showing attracted a large audience, and "Michael was treated like a film star."[37] After the premiere, Polanyi found the public presentation of *Unemployment and Money* to be a frustrating and disheartening affair. His dream of an institute dedicated to teaching economics by means of film and lectures never materialized. Perhaps fifteen individuals showed the film to about forty adult classes in England, including several Workers Education Association groups,[38] a few classes at the Huddersfield Technical College, some military classes, and a few academic and social organizations.

Polanyi had thought of going to New York to organize the distribution of the film himself, but the war prevented the trip. He asked for help from his sister, Mausi, from his brother Karl, who arrived in the United States in August 1940, from Toni Stolper, and from an old friend of Karl's, the Berkeley economist Jack Condliffe, but they managed to set up only four or five presentations. The American premiere took place at the New York Film Center on November 7, 1940. The film was subsequently shown in Washington, D.C. (September 10, 1942), at Bennington College where Karl was teaching (October 28, 1942), and at Sarah Lawrence College (April 23, 1946). The group at Sarah Lawrence included twenty labor union men from nearby Yonkers, New York, and a very lively discussion ensued.

The film project may have failed, in part, because it told a peacetime story to countries at war. Polanyi made two further drafts entitled "Money in War and Peace: Project for a film" and "The Money Circle in Peace and Wartime,"[39] but nothing came of them. Polanyi also wrote about thirty letters to individuals and organizations, hoping to find an institution that would carry forward his scheme of economic education, all to no avail. He took the failure of his grand vision philosophically, writing to Mausi: "Don't worry too much about the film. It is getting clear that only an expert and enthusiastic teacher can make proper use of it."[40] Mausi had already told a friend that the film was "dead as mutton...it would be grand if it could be revived again."[41]

The invasion of Denmark and Norway in April 1940 intensified Polanyi's fears for himself and his family: "The invasion of Norway this morning by

Germany is surely a slight beginning only of what will presently come."[42] That same spring, Polanyi assembled four of the essays he had written since 1935 on Soviet economics into a small book, *The Contempt of Freedom: The Russian Experiment and After*. In his preface, Polanyi argued that liberty "cannot be saved unless it again becomes a progressive idea. Those who have returned to its defense must now give it all their hearts and gifted minds, to make it again a conquering faith" (1940e, vi). While other scientists worked together to build the atomic bomb or to break encryptions, Polanyi's solitary and self-set assignment during the war was to consider how best to preserve the liberal tradition.

Michael and Magda decided to send 11-year-old John off to Canada with a group of Manchester children on a government program administered by Anna Oliver from the Manchester English Department, one of Magda's best friends. The University of Toronto placed John with the family of Dr. Michael Cameron, a physician. Preparations for John's departure were made during the evacuation of British troops from Dunkirk (May 26–June 4). The outlook was bleak. Polanyi was not sure the British government would ever aggressively attack the Germans. Six years later he recalled that time: "I am sitting ... in my little garden in full sunshine under a spotless sky. This place and this time of year will always remind me of the summer of 1940: Of fear and despair, of personal disaster rendered unbearable by universal shame."[43]

Apart from his son's departure and his sister's imprisonment in Austria, Polanyi's "personal disaster" included being judged unfit to help in war research because he was a foreigner who had relatives still in Europe. Polanyi had volunteered to join Hugh O'Neill at the London, Midland and Scotland Railway Laboratory, helping with materials testing and metallographic photography. He moved to Derby under the assumed name of Michael Pollard, with an identity card under that name furnished by the Foreign Office (George and John also used "Pollard" during the war years). He would not accept O'Neill's invitation to stay in his house but asked him to find him a room; after settling incognito, he got in touch with Hugh.[44] O'Neill's daughter, who was 14 at the time, later remembered the atmosphere of intrigue, mystery, and excitement when Polanyi came to Derby: "My memories of Prof. Polanyi get confused with pictures of Mussolini, demoted, in a trilby hat and overcoat, similar clothing and demeanour: hat pulled down, collar up—incognito and scared."[45] No work was found for Polanyi, and he spent his time lying on his bed all day before going to see the O'Neills in the evenings. He stayed only about two weeks, for news came that the British had destroyed the German-controlled French Fleet at Oran and Mers-el-Kebic, Algeria on July 3, 1940, and he returned to Manchester with renewed confidence in Britain's ability to fight the Germans. No one was the wiser about his secret trip to Derby because the university had closed down during the summer.

Polanyi was saddened by his Aunt Irma's death from a heart attack in Budapest on the fourteenth of July. She had been a confidante and second mother; her death meant the final rupture of his connection to Budapest and his parents' generation. His spirits were raised considerably by the success of the Royal Air Force in the "Battle of Britain" in August and September, even though Manchester was targeted by the German bombers. His exuberance was boundless when winning the war became a possibility:

> The horrible 100 days from May 11 to August 20th have passed— their danger was infinitely greater to humanity than that of the 100 days of 1815 ... and now we see for the first time, perhaps today, a new coastline appearing on the horizon, the heritage of our children, the world of a better future. People ... have not seen yet the new age into which they are entering this morning. So I sit alone in my office and feel as that solitary "watcher of the skies when a new planet swims into his ken" ... "full of wild surmise." ... we now know again that Progress and Civilisation, Reason and Liberty are real and that they will have to be maintained and spread everywhere by the might of tanks and planes.[46]

He now was confident that Hitler would be beaten even before he set foot on the island, "though it is a pity he did not try an invasion ... the spirit of the people has become invulnerable."[47]

Michael and Magda suffered no extreme physical inconvenience even at the height of the war, but they endured many minor annoyances with food, heating, and communication, particularly when they were providing a temporary home for their displaced relatives. More debilitating were their worries about the outcome of the war, so much so that they often asked each other to cease expressing anxiety. Moods of despair alternated with moments of euphoria, and they tired of the emotional upheavals. Magda and Michael were glad that John was safe in Canada during the bombing, but they missed him sorely. George and Michael became close companions at home, discussing politics endlessly while they washed the dishes. After George spent the summer of 1940 working on a farm, he and his father took a week's vacation together; that fall, he entered Magdalen College, Oxford. Magda worked at the Citizen's Advisory Bureau, supervising a rest center for bombed-out people and advising them on housing, money matters, and personal problems. Polanyi appreciated her gifts for this practical work and shared in the satisfaction that the work brought her.

For a short time, Polanyi and his two older brothers were reunited in England. With no prospects for employment in Britain or the United States, Adolf decided to go to Brazil. He and his second wife, Lilly, left at the beginning of June 1940. Karl managed to get a teaching appointment at Bennington College in Vermont, beginning in the fall of 1940, and Oscar Jászi arranged a lecture tour for him in early September. Karl was eager to complete a book he had been working on for many years, tentatively entitled *Anatomy of the Nineteenth Century: Political and Economic Origins of the Cataclysm*; he taught a seminar at Bennington that allowed him to develop his ideas. Ilona joined him later. Ilona had been invited to teach physics at Bennington for the school year 1941–42, but did not reach the United States until January 1942 because of problems with the exit permit and entry visa. Ilona not only taught physics but subsequently studied aeronautical engineering in the hope that she might serve in the Royal Air Force when they returned.

Polanyi continued to ruminate with his friends about the shape of the postwar world. In a conversation with Hugh O'Neill, he advocated taking an "imperial outlook" on Europe after the war, an idea that he knew was repulsive to most people but which expressed his devotion to the ideals of Western civilization. Where the first European empires were founded on military conquest, the new empire was to be established by means of persuasion: "The war will be very long and the struggle will have to go on indefinitely even beyond the defeat of Germany. We and the generation after us are dedicated to a re-conquest of this planet for the rule of the Anglo-American Civilization ... our task is to dig back to the sources of our strength [and to] revive the flow of inspiration."[48]

On November 19, Polanyi addressed the Manchester Classical Society on "Planning, Culture and Freedom."[49] He emphasized the social function of liberty, which "is to be distinguished from its commoner aspect of the protection of private life and private opinion from interference by other people, neighbors or government officials. There is beyond this a social purpose in liberty as the supreme method for co-ordinating cultural efforts."[50] Our present ideals of beauty, justice, Christianity, and science developed historically from· a coalescence of insights from Greece, Rome, Palestine, and Arabia. A few weeks later Polanyi addressed the Manchester Liberal Society on the same general theme. His talk, entitled "Planning, Efficiency and Liberty," contained an insight important for liberal economics: A fully planned society is "a system which destroys methods of ascertaining value [and therefore] is a system imposing economic chaos."[51]

In January 1941, Polanyi lectured on the topic "The Social Message of Science"[52] in the Advanced Science Series of the University of Leeds. He argued that "The conviction that some things are real and others unreal is the foundation for all other thought."[53] Polanyi took the position that the entire scientific, cultural, political, and economic order of society is suffering from the "destruction of faith started by people dazzled and misguided by the successes of science," but there is hope that a better understanding of the nature and limits of scientific method might re-vindicate the ideal of truth in all aspects, which jointly constitute the heritage of Christian civilization. . . . Much of our self-respect as civilised men rests on the pride in our heritage of scientific achievement. Wherever tolerance prevails; wherever questions of fact are judiciously separated from issues of opinion; wherever fairness and objectivity are upheld against passion, prejudice and oppression, there is a spirit at work in our society which is consonant with and historically not unconnected with the rise of modern science. Science forms an integral part of the way of life which the citizens of the West are pledged to defend and carry on. (1944a, 83)

This same month, Polanyi sent a short note to *Nature* taking issue with an earlier article in that journal (December 28) in which the editor had agreed with John Dewey that people should stop ascribing "peculiar holiness to scientific truth," should call for the social control of science, and should discard the idea of scientific detachment. Polanyi responded that he could recognize nothing more holy than scientific truth. In his view, scientific detachment was "of the same character as the independence of the witness, the jury, the judge; of the political speaker and the voter; of the writer and teacher and their public; it forms part of the liberties for which every man with an idea of truth and every man with a pride in the dignity of his soul has fought since the beginning of society" (1917b, 119). Ideally, the same virtues that make someone fit to do science would also equip them to act as responsible citizens in a free society.

Nature responded with editorials on May 10 and 24,[54] the first referring to *The Contempt of Freedom*[55] and the second to the Leeds lecture. The two unsigned editorials affirmed the importance of the fight for freedom in science and in all other intellectual activities, but criticized Polanyi for failing to recognize the interaction of science and society and for his refusal to accept the planning of science in order to address social needs. Polanyi composed a reply that *Nature* refused to publish.[56] He focused on the purpose of a democratic society, which is to cultivate "the ancient spiritual heritage of justice and human solidarity and their modern brother ideal: scientific truth."[57] In this time of crisis, the scientist who upholds the value of pure science "performs today an act of pivotal political significance." He thought it was absurd of *Nature* to suppose that anarchy would result from giving science its freedom, for "the worst examples of chaos and anarchy . . . are found under most complete government control both in this country and abroad." Polanyi described the viewpoint of the editorials as "a profound scepticism towards every basic idea of our civilization together with an almost unbelievable measure of gullibility in favor of practical quackery."[58]

In the fall of 1940, an Oxford zoologist, John Baker, decided to found a society to counter the influence of Bernal and the socialists who advocated placing scientific research under the control of a central authority. Baker hoped the new group would "so far as possible,... answer all their assertions with quietly stated, carefully reasoned arguments."[59] Polanyi had read Baker's "Counter-blast to Bernalism" the previous year, but had not yet met him in person.[60] On November 2, 1940, Baker proposed the formation of the Society for Freedom in Science in a letter addressed to forty-nine prominent British scientists. He suggested four propositions that should be the basis of the Society: (1) scientific knowledge is a value unto itself; (2) the benefits of science to society generally come from research in pure science, the application of which is often not obvious; (3) research workers should have as much freedom as possible to choose their own research subjects; and (4) researchers should decide for themselves whether to work alone or in a team.

Polanyi was delighted with Baker's proposal. Since his clash with Bukharin in Moscow in 1935, Polanyi had felt called to resist the spread of the utilitarian view of science: "Planning of science will be thrust upon us if collectivism wins out over individualism...we must join in this battle."[61] Polanyi met with Baker and Sir Arthur G. Tansley, professor of plant ecology at Cambridge, early in 1941. Two decades later, Polanyi identified that day as a decisive moment in his turn from science to philosophy: "I see myself arriving to our first meeting in Oxford, shaking hands with Tansley, being received by you and your lively Liena. I had written before a few essays on subjects of the kind, but it was your response which launched me finally in the direction of our mutual interests and brought me eventually to the entrance of my career as a philosopher. I had not realized until this moment, that this was the turning point of my life. At any rate the last of its turning points."[62]

Together the three men worked out a circular describing the aims of the Society: to defend scientific freedom against the agenda of the central planners, to spell out the rights and duties of scientists in a free society, and to marshal support for scientists in those countries that placed restrictions on research. Perhaps made wary by his disappointments with the film project, Polanyi at first sounded doubtful about the impact the circular would have: "The botanist, who is exceedingly eminent and rather old, is sending [the circular] round, the zoologist acts as a secretary, and I remain in the background. Unfortunately most of our adherents are convinced passivists, they will only approve in silence."[63]

The Society for Freedom in Science was organized in the summer of 1941 with Sir George P. Thomson, professor of physics at Imperial College, London, as president, Polanyi, Tansley, and Sir Henry Dale as vice-presidents, and Dr. John Baker as secretary and treasurer. The founders hoped that the Society would cultivate "a solid body of opinion ready to present the case for freedom if the threat to suppress scientific liberties should develop dangerously in the period of reconstruction after the war."[64] At first they found it hard to get their material published in standard journals. Along with the wartime paper shortage, there was a general (and accurate) sense that the Society represented a small minority of intellectuals; at its peak in 1946 there were around 430 members.

The advocates of planned science had many more allies than the fledgling Society. In September 1941, the British Association for the Advancement of Science arranged a highly publicized Conference on Science and the World Order, sponsored by the association's Division of Social and International Relations of Science with the help of members of the Association of Scientific Workers. This three-day gathering was attended by ambassadors, governments in exile, and cabinet ministers. Although the nominal purposes of the conference were to support the Allied war effort and to promote the planning of science, many saw the conference as nothing but a grandiose propaganda exercise—"a camp meeting for the Marxian religion."[65] Members of the Society had no opportunity to voice their objections at that conference, but over the next three years they managed to publish several articles and books. Not till the end of the war were they able to publish a series of their own "occasional papers." However, despite limited membership and modest publications, the Society for Freedom in Science was the beginning of the "cultural Cold War" against the scientific Left.[66] Polanyi was deeply pleased with the efforts the Society made to preserve the freedom of pure science. The group continued its work until 1962.

During the next two years, Polanyi also addressed himself to the question of applied science, particularly the structuring of incentives that would stimulate research, reward invention, and yet, at the same time, allow the greatest public access to the scientific and technical developments. As a solution to these difficulties, Polanyi proposed that inventors and their backers should be rewarded from the public purse and given "licenses of right" (1944e, 67), a practice that already had limited use in Great Britain. The awards would be made by a panel of technical experts and trade representatives who could make equitable assessments of the probable value of the patent to the public at large. The usual legal bases for assessment—novelty, utility, and inventive effort—would be the criteria. Users of the patent would pay license fees, instead of granting one company monopoly rights and excess profits. The average compensation to inventors would be close to that at present, but might also be larger because of the wider use that would be made of a productive invention under the new scheme. Polanyi characterized the proposal as moving from strict law to a system of equity, using public awards based on scientific and technical judgments. John Jewkes thought that Polanyi's proposals were intriguing but unworkable.[67]

April and May 1941 were very trying months for Polanyi. He was anxious about Hitler's forces taking Libya and Crete, and watched the skies for German planes during a new surge of night bombings. He was consoled by Rudolf Hess's escape to Great Britain and the sinking of the Bismarck, "but there was not much else until the Gods . . . suddenly decided to redress the balance by striking Hitler with madness and making him attack Russia. . . . It was a relief."[68] After the Germans attacked Russia, Polanyi tried in vain to send a cable to a family friend, the scientist Alexander Frumkin. He expected the Germans to get bogged down all through the winter, with more grim fighting to come in the spring. Michael and Magda felt oppressed by the prospect of seemingly endless destruction—"as if we just wanted to go to sleep for the rest of our lives, or join an embroidering club, or the Salvation Army."

In August 1941, Polanyi undertook a brief government assignment at a laboratory in Swansea, South Wales. The research project probably concerned reducing the telltale flames associated with gunfire.[69] After finishing his part in the project, Polanyi stayed on for a short vacation during the Bank Holiday, joining the crowds of others who flocked to the seashore for a "breather" in spite of the government's entreaties not to do so.[70] On his return, Polanyi gave his typist twenty-five pages entitled, "Beginning of a Book on the Scientific Life."[71] These notes pulled together and enriched the material in the "Chapters," the "Organization of Scientific Life," and the "Social Message of Science."

In September, Michael and Magda went to North Wales for a week. They stayed at the Oakeley Arms, an old coaching inn that was to become Polanyi's favorite spot to rest and to write. Located in hilly, half-mountainous country, at Tan-y-Bwlch in the small village of Maentwrog, the Oakeley Arms was frequented by a number of authors. Mrs. Mary Roberts, a slender, handsome woman, saw to it that "the bath water was always hot, the food well-cooked and the atmosphere of the place easy-going."[72] Polanyi was attracted by her literary and social acumen, as well as her gift for hospitality.[73] He liked room 12 with its view over the green valley, and Mrs. Roberts always gave it to him if it was available. Polanyi visited there often from 1941 to 1947. It was "a great stand-by to me during this war. . . . [I have] done more than one half of my writing at this window."[74]

Polanyi also did a lot of walking during his stay at the Oakeley Arms. In the countryside near the hotel there was a narrow, unused railway that ran above Maentwrog, along the hillside as far as Blaeneau Ffestiniog. Sometimes he might have three or four walking companions; the novelist Storm Jameson would often accompany him: "I have a vivid image of Michael Polanyi walking ahead of me through the pitch-black tunnel of a disused slate railway, toward the end of a strenuous climb across rocky hills. To lighten the way through the mud and the fatigue of falling in and out of unseen holes and jumping the wooden blocks between the rails, he repeated verse after verse of Verlaine, in an enchantingly gentle voice."[75]

With the development of his thoughts on social matters occupying more and more of his time, Polanyi needed a secretary to type up what he had written. On November 20, he hired a half-time personal secretary, Olive Davies, who had been working for an insurance company. She was to become Polanyi's indispensable factotum; she worked for him at Manchester in one capacity or another for the next seventeen years. Davies made his travel arrangements, saw to it that he arrived with the correct notes at the correct place, and replenished his numerous medical prescriptions, which often needed to be forwarded to him during his trips. Taking care of her absent-minded employer was no small matter. She frequently had to send the lab boy to retrieve items he had forgotten at home, and on one occasion she herself followed him to the train station and walked the length of the train to bring him some money he had left behind.

At times, Polanyi would isolate himself from the chemistry department for two or three days. Davies was usually successful in keeping the students from disturbing him; if she failed, they would generally find Polanyi unprepared to discuss their problems, or else he would only spend a small amount of time on chemistry and then return to his work in economics and social theory. He still had excellent ideas in chemistry—Warhurst remained in awe of Polanyi, "so extraordinarily versatile, such a profound intellect"[76]—but Polanyi usually left his colleagues and students to do the research.

Polanyi's interest in social analysis deepened his bond with George, who studied his father's work and stood by him loyally. In November 1941, George founded *The Liberal Review*, a journal which brought forth a flood of contributions. Polanyi thought that George showed a very genuine ability for this job and proudly sent the few available copies of the journal to friends and relatives in the United States. George surprised his parents at Christmas time by announcing that he had taken his final exams in history at Magdalen College, passing with distinction.

Polanyi gathered a huge collection of books from which, both in North Wales and back at Manchester, he distilled many notes on a whole range of subjects that intrigued him. Polanyi mentioned C. K. Allen, Aristotle, Bernard Bosanquet, Edmund Burke, G. D. H. Cole, Locke, Nicolo Machiavelli, Sir Henry Maine, F. D. Ritchie, R. H. Towney, G. M. Trevelyan, and A. N. Whitehead, among others.[77] He found himself "in closest agreement with the idealists Rousseau, Kant, Green, and Bosanquet, with Aristotle and Plato in the background, of course, as the first sources of wisdom."[78] In these early days of his philosophical career, Polanyi was already grappling with the themes that he developed in *Personal Knowledge* and *The Tacit Dimension*. His notes describe what he would later call "tacit knowledge": "It is one of the most striking abilities of the human mind that it can pursue a consistent course of action without being aware of the guiding principles involved."[79] As examples he listed elements of grammar, maxims of scientific method, rules of arts and crafts, and hunches that guide discovery. Polanyi also asserted the primacy of belief over doubt: "No skeptical Columbus has ever persevered on his way to the Indies."[80] He was also beginning to analyze knowledge in terms of Gestalt psychology, which showed that the perception of wholes "can be destroyed by persistent emphasis on the constituent elements, which releases them from the band which the mind instinctively clasps around them."[81]

In January 1942, Polanyi made several outlines and drafted four chapters for a book tentatively entitled *Science, Welfare and the State* that would use understanding of the scientific life as a model for a liberal society.[82] In a later essay entitled "The City of Science," Polanyi listed six achievements of scientific truth: science upholds standards, inspires the devotion of geniuses, commands the admiration of students, has universal and permanent convincing power, gains public confidence and interest, and produces useful knowledge and reasoning techniques.[83] On February 16, 1942, Polanyi started another outline for a considerably revised form of the book, which he now entitled *The Structure of Freedom*. In this manuscript, Polanyi sought to integrate his analysis of market economics with his view of the structure of science.

Polanyi took stock of himself at age 50 in a letter to his sister Mausi. On the one hand, he saw himself as quite fat, his face bloated, with "small eyes sunk behind beady dark rims."[84] He felt that young ladies looked right through him, as if he had turned into an Invisible Man. On the other hand, he now could sleep well most nights. He was content with six or seven hours of sleep, and his daily working capacity had increased to between 12 and 15 hours. His anxiety and depression had diminished and he was pleased with the direction his work had taken.

The fate of his sister Sofie and her family was never far from Polanyi's thoughts. For three years Sofie's husband, Egon Szecsi, had been held a prisoner in German concentration camps. Despite the Polanyis' strenuous efforts to free them, Sofie and her son, Karl, were trapped in Austria by the Nazi occupation. Fortunately, the two daughters escaped. Maria, the elder, had earlier settled in Chicago; the younger daughter, Edith, was allowed to come to London when the authorities learned she had tuberculosis. There had been a short-lived period of hope in the spring of 1940, when Sofie expected Egon to be released any day. There was no further word for six months until October, when Egon's suitcase was sent home with his clothes, but no message. It was not until July that Sofie learned Egon had died in Dachau on April 1, 1941.

Polanyi wrote consoling letters to Edith and Maria, but his feelings were more bitter than anything he told them. "To kill this poor little man like this... is more cruel and stupid than anything I have heard of."[85] He expressed outrage to Mausi: "The fact of [Egon's] Calvary and death remains to me the focus of all my most bitter thoughts . . . a certain race of thugs will have to be exterminated."[86] To Jászi he expressed the hope that "We may be able to destroy his murderers before long."[87] At about the same time they learned of Egon's death, the family heard that Sofie had been sent to Poland. Polanyi suggested to Maria that she ask his old colleague, Karl Bonhoeffer, to intervene on Sofie's behalf, but he was unable to win her release.[88] In January 1942, Polanyi was somewhat consoled when he heard from Ilona the news that there was a "fine and radiant spirit" in the Jewish community of the Polish camp where Sofie was confined, though he could scarcely believe the report that his sister was "very happy" there.[89] The family learned that Sofie was planning to marry a Jewish intellectual who had joined her in exile in Poland. In February, Edith, who was living in London, received a Red Cross telegram from her mother that said she was "gesund und wohlauf" ("alive and all right").[90] In another Red Cross message dated July 10, 1942, Sofie asked her relatives to write more often. The telegram did not arrive until January 1943.[91] Nothing more was ever heard of Sofie and her son.

George Polanyi came from Oxford to Manchester in March 1942 to take part in a conference of the Union of University Liberals. Since the film had failed to attract a following, George proposed his father now write a substantial treatise on the theory of unemployment. Polanyi began by talking over his plans with his favorite advisors in economics, John Hicks of the University of Manchester, J. R. and Barbara Hammond of the *Guardian*, and John Jewkes. Jewkes was then working with the war cabinet in London and appreciated Polanyi's willingness to travel by train despite continued German bombing. By the end of July, Polanyi had to set this work aside for about a year and a half because of his preoccupation with his manuscript on "Science and the State."

When Polanyi was finished with both his June classes and his writing, he set off for North Wales with an armful of books by de Tocqueville, M. Perkins, A. E. G. Robinson, Dicey, Gardiner, and K. A. Meyer.[92] In evaluating the conduct of the war, Polanyi judged that the English "will win if there is a chance, and if there is none, they will have saved their souls."[93] He was very impressed by the calmness and determination that the British exhibited during the war. During the night of October 23, 1942, he heard how the British victory at the battle of El Alamein saved Egypt from a German invasion. At breakfast at the university next morning, there were no shouts of joy, only the usual discussion of the weather. It was not until the end of the meal that somebody first mentioned the battle.[94]

In the spring of 1943, Polanyi began to suffer from inflamed vocal chords. Six weeks at the Oakeley Arms during the summer gave him some relief, but when Polanyi returned to his chemistry lectures during the fall term, the inflammation worsened and his voice began to be affected. His physician ordered him to give his voice complete rest. Forced to give up his lectures, he resorted to communication by writing notes, which led people to raise their voices. He finally put a sign on his desk that read: "I am not deaf."

Life in Manchester involved too much activity and too many temptations to talk. Polanyi returned to the Oakeley Arms for a prolonged stay, interrupted by a short trip back to Manchester when George was on leave from the Royal Air Force for a week. He enjoyed concentrating on his writing and found he rather liked his muteness, although the anxiety of not getting better began to weigh on him. During the dark winter days, he followed a simple routine, working through the morning, then setting out for an afternoon walk. In the evening, he would have a drink or two in the bar with the other guests, then return to his room to read and write.[95] During his recuperation, he wrote a manuscript entitled "Full Employment in Theory and Practice."[96] He wrote with a sense of "urgent obligation.... my main point is to say my say, so that at least nobody will be able to reproach me if the world goes down in the next economic collapse."[97]

By the spring of 1943, Polanyi had written fifty pieces in defense of the liberal tradition: five of them published, fifteen given as lectures, five incomplete manuscripts for books, and twenty-five fragments and short essays. He continued to promote the film and wrote a synopsis of it for a book on economics. He also kept up with his lecture course on physical chemistry and judged that he had kept up his "scientific work at a fair (if not altogether undepressed) level."[98] Polanyi thought he was ready to bring together all his ideas on "Science and Society" in one "magnum opus to deal with science and everything else in the world."[99] His goal was to lay down the main principles of a "'dedicated society,' i.e. a society constituted for the cultivation of its beliefs, embodied in tradition."[100] Polanyi spent the summer of 1943 on this project, "Science, Ideals and Society,"[101] and continued on into the school year, writing in his spare time every night and on weekends.

Although Polanyi was prohibited from working on top-secret projects, the Manchester laboratory was given some research to do. Many efforts had been made, principally in Germany and the Soviet Union, to produce synthetic rubber by polymerizing various types of unsaturated hydrocarbon molecules into long chains. Natural rubber consists of long chains of isoprene, a compound that is hard to synthesize in the laboratory. One attempt at synthetic chain production was based on the readily available isobutene, which yields butyl rubber, later found to be a superior product for making automobile inner tubes. By 1940, scientists knew that the polymerization proceeds very fast with a reagent that opened the double bonds in the isobutene molecule to link units together in a linear sequence; when the reagent is mixed rapidly with isobutene, the isobutene becomes completely polymerized in only a second or two. The resulting rubber could not be vulcanized by the usual process of combining it with sulfur at high temperatures in order to make the material elastic and eliminate its natural stickiness. To be able to vulcanize butyl rubber, 1 percent or 2 percent isoprene had to be mixed in with the isobutene.

The British had not been interested in synthetic rubber as long as they controlled Malaysia and its rich resources of natural rubber. When the Japanese overran Malaysia early in 1942, Britain turned to the United States for synthetic substitutes as well as initiating production at home. Imperial Chemical Industries at nearby Billingham was trying to produce butyl rubber, but they had problems controlling the rate of this very fast reaction and the length of the chain produced. The company sought to improve their production by funding some basic research. Polanyi's group seemed just the right one to study the reaction. A. G. Evans was able to take some time from his war work to try a few experiments.

One of the obvious features of the polymerization reaction that would affect its rate was "steric hindrance" between any two elements trying to join together. Every molecule has its own characteristic shape (or possible range of shapes under different conditions). In some chemical reactions, the shape of the molecules involved can get in the way of new bonds being formed—if the complex molecules collide at the wrong angle with each other, they will simply bounce away and not react. A. G. Evans and Polanyi had studied this phenomenon in their work on bond-energies. They first made a calculation of compressive forces for the tertiary form of butyl chloride compared to the case of butyl iodide, in which an iodine atom takes the place of the chlorine atom; to displace the chlorine atom, the iodine atom must bypass three carbon-hydrogen groups without bouncing away from the radical. Evans and Polanyi made a model with accurately proportional radii for the given forces of attraction (covalent, ionic, or Van der Waals), and estimated the compression energy involved in the reaction (1942a). In their study of how isobutene molecules are rearranged to form long chains of butyl rubber, Evans and Polanyi found two different paths that the reaction might follow (1943j). In one, there was no steric hindrance to the formation of carbon-carbon bonds. However, the overall heat of formation of the chain turned out to have a more stable value than for the other path, in which there was some steric hindrance. The physical model they had constructed showed that the whole system fit together very snugly.

As this research progressed, Polanyi was introduced to Peter Plesch, the son of his friend Janos Plesch, a Hungarian doctor who had taken care of the family in Berlin. Polanyi arranged to have him released from his industrial assignment and obtained an assistantship for him at Manchester. Polanyi asked Plesch, a Cambridge chemist, and Hank Skinner, an Oxford physicist, to tackle the problem of the runaway reaction. Neither had dealt with the organic chemistry of polymers. Skinner had been in the quantitative field of spectroscopy and commented that even after 30-odd years, the uncertainties of polymerization made it still an intuitive art.[102] Polanyi evidently hoped that the odd couple would bring fresh eyes and creative suggestions to bear on the question of how to control the rate of polymerization.

Plesch and Skinner conducted experiments with isobutene, using boron trifluoride as reagent and working under conditions designed to maintain high purity. Each time they started up the reaction, they were dismayed to see it come to an early stop before the isobutene was all polymerized—one could watch the solid rubber polymer emerge quickly but then grow more slowly. One day, after the reaction slowed down, J. H. Allen opened the vessel too soon, contaminating the mixture with air, whereupon the reaction re-started and used up all the available isobutene. This surprising result galvanized the group. Plesch and Skinner began careful experiments on all the different components of air (nitrogen, oxygen, carbon dioxide, etc.) to determine which one had changed the course of the reaction. Evans had already had some ideas about the possibilities, and Plesch and Skinner with further help from D. Holden and M. A. Weinberger narrowed the possibilities down to the water vapor in the air. Only a tiny bit was needed. The first article dealing with polyisobutene was published in December 1943, when it looked as if the war might soon be won; there was little chance that the Manchester research could be done in time to help the war effort, but the basic work might prove useful later. Nevertheless, it was announced at the end of the article that a part of the research would not be published until after the war was over.

Just as Polanyi had found the war years a time for intensive reflection on social issues, so had his brother Karl. After many years of labor, Karl finally finished his analysis of the social, economic, and moral foundations of European civilization. Karl wrote Michael that *The Great Transformation* "is one of the most stubbornly sustained arguments a born bore ever inflicted upon the race, and, perhaps for that reason I suspect it is my true portrait."[103] Polanyi was happy that his brother had completed the work, although he did not find it to his liking:

> Your own destiny has most fully, I should say romantically, fulfilled itself by this work. It gives expression to the thought and passion of a lifetime.... secures you at one stroke the position which is due to you.... The book is so intensely personal ... that clearly no-one would have thought it or written it, had you not done so.... And this brings up another curious thread of destiny. Here am I, connected with you by ties which are close and vital beyond, far beyond the perception of either of us; yet I doubt whether there is anybody more clearly born and bred, more thoroughly destined, to disagree with that particular, unique function which you have so dramatically fulfilled now.

He concluded that he would withhold further comments so as not to raise "intimate sentiments of a harassing kind" until he sees if there is something the public critics leave out.[104] To Mausi, Michael wrote, "I need not any more be a thorn in his side, undermining his self-confidence by my criticism. He has called the broad public into the lists and I can keep my views to myself in the future."[105] A month later, Michael wrote Karl about the tensions between them: "There is a good deal to clarify in this world, and some of it is given to you and me to elucidate at the expense of our peace of mind. Considering the way our insides must be torn from time to time we cannot wonder or complain if our mutual relations are strained as well."[106]

In January 1944, the Polanyis received word that John was coming home from Canada on a warship and was expected to arrive shortly. John, now a lanky 15-year-old, telephoned from Liverpool to say that he had arrived safely. The voyage from New York on an aircraft carrier had been a rough one. The ship had gone through severe gales, and John was rather shaken.

A growth was removed from Polanyi's vocal chords in February and a speech training program taught him to speak "in a low tone through my nose, a method eminently suited to increase my social prestige and economize my vocal chords at the same time."[107] While Polanyi was preoccupied with his own health, his young niece, Edith Szecsi, Sofie's daughter, was slowly dying of tuberculosis. The day before his operation, he attended her funeral. Polanyi's contact with this niece had been slight, but he had seen in her "the heavenly sweetness that Sofie possessed. We lose in her a token of that dear and eternally mourned being."[108]

On March 16, 1944, Polanyi was elected a Fellow of the Royal Society. Michael and Magda were both pleased and touched by the unexpected honor and by the many congratulatory letters from friends and colleagues which followed. Polanyi told Hugh O'Neill how much the honor meant to him: "I have been a vagabond all my life and the recognition by such a venerable body as the Royal Society does not really fit me. Perhaps I need it the more. Maybe this makes me also particularly happy in company of really settled people like yourself and Barbara, whose roots go deep into the soil of which I know only from books."[109]

The citation that appeared in the Royal Society's *Candidates Book* for 1944 catalogued Polanyi's work on the adsorption of gases on solids, the fibrous structure of cellulose, the rotating crystal method of analysis, the theory of the plasticity and strength of metal crystals, and reaction kinetics, especially the work accomplished in the dilute flame experiments. "Polanyi made the first theoretical calculation of an activation energy and with many co-workers has extended the theoretical basis of the transition state method of calculation of reaction rates."[110]

With George in training near Sheffield and free to come home on week-ends, the whole family was reunited. John had suffered an inflammation of the sinus before leaving Canada and fell ill again almost as soon as he arrived. The diagnosis was mastoiditis; an operation and a long stay in the hospital fol-lowed. John did not fully recover until the end of April, when he and his mother spent two weeks at the Oakeley Arms enjoying the beauty of spring.

That same month, Polanyi was invited to London to spend an evening with social theorist Karl Mannheim and his wife and collaborator, Julia. Two years younger than Polanyi, Mannheim was another exiled Hungarian. Like Polanyi, Mannheim had left his native Budapest for Germany when Horthy came to power, and then in 1933, he, too, became a refugee in England. Polanyi and Mannheim had known each other from university and from the Sunday-afternoon discussions held at Balazs's home in Budapest. Polanyi had kept up with Mannheim's career in Heidelberg and Frankfurt in the 1920s and later at the London School of Economics through conversations with Emil Lederer, an economist and the husband of Emmy Seidler, one of Polanyi's distant relatives. Polanyi had discussed Mannheim's work on social plan-ning and reform within the liberal state with Oscar Jászi only a few months before.[111]

Mannheim had just read two of Polanyi's essays, "The Autonomy of Science" and "The English and the Continent." As editor of the *International Library of Sociology and Social Reconstruction*, he wanted to publish a volume of Polanyi's essays in that series on the theme of "The Autonomy of Science." Polanyi agreed to write a new essay to introduce the collection.[112] He then wrote Mannheim to clear up "one or two personal points" raised in that "most stimulating evening":

> Your questions have made me think about my past and this is what I find. As a boy and young man I was a materialist and an eager disciple of H. G. Wells. My religious interests were awakened by reading *The Brothers Karamazov* in 1913. I was then 22. For the fol-lowing 10 years I was continually striving for religious understanding and for a time, particularly from 1915 to 1920, I was a completely converted Christian on the lines of Tolstoy's confession of faith.

> Towards the middle 'twenties my religious convictions began to weaken and it was only in the last 5 years that I have returned to them with any degree of devotion. My faith in God has never failed me entirely since 1913 but my faith in the divinity of Christ (for example) has been with me only for rare moments.

> As regards Marxism, etc., my earliest writing on politics (on European peace, 1917), was already an attack on the materialist conception of history. During the Communist Regime in Hungary

I dissented violently from the measures taken by the Government, e.g. I was the only male member of the University who refused to volunteer for the Red Army and was threatened in various ways in consequence.[113]

Polanyi objected to the way Mannheim used the phrase, "planning for freedom"; Polanyi thought that "planning" suggested central control, which he despised. He also criticized Mannheim's views on the limits of historical knowledge: "You seem inclined to consider moral judgments on history as ludicrous, believing apparently that thought is not merely conditioned, but determined by a social or technical situation."[114]

Michael sent a copy of his letter to Magda, who was vacationing in North Wales with John. She acknowledged that he had given "a true picture of your road until now," but was anxious that he had written to Mannheim "about such intimate matters": "As usual—I am afraid that you will be misunderstood and fear that you have wasted all that candour on a conceited fool. I hope I am wrong." But Mannheim responded warmly to Polanyi's self-disclosure. "My dear Misi," Mannheim wrote a few days later, "I am most grateful for your letter which more than anything shows that our meeting meant to you too, more than a conventional talk. I, also, had the feeling that, after a long time, I had an opportunity of exchanging ideas on a level of frankness which I have missed. This is, perhaps, the excuse for my having put personal questions which one usually avoids."

Despite the convictions which made them kindred spirits, Mannheim felt that Polanyi's social analysis was still too dependent on "emotional decisions, where still a further confrontation of evidence and argument is feasible."[115] Polanyi responded that evidence cannot either kill or create our fundamental beliefs. "We must choose in such a fashion that what we instinctively love in life, what we spontaneously admire, what we irresistibly aspire to, should make sense in the light of our convictions."[116] In tracing the nature of such personal commitments, Polanyi found them rooted in what he later came to speak of as the tacit dimension: "there remains fixed a deeper secret pivot of faith round which we keep revolving; we follow throughout a code of duty, of which we are so unconscious that we could not formulate one single syllable of it."

Polanyi's faith was put to the test by his younger son's brush with death. In August, John began to suffer from insistent pain in his right thigh caused by osteomyelitis of the femur. His health became a source of great anxiety for his parents. John was saved from death by the release of penicillin for civilian use.[117] At the end of the ordeal, John spent another period of recuperation at the Oakeley Arms, this time with his father.

Anxiety about John's condition did not keep Polanyi from pursuing his work in social and economic analysis. Earlier that year, after having written about 80,000 words, Polanyi had accepted John Jewkes's criticism that his economics project was too vast. He selected about a hundred pages of the material to use in a second draft of "Full Employment in Theory and Practice."[118] At the beginning of November 1944, Polanyi finished the final draft: "So at last I am free of any major intellectual care."[119] In the preface to *Full Employment and Free Trade*, Polanyi reaffirmed his sense of urgency that Keynesian ideas be put to use in time to avoid the next depression. Keynes himself was a creative writer of great speculative intelligence and sparkle, not a system maker. It has been said that no systematic account of Keynesian theory could possibly fit Keynes. Polanyi's focus on one practical point of controlling the volume and circulation of money provided a valuable method and outlook in economics. While he referred to his economics film in a footnote, he did not propose more efforts of this kind—he had learned his lesson about the limits of film as a teaching tool. Soon after publication of the book Karl wrote to say that the work was "worth doing" and congratulated him on the way the book threw into relief the "general social and political viewpoint" of Keynes's theory. Nevertheless, Karl called Michael's book "the most damning indictment of a market economy I have ever read (in my specific definition as including competitive markets for labor and land)."[120]

At Karl Mannheim's suggestion, Polanyi was invited to the June 1945 meeting at St. Julian's as a guest of the Moot, a discussion group founded by the distinguished theologian Joseph H. Oldham; Polanyi once referred to it as the "secret enclave of J. H. Oldham and T. S. Eliot." At the meetings of the Moot, Oldham himself was clearly in charge, still vigorous at the age of 70; he corresponded with Polanyi regularly for almost two decades and made many suggestions about the development of the Gifford Lectures and *Personal Knowledge*.[121] Kathleen Bliss recalled how he "controlled the meetings with well-regulated tolerance, circulating from member to member on his stool, with his vast hearing aid on his knee."[122] In preparation for a weekend's discussion, he would investigate the subject "with infinite care," carrying on an extensive correspondence, talking with members informally, and overseeing the circulation of the papers to be discussed.

A former missionary to India, Oldham had a passionate interest in helping Christians to practice their faith in the modern world. A layman himself, he had been honored by the universities of Edinburgh (1931) and Oxford (1937) for his missionary work. The Moot had grown out of his experience in organizing the World Conference on Church, Community, and State, held at Oxford in 1937, which brought together existing ecumenical groups and gave birth to the World Council of Churches. Because of his hearing problems, Oldham preferred small groups to large gatherings, where the cross-talk was impossible for him to follow. When he brought together the assortment of theologians, philosophers, poets, and educators who became the Moot, his goal was to think about problems of society "in a Christian way."[123] Oldham was interested in private dialogue and mutual support rather than publications or joint declarations. A clear distinction was made between the regular members and special guests who were invited from time to time; the decision about membership was left to an election by the group.

Oldham had been impressed by Polanyi's article "The English and the Continent," and had published an abridged version in the *Christian Newsletter* in December 1943. Because of shortages caused by the war, Polanyi was asked, like the others, to bring along a little butter, sugar, and bacon and—if possible—a sheet. Oldham told Polanyi about some of the other members of The Moot: "Sir Walter Moberly, whom you know, Mr. T. S. Eliot, Mr. Middleton Murry, Professor Hodges of Reading, Professor John Baillie, Sir Hector Hetherington and a few others."[124] At the next meeting, June 23–26 at St. Julian's, south of London near Horsham, Sussex, Professor Hodges was to present two papers on "the relation of Christians to a collective commonwealth, the coming of which he believes to be inevitable."[125] Polanyi told Eliot that he had found the meeting "most profitable."[126]

Oldham invited Polanyi to make a presentation at the December Moot. Polanyi agreed to discuss "The European Crisis," using one of the chapters from an unpublished manuscript.[127] Oldham also asked him and Mannheim to respond to a paper by Eliot, "Clerisy and Clerisies," which dealt with the duty of the intelligentsia to uphold and cultivate the heritage of civilization. Polanyi very much enjoyed the intellectual stimulation and the friendship he found in The Moot. "These things changed our lives," he wrote later.[128]

With *Full Employment and Free Trade* in the hands of his editor, Polanyi returned to the larger topic of how to preserve freedom in society. Although Hitler was near defeat early in the spring of 1945 and the power of the collectivist spirit was greatly weakened, Polanyi continued to explore his own vision of how a society preserves its traditions and yet encourages freedom and creativity. A BBC "Brain Trust" broadcast about the planning of science provided Polanyi the opportunity to debate with Bertrand Russell. To refute the claim that scientific research is generally inspired by social needs, Polanyi used the example of Einstein's development of the equation $e = mc^2$ in 1905 before any of its applications to nuclear physics were dreamt of.[129] Just seven months later, the annihilation of Hiroshima and Nagasaki revealed to the whole world how much energy could be released from nuclear reactions. For good or for ill, development of the atomic bomb showed how much could be accomplished by large teams of scientists working on behalf of the government.

Polanyi celebrated the surrender of Germany on May 7, 1945, by writing to Hugh O'Neill: "May I wish you a very happy V-E Day—without returns."[130] Polanyi wanted to thank all the British people, starting with Hugh and Barbara O'Neill, for what they had done for him and his family. He wrote that he and his sons would never forget the O'Neills' generous support. Although the death of Sofie and of others left enduring undercurrents of sorrow, Polanyi found much to be grateful for. Since he had not been able to do much war-related research, he had time to hammer out the fundamental ideas that would occupy him for the rest of his life.

With the danger of German invasion behind them, both John and George resumed the use of "Polanyi" as their surname. John, age 16, had fully recovered from his illness, and his parents greatly enjoyed his presence at home. At war's end, George was serving as a captain in counter-intelligence in Europe, pursuing his study of Russian language, and reading in his spare time. When George was released from military service, the Polanyis were reunited in Manchester. Michael wrote Mausi of those golden days. "For the moment we are forgetting even the Atomic Bomb and looking into the future once more with the eyes of confidence. These two boys are so full of life and kindness that we feel like pilgrims who after a life time's progress have reached their goal. For us the more serious business of life is now over."[131]

At Oxford, George changed his studies from history to Modern Greats, which consisted of studies in philosophy, politics, and economics. George specialized in philosophy. When Polanyi visited George at Oxford, he found him reading "like a man famished and ravenous for intellectual food, day and night...except for the rowing which keeps him fit."[132] When they were to-gether, the two of them "went on talking without pause about Plato, Leibniz, Tariffs, Monetary Theory, etc. etc. Great Happiness."

In the fall of 1945, Polanyi received an invitation to give the opening address to the Conference on Scientific Research and Industrial Planning held by the Division for the Social and International Relations of Science of the British Association for the Advancement of Science on December 7–8. Still thinking of the overwhelming prewar support of the planning of science by the Association of Scientific Workers and expecting another strong attack by the defenders of planning, he prepared a lecture entitled "The Social Message of Pure Science" (1945f). Polanyi described the movement calling for the planning of science as coupling disbelief in the human spirit with extravagant moral demands: "the chisel of scepticism driven by the hammer of social passion."

In November 1945, Polanyi's research group was finally able to disclose their finding that a co-catalyst was needed to keep the polymerization of isobutene going. Everyone involved in the wartime research had his name on the paper (1946a). In a note written in February 1946, and appended to a letter to *Nature* pointing out other similar cases, Polanyi reported that the reaction had been carried out at low temperature using titanium tetrachloride and a trace of water vapor (1946b). The reaction went on surprisingly fast at very low temperatures, which is counter-intuitive. On April 4 at a discussion meeting of the Institute of Mechanical Engineers in London, Polanyi's group suggested that the low temperature behavior, involving experiments between −30°C and −120°C, was explained by the fact that there was no hump to go over because the individual isobutene molecules approached each other in the correct geometry; the more random motion of the molecules at higher temperatures introduced steric hindrance to the reaction.

On May 14, Polanyi and some of the research group went overnight to Oxford to have a day's discussion on these problems with Hinshelwood's group. While the group knew how to find the train from Manchester to London, they were not sure which was the train for Oxford:

> The railways still showed many signs of the wartime removal of information of possible use to an enemy and it was ... very difficult to find out from which platform at London Road Station the appropriate train would leave.... Polanyi took charge after some early attempts failed.... [He said,] "We had better ask that railway man which platform it is. He's sure to know—he's very fat." This meant, presumably, that the person most likely to know would be a person of authority and not a low-level, hardworking porter. This would then correlate with bodily size.[133]

Whether or not Polanyi's reasoning was sound, the heavyset man was able to point the group in the right direction.

On June 19, 1946, the Polanyi group reported the results of further experiments. They cautiously called the needed extra catalyst "X" and made several tests with and without water (1946c). They found alternative co-catalysts besides water vapor, especially tertiary butyl alcohol. In addition they determined that cooling to liquid air temperature with careful attention to purity allowed the reactions to go to completion without any trace of a co-catalyst.

Polanyi sent a review copy of *Full Employment and Free Trade* to the Stolpers in September 1945, eager for advice, criticism, or comment. Toni replied in December that she had read the book once but, not being yet herself into the core of Keynes, she was unable to lose her uneasy feeling about quantifying the art of economics. By the next May, she and Gustav agreed that Polanyi had become "an economics expert instead of the brilliant amateur of ten years ago—an amateur, however, who approached the experts with gifts rather than with inferiorities."[134] Later she referred to Keynes's "illuminating contributions which you have presented so brilliantly and truly."[135] Toni Stolper put Polanyi in touch with Gottfried Haberler, an Austrian economist then teaching at Harvard, who was favorably impressed by the book. In the fall of 1946, Haberler requested that MacMillan reprint *Full Employment and Free Trade*, informing them that he was using it in his lectures; negotiations led to the publication of a U.S. edition in 1948, with a foreword by Haberler.

The University of Durham gave Polanyi a chance to consolidate his years of reflection on the liberal tradition when it invited him to give the 1946 Riddell Lectures, founded in 1928 in memory of Sir John Walter Buchanan-Riddell, Baronet, and given in alternate years. Polanyi was delighted with the chance to enter "the great struggle between the modern barbarians and their opponents upholding the ancient propositions to which we are dedicated."[136] In October 1945, he wrote to his friend Arthur Koestler[137] that he planned to incorporate in these lectures his "ultimate beliefs."[138]

Koestler had recently returned from Palestine and rented a cottage in the hills of North Wales at Blaenau Festiniog not many miles from Polanyi's favorite haunt at the Oakeley Arms in Tan-y-Bwlch. Polanyi came to the Oakeley Arms after Christmas to immerse himself in writing for the next seven weeks, with intermittent conversations with Koestler. He presented three lectures at the University of Durham in the first week of March, then published them as *Science, Faith and Society* (1946k). Polanyi ended his lectures by suggesting that growth in the power of our basic ideals, our spiritual heritage, comes from a deep source, "the same source which first gave men their society-forming knowledge of abiding things. How near that source is to God I shall not try to conjecture" (83). With the publication of the Riddell Lectures, Polanyi turned to what he now saw as his true vocation: "the pursuit of a new philosophy to meet the need of our age" (1975a, 1152). He wrote Mausi that the crisis of his life was over. After forty years of struggle, he had come at last to the point where his task was clear; it was now merely a matter of living to finish it.[139]

In the same month that Polanyi delivered the Riddell Lectures, George came to Manchester with Priscilla Sheppard, a married woman fourteen years older than he and the mother of two young boys. She was then three months pregnant with their child. Magda was understandably upset and seems never to have been completely reconciled to their union; years later, she was to describe George's relationship with Priscilla as the greatest tragedy in the family's history. Polanyi, always a gentleman, treated them courteously and escorted the young couple around the city. Without telling Magda, he provided the funds for Priscilla's divorce. He also did what he could to help George find a way to support his new family.

The baby, a girl, died three days after a premature birth. George and Priscilla were sustained by an intense love for each other, a love which endured through the years. After Priscilla obtained her divorce, they were married and received custody of Garth, the younger of the two boys from the previous marriage. With his new financial responsibilities, it was hard for George to complete his studies at Oxford. Michael reported to Mausi that George had "grown into a man over this affair" and had established his independence at last after years of "excessive dependence" on his parents' judgment.[140] After earning "golden opinions" in Oxford, he was being urged to embark on an academic career, but he had decided to shorten his course and look for a job as a journalist because he disliked "sitting on the fence of academic life" and wanted to "get cracking" with a job at the *Manchester Guardian* as soon as possible. Polanyi felt that "poor dear Magda was reviving again and all is set fair once more in our family." Later that year, he asked Mausi to congratulate the young couple: "Whatever warmth you can command to welcome her, however insincere, will be most useful in the public interest."[141] For some time, Polanyi helped support his son's new family, a situation made more trying because he felt that George and Priscilla lived beyond their means. Polanyi worried that George's wartime experiences may have "unbalanced his sense of reality." He shared his concerns with Mausi: "fortunately with John I feel no such apprehension.... There is so much legacy of excessive subjectivism in the family that I always feel inclined towards pessimism in these matters. I do not doubt that George will do very well in another 30 years or so, but that does not altogether reconcile me to the situation."[142]

Princeton University invited Polanyi to discuss the future of nuclear science as part of their Bicentenary Celebration in September 1946. He was also offered an honorary Doctor of Science degree to be given at a separate ceremony in October. The Rockefeller Foundation also offered him funds for an extensive trip across the United States. Polanyi wanted to survey American views on the general problems of scientific organization, make contact with American movements aiming at the "reestablishment of transcendent beliefs,"[143] and get a feel for American policy toward Marxism, Fascism, and the Soviet Union.[144] He also had many family members and friends to visit in the States.

Polanyi flew to New York on September 14. Mausi and Michael were anxious to see each other for the first time since the war began. She met him at the airport and took him to the Kings Crown at 520 West 116th Street. The hotel was adjacent to Columbia University and just a block or so away from his relatives: nephew Misi and his wife, Hilde Striker, at 600 West 115th Street, Sandor and Mausi next door at 604, and their daughter, Eva, and her husband, Hans Zeisel, at the end of the block.[145] Karl had lived in a rooming house in the same block until he moved into an apartment with the Hungarian political writer Nicholas Halasz at the opposite corner of the Columbia campus. Polanyi visited Mausi and the others on 115th Street each morning before he sat down to work on his speech for Princeton.

Before leaving New York, Polanyi visited the Rockefeller Foundation, which had arranged for air tickets and cash for his trip to Los Angeles, San Francisco, Chicago, Toronto, and Boston. After a week in New York, Polanyi took the two-hour train ride to Princeton to present "The Foundations of Freedom in Science" (1946g). He described several features of science important to its philosophy, noting Enrico Fermi's point that freedom in allowing the search by scientists for worthwhile problems ensures that all the holes in the edge of the web of science will be found and filled. The individual impulses of scientists in this process are primarily dedicated to the tradition of science, which is the heir of Greek intellectual honesty, Christian brotherhood, Roman legal reasoning, and the tradition of tolerance derived from Milton and Locke. These values form the dwelling place and provide the discipline for our romantic moral passions.

After his time at Princeton, Polanyi visited the California Institute of Technology, University of California at Berkeley, and Stanford. In Chicago, Polanyi spent an evening with Eva Zeisel, Adolf's son, Tom Polanyi, and his wife, Alice, Sofie's daughter, Maria, Mausi's son, George Striker, and his wife, Barbara. They all took turns signing a postcard of greeting to Mausi in New York. From Chicago there was a trip to Toronto for a day to visit Magda's brother, and four days in Boston to visit Harvard.

Polanyi returned to Princeton as a participant in one of the several honorary degree celebrations accompanying the Bicentenary; a total of 23 degrees were awarded on October 19. Among those honored were Niels Bohr, Emil Brunner, Reinhold Niebuhr, and Linus Pauling. The citation for Polanyi's doctorate called him "A physical chemist who has devised new tools to determine how fast atoms react; a veteran campaigner against those who would take from science the freedom she requires for the pursuit of truth."[146]

On his return to Manchester, Polanyi wrote an affectionate letter to Mausi: "Naturally there is rather a lot of work awaiting me here, but I am happy to be back and in a way I feel happy to be so happy."[147] The work awaiting him was to prepare four speeches to be given in four weeks. He delivered the first to the Economic Reform Club and Institute of London: "From Adam Smith to Keynes: Free Trade and Full Employment." The second address was a repetition of "The Struggle for Faith" delivered on Sunday, November 3, 1946, at the University Chapel at Aberdeen. The third speech was a university lecture in Manchester, entitled "Science: Observation and Belief," written at the request of the editors of *Humanitas* for their third issue (1947b). As in *Science, Faith and Society*, Polanyi argued that science goes beyond mere observation and depends on interpretations for which the scientist is held accountable; apart from such freely adopted scientific convictions it is impossible to justify the premises used or to give a formal proof for the claimed scientific result. To rely on pure empiricism would open the way to a Marxist interpretation because the uncertainties of empirical claims can be used to justify selectively those results consonant with the Marxist ideology. His fundamental philosophical point was that we must openly admit the role of belief and conscience in science rather than trying to hide the fiduciary dimension under the cover of formalisms.

The last speech, "The Foundations of Academic Freedom," was given the next day as the 1946 Lloyd Roberts Lecture at the University of Manchester (1947j). The freedom to promote happiness and the freedom to fulfill obligations fit together in a system of dynamic order. The dissemination of knowledge needs specialized academic opinion on the merits of the discoveries and abilities of scholars, their skill at evaluating hidden possibilities of mind and of making contact with spiritual reality. Although the Soviet Union was still challenging the liberal positions represented by these lectures, Polanyi saw grounds for hope (1947a). The task of bringing the Soviets into the company of civilized nations seemed less formidable because the "humanitarian adherents of politics by violence" had become less violent, the Soviets no longer demanded the immediate overthrow of capitalism, and the fascist forms of dictatorship had been defeated. Furthermore, Polanyi stated, the invention of the atomic bomb meant that equilibrium among fully armed states was no longer possible. Coexistence required adoption of the same principles of self-restraint and mutual trust that were the ideals of the Western nations.

Polanyi accepted an invitation from Friedrich von Hayek to a ten-day conference in Switzerland of economists and historians, starting April 1, 1947, for the "consolidation of liberal thought."[148] He longed "to get enough time to write a larger thing on philosophy." Hayek's conference was held at Mont Pélèrin, near Vevey on Lake Geneva, and, although the conference was not very satisfying to Polanyi, he had the good fortune to make a new and lasting friendship with Veronica Wedgwood, a historian and deputy editor of the weekly, *Time and Tide*, in which he had already published five articles.[149]

A few days later, on Easter Sunday, there was an overnight expedition to the town of Einsiedeln, east of Lucerne, for a visit to its early Baroque monastery. Wedgwood and Polanyi joined the other historians and economists along the path of the Easter procession, and at the point where worshipers were expected to kneel, they did, too. Although neither had been raised in a religious environment, the spirit of the ritual had touched them. Beyond mere courtesy to the believers around them, they had both felt moved to kneel.

In May 1947, Polanyi gave a talk at the invitation of the Manchester Grammar School on "What to Believe."[150] "The school children . . . have the advantage of not being surprised by anything, so one can seriously discuss with them the more heretical views without any false note of paradoxity."[151] He explained that we do not believe just on the basis of our senses, for a person brought up in a scientific culture would interpret their sense experience very differently from someone brought up to believe in witchcraft. What we get from our senses depends on what we understand and what we learn from our community, so there is always a social dimension to knowledge: "The knowledge of man relies decisively on his will to form a good society" (1947l, 10).

On May 23, 1947, Sir William Hamilton Fife, vice chancellor of the University of Aberdeen, invited Polanyi to give the next series of Gifford

Lectures. The opportunity for his wider piece of work in philosophy was suddenly at hand. Sensing that preparation for the lectures would require many months of time free from teaching and research, he asked the vice-chancellor at Manchester, Sir John Stopford, for a two-year leave of absence from the Chemistry Department. Polanyi then accepted the invitation to give the lectures, specifying two series of ten lectures each to be delivered in the fall of 1949.

Polanyi's proposal for a leave of absence meant that the Chemistry Department would probably not be able to hire someone of his stature to chair the physical chemistry department during his time away from the university. However, the vice-chancellor had already thought about the possibility of a permanent change in position for the university's "Erasmian man."[152] Stopford was well aware of Polanyi's interest in social science and philosophy, and he had become increasingly worried that Polanyi might be lured away to an American university. John Jewkes, Polanyi's friend in the Faculty of Economics and Social Studies, told Stopford that he would be delighted to have Polanyi in his department. Stopford observed in reply that the University of Manchester could put up with a number of high-flying balloons. When Stopford asked what Polanyi's title should be, Jewkes replied that it did not matter much—calling him Professor of Social Studies would allow him to do anything he liked. At that time Jewkes did not anticipate Polanyi's interest in philosophy, but supposed that he would continue his work on Keynesian ideas and patents.[153] Early in August, Stopford offered Polanyi the new assignment with few teaching duties, to take effect after the end of Lent term in March 1948. Stopford's proposal was ratified by the University Senate on November 11.

As he prepared to change from the sciences to the humanities, Polanyi wound down his work in the laboratory. The alternation of Polanyi's sharp-witted presence and complete absence in the laboratory led one research student to suggest "a change in the thesis acknowledgement from 'The author thanks Professor M. Polanyi FRS for his continual interest and advice' to 'strictly quantized interest and advice.'"[154] Polanyi, Evans, and Meadows published a one-page report on the efficacy of acetic acid as co-catalyst for the polymerization of isobutene (1947i). Polanyi reviewed the team's work on polymerization in a lecture given back in Berlin at the Technische Hochschule on December 2, 1947. For the next few years, A. G. Evans, Peter Plesch, and others continued the work, developing more evidence on co-catalysts, especially at low temperature, with some attention to other polymerizations.

In late November 1947, Polanyi embarked on a long-anticipated scientific trip to Berlin. It was his first visit to the Continent since the outbreak of the war. Polanyi consulted with people at the Kaiser Wilhelm Institute for Physical Chemistry on their new research program, meeting especially with the director, Hartmut Kallmann; Polanyi had written a letter on his behalf in

1946 when the occupying authorities were withholding permission for scientific research. He also met with British, American, and Russian authorities overseeing the German universities. Polanyi then lectured on polymerization at low temperatures at the T. H. Charlottenburg (1948a) and at Harnack House, the scene of so many pleasant memories from the 1930s. His schedule gave him time to visit with Karl Bonhoeffer and his former technician, Kurt Hauschild. Finally, for old time's sake, he visited the family's former home in Lichterfelde and the lot on Waltraudstrasse where the house they built had been destroyed by bombing.

For the Berlin newspaper *Die Welt*, Polanyi wrote "Aus der Welt der Wissenschaft," an essay on the current state of science. He expressed disappointment that so little research was being carried on—there seemed to be very little scientific passion left. Although there were a large number of publications in social science and philosophy, their scientific journals languished.[155] Polanyi noted the physical and political ruins left by the war: "I have just returned from Berlin where the rats are having a grand time under rubble, while the occupying powers of the two opposing sectors are playing at Red Indians around the Brandenburger Tor."[156] The visit sharpened his desire to understand the roots of the war: "I am glad I went here, for it gave me some important notions about Europe's disaster which must be our main concern for the next hundred years or more. It is the central problem, and marks the central task of the coming phase of humanity."[157]

Upon his return from the ruins of Berlin, Michael and Magda moved into a small and comfortable house at 10 Gilbert Road in Hale, a pleasant suburb twenty miles south of Manchester. Polanyi looked forward to being near the Jewkes, working in the garden, and walking through the village and the countryside. The increased distance from Manchester's academic and social life suited Michael more than Magda because his philosophical research kept him occupied. As Polanyi began to work on his lectures, he felt that the task would be "hopeless" unless he "put everything else aside."[158] To remedy some of his deficiencies as a philosopher, he began to study some modern logic. Using Tarski's *Introduction to Logic* (he had already read Russell and Carnap), he came to grips with Gödel's demonstration that no formal system powerful enough to deal with the question of truth could be proven to be consistent with itself. Polanyi drew the conclusion that every logical proof must ultimately have to rely on intuition.[159]

The Polanyis vacationed for a week with the Jewkes family in the Lake District. Polanyi then settled down by himself at the Oakeley Arms to make his first survey of the task he had set himself. Arthur Koestler lived nearby, and Polanyi found himself "more and more at home" with him.[160] At the Oakeley Arms, he began to work out the epistemology of personal knowledge: "My whole philosophy is built on the emphasis on discretionary factors permeating all our most securely accepted knowledge."[161] The desire to commit ourselves in the hope of achieving contact with reality is, he said, "the universal principle of faith beyond evidence, of love beyond desert, of gratuitously given confidence which the Gospels enjoin." As Polanyi wrestled with the implications of his own view, he realized that two years would not be long enough for him to prepare the lectures, so they were postponed until the spring of 1950.

While he was in North Wales, Polanyi explored the thought of Descartes, Hume, and Kant. Kant was a delight: "To have lived as a scholar and missed Kant would be like visiting Egypt and missing the Pyramids."[162] "I just read the *Prolegomena* and *The Critique of Pure Reason* for the first time and with enormous enthusiasm. Only the title today should be *Wahrheit und Dichtung* [*Truth and Fiction*]. After all, most of it is wrong; but what a gigantic concept!"[163] Polanyi also found time for Veronica Wedgwood's new book and reported to her: "I have just started reading your *Thirty Years War*. Very important for keeping in mind that human affairs have always been in a hopeless mess."[164]

In September, Polanyi and Magda spent nearly two weeks in the Koestlers' cottage at Bwlch Ocyn. Polanyi filled three notebooks with ideas about how his philosophy might "restore the whole damaged system of thought."[165] In thanking Koestler for his hospitality, he remarked, "I did as much work as in two months in Manchester and accumulated enough health to pay the cost of six months' living."[166] Despite the progress he had made, Polanyi still felt anxious about his new task and role: "To lay down at my age my personality as a scientist (or my impersonation of a scientist) does leave you for a moment a bit naked."[167] When Veronica Wedgwood requested comments on the Mont Pélèrin meeting on behalf of *Time and Tide*, Polanyi replied that he must not write anything other than his lectures: "I must try to think: why is a cow? and such like fundamental problems for my magnum opus. Having once found out everything about everything I shall be only too glad to give some details to your readers on this subject."[168]

Turning his notes into a finished product was difficult. Polanyi wrote to Mausi that his first draft for the Lectures "looks rather hopeless."[169] Two months later he told his sister he had just started to write on the growth of thought in society (1941e), which he planned "to be my Gifford Lectures in 1950"—this was the "little tail which was to wag a big dog."[170] At the end of 1948, he wrote Toni that the "Theory of Convictions" was to form the first series of lectures, to be given in the Lent term, 1950. Preparing these lectures was a terrible struggle. They absorbed all his energy and prevented a new visit to the United States. "Sometimes I am uncertain even of my mental balance."[171] He was very grateful for Magda's steady support for the project. Early in 1948, Polanyi again journeyed to the Koestlers' cottage in Wales with John and two of his friends. Polanyi pursued his lecture preparations while the boys studied for their upcoming examinations. Polanyi failed in his efforts to write the beginning of the lectures. Even though the boys kept out of the way and left him to his work, Polanyi felt he was spoiling their vacation. He was also concerned with the as yet undefined teaching responsibilities that would accompany his new position. Polanyi returned to Manchester a few days early and left the boys alone in the cottage until the beginning of the spring term.

Shortly after this vacation, Polanyi received a disturbing report that cast doubts on John's basic ability in science. On the strength of this report, Michael and Magda thought that "John will not be very successful in his profession."[172] For reasons that are now unclear, neither they nor John's teachers recognized at that time the talent that would surpass his father's accomplishments in chemistry and earn him a share in the Nobel Prize for Chemistry in 1986 (there must be a law of human nature such that for every Nobel Prize winner, there is at least one anecdote about a shortsighted professor who thought that the student was hopelessly inept). Michael and Magda's pessimism apparently lasted until John graduated from the University of Manchester and started to work on his doctorate under M. G. Evans, who was then chair of the Chemistry Department. For his dissertation, John studied a problem in pyrolysis, the breaking up of organic compounds at very high temperatures, a topic related to his father's contributions in the field of reaction kinetics.

Polanyi started his last series of chemistry lectures in the spring of 1948 with the announcement of his coming shift from Physical Chemistry to Social Studies. While it may have been a surprise to the students, his colleagues had seen the shift developing. When Michael Swarc asked Polanyi why he was giving up chemistry, he replied that at age 57 he had contributed as much as he could to that field but now had something worthwhile to contribute in other areas.[173] In 1945, fifteen years after its resurrection via quantum mechanics, Polanyi's multilayer theory of adsorption had finally come into its own through the collection of new data and a greatly expanded thermodynamic analysis that employed a graphical representation of energies, entropies, and detailed formulations of statistical mechanics. Stephen Brunauer gave an extended account of Polanyi's theory and judged that it was "eminently successful in accounting for the temperature dependence of physical adsorption....[It] applies to both unimolecular and multimolecular adsorption...the only theory...that can handle quantitatively adsorption on a strongly heterogeneous surface."[174] On the other hand, he said, the theory is limited in not attempting to formulate an isotherm equation. Polanyi's work has been subsumed into that done by Frenkel, Halsey, and Hill.[175] D. D. Eley in his obituary account of Polanyi's successes in chemistry reported some of the ongoing work.[176]

As his career in chemistry drew to a close, Polanyi had good reasons to feel satisfied with his long search for a fundamental theory of chemical reaction rates. He had started in Karlsruhe by studying molecular collision rates, the velocity constant and the equilibrium constant, the initial and final states of a reacting system, and the energy needed to activate a reaction, all within the framework of the statistical mechanics of gases. In Berlin, he had pursued the notion of the potential energy hump and the transition state at the top of the hump, and had worked with London and Eyring to calculate contour-line potential diagrams. With Wigner, he had produced a statistical theory of the transition state that allowed the calculation of the rate of passage across it, and with Evans he had developed this theory in parallel to the work of Eyring's group in Princeton. The electron-switch theory ("harpooning") was shown to have much explanatory power along with its ease of calculation for reactions with ions. Polanyi had made definite progress toward the goal of understanding the fundamental nature of chemical reactions.

With the benefit of hindsight, one might place some black marks on Polanyi's scientific record. In his attachment to a non-existent energy-transport mechanism, he obscured some of his own most original work in measuring reaction rates. Some of his suggestions were naive and lacked mathematical sophistication. His record is dotted with near misses: coming close to unraveling the full structure of cellulose, almost discovering (with Wigner) the indeterminate behavior of quantum phenomena prior to Heisenberg, anticipating London's understanding of dipoles, and failing to press forward with his findings on the nature of organic reactivity. He was also slow to recognize that he held the key to understanding the paradox of crystal strength and edge dislocations. He never dominated one area of research as did Langmuir, Eyring, Wigner, London, Calvin, or his own son, John. Polanyi did not break free from the pack, placing his name in the forefront of public consciousness, as did scientists like Einstein, Heisenberg, Nernst, Haber, or Planck. He was not drawn into the circle of bomb scientists or decoders who shared an extraordinary experience of big science during and after the World War II.[177] The very qualities that make him so interesting as a humanist—his intuition, his willingness to explore a broad variety of disciplines, his self-confident intelligence, his sense of being called to bring European civilization back to its senses—may have robbed him of the intense focus and lifelong concentration necessary to enter the highest echelons of science. Some say that the strongest force known to scientists is jealousy; Polanyi may simply have been too diffident about his own work to shoulder his way into the company of the greats.

Isaiah Berlin summed up the case against Polanyi's career change: "These Hungarians are strange ... here is a great scientist giving up the Nobel to write mediocre works of philosophy."[178] For those who knew Polanyi and worked with him in physical chemistry, a critical focus on what he might have done differently presents an altogether too negative picture of the man. Polanyi made seminal contributions to a wide number of different fields and left others to gather the harvest.[179] His work on atomic reactions, backed up by the sodium flame experiments, was the kind of deep, original, and fruitful research for which the Nobel Prize is often awarded. As Polanyi made the turn from the physical sciences to the humanities, he could look back on his accomplishments with a great deal of pride. Nevertheless, his own judgment was that, in time, the work he had begun to do in philosophy would far outweigh his contributions to physical chemistry.

8

Personal Knowledge:
1948–1959

The time for the final goodbye to physical chemistry was approaching. By the end of Lent term, March 18, 1948, Polanyi had already taken up an office in the Faculty of Economics and Social Studies. The Chemistry Department gave him a joyful farewell party on March 20. Polanyi's first impression of his new department was that it was lively and energetic. There were four professors and about twenty members of the junior staff, all of whom met twice a week for conferences, which Polanyi found "quite a strain to attend and digest."[1] Polanyi did not intend to shape himself to the mold of Economics and Social Studies: "I am taking a rather high-handed attitude and consider myself a research professor until proof of the contrary."[2] Although he felt unqualified to teach any part of the subjects offered by the department—and therefore anticipated that he would not be called on to do so—he was asked to lecture in the fall term on "Problems of Planning" and conduct a few informal seminars. "Even a great-hearted university like Manchester demands its pound of flesh."[3]

Polanyi dedicated the summer of 1948 to preparation of his economics lectures and a collection of essays, *The Logic of Liberty*. At the end of the summer, when Polanyi felt he was getting badly bogged down again, he and Magda went on a vacation to Arles and Avignon in Southern France. It was just what they needed. "Basking in the sunshine of Provence, Manchester seems... remote," Polanyi wrote in a postcard to Olive Davies. "It is only a week that we left but here one loses oneself in the vestiges of twenty centuries."[4]

Polanyi was still on vacation when his talk, "Ought Science Be Planned? The Case for Individualism," was broadcast by the BBC on September 1.[5] Polanyi finished preparing an economics lecture related to the theme of the book, "Profits and Private Enterprise," which was given in London after his return to Manchester (1948h). That same month, Polanyi accepted the Alexander White Visiting Professorship for the spring term of 1950 at the University of Chicago; he planned to lecture on the topics he had explored in *The Logic of Liberty*. The book described the role of liberty in the growth of knowledge and in the maintenance of dynamic order in the economy: "A free society is not an Open Society, but one fully dedicated to a distinctive set of beliefs" (vii).

In October, Polanyi had a group of twenty or thirty Manchester students following his lectures on Social and Economic Theory. He dealt with the large questions, the area that later became the field of macroeconomics, but he did not provide much of the sort of detail that students were seeking[6]—not surprising from a man who tended to work up the details that had a bearing on his favorite proposals. Some of the material from the course appeared in "Planning and Spontaneous Order" (1948g). Within a month, Polanyi was plagued with exhaustion and insomnia. He attributed his health problems to the strain of lecturing in an area in which he was unqualified. In December, the university agreed to let him withdraw from teaching, and he plunged back into work on the Gifford Lectures, taking his theory of convictions as his starting-point.

In mid-May, Joseph Oldham had written Polanyi about the next meeting of his group, which would continue "our conversations about God, approached from the standpoint of modern atheism." By this time, the Moot seems to have formally disbanded, but Oldham continued to invite many of the old members along with interesting newcomers to weekend discussions following the traditional pattern. Hendrik Kraemer, the distinguished Dutch theologian, had been visiting Oldham and expressed "immense interest" in what he and his colleagues were doing, pointing out that contemporary doubts were quite different from "the traditional doubts about the existence of God."[7] The new atheism represented "serious attempts to organise life on the assumption that God does not exist." Oldham believed the only way to meet this challenge was for "Christians to discover what it means to build our lives on the faith that God does exist."

In his response to this invitation, Polanyi noted that he was becoming steadily more uneasy about the influence of Marxist thinking among Christians, though he doubted whether he would have anything to contribute to the discussion. "Our meeting leaves me increasingly with a feeling that I have no right to describe myself as a Christian. So perhaps I may play the part of the outsider in the discussion. But my dominant sentiment is really this: Whatever meeting you may call and invite me to, I shall certainly attend. I don't think the subject will make very much difference to the benefit which I will derive from such a meeting."[8]

Despite his reservations, Polanyi met with Oldham and the group in December. Their friendship had deepened over the years, primarily through correspondence.[9] Polanyi appreciated Oldham's views on fundamental issues and his concern for faithful participation in the crises of the times. The two men shared a commitment to the kind of rigorous examination of beliefs that nevertheless treated the act of faith with respect. It was Oldham who gave Polanyi his first book on theology, a work by John Oman,[10] the first specialist theologian whom Polanyi studied. It was probably through the Moot that Polanyi became acquainted with the theology of Paul Tillich and Reinhold Niebuhr.[11]

The weekends with Oldham and his group provided Polanyi not only with the rare, perhaps for him unique, opportunity for serious discussion in a community of religiously oriented scholars, but also with a new experience of prayer. Worship was part of the gatherings of Oldham's group; members regularly took turns in offering a brief prayer at the beginning and end of the day. Kathleen Bliss remembered these prayers as sometimes going very deep.[12] Polanyi was introduced to the Anglican Book of Common Prayer, which he subsequently carried in his breast pocket.[13]

Polanyi sent Oldham a five-page, single-spaced set of notes entitled "Forms of Atheism" in preparation for the weekend (1981). He began by stating his agreement with Père Henri de Lubac that "we need not concern ourselves with atheism that is merely verbal. There were always people who made fun of priests and doctors, and yet continued to fear the gods and take medicines. We are concerned with the convinced repudiator in modern times of God as manifested in the Bible, rejecting him in favour of other gods" (5). Polanyi expressed his sympathy with "the horror of religious fanaticism," which dates back to Lucretius and Democritus, a horror that remains "one of the most powerful forces opposing the acceptance of any theological authority based on revelation." Polanyi wrote, "I am, myself, very responsive to this kind of horror and never feel at my ease when told that religion *is* the blessed sacrament or that the decisive fact of Christianity is that 'the tomb was empty'" (5).

After this prologue, Polanyi explained his own standpoint on questions of faith. First, he rejected "doubt as a supreme guide, because it logically cannot justify the empiricism which it wishes to promote." He then criticized "all categorical forms of assertion" as "misleading (no matter whether they assert a certainty or a probability)":

Only the fiduciary mode, used in the first person "I believe this or that" can be self-consistently upheld. I am ready to claim universal validity for my beliefs, even though I recognise that such

commitment inevitably transcends evidence. I take this jump
trusting that God demands it of me and hoping that I may succeed
for reasons that pass my limited understanding. Such is the paradox
of faith: it demands that we do now what on further reflection must
seem unjustifiable.... My beliefs are surrenders, accepted to avoid
further delay which I believe unjustifiable.... I hold it to be fully
consistent with my belief in the transcendent origin of my beliefs that
I should be ever prepared for new intimations of doubt in respect to
them. (6)

Because "the number of questions we can ask about God...seems to me
greatly in excess of the range that is likely to possess meaning," Polanyi held
that "when we pray 'Thy will be done' we should offer to surrender to the will
of God all our specific beliefs, excepting only what is logically implied in this
act of surrender. In this sense I concur with much of the tendencies that find
expression in rationalist atheism of the kind I have put down to Athene" (7).
In his final analysis, he found that he could not rest easy with the "substitute
deity" of rationalism because of that "Christian love," which Eliot called "the
intolerable shirt of flame, which human power cannot remove" (13). Such
concern for the welfare of others would keep us from adopting "that indifference to human suffering at the price of which the mind of antiquity (from
Socrates to Marcus Aurelius) secured its serenity" (8).

Polanyi gave 1949 over to writing, concentrating mainly, but not exclusively,
on the Gifford Lectures. He spent four different periods at the Oakeley Arms,
a week beginning the first of February, three weeks in March to April, most of
September, and a week at the end of November. Once again he was grateful
for the uninterrupted peace of his favorite country inn. The work was often
discouraging. In February 1949, Polanyi told Mausi the task before him was
too much for him to carry out and that he needed to find a compromise. In
March, he reported to Karl that he was again up to his neck in logic and
mathematical philosophy, and that he had postponed the lecture dates once
more, this time until Autumn 1950 and Summer 1951. He felt at times that
he was "on the point of going down the drain";[14] when the work went well, he
felt he could see Mt. Ararat emerging from the flood. To his old friend Gyula
Hollo he wrote that he seemed to be back to square one: trying to get properly
started on his magnum opus, needing to write two volumes in 18 months, and
squandering his last years "on a supreme wild-goose chase."[15]

The complexity of Polanyi's vision engendered continuing delays. In
September 1949, he wrote the new vice-chancellor at Aberdeen, T. M. Taylor,
that he had two-thirds of the work complete. However, despite his confident
report of a few weeks before, he found he could not meet the latest schedule.
Now, he told Taylor, he would rather resign than put Aberdeen to the trouble

of another postponement. Polanyi explained that undoubtedly Aberdeen had expected him to lecture on past work, meaning the essays on the free society in *The Logic of Liberty* (heading for publication at long last). By contrast, he hoped to use the lectures to elucidate the fundamental implications of his beliefs. After two and a half years, he thought a draft might well be done by Christmas. It would then need to be reconsidered and recast—all the factual material (logic, mathematics, psychology, etc.) would need to be discussed with experts. Polanyi did not intend to rest until he could say, "This is as much as is required of me."[16] Because of the magnitude of what he wanted to accomplish, he felt unable to meet the terms of his contract. Taylor refused to accept Polanyi's resignation and urged him to continue the work. Polanyi answered that Aberdeen's response made "all the difference" to him.[17]

In addition to his work on *The Logic of Liberty* and the Gifford Lectures, Polanyi agreed to participate in the Manchester Conference entitled "The Mind and the Computing Machine." Polanyi prepared a paper, "Can Mind be Represented by a Machine?" which drew on the ideas of Gödel and Tarski to show that the use of intuition and judgment, which is essential to even the most formal of logical procedures, cannot be represented by any kind of mechanism.[18] The conference itself was held at the university on October 27, 1949, with Polanyi joining in discussion with Alan Turing, M. Newman, M. B. Bartlett, J. Z. Young, and D. N. Emmett, among others.

In order to get on with writing and to conserve his strength, Polanyi went away for ten days in early January 1950, this time to the Eastern Court Hotel in Chagford in the middle of Devon. He was attracted by an advertisement that offered "strong tables for writers." He was given room #1, the same room in which Evelyn Waugh had written *Brideshead Revisited*.[19] This time the combination of writing and resting did not work. Polanyi came home near to a state of breakdown. He felt knocked out by even a few hours of work, but slept badly, both in Devon and at home. Even two kinds of sleeping pills at maximum dose did not help.[20] At the end of January, he went to a psychiatrist, who ordered him to take time off. Polanyi gave up on several reviews he had agreed to write for *Time and Tide*, canceled his economics lectures, asked for sick leave, and postponed the first Gifford Lectures to the summer term of 1951.

After taking the prescribed break from his work, Polanyi set out for the lecture series in Chicago. While en route, he stopped in London to talk with Hayek and Robbins "about the appalling mischief for which we are making ourselves responsible"—he disagreed with the "regime of harshness and financial orthodoxy which threatens to undermine social peace." Polanyi feared that the current round of unemployment in Germany would trigger yet another world war or another violent revolution on the Soviet model. "I have been pushing Jewkes in vain for some time to do something about it."[21] After the discussion with Hayek and Robbins, the Polanyis sailed on the *SS Washington* from Southampton on March 12 and arrived in New York eleven days later after one of the stormiest periods on record in the Atlantic—the ship passed through nine large storms and came into New York Harbor three days behind schedule with an exhausted load of passengers.[22] Michael and Magda visited briefly with Mausi: "I shall never forget either your face at the barrier on 23 March or the wave of sweetness which met me in entering your flat with its veritable symphony of loving deeds and symbols."[23]

A few days later, the Polanyis arrived in Chicago and took an apartment of three small rooms plus bath at the Hotel Windermere just off the campus of the university. They were tired, and both had caught a cold. Magda remained in bed for several days, but Michael recovered well enough to get settled at the university and start his once-a-week lecture series on April 12. The relatively light schedule in Chicago allowed Polanyi the rest prescribed by his psychiatrist and his health improved. There were lunches at the university about three times a week, as well as frequent sherry parties and dinners with colleagues. The one sour note was his inability to make sense of the Chicago newspapers, which, for him, concealed more than they revealed about life in the United States.

Polanyi's lectures went well and attracted larger audiences as the term went by. He worked steadily after each lecture preparing the next. In the absence of his secretary, Magda took over the task of typing his manuscripts. In addition to the ten *Logic of Liberty* lectures Polanyi gave a related speech in April at the university on "Freedom in Science" (1950b). It contains some of his earlier material on the structure of belief, commitment, and opinion in science. In an after-dinner address to the Chaos Club the following month, Polanyi recalled his memory of World War I and its consequences: "Only those who knew the Continent in its incomparable glory can know the depth of the abyss and the measure of the chaos into which Europe has fallen." He agreed with Friedrich Meinecke's account of the philosophic disaster that overtook Germany ("Die Idee der Staatsraison"). The source of the trouble was the idea that the Prince, the leader, is not tied to moral obligations: "And it is the tragedy of Germany that her thinkers and people had the courage and profundity to pursue it to its ultimate consequences."[24]

Polanyi made the acquaintance of Marjorie Grene through the lecture series. Her husband, David Grene, a classicist, had heard one of the lectures and encouraged her to attend. Polanyi sensed Marjorie's brilliance in philosophy, the congeniality of her views, and her intense interest in what he was doing. He asked if he could send her some of his papers to criticize. It was the beginning of a lifelong friendship. Grene thought that "if I had anything to say in philosophy, five years' work with M. would help me say it, and if I hadn't, I couldn't do any better with what talents I had than to help him."[25]

After their stay in Chicago, the Polanyis vacationed in London, Paris, and Capri. Toward the end of August, they moved into Arthur Koestler's house at Verte Rive, near Fontaine-le-Port. The Koestler's factotum, Anna, took care of the Polanyis, and they in turn took care of Koestler's two huge dogs. They did quite a bit of sailing and paddling in Koestler's canoe and used the row boat every day. John lived with them from the middle of September till the end of their stay on October 9. The working conditions were ideal for Polanyi. He produced three chapters of the Gifford Lectures under the heading "The Justification of Belief."

Early in 1950, Polanyi thought that he might receive a permanent appointment to the University of Chicago.[26] He had talked with Edward Shils, a sociologist and secretary of the University's Committee on Social Thought. Shils offered Polanyi a permanent chair in social philosophy sometime that summer. Polanyi accepted the position, which was to begin in October 1951.[27] Once again, this meant more correspondence with the long-suffering Taylor at Aberdeen concerning the dates of the Gifford Lectures. Polanyi had hoped Taylor would allow him to push the first lectures up into June and limit informal discussion to the second series. Taylor resisted on both counts. It was finally settled that eight lectures should be given during the month of May, with the last two early in June, and that arrangements would be made for informal discussion groups during the same period.

By late January 1951, everything seemed to be in order for both the lectures in Aberdeen and the chair in Chicago. Polanyi applied for a U.S. immigration visa and then concentrated on polishing the first set of Gifford Lectures. During this period, three of his publications were translations or simple modifications of previous work and took little time or effort (1950a, 1950d, 1951a). "The Hypothesis of Cybernetics" was part of a discussion on calculators simulating minds (1951b). Polanyi pointed out that all our formalized thinking rests on unspecifiable judgments about symbols and operations. The conviction that "All knowledge is ... either tacit or rooted in tacit knowing" became the backbone of Polanyi's theory of personal knowledge (MNG, 61).

On March 12, 1951, Polanyi celebrated his sixtieth birthday. M. G. Evans arranged the dinner at the University of Manchester with Magda, Michael, John, and many old friends, including three of his pupils: "There was a birthday cake with 60 candles! and a lovely red-leather bound volume of papers collected for the occasion by my pupils in England. ... Quite a number of the participants had come from a distance for the occasion and it was extraordinarily friendly—Magda and I really enjoyed it."[28] The next day there was a quiet celebration at home with John, George, and Priscilla—"much more peaceful and comforting than I would have ever expected."

After four years of intense preparation, Polanyi presented the first of the Gifford Lectures on May 7, 1951. Lord Adam Gifford, who had endowed the lectures in 1885, was "deeply and firmly convinced that the true knowledge of God . . . when really felt and acted on, is the means of man's highest well-being, and the security of his upward progress." It was his wish that the lecturers "treat their subject as a strictly natural science, the greatest of all possible sciences, indeed, in one sense, the only science, that of Infinite Being, without reference to or reliance upon any supposed special or exceptional or so-called miraculous revelation." He envisioned lecturers of "any denomination whatever, or of no denomination at all," since "many earnest and high-minded men prefer to belong to no ecclesiastical denomination." The essential requirement of the lecturers was "that they be able reverent men, true thinkers, sincere lovers of and earnest inquirers after truth."[29]

The first three of Polanyi's ten lectures provided a map of the ground Polanyi would cover in the series: "Philosophy must voice today our decisive beliefs."[30] Polanyi's fourth lecture addressed the pervasiveness of belief. He called it "The Fiduciary Programme." The fifth lecture, "The Self-Destruction of Objectivism," traced the history of the Enlightenment showing how radical skepticism grew from the doubt that had cleared the ground for the progress of science. When truth, justice, and charity became objects of doubt, the way was opened to Nihilism and Marxism and then to denial of objectivity itself. Polanyi repeated his brother's suggestion that there has been a Second Fall in which the very knowledge of good and evil has been rendered unintelligible.

Under the title of "The Doubting of Explicit Beliefs" (lecture seven) Polanyi examined how common-sense doubting is useful in science. The Gifford Lecturer is supposed to treat the question of the existence of God. Polanyi said that in place of the claim that we must either live with God or live without him, "there are any number of grades between these two . . . I believe we must decide what service we owe to God without any proof of his existence."[31] Any being that could be observed scientifically would merely be an idol, not a real god.[32] For Polanyi, the supreme being must always be beyond all telling.

The eighth lecture took up the topic of doubting implicit beliefs. The first half of lecture nine was directed against the kind of comprehensive or universal doubt proposed by Descartes and still held, in Polanyi's opinion, by a number of philosophers. He attacked universal doubt on grounds of inconsistency and announced: "Thus the programme of comprehensive doubt collapses and reveals by its failure the fiduciary rootedness of all rationality."[33] In Polanyi's last lecture (June 4), "The Personal, the Universal and the Subjective," he discussed how a child develops commitments and begins to have a sense of self versus non-self. He ended with a sort of postscript on the impossibility of ever having enough time and data for strict proof of our intuitions, which we have no business forsaking in our tumultuous world. We commit every second of our lives one way or the other as time passes. We must form our convictions, knowing their limitations, and do the best we can.

The lectures were well received. Polanyi was pleased with the questions and discussion in the accompanying seminar sessions. The years of anxious preparation and hard work had borne good fruit. The summer in Manchester between the two sets of Gifford Lectures was a time for Polanyi to rest and look ahead. He and Magda booked passage to the United States for September and made preparations to move to Chicago. In July, Polanyi went off to the Oakeley Arms, taking along Katz's *Gestaltpsychologie* and Cassirer's *Philosophie der symbolischen Formen*. By the middle of August, the Polanyis began to worry that their visas had not come through. They put off their voyage to America until October and embarked instead on a Mediterranean vacation with visits to Capri and Nice. Polanyi found a picture of a tree known as "Tormented Olive" and sent it to Olive Davies in affectionate recognition of the problems he had caused her over the years.[34]

By September, the visas had still not arrived. Polanyis' move to Chicago was rescheduled for January, but he was to leave the payroll of Manchester University at the end of September. With no visible progress being made on the visa, in November Polanyi resigned from his appointment in Chicago. Fortunately, Sir John Stopford had also been worried about the visa problem and had kept Polanyi's position open at Manchester; to Polanyi's relief, he was back on the Manchester payroll in a couple of weeks. The visa was not granted for another two years; in the interim, Polanyi wrote a letter to the editor of the *Manchester Guardian* in which he was sharply critical of the interrogations he had to endure: "This is the way to build up a world of phantoms in which men are lost in a maze of mutual suspicion."[35]

Sir Henry Clay, who had been influential in getting Rockefeller support for Polanyi's film project, was delighted that Polanyi was to remain in England. Clay felt that Polanyi's background and insights would make it particularly valuable for him to remain in contact with Europe. Besides, Clay was afraid that Polanyi would have been antagonized in Chicago by "the rather arid atmosphere of rationalist liberalism."[36]

With the help of a Rockefeller grant, Polanyi brought six visiting lecturers to Manchester in 1952: Jean Piaget lectured on "Intelligence and Logic," Raymond Aron explored different contemporary meanings of the opposition "Left" and "Right" in our time, Hannah Arendt and Czeslaw Milosz lectured on "Totalitarianism," Dennis Gabor discussed the "Theory of Communication," and Nandor Balazs spoke on the "Theory of Probability." Polanyi attended a conference in Paris, where he talked with Bertrand de Jouvenel, Gabriel Marcel, and Milosz. He arranged a Manchester conference on computer intelligence with Ilya Prigogine, M. G. Evans, Alan Turing, William Byers Brown, and Michael Swarc, and contributed to a weekend conference in Oxford arranged jointly with Jewkes where Polanyi gave a talk on "Economic and Political Illusions."[37] The same grant also paid Polanyi's expenses to go to the Oxford Political and Economic Society in March, the Institute for Advanced Studies in Dublin in May, the Socratic Society in Oxford and the British Society for the Philosophy of Science in June, and the Present Question Conference in August, where he presented his essay on "Science and Faith" (1952c).

One of the most important effects of the Rockefeller grant was securing Marjorie Grene's assistance. Since their meeting in the spring of 1950, Grene "had contributed to a major extent" to Polanyi's work through "almost daily" correspondence and by spending "two extensive periods in Manchester during the past session."[38] The Rockefeller Foundation funded Grene's trip to Manchester during the spring of 1952 so that she could give Polanyi her full-time assistance. Grene spent about six weeks on critical bibliographical research and editorial work for the second set of Gifford Lectures. By all accounts, Grene was the dominant figure in the development of Polanyi's philosophical skills. She was trained in science and philosophy, had translated some of Heidegger, and was familiar with the German existentialists. She kept a weather eye on Polanyi's use of philosophic terms, frequently correcting him and challenging his interpretations. Once she had volunteered to help Polanyi with his work, it went forward much more rapidly and directly than when he had worked alone.

In the months between the two series of Gifford Lectures, Polanyi accepted Professor Dorothy Emmet's invitation to start teaching a weekly seminar during the winter and spring terms sponsored by the Philosophy Department of Manchester—"to which I have at last managed to gate crash."[39] The weekly seminar in the spring of 1952 gave him the opportunity to try out some of his ideas: "I wish I knew what to tell them," he wrote Karl and Ilona. "But it will at any rate serve as a dress rehearsal (including probably of the emperor's clothes) for the Second Series of my Gifford Lectures."[40]

The Polanyis returned to Aberdeen in November 1952. In the first lecture, "Meaning," Polanyi dealt with the ultimate frames of reference that we accept as our guides for thought and action. The second lecture, "Objectivity," showed how the human desire for objectivity has moved from a view that satisfies direct sense impressions (Ptolemaic geometry) to our theoretical delight in ever-more abstract mechanical and mathematical schemes. Lecture three, "Personal Knowledge," was concerned with fixed frameworks of belief and their modification, either by a complete rupture between frameworks or by gradual development of a view through deeper insights.[41] Polanyi said little about scientific verification in the third lecture because he was going to devote his next talk, "Chance," to the validating aspects used in much of science, taking up cases where substantial unverifiable personal judgments need to be made, namely cases with substantial degrees of experimental inaccuracy or probabilistic behavior.

The fifth lecture, "Order," was almost entirely taken up with the regularity of crystals; 32 crystal classes and 230 space groups are derived from symmetry arguments and from the translational and rotational invariance of atomic and molecular arrangements. The sixth lecture, "Skill and Connoisseurship," dealt with skillful performance and expert artistic judgment, which rely far more on unspecifiable personal activities than the scientific endeavors of the previous lectures. Lecture seven, "Two Kinds of Awareness," brought forth, finally, the solution to Polanyi's problem about the unspecifiability of doing and knowing. More than a year earlier during the first Gifford Lectures, he had referred to many small "impressions which we do not know in themselves" caused in us by the sight of a flying bird.[42] Reflecting on these vague impressions led him to develop new terminology for two kinds of awareness: *focal awareness* for what comes to our attention as we focus on doing or seeing something, and *subsidiary awareness* for all the other relevant things we notice only peripherally at the same time. This became a key distinction in Polanyi's theory of tacit knowing.[43]

In lecture eight, "Living Beings," Polanyi observed that living beings are coherent wholes with significant parts, the meaning of which "can exist only if sustained by an intelligent personal effort of an integrating mind."[44] In the ninth lecture, "Living Action," Polanyi moved from considerations of shape among living things to the activity of life. Polanyi treated the higher levels of "Intelligence and Responsibility" in the last lecture.

Polanyi's Gifford Lectures attracted members of the community as well as students and faculty, averaging fifty or more persons at each session. He focused attention on matters of intelligence, philosophy of science, and the grounds of knowledge, rather than on theology. Although he was heartened by his attentive audiences and the Vice-Chancellor's enthusiastic appreciation, Polanyi was disappointed in not having excited any substantial controversy. What he believed to be a fundamental and revolutionary contribution to the philosophy of knowledge had evidently not been recognized as such. When he and Magda returned to their quiet house and garden in Hale, Polanyi set to work on a careful consolidation and further development of his philosophy. He recognized that he had treated the area of language far too briefly in the lectures and that an extensive account of this topic would be needed to describe the distinctive character of human life. The concept of focal and subsidiary awareness also needed further development.

Polanyi's sons were both doing well. John enjoyed living in his own apartment and was continuing his Ph.D. research on pyrolysis. George was earning a living writing on economic and social thought. Although Michael and Magda were still anxious about George's prospects, they were delighted to see the progress he was making. Magda's translation of textile chemical prospectuses had led her to compile a multilingual dictionary of textile terms. This extensive project demanded many hours of work in the university library and gave her considerable satisfaction—it was a pleasant change from her role as homemaker.

In January 1953, Polanyi became involved with the Congress of Cultural Freedom. This anti-Communist organization had been founded by the American writer Melvin Lasky in West Berlin in June 1950. Bringing together writers, artists, philosophers, and scientists from twenty-one countries, the new organization was created "to combat totalitarian threats to freedom of critical and creative thought wherever they might appear in the world." Arthur Koestler played an influential role in starting the Congress and in its first gathering, which reportedly attracted fifteen thousand participants. Polanyi was invited to join a small international committee in Paris at the office of the Congress to draft plans for a conference on how to sustain freedom of inquiry in the face of Communist ideology. Alex Weissberg, former husband of Polanyi's niece, Eva Zeisel, came to Manchester to persuade Polanyi to chair the Committee on Science and Freedom. Polanyi had long been aware of the denial of freedom in Eastern Europe. He felt that the agenda of the Congress of Cultural Freedom and the Committee on Science and Freedom was worth a substantial commitment of his time and energy.

At first, the organizing committee consisted of Polanyi, Weissberg, and Nicolas Nabokov, who was secretary-general to the Congress. By April, Polanyi had enlisted the support of John Baker, Theodore Dobzhansky, Jacques Maritain, Ernst Nagel, Bertrand Russell, and Nobelists H. J. Müller, James Franck, and Max von Laue. Polanyi prepared his keynote speech on pure versus applied science (1953a).

Edward Shils, who had secured the Chicago appointment for Polanyi, came to Manchester University to lecture in Lent term, 1953. Polanyi loved the lunchtime conversation with Shils and the other social scientists gathered together at the big round table in the university dining room. The pleasure of these conversations drew Polanyi to work in his social studies office rather than at home in Hale. In April, Michael and Magda embarked on a vacation to Italy. They traveled first to Rome, then spent some time in Palermo, Sicily. They returned through Karlsruhe for a nostalgic overnight stay, reliving memories of their courtship some thirty years before. By the end of the month, they were back home in Hale.

That summer, the difficulties with Polanyi's American visa were finally cleared up. They stemmed from his association with two Communist organizations. The first group was the League for Free German Culture. Polanyi had given a lecture to the League on December 12, 1942, knowing it was anti-Nazi but not that it was pro-Soviet. His lecture attacked totalitarian views of science, including those of the Soviets, and upset the League leadership so much that they sent him a letter of censure. Before the lecture, however, he had agreed to be a patron. The presence of his name on the League's letterhead led the State Department to believe that he was a Communist himself. Although Polanyi had mislaid his correspondence and had forgotten his "patron" status, this first charge against him was eventually cleared up.

The second accusation was not settled so easily. Polanyi was a member of the Society for Cultural Relations between the Peoples of the British Commonwealth and the USSR from June 1946 to June 1947. He joined because he wanted to share Western ideas with Soviet writers and because he was confident that the Society's leading members were not Communist. The president was J. B. Priestley. Other members included Margaret Storm Jameson, Somerset Maugham, H. G. Wells, G. K. Chesterton, A. J. Cronin, Agatha Christie, Grahame Greene, and Daphne du Maurier. The Society helped Polanyi with the translation of some important Soviet documents. When he realized that the discussions were biased toward Communism, Polanyi resigned from the group.

In January 1952, Polanyi traveled to Liverpool for a two-hour interview at the American consulate. Although he was told the Liverpool meeting was to be decisive, the State Department transmitted a series of requests for more information month after month. Michael and Magda spent Easter vacation soaking up the mild Mediterranean light on Mallorca while their family and friends did their best to protect Polanyi from guilt by association. Polanyi provided the American inquisitors full anti-Communist credentials, but his testimony fell on deaf ears. The fact that Koestler's strongly anti-Communist book *The Yogi and the Commissar* was dedicated to Polanyi carried no weight in the argument because none of the American officials had ever heard of the book. At one point, Polanyi changed his request from an immigration to a visitor's visa, but that made no difference. On June 26, 1952, J. F. Huddleston, consul general for the United States, wrote that on the basis of the information submitted and "other available data," Polanyi was "ineligible to receive an immigration visa as a person inadmissible into the U.S."[45]

In 1953, there was finally a change of attitude on the part of the U.S. government. Acting under the new McCarran Act, the attorney general unofficially informed Polanyi that his visitor's visa could now be granted without further investigations. The consul general in Liverpool pursued the matter through the thickets of bureaucracy. The visa was granted on June 29, 1953, and the way was now clear to accept Chicago's invitation to lecture during the winter of 1954. Since they were planning a series of trips before the voyage to America, the Polanyis decided to lease their home in Hale for the coming year. Magda was especially pleased to have a sabbatical from her household chores.

The Polanyis' first trip was to the Conference on Freedom in Science in Hamburg on July 24–26. Although the organizing committee had feared disruptive demonstrations, the conference was a success. There were five sections with a total of twenty papers, in addition to twelve plenary speeches. In his concluding remarks (published as a preface to the *Proceedings*), Polanyi observed that many different people had come together because of the collapse of a messianic ideal: the conception that universal justice and plenty

would be instantly achieved by means of a single political change. This expectation, which had dominated Europe since the French Revolution, had
been demolished by events in the Soviet Union. Polanyi hoped that the work
of the Committee on Science and Freedom would reveal the suppression of
intellectual freedom in the totalitarian regimes and provide a means of pre-
serving and extending that same freedom in the West. He later confessed that
"I suppose I have been tempted by the restless American imagination which
is ever trying to put things right altogether."[46]

After the conference, Polanyi spent the month of August working in close
collaboration with Marjorie Grene in Ireland. Grene had recently moved from
a farm in Illinois to a farm in Clash, Rathdrum, County Wicklow. Polanyi very
much appreciated the countryside and the opportunity the visit gave him to
concentrate on the manuscript. Polanyi concentrated on his book from October to Christmas, although other matters drew his attention as well. He
wrote to support the formation of the Northern Section of the British Society
for the Philosophy of Science. He sought to get the poet Czeslaw Milosz out of
a Bulgarian jail and safely into Great Britain. Polanyi also found time to write
reviews of *The Counter-Revolution of Science* by F. A. Hayek, *The Estrangement
of Western Man* by Robert Strauz-Hupe, *Science and the Social Order* by Bernard Barber, and *Sociology of Communism* by Jules Monnerat.[47] He used a
Rockefeller grant to finance visits to Manchester of Professor Paul Radin of
the Bollingen Foundation, of Professor E. E. Evans-Pritchard of Oxford, and of
Professor M. Fortes of Cambridge. Before the end of the year, Polanyi published an article entitled "On the Introduction of Science into Moral Subjects"
in which he showed the fallacy of the fact-value distinction and the Laplacean
ideal of purely mechanical knowledge, which has no way of treating subsidiary awareness and the formation of Gestalts (1954a). Polanyi argued for the
validity of personal knowledge within the moral order: "As we know order
from disorder, health from sickness, the ingenious from the trivial, we may
distinguish with equal authority good from evil, charity from cruelty, justice
from injustice" (15).

Michael and Magda flew to New York on December 23, 1953, to celebrate
Christmas with Mausi's family and with John, who was visiting from Ottawa,
Canada, where he was a postdoctoral fellow. They spent a pleasant week
together, then flew to Chicago to prepare for the new term. Polanyi's program
was sponsored by the university's Committee on Social Thought. He was to
deliver a series of eight weekly lectures (from January 5 to February 26) on the
subject of his current research. After spending nine months on the Gifford
Lectures, he hoped the lectures and seminars would help him cast his
thoughts into a more precise shape. He had shipped forty-five books on a wide
variety of topics to Chicago from England, mostly from his own library.
Marjorie Grene arrived from Ireland to help Polanyi with his lectures. She

gave her own course of lectures for the Committee on Social Thought, including a lecture on the historical setting of Polanyi's work.

Mausi came to Chicago for the lectures. She enjoyed hearing her younger brother explore matters close to his heart. In turn, Polanyi was grateful for the presence of a sister who had been such "a great treasure" for him. Polanyi thought the lectures had been quite successful. "It was a considerable job to keep that audience from running away altogether," he joked. "The result has been very useful to me for it led to a sharpening of my points and tightening of my argument."[48] Nevertheless, it was hard work. At the end, he was "just about dead beat."[49] On the way home, he lectured on "Objectivity in Science from Copernicus to Einstein" at Princeton University (1955b): "Very good meeting... 300 people," he wrote to Mausi, adding, "Well, these are vanities."[50] Shortly afterwards, the Polanyis flew back to Manchester for a month's work. They then vacationed in Agrigento on the southern shore of Sicily.

In July, Polanyi lamented that "I am still struggling with the burden of my life's work on my shoulders. But I hope to have done with it by the end of year."[51] That same month, Polanyi accepted the chairmanship of the permanent Committee for Science and Freedom of the Congress of Cultural Freedom and arranged a Rockefeller grant of $12,000 to fund the work of his committee and to provide for the publication of *The Bulletin of the Committee on Science and Freedom* and *Special Supplements*. The Committee on Science and Freedom soon developed into a working group of fifteen, with seventeen honorary sponsors, including Jacques Maritain, Bertrand Russell, Robert Oppenheimer, James Franck, Romano Guardini, Karl Laspens, Lise Meitner, Ernst Nagel, and Salvador de Madriaga.

In August, Michael, Magda, and John traveled through Germany, Austria, and South Tyrol. He toured the Rosengarten in South-Tyrol with his colleague Karl Bonhoeffer, "his only German friend."[52] The Polanyis felt at home in Austria. They were especially attracted by the milieu in Alpbach where the whole family took part in an international summer school, the Österreichische College. Magda and John signed up for a course on the modern novel, taught by poet Elizabeth Sewell, but Magda soon dropped out, not wanting to be in the same group as her son. But when she later saw Sewell by chance on the village square Magda seized the opportunity to become better acquainted. During their conversation over coffee Magda suggested that Sewell should apply for a Simon fellowship in Manchester. Sewell met Polanyi only once or twice that summer in Alpbach. She found him very shy and assumed that he did not like her. But later she picked up on Magda's suggestion and applied for and received the Simon fellowship for the following year.[53]

In December 1954, Polanyi finished the draft of the chapter on "Articulation" and sent a copy of his manuscript to Marjorie Grene for her criticism and review. The Polanyis sold their house in the village of Hale and moved into much more convenient quarters back in the Didsbury section of Manchester.

Although Michael loved the large garden and the quiet atmosphere of their old home, Magda found the suburban setting increasingly inconvenient to her work in the university library. She also regretted their isolation from the wider social life of Manchester. The Polanyis moved into the former servants' quarters in the attic of "Mayfair," a large house in Fielding Park. They had to get rid of many household goods in order to fit into the "studio flat"; the "three theoretical but only two practical rooms" had too little wall-space to hold two large family paintings, treasures which the Polanyis parked nearby at the house of their friends, the Armitages.[54] The simplicity of the smaller quarters suited them well.

Polanyi returned to Chagford in Devon for a short stay at the turn of the new year; winter was always more pleasant near the coast in southwest England than it was in Manchester. He stayed there through most of April 1955 as well. Olive Davies shipped Tillich's *Courage to Be*, Whitehead's *Dialogues*, and books on astronomy and the philosophy of science to him. When he returned to Manchester from Chagford, Polanyi became involved in a conflict between Göttingen University and the government of Lower Saxony, which had appointed Herr Schlüter, a neo-Nazi, to the post of minister of education. As chairman of the Committee on Science and Freedom, Polanyi sent a telegram of support for the university in its stand against the appointment; the telegram was signed by members of the Committee and was addressed to the rector of the university and to the prime minister of Lower Saxony. Schlüter was forced to resign.

During his years in Manchester, Polanyi had made many friends in the university; however, few took him seriously as a philosopher. In 1955, he made such a friend in Bill Poteat, a philosopher of religion who had come upon Polanyi's essay on the Azande ("The Stability of Beliefs," 1952d) while writing his dissertation. Poteat had recently been appointed to an assistant professorship and was grateful for Polanyi's interest in him. He felt very young and insignificant when he attended a soirée at Michael and Magda's apartment. There he met a most impressive collection of people from all walks of life. To Poteat's surprise, Polanyi's friends and associates seemed unaware of his work in philosophy. In spite of his cordial relationships with them, Polanyi was something of an outsider among them. As Poteat was leaving to catch the train back to Oxford, Polanyi gave him three or four chapters of what was later to become part of *Personal Knowledge*. Poteat was terrified of losing the manuscript, since he had not had the presence of mind to ask whether another copy existed. He started reading while on the train, his excitement rising all the while.[55] Poteat's enthusiastic response must have been a great comfort to Polanyi.

Michael wrote Karl that his book was "making reasonable progress" and might be completed by the next Easter.[56] That same year, Magda finally finished her dictionary; she had become an acknowledged expert in textile literature, "a situation which she enjoys with gusto."[57] Magda and Michael traveled to the Continent in mid-August for a leisurely trip through Paris, attending a Picasso exhibition there, then journeying to Basel and Goldiwil, a resort town near the Lake of Thun where they spent a week relaxing and enjoying the view of the surrounding Alps. As they traveled, they reflected together on retirement after the book was done, debating whether they should go to Switzerland or some other place on the Continent. Polanyi was reluctant to give up the "homeliness" of England. He also feared his philosophical career might be endangered if he left the British milieu.[58]

In September, the Polanyis journeyed to Milan where they were welcomed by the youngest descendent of the Italian branch of Pollacseks, Giorgio Vedres and his wife. The International Congress on the Future of Freedom, supported by the Committee on Science and Freedom, met in Milan. Polanyi again gave the opening address, "This Age of Discovery" (1956a). Just as Columbus had sought the Indies but stumbled across the Americas, our age had sought peaceful progress and found terror instead. Polanyi concluded the conference with a talk on "The Strategy of Freedom."[59] He expressed appreciation for the delegates from Asia, Africa, and South America who helped shift the emphasis away from European concerns. Polanyi claimed that the argument between planning and free trade had been settled in favor of the latter, with the proviso that the state should intervene to maintain full employment. Thus, the socialist and the liberal forces of progress seemed to be joining hands: "this Congress has consolidated the intellectual and moral forces which the free world can throw into battle for the intellectual and moral conquest of men's minds throughout the world" (2–3).

Polanyi spent much of 1956 in the last great push on *Personal Knowledge*. For the most part, he worked steadily on the manuscript. During this time, Marjorie Grene was in Manchester, reading, cross-checking, and indexing the manuscript. Elizabeth Sewell, who had taken up her Simon fellowship the previous fall, was working on a study of poetry that later appeared as *The Orphic Voice*. Polanyi and Sewell spent many Saturdays engaged in hours of furious talk at the Rendez-Vous Café in Didsbury. Sewell appreciated Polanyi as "a highly poetic and imaginative man." They thoroughly enjoyed their marathon conversations, although Sewell felt that they were talking to each other "out of their respective galaxies."[60] When Sewell gave the Simon lecture at Manchester, Polanyi heard someone behind him say "The woman is mad." Polanyi turned around to reply: "That is her professional privilege."[61]

At about the same time, Polanyi discussed the intense and peculiar attraction that Marxism had for the modern intellectual in "The Magic of Marxism" (1956e). The coercive logic of Marx was again his target, that system that coupled a moral passion for a better society with a scientific outlook insistent on purging from modern thought any reference to moral demands and values. Polanyi believed the Marxist conviction of the "true" objectivity of science bolstered dynamic fanaticism with its moral context; he called this relationship both a "dynamo-objective coupling" (213) and a "moral inversion" (232).

The first leg of the Polanyis' summer trip took them to Paris to pursue anti-Communist concerns. They spent a week at the offices of the Congress; "ring us up at Europe 5515," Polanyi wrote to Mausi.[62] He arranged a study group on Science and Freedom, which brought together university scholars from France, Britain, the United States, Australia, Germany, Yugoslavia, Spain, and Italy to discuss academic freedom and responsibility and to establish "a sense of community of ideals and objectives."[63] Michael and Magda then spent two weeks in Bandol near Toulon on the French Mediterranean coast. Polanyi wrote every morning and enjoyed the seaside for the rest of the day. It was a happy, relaxed time.

As Polanyi worked in opposition to Communism, he occasionally toyed with the thought of returning to Hungary.[64] He kept in touch with the Petöfi Circle, a literary group named for a poet who had played a crucial part in the Revolution of 1848. In June, an overflow crowd of six thousand citizens of Budapest listened to a series of Communist writers pledge that they would write no more lies for the party. When open warfare began later in the year, Polanyi tried to disseminate information and generate support for the revolutionaries: "I am just going to a meeting of Senate to which I shall communicate the latest reports from Hungary. The reports are terrible. I hope our university will respond in some manner."[65] Apart from anxiety for his homeland, Polanyi was also concerned for the safety of Mausi's younger son, George Striker, who remained in Budapest with his wife and their two young children. George was an engineer who specialized in international standards of measurement; he and Barbara had returned to Hungary after spending the war years in Chicago.

Polanyi organized a meeting of the Congress of Cultural Freedom for November 10 in Hamburg to assist the 160,000 refugees who had escaped from Hungary before the border was closed. The Congress also called on the Soviet Union and the Hungarian government to restore intellectual freedom to the Hungarian people; the petition was signed by twelve hundred faculty members from universities in twenty-four countries.

At the end of the year, Polanyi flew to New York to address the annual meeting of the American Association for the Advancement of Science. By this time, a large part of Personal Knowledge was finished. Polanyi drew material from the manuscript for his presentation, "The Scientific Outlook: Its Sickness and Cure" (1957a). As usual, Polanyi took advantage of the trip to spend time with Mausi, Eva, Misi, and their families. Polanyi went on to Toronto to see John, who had just started lecturing in chemistry at the University of Toronto. He also saw Karl, who was suffering from a bladder problem that would later be diagnosed as cancer.

Before returning to England, Polanyi gave the Oscar Jászi lecture at Oberlin College on January 7, 1957. Jászi was too ill to attend; he died on February 13. Polanyi had proposed to speak on "Jászi and the Future of Liberalism," but was asked instead to address "The Future of the European Tradition in Europe." He recalled Jászi's role in the cultural milieu of his youth, how this liberal tradition became eclipsed, and how its principles were now being renewed in intellectual movements opposed to Communism (1957b). In February 1957, Polanyi made an unsuccessful attempt to bring George Lukács to England. Lukács was a Communist theoretician who had defected at the time of the Hungarian Revolution. Polanyi had hoped to free him from internment in Rumania by nominating him for a Simon Visiting Professorship in Manchester.

After his return from the United States, Polanyi labored at home on the final part of *Personal Knowledge*. He would work hard for a spell, then take time out for a walk; he liked to join friends for lunch or dinner. He relied on sleeping pills to relax after the stress of the day's writing. As the end came in sight, the work intensified. He was especially tired on the 19th of March when he wrote the last page. In the morning, he decided that the only thing to do was to stay in bed all day. Besides the benefits of rest, it was also a comfortable place to catch up on the letters he had set aside while working on the manuscript.[66] When he and Magda traveled to Sicily for the Easter vacation, Polanyi encouraged Olive Davies to rest, too: "Please take as much as you can, so far as my blessing can grant it to you."[67] Michael and Magda spent the Easter holidays in a feverish round of sightseeing. Then, with Marjorie Grene's help, Polanyi set himself "to plough through all my 200,000 words and make sure of each single one of them."[68]

Besides Grene's input, Polanyi also received comments from Oldham, who had read the draft: "Of all the books I have read in recent years none has taken so powerful a hold on me. . . . you have by the comprehensiveness of your thought brought to the birth in me a way of seeing things as a whole that up till now has existed only in a very embryonic and incomplete stage."[69] Nevertheless, Oldham thought the book was uneven in quality. He disliked Polanyi's use of "conviviality" to describe the communal sharing of scientific activity and resources. He recommended "living together" as a more apt expression (!). Oldham was also critical of the last chapter, "The Rise of Man." Polanyi's view of evolutionary theory appeared to be an addendum whereas Oldham thought it should be given a more extensive and more integrated treatment. He urged Polanyi either to omit Teilhard de Chardin completely or to explain Teilhard's ideas in two or three pages rather than just two paragraphs. He also advised him to restate his fiduciary philosophy, possibly relating the argument to his own grand scheme of human evolution. For the most part, Polanyi accepted these criticisms; Marjorie Grene, who had suggested similar changes, later remarked that Polanyi would accept them from Joe Oldham and not from her. Polanyi finally rewrote the last chapter at the beginning of July when the book was already in press at Routledge.

After completing the preface at the beginning of August 1957, the pressure was off. Polanyi was glad to enjoy a period of "free-wheeling." He relaxed by reading some philosophy of history: R. G. Collingwood, Pieter Geyl, Marc Bloch, and Wilhelm Dilthey.[70] In the middle of August he left for Alpbach with Koestler to take part in discussions and study groups of the Österreichische College. He saw Erika Cremer, his former student in Berlin and now professor at Innsbruck University, for the first time in twenty-four years. They hiked together for several hours, reminiscing about Berlin and the work at the Kaiser Wilhelm Institute.

The proofs of *Personal Knowledge* began to arrive by the end of October. The final publication date was June 20, 1958. A week later, the University of Chicago Press brought out an American edition. Polanyi's goal in *Personal Knowledge* was to establish an alternative to "a mistaken ideal of objectivity" (7), which "exercises a destructive influence in biology, psychology, and sociology, and falsifies our whole outlook far beyond the domain of science" (vii). He did not want to discard or diminish the accomplishments of the Enlightenment, the age of critical reason, but he sought to restore awareness of the "tacit and passionate contribution" made to the act of knowing by the knower (312).

Polanyi realized that there was a self-referential character to all of his thinking about thinking and speaking about speaking—he did not want to fall into the trap of acting as if he were an impersonal observer when that was the very model of knowing that he was attempting to overthrow: "we can voice our ultimate convictions only from within our convictions" (267). He therefore explicitly took responsibility for the set of beliefs on which *Personal Knowledge* was founded:

> When I gave this book the sub-title "Towards a Post-Critical Philosophy" I had this turning point in mind. The critical movement, which seems to be nearing the end of its course today, was perhaps the most fruitful effort ever sustained by the human mind. The past four or five centuries, which have gradually destroyed or over-shadowed the whole medieval cosmos, have enriched us mentally and morally to an extent unrivalled by any period of similar duration. But its incandescence had fed on the combustion of the Christian heritage in the oxygen of Greek rationalism, and when this fuel was exhausted the critical framework itself burnt away. (265–6)

Following Descartes, the orientation of the Enlightenment was to doubt everything. In Polanyi's view, this project had undercut itself, so he argued that "We must now recognize belief once more as the source of all knowledge" (266). Because the grounds of knowing run deep in the structure of the person and cannot be wholly formalized, "to destroy all belief would be to deny all truth" (286).

In contrast to the Enlightenment's dictum that we must not believe what cannot be proven, Polanyi held that "We may firmly believe what we might conceivably doubt; and may hold to be true what might conceivably be false" (312). Polanyi offered no strict proof that the concept of strict proof is self-defeating and poisonous to society. He tried instead to exhibit the principles of thought on which his own view of reality was based and to persuade the reader to adopt a similar "interpretative framework" (172). When Polanyi claims, for example, that "thought proceeds largely by an irreversible process of comprehension and not according to specifiable rules" (333), the laboratory for testing that claim is in the reader's own mind and personal self-awareness. Though it may sound to some as though Polanyi is abandoning rationality, he saw it otherwise: "This position is not solipsistic, since it is based on a belief in an external reality and implies the existence of other persons who can likewise approach the same reality. Nor is it relativistic" (316).

There were more than twenty reviews of *Personal Knowledge* from 1958 to 1960. Opinions were divided. Polanyi showed to most reviewers' satisfaction the absurdity of requiring all knowledge to be objective, but some reviewers felt that Polanyi was unable to pin down his claim that the personal element was present everywhere in the knowing process. Edward C. Moore connected *Personal Knowledge* with a tradition in science that built on Plato and Spinoza and the modern metaphysics of Charles S. Peirce and Alfred North Whitehead.[71] However, Alan R. White in a lengthy review in *Philosophical Quarterly* attacked the book as a case of "misplaced erudition."[72] White judged that Polanyi's "references to recent philosophy are usually based on misunderstanding and sometimes on petulance." Polanyi's language was described at the one extreme as having a "luminous beauty"[73] that gave it rank as literature no less than as science, at the other as having a "vagueness and diffusiveness" that made it unintelligible.[74] Other reviewers pointed out that Polanyi's unusual terminology created difficulties for the reader. C. A. Coulson hoped that Polanyi would carry his story further because he saw in Polanyi's "monumental book" the "germ of a new Christian apologetic, relevant to the twentieth century."[75]

After completing *Personal Knowledge*, Polanyi was eager to explore the ramifications of his position in related fields. His first priority was to work out his own conception of the meaning of history. He also hoped to explore jurisprudence, political theory, ethics, art criticism, and the social sciences.[76] Polanyi opposed envisioning the humanities, especially the discipline of history, as radically different from the natural sciences. Instead, he believed that the many levels of reality revealed by tacit knowing provide for a continuum of disciplines from physics and chemistry through biology to the behavioral sciences and the humanities.

The University College of North Staffordshire (later Keele University) invited Polanyi to give the first Lindsay Memorial Lectures in March 1958. The lectures had been established to honor the memory of Alexander Dunlop Lindsay, the distinguished former Master of Balliol College, Oxford, who had provided leadership for the new experimental university at Keele in the potteries at Stoke-on-Trent. A person of tremendous moral stature, Lord Lindsay was both a political philosopher and an active participant in politics, as well as a devoted supporter of worker education.

Polanyi plunged into his preparations for the lectures. During that era of continuing Cold War tensions, he was aware of the concern among intellectuals to counter the threat of atomic warfare, a threat that overshadowed much of the discussion on the future of humanity. Knowing Karl's impassioned position on this issue, Michael promised that he would make "an absolutist anti-atom statement."[77]

At Keele, an audience of fifty to sixty persons assembled in uncomfortable chairs in a temporary lecture hall on the three cold, windswept March evenings. Polanyi used "The Study of Man" as a synonym for "history" and devoted his first two lectures, "Understanding Ourselves" and "The Calling of Man," to a popular account of tacit knowing and the embodiment of subsidiary particulars; he conceived this fundamental recapitulation of his theory of personal knowledge as essential to the development of his thought in the third lecture, "Understanding History" (1959c). By justifying "understanding as a valid form of knowledge" he sketched "a path which would lead smoothly from the exact sciences to the study of man, and even further to a confrontation with man, engaged in responsible decisions under a firmament of universal obligations" (41).[78]

Polanyi concluded the second lecture by reminding his audience of the human vocation to engage in "works of the mind": "For so far as we know, we on this earth are the only bearers of thought in the universe.... If this perspective is true, a supreme trust is placed in us by the whole of creation, and it is sacrilege then even to contemplate actions which may lead to the extinction of humanity" (69–70).

In his last lecture, Polanyi described his idea of a university, which he believed might "claim close kinship with that embodied by Lord Lindsay in this University College" (69). He stressed the role of the universities in "the framework which shapes the modern man. University teachers are today the chief transmitters and interpreters of the heritage which defines the duties of men and sets up the standards that society must respect. The principal obligation of universities is to teach young people, and among them our future leaders, the basic truths to the service of which a free society is dedicated" (99).

The three Lindsay Lectures were collected into a slim volume entitled The Study of Man (dedicated to Joseph Oldham), to which Polanyi added a brief bibliographic note, some critical comments on Collingwood's Idea of History, and a word of appreciation for Dilthey. Polanyi credited Dilthey and his work in phenomenology and existentialism with transforming "the whole climate of philosophy on the Continent of Europe. Out of it has issued modern Gestalt psychology, which I myself am trying to restore to its function as a theory of knowledge adumbrated in its philosophical origins. Many of my statements are reminiscent of this movement; but let me recall that its thought was based throughout on the exclusion of the natural sciences from its scope" (102).

Polanyi sent the manuscript for *The Study of Man* to Veronica Wedgwood, asking her to tell him what she thought of his analysis of history. A month after the Lindsay Lectures, he wrote her that he was "still indulging" his interest in books on historiography.[79] In London a few weeks later, he called to say he had just gotten his copy of *Personal Knowledge* and had "spent the night hunting for misprints and grammatical mistakes."[80] After that ordeal, he was ready to celebrate: "Could you think of some absolutely wild idea for our outing on Monday night? . . . Can I make you share this 2nd adolescence? Alas, you are too young for it."

Polanyi devoted the month of May 1958 to his duties as chairman of the Committee on Science and Freedom. He visited Tunis in May to organize a meeting on "Science and Freedom" for the coming year. One purpose of the meeting was to broaden the focus of the discussion to include African and Asian perspectives. Tunisia was chosen as the site for the meeting because it was trying to develop an independent national policy and to strengthen its contacts with non-Communist countries. Since the government intended to establish a new university in Tunis, the study group meeting would also help to clarify the relationship between the university and society.[81]

Polanyi delighted in the glorious weather and ancient surroundings of Tunis. "Politically, a joy to find myself for once in tune with an authoritarian dynamism," he wrote Wedgwood enthusiastically.[82] "The restrained dynamism of the new generation of rulers led by President Bourguiba in Tunis has deeply impressed me." In Beirut, Polanyi met with Jawad Bulos, a distinguished Arab historian who clarified the dynamism that Polanyi had found so impressive. Bulos explained that Arab civilization was not territorial but tribal, that no tribal people could understand the principles of self-government, and that the conception of the tribal ruler was incompatible with any opposition to his commands. The two men also talked about the armed clashes that were taking place just then throughout Lebanon. Polanyi admired "the science which kept the consequences of this division under control" (1958f, 16).

Polanyi returned to Manchester with a marvelous suntan, much to the surprise of his friends who had been reading newspaper reports of the Lebanese revolution. Polanyi had enjoyed sunbathing on the beach, despite the gunfire behind him in the city.[83] After his tour of Tunis, Beirut, and Baghdad, he felt "a complete reorientation of my conceptual framework . . . here [is] a teeming civilization, more ancient than Europe with modernity superimposed on it."[84]

Polanyi retired from the University of Manchester in 1958. Although Michael and Magda had enjoyed their time in Manchester far more than they first anticipated, they decided to make their retirement home in London.

Preparations for the Congress of Cultural Freedom meetings in the coming autumn led them to delay the search for a place in London. Instead they put their furniture in storage, quit their studio flat, and headed for the Continent. There they spent two weeks at Alpbach with the European Forum, three weeks vacation at Ronchi Poveromo, Italy, and then visited Paris, where Polanyi prepared his papers for the upcoming Congress of Cultural Freedom seminars.

At summer's end, they traveled to Vienna for a Congress devoted to the topic of "Workers' Participation in Management." The conference was chaired by T. E. Chester of the University of Manchester and supported by the Ford Foundation, with cooperation of a number of Austrian institutions. While in Vienna, Polanyi met with his niece, Maria Szecsi, now a government economics statistician. Maria had managed to find refuge in the United States during the war and was the only member of his sister Sofie's family who was still alive.

At the beginning of October, the Polanyis visited Athens and Rhodes for a seminar sponsored by the Congress of Cultural Freedom entitled "Tradition and Change—Problems of Progress, Representative Governments, and Public Liberties in the New States." Polanyi had prepared two papers during his short stay in Paris, dealing with recent events in France, Algiers, Lebanon, and Iraq.[85] In his discussion-group paper, "Tyranny and Freedom, Ancient and Modern," Polanyi observed that our planet has been in turmoil for more than fifty years, not because of technological change but as a result of one tenacious idea: self-determination, the freedom for nationalities to re-shape their own societies as they separately see fit (1958f). Never before has there appeared such a zeal for social improvement, whether by reform within the rule of law or by revolution that puts down the rule of law in favor of an omnipotent and violent center of power.

The Polanyis returned from Rhodes and the Continent in October. After a temporary stay in the Athenaeum, Polanyi's favorite London club, they headed to Toronto to pay their first visit to John and his wife, Susan, whose wedding they had been unable to attend. Michael and Magda were both very happy about John's marriage. Polanyi was delighted with the work his son was doing. John had recently made important discoveries in the field of re-action kinetics. "John will be good at his profession. . . . He has now discovered that a mixture of H-atoms and C_{12}-gas reacts to form HCl with a larger portion of the exothermicity poured into vibrational energy of the nascent HCl. This is shown by an intense infrared luminescence of the HCl bands."[86] To his brother, Polanyi wrote: "He is about to solve problems I have tried to crack open and failed. That is nice."[87]

Polanyi also met with Karl while he was in Toronto. In contrast to many stormy occasions in the past, he found their meeting pleasant, peaceful, and happy: "It is undoubtedly sad that men are, despite of Donne . . . islands to each other. But even so, there has been an easy communion of minds between us, as not before. Let us gratefully remember this ever after."[88] Nevertheless, Polanyi left Toronto without saying goodbye to his brother because he found such gestures increasingly hard to make.

Magda returned to Manchester while Michael traveled to Chicago, where he met the economist Friedrich von Hayek and lunched with the Committee on Social Thought. Thence, he flew to Palo Alto and Stanford, where he visited the Center for Advanced Study in the Behavioral Sciences, and finally to Austin, Texas, where William Poteat was teaching at the Episcopal Seminary. Polanyi arrived unannounced. Dismissing his taxi at 6:30 A.M., he found Poteat's office still locked. Eventually he located a janitor, who let him in. At about 8:00 A.M., Poteat opened his office door to find Polanyi sound asleep, with his head propped on the handle of an umbrella braced between his knees.[89] After Polanyi's visit to Austin, he flew to New York to celebrate Christmas with his family. Mausi was not at all well, but was released from the hospital in time to preside over the family gathering. Polanyi spent New Year's Eve in Princeton with Hugh Taylor, who had just recently lost his wife. After a short time together in London, Michael and Magda arranged a trip to Brazil to visit Adolf and his wife, Lily. En route, they passed through Mexico, Costa Rica, and Venezuela. Michael reported to Karl that their older brother was weak, "passionately nostalgic," and "tainted by an exaggerated dislike of his South American surroundings."[90]

Michael and Magda returned briefly to England, then departed for Tunis in April to take part in the Congress of Cultural Freedom seminar on "Freedom and Responsibility: The Role of the Scholar in Society." After a short holiday in Rome and Perugia, Michael and Magda moved in early May into 70 Cheyne Court, London. At the end of nearly 10 months of travel and temporary arrangements, they were happy to settle into a place of their own. In their last years at Manchester they had given much consideration to the ideal setting for their retirement. Now they were ready to take advantage of all of London's theaters, concert halls, museums, galleries, gardens, and restaurants. "I feel so exhilarated by London that I feel quite carried away by it."[91] The exhilaration did not last long. To their surprise, the Polanyis found daily life in the great city much less fulfilling than they had expected it to be. In contrast to the familiar circles of university and community friends and colleagues that they had enjoyed in Manchester, Magda and Michael now found themselves cut off and dependent on one another for companionship. They were surprisingly lonely. Their friends were scattered over the vast region of London and its suburbs, and they found that the marvelous cornucopia of urban culture did not replace the satisfaction to be found in everyday relationships.

In early June, Polanyi had lunch with C. P. Snow, the prominent Cambridge physicist-turned-novelist who had argued in his essay "The Two

Cultures"[92] that the influence of science on the rest of culture was too slight. In an essay of the same title, Polanyi responded that, on the contrary, science had established itself as the supreme intellectual authority and made many valuable contributions to culture before it turned to social revolutionary zeal under the inspiration of Marx and Freud (1959b). He maintained that Marxism left a widespread view of the person as the product of amoral appetites. But, since about 1950, Polanyi saw social zeal declining. He felt the time was ripe to discard the absurd ideal of impersonal objectivity and to renew "the great work of the Enlightenment" (4).

PART IV

Scholar at Large:
1959–1976

9

Merton College, Oxford: 1959–1961

On June 23, 1959, Polanyi was elected a Senior Research Fellow at Merton College in Oxford University. Polanyi's friend, economist John Jewkes, had moved to Oxford from Manchester and suggested to the warden, G. E. Mure, a philosopher, that he should read *Personal Knowledge* and consider appointing Polanyi to the vacant post. Mure talked to other Oxford economists, as well as to Alister Hardy and several other of the university's scientists. In general, there was strong support for Polanyi, more for the general caliber of his mind and reputation than for the work he had done in *Personal Knowledge*. The appointment was not universally admired, however. Polanyi's consistent anti-Communist stance was well known. When a famous, left-wing Hungarian economist in the Balliol Senior Common Room heard the news of Polanyi's honorary research fellowship at Merton, he exclaimed, "What! That charlatan coming to Merton?"[1]

Upon his appointment, Marjorie Grene, who corresponded frequently enough with Polanyi to have become an astute and critical observer of his prose, sent a poem entitled "Lines Respectfully Addressed to a Neo-Peripatetic Neo-Augustinian Philosopher." Grene lamented:

> Oh, where have you left your English?
> In Baghdad, Berlin or Brazil?
> The language of Shakespeare and Newton
> You used to write better than Mill.
>
> *Where* have you left your English?
> Though good Magyar this may of course be,

With its "never suspected"s and "deeper"s
It sounds rather Teutonic to me.

Where *have* you abandoned your English?
Is it buried in Athens or Rome?
But in such foreign parts, it's apparent,
Great Thoughts are no longer at home.

Oh, where have you left your good English?
On what cont'nent to East or to West?
This may be an insular island
But its language is clearly the best.

In short, you had better cease travel;
The lesson's exceedingly plain;
If you're going to settle in OXFORD,
YOU HAVE GOT TO LEARN ENGLISH AGAIN!

Polanyi described his appointment to Merton as a "job which entails no obligation beyond occasional dining" but "does morally oblige me to avoid long absences from Europe."[2] Though his position at Merton College was not tied to residence in town, he wanted to move to Oxford and participate fully in the life of the university. Over the next few months he often stayed at Merton, enjoying his comfortable new college quarters during the week and returning to London on the weekend. The change from London lifted Polanyi's spirits. His desk was "facing the Fellows Garden with Magdalen Tower peeping in from (the) other window.... It makes me feel as if I had died and found my soul dwelling in some scholars' Elysium."[3]

The honeymoon with Oxford did not last. Polanyi had joined Merton College in the hope of taking a prominent part in the discussion of philosophy, but he found it difficult to establish the intellectual contacts he yearned for. On Sunday nights, tuxedo-clad dons and their guests in the Senior Common Room engaged in bright, witty conversation, but neither then nor during the week did Polanyi find much opportunity for serious discussions of the questions that concerned him. Nor did Polanyi enjoy anything like the prominence that he had experienced in Manchester. An in-house scholar with unconventional ideas got little notice in comparison to the steady stream of world-renowned thinkers invited to lecture in the various colleges.

It was not surprising that Polanyi had difficulty communicating with the Oxford philosophers. His approach to philosophy was grounded in his years of work in medicine and chemistry, not in any formal philosophical training. He felt sure it had been beneficial for him to start off "with little or no schooling," because "a sound knowledge of philosophy makes the necessary radical advances extremely difficult"; but he used common philosophical terms in unusual ways and did not always define his concepts with the precision the academic philosophers expected. He had apprenticed himself to no master and therefore had no mentor to guide his entry into the field. In the humanities, Polanyi's self-set standards and reluctance to frame his concerns in others' language cut him off from the intellectual companionship that he desired. He liked to mix his philosophy with observations from a wide range of other fields, often indulging in prophetic homilies and ethical generaliza-tions. And—as with so many of us academics—he seemed to be inclined to live among his admirers and to shun his critics.

Oxford philosophy was dominated at that time by strongly entrenched pillars of logical positivism and of linguistic philosophy. An observer of the Oxford scene, Robin Hodgkin of the education faculty, later recalled that the university was "the intellectual home of many of the philosophical positions which Polanyi had been criticizing":

> In the nineteen-sixties the student population had begun to ask for more substantial philosophical food than the logic of A. J. Ayer or the conceptual clarity of Gilbert Ryle could offer; but the response to this need was slow to develop. When Polanyi arrived on the scene he had already articulated a radically new conceptual scheme in which many familiar philosophical problems would lose their hold and new ones would appear. Here was this quiet polymath, 'unqualified' in philosophy, asserting that the dichotomies of fact and value, thought and action must be closed and showing how this could be done with a bewildering range of metaphor, scientific example and rhetorical flourish. He questioned the centrality of scepticism and of objectivity in science and reinstated commitment and even therefore certain kinds of faith as prior conditions for effective action and understanding. Through it all came a calm confidence which must have disconcerted critics who shared neither his breadth nor his conviction.[4]

Although his own epistemology explains quite well why people dwelling in different interpretative frameworks necessarily have difficulty communicating with each other, such irenic abstractions seemed to provide Polanyi no balm for the sting of being neglected.

Lady Drusilla Scott, daughter of Lord Lindsay, was drawn to Polanyi's ideas and was sensitive to his feeling of isolation. She saw that he was not accepted by the Oxford philosophers. "They mistrusted him, he did not stick to their strict division of subjects, but used psychology, religion, medicine or any other subject to expound his ideas. He did not use their language, he was not asking the sort of questions they were interested in. . . . I remember that once he sent me a paper he had just published, and I wrote back to say that I found it very convincing but I should like to see the arguments against it— could he tell me of anyone who had written on that side? He replied rather sadly, 'They don't argue against it, they just ignore it.' "[5] Polanyi found support and acceptance primarily among the friends with whom he kept in touch through correspondence and occasional visits, notably Arthur Koestler, Marjorie Grene, Veronica Wedgwood, John Jewkes, Hugh O'Neill, Edward Shils, Joseph Oldham, Karl Mannheim, Elizabeth Sewell, and the members of the Committee for Cultural Freedom.

In September, Polanyi traveled to Paris and Basle on behalf of the Congress of Cultural Freedom, then joined John and Sue for a ten-day vacation in Rome and Taormina. Polanyi then traveled to New York to receive the Lecomte du Noüy award for *Personal Knowledge* and *The Study of Man* on November 17. The award was presented in recognition of Polanyi's contribution to contemporary spiritual thought, particularly in relation to the compatibility of religion and science. On this trip, Polanyi was able to rehearse his Eddington Lecture, "Beyond Nihilism," which he was to give at Cambridge in February (1960b). The terms of the appointment required that a printed version of the lecture be on sale in Cambridge the day after the presentation, which meant that Polanyi had to deliver his final draft to Cambridge by November 16. Polanyi delivered early versions of the lecture at Princeton, Harvard, and Yale.

It was at the Yale event that Bill Scott first met Polanyi. Although Scott had purchased *Personal Knowledge* and *The Study of Man* on the recommendation of a friend, the books were still unopened on his shelf when he was invited to a faculty dinner for Polanyi. Since Scott was supposed to serve as Polanyi's host at breakfast the following morning, he was driven to a hasty reading of *The Study of Man* over the weekend. Although he was intrigued by Polanyi's topic, "Beyond Nihilism," and attended his evening lecture with interest, he failed to comprehend his account of how life transcends physics and chemistry—it did not fit Scott's lifelong grounding in physics. In conversation at breakfast, Scott began to see how Polanyi had constructed a bridge between authentic science and authentic faith.

In his lecture, Polanyi reiterated his claim that we have in Western society an excess of moral zeal and passion, such as was known in antiquity only among the Hebrew prophets; in contrast, among the Greeks moral rectitude was associated with serenity. Polanyi declared, "The idea that morality consists in imposing on ourselves the curb of moral commands is so ingrained in us that we simply cannot see that the moral need of our time is, on the contrary, to curb our inordinate demands which precipitate us into moral degradation, and threaten us with bodily destruction" (KB, 4). At the Lecomte du Noüy award ceremony, Polanyi was praised for his concept of personal knowledge and his work for human freedom. He responded that in his youth, he and his friends developed a concern for the world as a whole. His abandonment of chemistry for "economics, sociology, philosophy and the like" was just "a desire to go back to normal" (1960c, 57).

Before concluding his American visit, Polanyi spent a long weekend with Mausi at the country home of her daughter, Eva Zeisel, in New City, outside of New York. After years of spending her energy on the needs of her family and on her concerns for peace and justice, she had returned to the field of her graduate studies at the University of Budapest. Although Mausi was confined to bed with what was to be her last illness, she was still pursuing her historical research, dictating her recent discoveries concerning Captain John Smith's early journeys in Hungary. Polanyi was not to see her again. He heard from John of Mausi's death on December 23. He had lost both a sister and an intimate confidante. Although there was no one who could take her place, Polanyi accepted her death stoically: "at our age, so near to our own end, it behooves us to be passive in meeting death ... our pain needs no expression."[6] Christmas of 1959 was the first that Michael and Magda had spent alone in nearly forty years. Despite their sorrow, they were in good health and pleased to be moving to Oxford. Polanyi reported that they were both "well and cheerful, and not yet too old."[7]

At the beginning of 1960, Polanyi reviewed a translation into English of Teilhard de Chardin's book *The Phenomenon of Man* (1960a). Polanyi had long been impatient with the more mechanistic formulations of neo-Darwinism and had argued in the concluding chapters of *Personal Knowledge* for a complementary morphogenetic influence playing a part in evolution. In his review, Polanyi asked whether the high praise for Teilhard by Sir Julian Huxley in the introduction presaged the end of the obscurantism of the mechanists. Polanyi himself resonated to Teilhard's poetic vision of "the grand orthogenesis of everything living toward a higher degree of immanent spontaneity." However, he deplored the way Teilhard avoided many decisive issues and left key problems unresolved. Teilhard admitted his ignorance of how character is formed and simply said that "the blind determinism of the gene plays a subordinate role" (21). Polanyi was disappointed that Teilhard did not go beyond his statement that "the progressive leaps of life" must be interpreted "in an active and finalistic way." During the first few months of 1960, Polanyi had several more occasions to present his understanding of philosophy. In addition to the Eddington Lecture at Cambridge, he gave a lecture series at Merton[8] and presented a talk on "The Process of Knowing" at the Philosophy Club. Reverend Thomas Torrance invited him to deliver the Gunning Lectures at the University of Edinburgh. Polanyi spoke on "Perspectives of Personal Knowledge" in five lectures, February 28 to March 4.[9] He argued that we enter into an enlarged conception of being by virtue of recognizing our part in tacit knowing.

In the first week of April 1960, Michael and Magda moved into 22 Upland Park Road, a comfortable little house with a small garden in North Oxford. They hung a dramatic portrait of Michael's father in their parlor, arranged their furniture and other treasures, and moved Michael's books and papers into the upstairs study. The house on Upland Park Road was to be their home for the rest of their lives.

June marked the tenth anniversary of the founding of the Congress for Cultural Freedom. The General Assembly in Berlin drew more than 200 scholars, writers, and intellectuals to discuss "Progress in Freedom." Polanyi became acquainted with Mayor Willy Brandt during preparations for the Congress. He found him "an impressive person full of life, humor and courage."[10] At the June session, Brandt came specifically to hear Polanyi's address, "Beyond Nihilism" (1960b). This address served as an introduction to the section devoted to "Progress of Ideas," which was held under Polanyi's direction.[11] As one of six speakers at the closing session, Polanyi extolled "the unexpected strength of the truth" that was revealed during the ten years since the founding of the Congress (1960e, 6). He affirmed his hope that just as liberal ideas were taking root again in Hungary, Poland, and Russia, so, too, the "dehumanization of the intellect" could be halted in China.

Back in Oxford, Polanyi sought to build on the foundation he had laid in *Personal Knowledge*. He continued to publish articles and lectures exploring ramifications of his scientific thought and his theory of tacit knowing. In October, he discussed matters of judgment and intuition in science in a seminar led by A. C. Crombie, Professor of the History of Science in Oxford. Polanyi focused on "The Unaccountable Element in Science," the tacit power which underpins all articulation (1961e). In keeping with his understanding of the vital role that the Western tradition of freedom plays in research, Polanyi continued to work for the Congress of Cultural Freedom in order to "better our prospects of survival."[12] From the middle of December to the beginning of January 1961, he traveled to Egypt and India for a series of international seminars and private conferences. He repeated his lecture on "The Unaccountable Element of Science" at the Bose Institute in Calcutta and discussed his recent article, "The Study of Man" (1961a), at a Bombay Seminar on "The Place of Science and Humanities in Higher Education." Upon his return from India, Polanyi gave a series of eight lectures on "Unspecifiable Elements of Knowledge" at Oxford during the Hilary term, January to March 1961.[13] These lectures were a considerably expanded version of the single lecture he had delivered in Crombie's seminar.

The Oxford lectures were completed just before Polanyi's 70th birthday (March 11, 1961). Marjorie Grene and Veronica Wedgwood arranged a grand celebration in London at the Rembrandt Hotel. At the dinner, Polanyi was presented with a Festschrift, *The Logic of Personal Knowledge*, a collection of nineteen essays that paid tribute to Polanyi's career in science, his philosophy of freedom, and his epistemology.[14] Many of the authors were able to attend, including Paul Ignotus, Arthur Koestler, Ely Devons, and D. M. MacKinnon. Other friends present were John and Sylvia Jewkes, Sir Charles Reynolds,

Ruel Tyson, Colin Franklin (for Routledge), Walter James, John Baker, and Mrs. Melvin Lasky. Polanyi felt fine: "I am grateful to say that we are both in good health and spirits. This period between the beginning of the end and the end of the end appeals to me by its formless joys and muted passions.[15]

Later that March, Polanyi gave the fifty-first May lecture on science in industry at the Royal Institution of London: "Science: Academic and Industrial" (1961b). Polanyi noted that the study of technology and the study of humanities are comparable because both study the products of human ingenuity. He pointed out that both technology and the humanities (language, literature, history, arts, philosophy, etc.) can be studied only at second-hand at a university because their development goes on mainly outside the university. The fields of tacit knowing that ground articulation and theory extend far beyond the bounds of academic disciplines.

In the spring of 1961, Polanyi was invited to address the World Student Christian Association in Louvain, Belgium. While preparing his talk, Polanyi read Josef Pieper's *Scholastik*, which traced the history of the faith-reason relation back beyond medieval times to early Greece and then set out Pieper's analysis of contemporary obstacles to faith. Polanyi wrote an essay entitled "Faith and Reason," which was published on the Continent as "The Scientific Revolution." Polanyi argued that "all true knowing is inherently hazardous, just as all true faith is a leap into the unknown. Knowing includes its own uncertainty as an integral part of it, just as, according to Tillich, all faith necessarily includes its own dubeity" (1961c, 244).

In speaking to the students at Louvain, Polanyi shared his favorite reference to St. Paul's vision of faith, hope, and grace, applying it to scientific discovery: we carry out extensive labor, which of itself cannot make a discovery, in the hope that powers beyond our own will lead us to new, as yet hidden meanings. His own vision of the coming of Christ was of that of a man set free from the bondage of human affliction who was able to point the way to redemption: "This is the event, whether historic or mythical, which shattered the framework of Greek rationalism and has set for all times the hopes and obligations of man far beyond the horizons of here and now" (KB, 43–44). That same spring, Irving J. Good persuaded Polanyi to contribute to a collection of essays entitled *The Scientist Speculates: An Anthology of Partly-Baked Ideas*. To fulfill his promise, Polanyi wrote "Clues to an Understanding of Mind and Body" (1962d). Over the next few years, Polanyi continued to argue that his theory of tacit knowing could resolve Descartes's mind/body problem.

During the week of July 9, Polanyi took part in the Symposium on the Structure of Scientific Change, which was held in Rhodes House at Oxford University under the auspices of the International Union of the History and Philosophy of Science. Thomas S. Kuhn of the University of California at Berkeley had invited Polanyi to be one of two commentators for his paper "The Function of Dogma in Scientific Research." Kuhn had heard Polanyi speak on tacit knowing in November 1958 during his brief visit to the Center for Advanced Study in the Behavioral Sciences in Palo Alto; Kuhn was in residence there at the time.[16] He had also read some of Polanyi's work, including *Science, Faith and Society, The Logic of Liberty*, and *Personal Knowledge*. Polanyi began by observing that "The paper by Mr. Thomas Kuhn may arouse opposition from various quarters but not from me" (1962e). He agreed with Kuhn's statement that research is dependent on a deep commitment to established beliefs. However, Polanyi did not accept Kuhn's simple dichotomy between normal science conducted within a standard paradigm and revolutionary science that creates new paradigms because remarkable advances have been made by just taking current paradigms seriously. He also felt that Kuhn failed to account for the inner heuristic urge that drives scientists toward discovery.

Later in the month, Polanyi spent a week with Gretl and Ervin von Gomperz (who later changed their name to Dentay) at their favorite resort, the Hotel Waldhaus in Sils Maria in the Swiss Engadin. Several other friends of Gretl and Ervin stopped by, among them Silvia Kind, a vivacious Swiss-born professor of music who had heard Polanyi speak at the Congress in Berlin the summer before and had been very impressed by his presentation.[17] The two became good friends and began to correspond regularly.

10

At the Wheel of the World:
1961–1971

Because of his age, Polanyi was forced to retire from his Senior
Research Fellowship at Merton at the end of July. He remained
young intellectually and was now free to spend more time with the
large, appreciative audiences he found in the United States. On the
whole, his American students seemed less wedded to the analytic
school of philosophy and more open to the logic of personal knowledge. The University of Virginia named Polanyi a Distinguished
Visiting Scholar in the Thomas Jefferson Center in the fall of 1961.
During his residence, he delivered a series of lectures entitled
"History and Hope: An Analysis of Our Age."[1] In his initial address,
Polanyi gave a "two sentence history of hope: There were centuries of
culture that accepted custom and law as foundational. Then there
were the American and French Revolutions that instituted the deliberate continuing of unlimited social improvement as the dominant
principle." In the Western countries, the most humane and free
societies developed from this principle, whereas in the Soviet empire,
the same commitment to social improvement led to very different
results.[2] In the conclusion of the lectures, he suggested that we must
now revise the ideals of the French Revolution, using the tacit
dimensions of the scientific community as a new model for
the development of moral and political responsibility. Although great
discoveries are rooted in the tacit knowledge of the knower, they are
intended to become the common property of the whole scientific
community. Personal knowledge is the foundation of public knowledge, not its enemy. Those who have dwelt in the scientific worldview
deeply enough to make a new breakthrough feel a moral obligation to

persuade others in the scientific community of the value and worth of their discoveries. In turn, the scientific community needs to share its heritage of free inquiry and responsible personal judgment with the larger society that upholds the scientific enterprise. After leaving Virginia, Polanyi visited with John and his family in Toronto, then traveled to Chicago to lecture on "The Republic of Science: Its Political and Economic Theory" (1962b). Polanyi hoped to throw light on the operation of science from the politics and economics of a free society, and, vice versa, to show what help can be found for the latter from the success of the former. Philosopher Stephen Toulmin commented that in this presentation, Polanyi had undertaken a discussion of the social aspects of science long before it had become a fashionable topic in the history of science.[3]

In February 1962, Polanyi repeated his Virginia lectures on "History and Hope" as the McInerny Lecturer at the University of California at Berkeley.[4] He also visited the Pacific School of Religion, where he met with Charles McCoy's graduate seminar on Christianity and Contemporary Intellectual Movements. Following a conversation with Polanyi, one of the graduate students, Richard Gelwick, decided to write his thesis on Polanyi's philosophical work, the first of many doctoral dissertations to deal with Polanyi's thought.

Over the two previous years, Polanyi had corresponded with Dennis Gabor and Eugene Wigner about physics and philosophy. In June he sent Gabor an article entitled "Tacit Knowing: Its Bearing on Some Problems of Philosophy" (1962c). Polanyi took up the question that Lord Brain had been trying to answer recently: "How do we come to know external objects, if our awareness of them is altogether internal?" Polanyi's approach to an answer lay in a proper grasp of the tacit dimension of our contact with reality. The body participates fully in both the life of the mind and the reality of the external universe. We use the body as an instrument of contact with reality by dwelling within it and attending from it to what we wish to explore. "Tacit knowing now appears as an act of *indwelling* by which we gain access to a new meaning. . . . since all understanding is tacit knowing, all understanding is achieved by indwelling. . . . indwelling is less deep when observing a star than when understanding men or works of art" (KB, 160).

In the summer of 1962, as was his custom, Polanyi combined study, travel, and visits with friends. He went to Alpbach to spend some time with Koestler, vacationed for two days in Sils Maria, and joined Silvia Kind on a trip from Italy to Winterthur in Switzerland, where they stayed with her sister and visited art exhibits. During this period, Polanyi was reading Hegel, which caused him to muse about the history of his time and his place in it:

The decline of late antiquity into the rise of Early Christian Art, this "perish and rebirth" ("Stirb und Werde") from which we have

both, you and I, emerged, has been fascinating me for years. Aren't
we again in the process of a similar explosion? Maybe I'm influenced
in this feeling by the reading of Hegel. I have suspected myself
for a long time of actually being a Hegelian, but to me he seemed to
be always much more crazy than I. Only in the light of my ideas
developed a short time ago (and still unpublished writings) I have
begun to doubt that. The amount of my craziness seems to
approximate his.[5]

The Center for Advanced Study in the Behavioral Sciences, in Palo Alto
near Stanford University, invited Polanyi to become a Fellow in 1962–63.
Polanyi was also invited to deliver the annual Terry Lectures at Yale University
in October 1962. During his time at Palo Alto, Polanyi concentrated on
synthesizing the new insights he had gained into tacit knowing since he had
finished *Personal Knowledge*. Polanyi wanted to make the most of his opportunities at Yale; he was convinced that he had found "a novel idea of human
knowledge from which a harmonious view of thought and existence, rooted
in the universe, seems to come into sight" (1962g, 4). Polanyi had written in
Personal Knowledge of how we take the subsidiary particulars into ourselves by
acts of indwelling or interiorization. In the first Terry Lecture, he further
explored the subject of indwelling and its illumination of the bodily roots of all
thought. Our own body is the only thing in the world which we almost never
experience as an object, but instead experience as a tool for intelligent use to
attend to what is outside. Indwelling, said Polanyi, goes on in subtle ways in
science, more strikingly in the humanities and in the works of the creative
artist, and even more in the interiorization of moral teachings. In the conclusion of the series, Polanyi argued that tacit knowing requires immersion in
our intellectual tradition, in which we believe before we know, combined with
new contacts with reality, contacts found in discovery and in dialogue with
others. Polanyi expressed the hope of reconciliation between critical lucidity
and moral demands, a task which he considered to be ultimately a religious
matter, but one to be carried out in the secular world first.

Polanyi shared his first impressions of the Center for Advanced Study
with Arthur Koestler: "It is a collection of specialists, a nice collection, occasionally instructive, but still only a replica of the academic mind, or lack of
mind. Comprehensive issues cause a dreamy look to come into their eyes. 'It
is not something one can get one's teeth into'—not their kind of teeth. I enjoy
it, for I am used to the tribe; and at least there is an effort of keeping the
conversation going, instead of just ducking behind the screen of expertise and
academic routine problems. Yes, I like it very much but doubt you would."
Polanyi declared that he did not mind making small talk and forgetting his
own interests, but he saw his friend Arthur as "an intellectual go-getter" and
doubted that he "could stick it for 9 months."[6]

During his time at the Center, Polanyi continued to develop the material he had prepared for the Terry Lectures. In contrast to his somewhat lonely experience at Merton College, life in the idyllic California countryside was rich and satisfying; the windows of his office looked out on farm fields and dairy pastures. He and Magda had their own small apartment nearby. Magda once again took up driving, and Michael was able to regularly take part in discussions at lunch and in many other meetings, both planned and unplanned. Polanyi enjoyed exchanging ideas with Erik Erikson, Meyer Shapiro, John McCarthy, Abraham Maslow, Peter Uttley, and Yehezkel Dror, but he was specially drawn to the humanist psychologist Carl Rogers. Discussions with Rogers led Polanyi to trace his philosophy back "to the corresponding ideas of the existentialist movement."[7] In February of 1963, Polanyi also noted discussions with McCarthy, Uttley, Shapiro, and Grene on problems of body and mind.

Richard Gelwick, the young student from the Graduate Theological Union in Berkeley, soon became a regular visitor to the Center. To Gelwick's amazement, the 71-year-old Polanyi asked his opinion on the draft of the Terry Lectures. Polanyi greatly valued Gelwick's interest in his work; he was delighted to have a disciple, and the two spent hours together in Polanyi's office. When Gelwick expressed his gratitude for the time they spent together, Polanyi said: "Old men are in greater need of the young, than vice versa."[8] Polanyi introduced him at the fellows' luncheons as "Gelwick from Berkeley." Gelwick was touched by Polanyi's easy, egalitarian manner.

Gelwick's wife, Beverly, and Magda became friends, too. Both Polanyis took an interest in the Gelwicks' two small children. The family often took the Polanyis on expeditions into rural California and the redwood forests; they soon learned that whenever Michael and Magda disagreed about directions, Magda was invariably correct. Magda and Beverly shared an interest in the art of the Etruscans, and Magda, thwarted in the professional ambitions of her own youth, also developed an abiding interest in Beverly's career. Perhaps Magda saw in Beverly another young mother whose work was overshadowed by her husband's achievements. Although Magda had continued her own writing in the field of chemical technology, it was far from the brilliant career she had envisioned for herself when she began her doctoral program in chemical engineering at Karlsruhe.

Gelwick questioned Polanyi about his publications on social and philosophical issues. Polanyi had never systematically collected these papers. He estimated that he might have about twenty-five of these short, non-scientific writings; it was clear that he had never given them much attention after they were published.[9] Gelwick had encouraged Polanyi to bring his collection of these non-technical articles to Stanford. Gelwick began a compilation that was later to occupy him for a full year and to result in a bibliography of some 120 essays on social and philosophical topics, a research project that proved invaluable to later students of Polanyi's thought.[10] Polanyi did not have a complete collection of the nine books he had published. The University of Chicago Press was having difficulty finding a clean copy of Science, Faith and Society in preparation for the publication of a new edition.[11] In his enthusiasm for sharing his ideas, Polanyi had given away all of his own copies of the book.

When Polanyi learned from Gelwick that Paul Tillich would be delivering the Earl Lectures at Pacific School of Religion in Berkeley in February, he asked Gelwick to arrange a private meeting between the two of them. Over the years he had found many of Tillich's ideas congenial. He had read the British edition of Tillich's Systematic Theology when it appeared in 1953 and copied a quotation from the text on the inside back cover: "The question of the existence of God can neither be asked nor answered."[12] Professor Charles McCoy of the Pacific School of Religion, Tillich's host and Gelwick's thesis advisor, arranged an informal evening meeting after the lectures on "Religion, Science and Philosophy," and "Irrelevance and Relevance of Christianity." Tillich was winding down after the day's lectures with a glass of schnapps. Polanyi, on the other hand, was eager to have a serious discussion and wanted to confront Tillich on the points where he felt he was mistaken, especially on the issue of the "method of absolute detachment," which Tillich ascribed to science in contrast to the methods of philosophy and religion.[13]

In "Points from a Conversation with Paul Tillich on February 21, 1963," Polanyi wrote a detailed record of his own comments and a brief account of Tillich's replies.[14] In his side of the dialogue, Polanyi explained the need for basic revision of Tillich's perspective by recognition of the logical functions of participation, that is, indwelling, tacit knowing, and the rest of Polanyi's own theory of knowledge. When Tillich asked about the relation of Polanyi's views to Gestalt psychology, Polanyi responded that he was "deeply indebted to Gestalt psychology," but that "it lacks the element of active participation on the part of the knower," and "has run away from its own philosophic significance" (2).

Polanyi also cited his own relationship to the pragmatism of Dewey and to modern existentialism and phenomenology. According to Polanyi, Dewey "recognized and vividly described the process by which we shape our own knowledge" (2). However, Dewey relied on the power of reason and progress without guessing that totalitarian states would use the elements on which Dewey relied in order to subvert the notion of truth. Polanyi recognized that his theory of indwelling also resembled existentialism, except that the existentialists treat the human situation "with an anxiety bordering on despair." Although he shared the existentialists' alarm at the collapse of the assumptions that had shaped European culture, he was nevertheless convinced that a proper understanding of the nature of science could restore the possibility of belief.

When Tillich asked whether Christianity has "any relevance to this project," Polanyi replied:

> You have said that the irrelevance of Christianity can be overcome only by passing through the darkness of existentialist despair. You have said that the faith which rises from this depth will embrace its own doubt. It will live as a perennial, unresolvable tension in us. My theory of knowledge takes this as its paradigm. It is shaped in the image of what I understand to be the Pauline scheme of redemption. Having to face the fact that no knowledge can be set free of conceivable doubt, and that the most distinctive form of scientific knowledge, the vision of great scientific originality, is a solitary knowledge ready to face universal doubt, I conclude that it is of the essence of knowledge to be held to be true by a man's mental effort. Such is the nature of that active indwelling by which we make sense of the world. (3)

In a further response to Tillich, Polanyi also published an article, "Science and Religion: Separate Dimensions or Common Ground?" (1963a). In this article, Polanyi elaborated on his conception of indwelling, which he said corresponds roughly to the existentialist vision "of being in our body and in the world" (8). If indwelling is accepted as the way for acquiring and possessing all knowledge, then "this may open up a cosmic vision which will harmonize with some basic teachings of Christianity" (11). Polanyi also argued that evolution is based on emergence, where each higher level arises from a lower but is not accountable by the levels below it. Only through creative power can we exceed our capacities and create novelties beyond ourselves. After reading this article, Tillich wrote Polanyi that he was happy to find how much they were in general agreement. Tillich especially appreciated Polanyi's comment: "[Tillich] has fought for the purification of faith from religious fundamentalism; I would supplement this by purifying truth from scientific dogmatism."[15]

While Polanyi was still in residence at the Center, Scott invited him to come to the University of Nevada for a lecture and meetings with his colleagues and students. Despite his seventy-two years, Polanyi's alertness and energy were everywhere apparent during his two-day visit to Reno. As always, he had a keen interest in new experience. His visit began with a trip to Pyramid Lake and the Paiute Indian Reservation, followed by a brief nap and dinner. Then he presented the lecture he had composed in 1961 on "Science: Academic and Industrial" (1961b) to the Desert Research Institute. He disappeared from the reception for a few minutes to follow his regular practice of calling Magda to tell her about the day's events.

At the end of the year at the Center, the Polanyis returned to England via New York and Canada. Besides visiting John and Sue in Toronto, Polanyi gave a lecture on "The Metaphysical Aspects of Science" at the World Student

Christian Federation at St. Anne de Bellevue in Montreal. "It was a great experience to be thanked for telling them so much more than I could possibly know. I certainly don't know, as I realized when finding their theological discourses arid and almost repulsive. Perhaps I am a child talking with an adult, a one-sided conversation."[16]

Back in Oxford, Polanyi was touched to receive a record from Silvia Kind of her own harpsichord recital. Despite his family's devotion to drama, literature, and dance, and although Magda was a good pianist and had always been much interested in music, Michael had considered himself unmusical. He had occasionally accompanied Magda to concerts when they were newly married in Berlin, but the music had not moved him deeply. He thoroughly enjoyed listening to Kind's recital and began to play a record every evening. He was delighted with the awakening of this new passion.[17]

In September, the Polanyis settled back into the routine of life at Upland Park Road. After his year in California, he found Oxford overspecialized and petty. To his disappointment, he received little notice from Oxford scholars; he gave only one lecture that fall, an address to Merton students on "The Republic of Science," which he had originally presented at Roosevelt University in Chicago (1962b). Polanyi continued to make valuable contacts outside of Oxford. He kept up an extensive correspondence on various topics, for example, with W. H. Thorpe on Elsasser and information storage in the DNA, with Chaim Perelman on his book *La Nouvelle Rhetorique*, with John Beloff on the Terry Lectures and the notion of indwelling, with Gerald Holton, proposing a publication of a collection of anti- or post-positivist essays, and with Nevill Coghill concerning physiologist Pirenne's opinions on *trompe l'oeil* and Polanyi's own ideas on a theory of poetry. Along with his dominant humanistic concerns, his retrospective article in *Science*, "The Potential Theory of Adsorption: Authority in Science Has Its Uses and Dangers" (1963b) resulted in eighty requests for reprints, some accompanied by warm letters of support.[18]

The fall of 1963 brought sad news from his brothers. Adolf, so recently in good spirits on his eightieth birthday, had suffered severe injuries in an accident and was recuperating in São Paulo. Frida, Adolf's first wife, had died after a brief illness. Michael, who had not seen his former sister-in-law for more than fifty years, wrote his nephew Tom that he remembered her very well from their early Budapest days. "With her passed away yet another symbol of another world. . . . her long life was very much of our times. Such losses, anxieties, fantastic escapes, her surviving relatives scattered."[19] Polanyi sent Adolf and Karl a color photograph of the family portrait of the five brothers and sisters that had been painted sixty-eight years previously. He thought they, too, might like to be reminded of their childhood. Karl was in increasingly poor health. He made a farewell visit to Hungary, staying with his nephew, George Striker, and visited old friends, especially members of the

Galileo Circle whom he had known for fifty years. From one of these friends, Kende Zsiga, Michael heard that he was much on Karl's mind. In response, Michael suggested that instead of puzzling about each other they should "cultivate our brotherly love as our garden, á la Candide."[20]

Bill Poteat nominated Polanyi to serve as the James B. Duke Distinguished Professor at Duke University in Durham, North Carolina during the spring of 1964. Polanyi was delighted to leave Oxford to share his ideas with another American audience. Before his departure, Polanyi met with Dennis Gabor, the innovative Hungarian engineer, to further explore information theory; Polanyi hoped to write a synopsis of that field as a guide for the Congress for Cultural Freedom in the years ahead. Magda remained in Oxford to complete her work on a textile dictionary. This was to be the longest time they spent apart since their marriage more than forty years before.

Polanyi's chair was in the Department of Religion: "If you think this is paradoxical, I should reply that I find more people in that department with a deep interest in important matters than in any other part of the University."[21] Polanyi's presented a series of five public lectures entitled "Man in Thought" on successive Monday evenings during February and early March; each lecture was followed by an informal discussion the next afternoon. Polanyi reported to O'Neill that the lectures were attended by about three hundred people, "absolutely Catholic," and the next day, most of them would be present for the follow-up discussion. In his first lecture, entitled "The Metaphysical Reach of Science," Polanyi tried to define the mental powers by which scientific discoveries are made, using the Copernican revolution as an example.[22] The other four lectures ("The Structure of Tacit Knowing," "Commitment to Science," "The Emergence of Man," and "Thought in Society") were essentially a repetition of the Terry Lectures he had given at Yale more than a year before.

Polanyi found the living arrangements at Duke very attractive; he was housed in a pleasant faculty apartment on the third floor of an experimental women's dormitory in what was then the women's campus. The resident students were charmed by the guest professor from Oxford and they were soon knocking on his door to engage him in long conversations on subjects ranging from French Existentialism to a broken romance. Polanyi relished his new role as a sort of father confessor to a host of fascinated and fascinating young women. Magda, keeping track of affairs through Michael's letters home to Upland Park Road, wrote Gelwick that she was happy to hear about all the young ladies "buzzing around" her husband.[23]

Bill Poteat took good care of Polanyi during his stay in Durham, seeing to the everyday needs that Magda generally managed when the Polanyis were together. Because he was now showing more and more signs of his "otherworldliness," as his friends called his increasing absentmindedness, it was evident that Polanyi did indeed need attention. He often went the wrong way and got lost. At the end of a luncheon one day, he abruptly wheeled from the table and disappeared; his colleagues eventually found him in the kitchen.[24]

Polanyi felt he was receiving a hearing at Duke such as he had not received before: "I am no longer an invisible man."[25] The experience sealed his affection for the United States: "To love America is not only happiness but a gain for truth and the future."[26] At the same time, he felt doubtful about his success. After the last seminar at Duke, he was talking with Poteat, Gelwick, and Grene when he suddenly sighed; "The romance has gone all out of it," he told them.[27] The opponents he had once thought influential, innumerable, and invincible now seemed inconsequential, as if they were hardly worth noticing anymore. "God knows, in the end one might tell me I'm trying to beat down open doors."[28]

Besides his five public lectures, Polanyi addressed several other audiences during his stay. Poteat took him to the Junior Honors Seminar that he was directing at the University of North Carolina at Greensboro, where Polanyi lectured informally on *Personal Knowledge*, which Poteat's students had been studying throughout the term. Polanyi also addressed the Duke Divinity School and gave a lecture entitled "On Body and Mind" to approximately two hundred people in the Psychiatry Department (1969a). Polanyi told the psychiatrists about his theory of tacit knowledge: "all communication relies to a noticeable extent on evoking knowledge that we cannot tell, and that all our knowledge of mental processes, like feeling or conscious intellectual activities, is similarly based on a knowledge which we cannot tell" (196).

Douglas Adams, a Duke undergraduate at the time, was standing with Polanyi and Poteat on the steps of the Faculty Apartments after a class. Polanyi became fascinated by a frisbee that some students were throwing back and forth. When Polanyi commented that he should do a study of frisbees, noting some interesting aspects of their movements in flight, Poteat turned him around and led him back into the classroom saying "You work on the mind/body problem instead!" At other times, when Polanyi would express a desire to study the Russian Revolution, Poteat would say, "Stick with the mind/body problem."[29] Like many others at Duke, Adams admired Polanyi's willingness to talk with students, treating them with attention and respect. He questioned Polanyi about what he meant in *Personal Knowledge* when he said that "The Bible and the Pauline doctrine in particular, may still be pregnant with unexpected lessons" (PK, 285). Polanyi replied, "Oldham had suggested that."[30] As Adams was then studying Eastern Orthodox theology, he also spoke with Polanyi about "how the via negativa is a paradigm for the epistemology he was suggesting." He also questioned Polanyi about Wittgenstein's thought and its evolution, but "Polanyi was less inclined to see similarities between his thought and Wittgenstein's thought (even after the latter's thought had changed so greatly) than he was to see their differences."

Polanyi spent much of April traveling up and down the East Coast, first to vacation with friends and family in New York and Toronto, then to lecture at MIT on "The Metaphysical Reach of Science" and "The Structure of Tacit Knowing," and finally to address the American Academy for Arts and Sciences in Boston on "The Place of Man in the Universe." Polanyi also visited Elizabeth Sewell in Tougaloo, Mississippi. They had resumed their spirited correspondence after a visit together in New York the year before. Sewell wanted to correspond "rather more fully and personally";[31] in the months that followed, they exchanged ideas on poetry and modern drama and Polanyi read with interest Sewell's descriptions of life at Tougaloo Southern Christian College, an institution with a student body that was largely African-American. The twenty whites on campus in 1963–1964 made it one of the few desegregated areas in the State of Mississippi. Sewell introduced Polanyi to her classes by saying that, in view of the things he said, his friendly way of lecturing always seemed to her like politely asking for permission to saw off her right leg. She was somewhat anxious that his lectures might be too abstruse,[32] but her students listened attentively. Polanyi was pleased: "They seemed to feel the momentous implications of what I was saying."[33]

Shortly after his return to Durham, Polanyi received the news that his brother Karl had died on April 23. Karl had just finished *Dahomey and the Slave Trade*, and he and Ilona had published an anthology, *The Plough and the Pen: Writings from Hungary, 1930–56*. Polanyi left immediately to attend the funeral in Toronto. Now only Michael and Adolf remained of the six Polanyi children.

In May, Poteat invited Gelwick to come from Berkeley to lecture on the theological significance of Polanyi's theory, a subject which had hardly been discussed during Polanyi's stay at Durham. Gelwick spoke on Polanyi's theory of cognition and then the whole group joined in discussing the possibility of a new theology. That same month, Polanyi addressed physicists at the University of North Carolina, Chapel Hill, on "Science and Man's Place in the Universe" (1964d). Polanyi's theme was how humans had evolved to the highest place in a many-leveled universe. The lecture was repeated a few days later at Johns Hopkins University in Baltimore.

Before he returned home, Polanyi's friends in the dormitory gave him a going-away party; he reciprocated by hosting a champagne reception. He had very much enjoyed their friendship, and he was delighted to squire some of them around Oxford when they visited the following summer. Four days before his departure, Polanyi gave a farewell dinner for fifteen guests. "We drank 8 bottles of St. Emilion 1959 and praised me heartily."[34] In many ways, Polanyi felt that this semester at Duke marked the high point of his career as a philosopher.

While in residence at Duke, Polanyi prepared a paper for the International Congress for the Philosophy of Science, which was to meet in Jerusalem in August 1964. He sought to show the connections between his work and that of Husserl,[35] Merleau-Ponty, Erwin W. Straus, and other contemporary philosophers.[36] He hoped that making these connections would reduce his isolation and substantiate the work he had done. The month before the conference, he was heartened by an enthusiastic letter from Princeton psychologist Hadley Cantril; Cantril reported that he had just read *Personal Knowledge* and called that experience "a page by page communion" with Polanyi.[37] Polanyi replied that he was working in the same vein as Erwin W. Straus, Carl Rogers, and Arthur Koestler.

Polanyi entitled his Jerusalem lecture "The Logic of Tacit Inference" (1966a). Polanyi associated his theory of tacit knowledge with the phenomenology of Husserl and Merleau-Ponty and with Gilbert Ryle's "informal logic" of science. He recognized the similarity between his notion of indwelling and the ideas of Dilthey and the existentialists. He argued that his concept of an active knower was consistent with Kant's vision of the moral person in the "Second Critique" and the *Metaphysics of Morals*. As had happened so often in the past, Polanyi was disappointed by the apparent apathy of his professionally trained audience.[38] He found only a few sympathetic listeners in the group.

After the conference in Jerusalem, Polanyi spent a working vacation on the island of Rhodes. He made some notes on the philosophy of finalism before returning to England to finish a lecture he had promised for the opening of the Senior Center at Bowdoin College in Maine in October 1964. He entitled his lecture "On the Modern Mind," describing his theory of knowledge based on indwelling (1965a). Although there was not much new in the lecture itself, he was delighted to be speaking at the invitation of Edward Pols, chairman of the Philosophy Department at Bowdoin.[39]

Pols had first read *Personal Knowledge* the year before, when Pols's *Recognition of Reason* was in press. Pols was struck by the similarity of their views and realized he would have been helped substantially had he seen Polanyi's book earlier. He added a footnote to his book to that effect and sent a copy to Polanyi when the book appeared.[40] Polanyi was excited and amazed to see how Pols had duplicated the fundamental ideas of *Personal Knowledge* in spite of an entirely different background—"with no science to speak of and a great deal of philosophy I lack."[41] Polanyi went so far as to call Pols a "Doppelgänger"[42] and an alter ego who expressed the same ideas as Polanyi in a totally different language. The meeting between Pols and Polanyi at Bowdoin was as congenial as their correspondence had been. The two later collaborated on conferences on the unity of knowledge.

Polanyi returned to Oxford in good spirits. The encounter with Pols had given him a new feeling of importance, as if he were "an impersonal power in

which perhaps hundreds partake."[43] Despite the cool reception he had received from the professional philosophers in Jerusalem, he was grateful for
the widening circle of followers around the world. At this time, *The Tacit
Dimension* and several articles were in press, the new edition of *Science, Faith
and Society* had just come out, and the latter book and the article "On the
Modern Mind" were being translated into Italian. At last Polanyi began to feel
confident that his thoughts would endure. A growing number of students
were working on his writings and he hoped to be able to provide them with
further material to work with. Even some at Oxford responded with appreciation when he repeated his lecture, "Science and Man's Place in the Universe" (1964d). He considered this to be his first success in his own university.
Polanyi felt rejuvenated by the work he was doing: "Here I am today an old
man but a young thinker. A prophet of new ideas, which might be able to help
humanity somewhat."[44]

In November 1963, Polanyi had visited the Koestlers in London. He and
Koestler discussed publishing an anthology from a like-minded group that
would include all branches of scholarship and show the unity of knowing in its
various fields. In the summer of 1964, he suggested that they ask the Congress to support a seminar to bring this group together to spell out the aims of
the movement under the title, "Man the Center,"[45] which he later changed to
"Unity of Culture." Polanyi hoped to overcome "the blight of scientism by
reconsidering the position of man . . . from one comprehensive point of view.
For we must aim at a metaphysical renaissance, a unified vision transcending
the irrelevances of the modern academic mind."[46]

After talking to Edward Shils, Mike Josselson, Marjorie Grene, Irving
Kristol, and Sigmund Koch, the consensus was to prepare annual meetings
that first were called "Study Group on Foundations of Cultural Unity" but
later were named "Study Group on the Unity of Knowledge." Marjorie Grene,
who had just been appointed professor of philosophy at the University of
California at Davis, joined Pols as the coordinator of the group.

At the end of December 1964, Polanyi flew to New York to meet with
Grene and Pols to plan the first Study Group conference, to be held the following August at Bowdoin College. Sigmund Koch attended the planning
session. He was a professor of psychology from Duke and had recently joined
the Ford Foundation in New York, taking over the Humanities and Arts Program. Ford agreed to sponsor the first meeting and to publish the proceedings.

Polanyi, Grene, and Pols drew up a statement of the general purpose of the
new group. They set themselves against the prevailing conception that all
things whatsoever are to be understood ultimately in terms of the laws of
inanimate nature: "the finalistic nature of living beings, the sentience of animals and their intelligence, the responsible choices of man, his moral and
aesthetic ideals, the fact of human greatness seem all of them anomalies that
will be removed eventually by further progress. Their existence—even the

existence of science itself—has no legitimate grounds; our deepest convictions lack all theoretical foundation."[47]

The Organizing Committee stated that "there are signs of new centers of resistance among scholars, scientists and writers in almost every region of knowledge.... Many share the conviction that a deep-seated philosophical reform is needed—one that would radically alter prevailing conceptions, not only of the nature of knowledge and of creative achievements in general, but of the human agent who inquires and creates, and of the entire fabric of the culture formed by such activities." Because they had seen a "convergence of ideas separately developed in various fields," they proposed a meeting for those who were opposed to "scientism, and the related methodological and ontological oversimplifications, which in one or another form are ascendant in every field of scholarly and creative endeavor" (ix–x).

Before returning to England, Polanyi spent a week in Toronto with John, Sue, and the grandchildren, then flew to São Paulo for Adolf's eighty-second birthday. In January 1965, Polanyi began to draft "The Creative Imagination," which he planned as the opening address for the first Study Group (1966b). He decided to try out this "completely new theory," throwing it "like a true atom bomb...at a hostile public"[48] at the University of London in May.

Later that month, Polanyi presented a thoroughly revised version of "The Creative Imagination" at the University of Notre Dame in Indiana, where he was given an honorary doctorate. In his talk, Polanyi described the role of imagination in intuition, an important new development in his theory of tacit knowing. Intuition can suggest an approach to reality, but, Polanyi explained, it needs the creative imagination to provide the actual power to find hidden realities. Polanyi called "all thoughts of things that are not present, or not yet present—or perhaps never to be present—acts of the imagination" (type-script, 15). The "imagination sallies forward and the intuition integrates what the imagination has lit upon" (19). The two aspects of tacit knowing work together: "The intuition informs the imagination which, in its turn, releases the powers of the intuition" (22). The result is a vision, which then needs to be tested to determine the extent to which it represents reality.

Polanyi found the visit to Notre Dame especially rewarding. Some Catholic philosophers there had read his work but had not endorsed it. He observed that these scholars acted just like the proverbial farmer who saw a giraffe for the first time and cried out: "There is no such animal."[49] However, in his lecture and subsequent discussions, Polanyi was able to convince some skeptics of the value of his approach. Even those who disagreed with him did so with a measure of respect that Polanyi found heartening. These agreeable dialogues provided Polanyi with a chance to communicate his vision in a way that his writings had not. He discovered that the greater openness to his thought also put him under more pressure to work harder.

He was not sure that his failing powers could meet the rising expectations that he placed on them.

During the rest of May, Polanyi worked on "The Structure of Consciousness," a contribution to an issue of *Brain* honoring the biologist Sir Francis Walshe (1965b).[50] Using the logic of tacit knowing, Polanyi supported Walshe's opinion that there must be integrative mental powers that are not explicable by anatomic structure. When he finished this short article, he plunged into Thomas Mann's *Death in Venice*, a book he had heard much discussed. He found Mann's German so refreshing that he read a good part of the book out loud to himself. While on vacation in Sils Maria with Magda, he also read *Mein Name sei Gantenbein* by Max Frisch; he found it both amusing and deep, like Ibsen's *Peer Gynt*.

During the summer of 1965, Polanyi took stock of his achievements in philosophy. He hoped to build a structure sturdy enough to support an application of his ideas to many areas that he could not explore. He saw himself laying the groundwork for a new synthesis: "We are," he said, "after the completion of the great Copernican epoch of four centuries, on the threshold of a complete renewal of Western thinking."[51]

The first Unity of Knowledge conference at Bowdoin attracted a diverse group of twenty-eight scientists, scholars, and writers from the United States, England, and Europe. On the evening of August 23, 1965, the participants gathered for dinner and the beginning of six days of very congenial dialogue. The participants included philosophers Marjorie Grene, Charles Taylor, John Lucas, and John Silber; psychologists Henry Murray and Sigmund Koch; scientists Eugene Wigner, C. F. A. Pantin, and Bill Scott; theologian Bill Poteat; graphic artist Donald Weismann; novelist Herbert Gold; and poet Elizabeth Sewell. Arthur Koestler had been invited, but could not make it to the conference. Polanyi introduced the first meeting with the latest version of his talk, "The Creative Imagination," and throughout the conference, his ideas were central to the discussion. For Scott it was an extraordinary week, providing the sort of warm and spirited interdisciplinary dialogue notably lacking in most universities. Conversations spilled over from the seminar room to the common meals and the cocktail hour, and even to a jaunt to the beach, where Polanyi led the shivering scholars into the frigid Maine surf.

The *New York Times* reported the conference in an appreciative article headlined "In Fear of Reductionism: Scholars Foment Gentle Revolution under Bowdoin's Towering Pines." Joseph Herzberg noted that the deepest concern of the conference participants seemed to be with the problem of epistemology as they sought "a philosophy that would encompass not only the whole nature of knowledge, but equally of man's thought, his creativity and the cultural fabric he creates." He also commented that "there were times when the debate appeared to be guided by the injunction, attributed to Sir Arthur Eddington, never to trust a fact unless it was supported by a theory."[52]

Polanyi himself felt that the participants in the conference were enthusiastic and would help enlist further support for his cause.

Marjorie Grene thought that the conference had been a gamble, but "a gamble that paid off." She considered the conference

> to have laid the foundation for continued contact and collaboration on a number of particular problems which had opened up as material for further discussion. The problem of the nature and role of the imagination, from scientific discovery in general, through biology (in particular, taxonomy), to the arts, was one such theme. Another which kept recurring was the question of levels of explanation and levels of reality: a central question not only for philosophy, but for the relation between the sciences of life—man, on the one hand, and physics, on the other—and indeed for the interpretation of the art object as well—the problem of its reality and its capacity to teach us about ourselves and our world.[53]

After the gathering, Polanyi concentrated on a lecture series that he was to give at the Center for Advanced Studies at Wesleyan University the next month.[54] He had been invited to Wesleyan University as a Senior Fellow for the fall semester of 1965 and he planned to give an expanded version of the Terry Lectures from the end of September to the end of January. Magda flew from England to join Michael at Wesleyan. He had asked the university for a study for each of them, since Magda was immersed in her own work in technical writing in the textile field. Polanyi entitled his lecture series "Man's Place in the Universe" and gave weekly talks that were open to the Middletown, Connecticut community. The first five weekly lectures were entitled "Science and Reality," "Structure of Tacit Knowing," "The Creative Imagination," "The Growth of Science in Society," and "Levels of Reality."[55]

By mid-November, after the first five lectures at Wesleyan and two additional speeches in Buffalo and Seattle, Polanyi felt unwell; he decided to cancel the last three lectures in his Wesleyan series. Although he partially recuperated during Thanksgiving vacation, he remained unable to work. Hoping that the sunny seaside setting of Key Biscayne, Florida would renew his strength, he and Magda embarked on a ten-day vacation trip. Gradually he healed. When the university asked if he would consider staying on for the spring semester, he agreed. Both he and Magda loved Wesleyan.

Polanyi used the month of January 1966 to put the finishing touches on *The Tacit Dimension*, a slim volume which, in spite of his numerous attempts at revision during the previous three years, contained the nearly unchanged text of his first two Terry Lectures, "Tacit Knowing" and "Emergence" (1966e). As Polanyi said in his introduction, he had come during the intervening period to feel assured that his reply to the *Meno* in the Terry Lectures was right, and he had further resolved that point in "The Creative Imagination" (1966b). The third Terry Lecture, "A Society of Explorers," contained a more detailed description of the pursuit of science in society as a model for human endeavor in all fields.

The final paragraph of *The Tacit Dimension* revealed Polanyi's renewed interest in spirituality. A year earlier, he had written: "For a long time I did not take part in prayer and this renewal made me deeply happy. My earlier writings were much more moved by religious belief; possibly that will come back now."[56] He now concluded *The Tacit Dimension* with the assertion that "Men need a purpose which bears on eternity. Truth does that; our ideals do it; and this might be enough if we could ever be satisfied with our manifest moral shortcomings and with a society which has such shortcomings fatally involved in its workings." Polanyi thought that this problem "cannot be resolved on secular grounds alone. But its religious solution should become more feasible once religious faith is released from pressure by an absurd vision of the universe, and so there will open up instead a meaningful world which could resound to religion" (TD, 92).

In Polanyi's view, the theologians with whom he was familiar had not yet developed a "reasonable" theology. He criticized Tillich because he, like most of modern theologians, attributed too much significance to the current scientific view of the world and therefore exaggerated the distinction between science and faith. For his part, Polanyi thought the structure of science was akin to that of religious faith, as he explained to Raymond Wilken, an American educator.[57] He later elaborated on this subject in "Prospects of Theology Today," in which he said that it was not science that confronted religion but scientism, the systematic objectivism that had developed since the 1850s and that menaced science itself.[58] Religion could only be defended by repairing the damage done by applying mistaken standards of absolute, impersonal detachment to all of human knowledge.

Polanyi did not want to go further than this in his comparison of science and religion. When he received an invitation from the University of Sussex to talk on the relationship between religious knowledge and other kinds of knowledge, he refused, saying that he found the theological evaluation of his writings in some articles and dissertations "far beyond his scope."[59] Asked by Wilken about his own belief, Polanyi reiterated what he had said to Karl Mannheim in a letter in 1944; namely, that after a "completely unreligious upbringing" his "gradual attraction to Christianity" began when he was about 20.[60] The decisive point that brought him into very close relationship with the Pauline scheme of redemption was the reading of Reinhold Niebuhr's two-volume work *The Nature and Destiny of Man*.[61] He had been reminded of this influence while preparing the opening address for a celebration in Niebuhr's honor in New York a few months before.

When Wilken asked whether the "cosmic field" Polanyi referred to in the last paragraph of *Personal Knowledge* had any implications for a life hereafter,

Polanyi said he did not think so. He certainly did not mean it to have a direct bearing. At most it was intended as "a back drop against which the scene of immortality can again be made apparent" (3). He was equally careful in talking about the existence of God and his own relationship to God, explaining that various relationships to God are possible that imply the existence of God but which do not allow the conclusion that "God exists." He explained, "I could well imagine the paradoxical situation that one can pray to God, or that one can love God, or that one can serve God, which is probably the nearest which I could imagine, myself, that could be accepted, without saying that God exists, because it would seem an unnecessary and foolish thing to add" (1).

There is a one-page typescript from January 5, 1966, that elaborates on this theme. The title is "Paradox in Science and Religion" and reads in its entirety:

> The unobserved electron exists at no particular point. It has a definite probability to be found at any particular point, but is there only when it is found there.
>
> The unloved God exists at no particular place. He has a probability to be found at any place, but can be there only when found there: as long as he is not found he exists nowhere.
>
> We must love him so that he may exist, not love him because he exist[s]. He can be loved but not observed.
>
> It is wrong therefore to demand logical consistency in religion. If consistency must be set aside in science in order to achieve a conceptual innovation that corresponds to the facts, we might set it aside also in order to form religious conceptions that correspond to the facts of religious faith.[62]

In this meditation, Polanyi is clearly striving to stay within the bounds set by Tillich's dictum that "the question of the existence of God can neither be asked nor answered."[63]

At the beginning of March 1966, Polanyi spent several days at Carl Rogers's home while attending a conference on "Man and the Science of Man" in La Jolla at the Western Behavioral Sciences Institute. Immediately after Polanyi's arrival on Saturday, a videotape was recorded of a dialogue between Polanyi and Rogers for presentation on educational television stations (1966c). Polanyi delivered his lecture on "Body and Mind Relation." Yehoshua Bar-Hillel responded to the paper. Papers by Rogers and Jacob Bronowski rounded out the Sunday Symposium. Polanyi also gave a public lecture on "The Growth of Science in Society," first at the University of California at San Diego and again in the evening in La Jolla (1967a). He

explained his ideas on the way science grows by showing why scientists sum-
marily and properly rejected Immanuel Velikovsky's book, *Worlds in Collision*.
Since scientists cannot investigate all possible theories, they must be guided by "a
broad exercise of intuition guided by many subtle indications, and thus *it is
altogether undemonstrable. It is tacit*" (KB, 76). Polanyi noted that his work on
adsorption had, for a time, been treated as implausible due to the intuitions
derived from the understanding of inter-molecular forces when he first proposed
his theory. "But I did not complain about this mistaken exercise of authority. Hard
cases make bad law. The kind of discipline which had gone wrong in my case was
indispensable. . . . Science cannot survive unless it can keep out such [nonsensi-
cal] contributions and safeguard the basic soundness of its publications" (78–79).

From San Diego, Polanyi flew to Toronto for the celebration of his seventy-
fifth birthday. Sue had written a song of praise, which was delivered "loudly
and joyfully as befitting the occasion to the tune of The British Grenadiers:"

Oh first he was a doctor
And then a great Chemist
We can't find one profession
That isn't on his list.
There is no doubt about it
For versatility
There is none so rare that can compare
To our Michael P.
Then he tried Economics
And solved it in a year.
He took on Social Science
Without the slightest fear.
Philosophy's his triumph now,
But knowing what he's got
We'd like to know
Why he's so slow
In being an astronaut![64]

The celebration continued on Polanyi's return to Wesleyan University. Polanyi was delighted with the kind words that were showered on him.[65]

At the end of the academic year, the Polanyis packed to return home.
Their experience at Wesleyan, their first year abroad together since their trip
to California in 1962–1963, had proved satisfying to both of them. They had
thoroughly enjoyed the university community. Polanyi had taken advantage of
Wesleyan's location near the metropolitan centers of the East Coast and Magda
had accomplished much work of her own; then "in her spare time," Michael
noted, "she reorganized the university."[66]

In June, shortly after Michael and Magda returned to Oxford, John and
his family came for a visit. They learned that Adolf had died in Brazil and that

his wife, Lilly, had committed suicide. When Polanyi had visited Adolf in December, his brother had been in good spirits over an increase in salary and the prospect of the revival of the Brazilian economy. Now only Karl's widow, Ilona, and Michael and Magda were left from their generation in the family. For Polanyi, "the feeling of being at home among the dead arose easily but not overwhelmingly."[67]

Polanyi's expectations continued to rise. When a professor said that *Personal Knowledge* would be required reading for the next twenty-five years, Polanyi joked: "In 25 years I thought one will only just begin to understand me properly! Impertinence! (mine or his?)."[68]

Polanyi was disconcerted to find that he was having difficulty putting his thoughts on paper. He hoped that ten days at the Koestlers' home in Alpbach would refresh him. He had long talks with Arthur that "were not smooth but always worth the effort; he has forgotten that one can contradict him."[69] During the visit, Polanyi did manage to write a short, informative, and revealing sketch of his life for *World Authors* (1975a). After a few more days of vacation in Sils Maria, Polanyi took part in the second meeting of the Study Group on Foundations of Cultural Unity at Bowdoin College.

On September 22, the University of Manchester conferred the degree of Doctor of Science (*honoris causa*) on Polanyi during the John Dalton bicentenary celebrations. Michael Evans, Polanyi's namesake and the son of M. G. Evans, attended the ceremony. Afterward, he offered Michael and Magda a ride back to the Piccadilly hotel in his very tiny, second-hand van. The Polanyis were grateful for the lift and perched on shallow ledges in the back of the van. When Evans pulled up at the main door of the elegant hotel, the doorman opened the back of the van, and Magda and Michael climbed out of the makeshift limousine, with Michael still dressed in his doctoral gown.[70]

Polanyi's next project was "Sense-Giving and Sense-Reading," a paper for the Eighth German Congress for Philosophy at Heidelberg at the end of October (1967d). The main theme of the Congress, language, fit well with Polanyi's desire to extend his theory of tacit knowing. He had covered much of this field in *Personal Knowledge*, particularly in the chapter on "Articulation." During the summer he had tried to expand his earlier thoughts on language by reading and by talking with friends and authorities in the field;[71] he often crossed Upland Park Road to discuss his ideas with his neighbors, Angela Bolton and her husband, a don in Classics at Queen's College. During the writing of "Sense-Giving," Polanyi borrowed some books from them. As the days before his departure became too hectic for visiting, he resorted to sending notes, one written "Sunday before dawn."[72]

Polanyi wanted to impress the audience of philosophers. He tried to link "the calling for exploring the outer world to the calling for our own existence," but could not explain his insight to his own satisfaction.[73] However, he thought he could answer two of Noam Chomsky's questions: how a child picks up the rules of grammar and how an adult can understand and form novel sentences almost instantaneously. Polanyi argued that the use of language is a tacit performance and that "the acquisition of language is accordingly explained by the dynamics of tacit knowing" (KB, 206).

The lecture went well in Heidelberg. The German philosophers seemed more receptive than his Oxford colleagues; there was even sufficient public interest for the Hessian Radio station to broadcast the lecture the next summer (August 22, 1967). Chomsky, who had been following Polanyi's work for years and found it a "constant source of great stimulation and insight," wrote that he was not sure he completely understood Polanyi.[74] In fact, he firmly disagreed with a fundamental premise of Polanyi's epistemology: "Clearly . . . one cannot conclude from the fact that mental operations . . . are unconscious that they are not specifiable in perfectly precise and explicit terms."

Chomsky was committed to the idea of an inherited "innate grammar," a pre-established pattern in the brain that explains the astonishing speed with which an infant learns language. Polanyi resisted the idea that such grammatical patterns could be heritable; instead, he held that humans, both infant and adult, have an appetite for meaning, pattern, and sense which enables them to build up structured systems (e.g., building blocks, phonemes, or musical sounds) without possessing any explicit rules of inference: "We are no longer faced with the question [of] how people who learn to speak a language can identify, remember and apply a set of complex rules known only to linguists. [Infants] do not identify these rules . . . and explicitly apply them, and do not need to do so. According to the dynamics of tacit knowing, the rules are acquired subsidiarily, without focal knowledge of them" (KB, 204). Polanyi believed that children observe patterned behavior, absorb the embedded rules of language, and then by a process of trial-and-error develop the skill to use those rules tacitly in speaking for themselves.

From Heidelberg, Polanyi went to Basel to hear Silvia Kind present a public lecture on musicology and ornamentation. Her latest lecture made a lasting impression on him: "Orpheus only tamed wild animals. To move me through music, to have me recognize at one blow the greatness of an artistic performance is much harder to achieve."[75] During a subsequent meeting in Innsbruck, Kind and Polanyi also spent several hours discussing the Dadaists, another new interest for Polanyi. Even at 75, "Misi's mind was wonderfully young."[76]

In the fall of 1966, work got underway to add a downstairs bedroom and bathroom. The new addition, which Polanyi called "the geriatric wing," was destined for Magda. Among other things, she was finding climbing the stairs increasingly difficult. During Polanyi's next trip to the States in the spring of 1967, Magda stayed in Oxford to supervise the construction of the extension. Polanyi flew first to Ithaca to repeat his Heidelberg lecture at Cornell

University, then traveled to New York to see old friends and family before spending the months of April and May in residence as visiting professor at the University of Chicago Center for Advanced Study in Theology and the Sciences. He was glad to be back in Chicago, with easy access to the excellent collections and quiet environs of the university library. He also enjoyed his stay at the Quadrangle Club and was gratified by the big audiences at his lectures.

Returning from the States in early June, Polanyi felt so exhausted that he flew off to the Koestlers' home in Alpbach to recuperate. He began to write again almost immediately. On his return to Oxford, he was able to keep up the momentum of his work, but he knew his career was coming to a close: "Certain weaknesses...indicate a not too distant end to my full ability to work."[77] That summer, in spite of getting rather tired from time to time, Polanyi felt well enough to continue work on "Logic and Psychology," the opening address to the American Psychological Association that he was due to give on September 1 in Washington, D.C. (1968a). The hall in which he was to give the speech could hold 5,000 people. Even though he knew the hall might not fill up completely, he felt it was a great opportunity to share his ideas with a new audience. He was grateful to Abraham Maslow, the president of APA, for the invitation.

Polanyi decided to show how scientific progress is determined by undefinable powers of thought and informal rules of inference. He pictured the structure of tacit knowing as a triangle with the three corners: the subsidiaries, the focal target, and the knower who brings the subsidiaries to bear on the focal point. He then explained his concepts of tacit inference and indwelling, how we know another mind and how visual perception is to be interpreted as tacit knowing, concluding that mind and body form two jointly operating principles: "Though rooted in the body, the mind is free in its actions—exactly as our common sense knows it to be free" (40). Marjorie Grene visited Oxford to assist Polanyi with the project.

After the meeting of the American Psychological Association in Washington, Polanyi flew to Liège to address the Institut International de Philosophie. A few weeks later he was back in the United States to take part in the meeting of the Study Group on the Unity of Knowledge at the Massachusetts Institute of Technology. The topic was "Artificial Intelligence."[78] Polanyi did not present a paper.

In October, Polanyi found it necessary to resign from the Congress for Cultural Freedom. Five months earlier it had come to light that the Congress of Cultural Freedom had been partially supported by the U.S. Central Intelligence Agency and that the Executive Secretary, Mike Josselson, had secretly accepted this support throughout the seventeen years of the Congress' existence. Polanyi seemed not to grasp the full dimension of the scandal—he hoped that Josselson could remain in the group despite being a paid agent of a covert organization. Polanyi asked Raymond Aron, "What kind of battle line are we holding by accepting the standards of culpability proclaimed by our chronically misguided opponents?"[79] Polanyi apparently did not think that covert government funding tainted the ideals of freedom to which he and the society had been dedicated. In his own philosophy he had developed a defense of the autonomy of intellectual life against political interference. In acting as a paid agent for the CIA, Josselson had betrayed that ideal. Nevertheless, Polanyi resigned from the Congress of Cultural Freedom when Josselson was expelled. Polanyi's resignation became effective in October, the same month in which the Congress gained support from the Ford Foundation for another five years.

Because of declining strength, Polanyi canceled his plans to be a visiting professor at Berkeley in the spring semester of 1968. He was still able to give individual lectures. In November, he gave a talk for the Bavarian Broadcasting Corporation, based in Munich. A studio audience of four hundred was present for his lecture, "Wider die Skepsis des Modernen Denkens" ("Against the Skepticism of Modern Thought"; 1968b). That same month, Polanyi traveled to Toronto to lecture on "Sixty Years in Universities" and to receive an honorary doctorate on November 24. He then spent a week with Marjorie Grene at the University of Texas, Austin, paying a visit to the Chemistry Department.

At year's end, he presented "Life Transcending Physics and Chemistry," at one of the General Symposia of the American Association for the Advancement of Science in New York City, December 30.[80] In this paper, an abbreviated version of a lecture he had given in May at Chicago, Polanyi added another step to his development of the concept of boundary control, explaining that the operational or organizational principle of a coherent entity cannot be accounted for by the laws governing the parts from which the whole is formed. "The irreducibility of machines and printed communications teaches us that the control of a system by irreducible boundary conditions does not interfere with the laws of physics and chemistry. A system under dual control relies in fact for the operation of its higher principle on the working of principles of a lower level, such as the laws of physics and chemistry. . . . The principles of mechanical engineering and of communication of information, and the equivalent biological principles, are all additional to the laws of physics and chemistry" (KB, 231). Polanyi hoped that "the recognition of the impossibility of understanding living things in terms of physics and chemistry, far from setting limits to our understanding of life, will guide it in the right direction" (238).

In January 1968, Polanyi gave three lectures at Berkeley: "Science and Reality,"[81] "Logic and Psychology,"[82] and "Science: Academic and Industrial."[83] During this period, Marjorie Grene and Polanyi were often in touch with each other, partially because of their mutual involvement in the Study Group but increasingly because Grene was editing a collection of Polanyi's essays. Grene aimed to trace the further consolidation and expansion of Polanyi's theory of knowledge from its first foreshadowing in *Science, Faith and Society* (1945) and its systematic development in *Personal Knowledge* (1958) through a group of papers written between 1959 and 1968. She grouped the fourteen selections into four parts: "Society and the Understanding of Society," "The Nature of Science," "Tacit Knowing," and "Life and Mind," and provided the reader with a nine-page introduction to Polanyi's thought. Although she excluded articles that Polanyi himself would have liked included, he recognized the quality of her editorial work and was pleased with the volume that emerged: *Knowing and Being: Essays by Michael Polanyi* (1969c).

Thomas A. Langford and William H. Poteat were editing another collection of essays to be published for the Lilly Endowment Research Program in Christianity and Politics by Duke University Press. The new volume was entitled *Intellect and Hope: Essays in the Thought of Michael Polanyi*.[84] It included Polanyi's "Sense-Giving and Sense-Reading," Richard Gelwick's bibliography of Polanyi's social and philosophical writings, and essays by fourteen other scholars. The book demonstrated the influence of Polanyi's ideas not only in Great Britain and the States but also in France and Germany.

Intellect and Hope brought together essays by a number of the scholars who had participated in the Study Group on the Unity of Knowledge—Marjorie Grene, Edward Pols, Bill Poteat, Bill Scott, Helmut Kuhn, and Donald Weismann—but Elizabeth Sewell was not among them. When Poteat had asked for a contribution, she had refused. Disdaining the Study Group gatherings as meetings for "Cultural Whatnot," she preferred to follow her own path. Instead, as she explained to Polanyi, she would go on with her present work "into which, naturally, your thought and presence is as interwoven and vital as food and drink into the living body. . . . my infinite and loving debt to your thought is that it empowers me towards my own vision. So the poems say, which are, as they should be, the real expression of the gratitude."[85]

At the end of January, Polanyi returned from Berkeley to Oxford. He spent a month at home with Magda before traveling to Bellagio on Lake Como for a meeting organized by Paul Weiss of the Rockefeller Foundation (March 10–14, 1968). There Polanyi found a sympathetic reception to his paper "Life Transcending Physics and Chemistry." Magda was still heavily engaged in volunteer work, giving much of her time to an Oxford agency supporting families of mentally disturbed people. She joined Michael for a ten-day holiday in Italy where they helped celebrate Leo Szilard's seventieth birthday.

By mid-April, Polanyi was back again in the United States, flying first to Austin, Texas for a meeting of the Study Group on "The (Ir)reducibility of Biology to Physics and Chemistry," then to the University of Chicago for a month, and finally to Cambridge, Massachusetts, for the Symposium on

Transcendence in Contemporary Culture sponsored by the Church Society for College Work. He had promised the Reverend Myron B. Bloy, the organizer of the Cambridge gathering, a paper to be published in a volume on the symposium. To Bloy's disappointment, Polanyi's contribution simply summarized his philosophy without adding anything new. Ruel Tyson, an American graduate student who had studied under Polanyi at Manchester, was present at the symposium. He prepared Polanyi's contribution for publication in *Soundings* and also suggested its title, "Transcendence and Self-Transcendence" (1970b). Late in 1969, Polanyi was asked to contribute to a Festschrift for Raymond Aron. He felt "rather disgusted with doing anything with my brain for the moment."[86] He submitted the text of his Cambridge talk, having forgotten its pending publication in *Soundings*.

Shortly after Polanyi's seventy-seventh birthday in March 1968, Harold Osborne, editor of *The British Journal of Aesthetics*, had invited him to address a meeting of aestheticians on November 5, 1969. Polanyi decided not to approach the visual arts directly but instead to apply his theory of language acquisition "to the analysis of metaphor, ritual and myth and then to expand this to include visual representation and expression."[87] After traveling to Austin, Chicago, and Cambridge in April and May, Polanyi vacationed at a thirteenth-century hotel, the Cappucini-Convento hotel, in southern Italy. He brought with him books by Rudolf Arnheim on the psychology of pictorial art. On one glorious June day, as he was sitting on the balcony of his hotel, he was overcome by the beauty of life. The experience invigorated him; he hoped he might be able to find his way back to this same balcony the next June.[88]

Polanyi presented a paper entitled "What is a Painting?" to the Study Group on Art and Perception at Bellagio (1970c). He was not satisfied with the paper. Poor health frustrated his efforts to improve it; by mid-August, he had not yet made any revisions. Instead, he found it necessary to enter the hospital for medical tests. Back in England he ordered several books from the London Library to help him clarify some of his ideas.[89]

Polanyi was also working on a related project, a study of visual perception that was to serve as a foreword to Maurice Pirenne's book, *Optics, Painting and Photography* (1970a). In 1964, Polanyi had begun a dialogue with Pirenne, a lecturer in physiology at Oxford, about structure of perception in art. Pirenne held that an observer of a work of art is usually aware of the canvas and therefore does not interpret the painted figures as if they were real. Polanyi reasoned that "our noticing of the canvas . . . will lend independent reality to the picture."[90] Polanyi and Pirenne had many subsequent discussions about visual perception; in fact, Pirenne included an explanation of Polanyi's concept of focal and subsidiary awareness in the second edition of his *Vision and the Eye* (1967).

On August 20, 1968, Michael and Magda were visited by Michael Evans and his wife. The day began pleasantly, but in the later afternoon, as they were enjoying tea in the garden, news of the Soviets' invasion of Czechoslovakia came over the radio. Polanyi's attention was riveted to the news. Normally very reserved and soft-spoken, Polanyi became very agitated, calling the Russian invasion a disaster so great that it could trigger a third world war.[91] Polanyi saw the event as "the sequel to fifty years of intellectual disaster, for most of the time aided by the admiration of Europe's most distinguished intellects."[92] A few weeks later, he attended a meeting of the Frensham Group at Dorking. In reply to an address by John C. Eccles, "Facing Reality," Polanyi presented a talk entitled "Why Did We Destroy Europe?" (1970e).

In the fall of 1968, three Americans came to Oxford to work with Polanyi: Donald T. Campbell, Paul Craig Roberts, and Harry Prosch. Campbell, a psychologist from Northwestern University and a Fulbright scholar, saw Polanyi mainly at his home for a series of talks on topics that Campbell suggested, including evolution, transparency of language, and the theory and sociology of science. His first reading of *Personal Knowledge* had affected him deeply, and he wanted to make sure he understood Polanyi's view.[93]

Roberts had been associated with Polanyi for seven years, mainly in connection with Polanyi's work on economics. He had hoped to work with Polanyi at Berkeley in 1967, but Polanyi's poor health prevented their collaboration. Roberts subsequently obtained a grant from the Penrose Fund for the fall of 1968. Polanyi and Roberts intended to develop a historical account of the intellectual process that led from the original ideas of the Soviet Revolution to present policies. Polanyi was delighted with the opportunity to consolidate his earlier work on this theme.[94] When Roberts published *Alienation and the Soviet Economy*, Polanyi considered it a continuation of his own thought. Roberts found in Polanyi's work in economics the same kind of strength and weakness that Polanyi showed in science and philosophy: "Being untrained as an economist allowed Polanyi to avoid pitfalls that confused economists. It also left him unaware of the magnitude of his achievement. He saw himself as a Keynesian, but in fact he achieved in the early years of Keynesianism, before the monetarist critique, an integration of . . . two approaches that economists did not reach until the 1970s. Needless to say, Polanyi got no credit for his achievement."[95]

The third American, Harry Prosch, was on sabbatical from his post as chair of the Philosophy Department at Skidmore College. Prosch's original plan was just to study Polanyi's publications in consultation with him, but in the course of the year, the idea to write a book about Polanyi's philosophic work took shape. Polanyi was preparing a series of lectures for audiences at the Universities of Texas and Chicago. As part of his new work on aesthetics, he read Mircea Eliade's four volumes on mythology. One by one Polanyi met the visitors over lunch and in conferences at home in his study. Magda was generous with her time, cheerfully taking charge of Prosch's wife and introducing her to the year's cycle of Oxford activities.

In December, Polanyi traveled to Berlin to take part in the 100th anniversary commemoration of Haber's birthday, stopping in Munich to continue negotiations with the Wilhelm Fink Verlag about a translation of *Personal Knowledge* into German. From Munich, Polanyi went to Vienna to visit his former co-worker, Helmut Schmid, and his niece, Maria (Szecsi) März, his sister Sofie's sole surviving daughter. Maria, who shared her uncle's anguish over the invasion of Czechoslovakia, despaired of ever seeing any "liberalization of the Eastern European States." She did not have high hopes for Polanyi's own approach: "Well, I suppose we all need a straw, and you yourself are holding fast to the thinnest one there is—a radical change out of spiritual conviction. Has that ever happened before?"[96]

At the beginning of the new year, 1969, "undisturbed by inner zeal and outer encounters," Polanyi reflected on how much wisdom had passed away with the loss of the ancient myths. Only the arts survived. He deplored his ignorance about music, which might well preclude a complete rounding off of his work in aesthetics. "But it will have been worth it to make the attempt."[97]

In mid-February, just before he was due to leave for the United States, Polanyi checked out ten books from the London Library for subsequent study along with the four volumes on myths he had begun to read in the fall.[98] He flew first to New York, then to the University of Texas at Austin, where Donald Weismann, the University Professor of Art, had made arrangements for his visit. There the lectures Polanyi had labored over during the fall of 1968 became the basis for a seminar for the Department of Comparative Studies. Polanyi described his course as "an attempt at a theory of art."[99]

While delivering the Austin lectures, Polanyi developed so many fresh insights that he made numerous changes in his original manuscript. Articulating his new ideas provided a fitting, though exhausting, way to celebrate his seventy-eighth birthday. After three weeks of teaching, he relaxed at the 40 Acres Club, where he enjoyed "the cool sunshine over the campus and the beds of amazing azaleas."[100] At the end of March, he took part in the Study Group meeting in Austin on "Scientific Knowledge and Discovery" with Bill Scott, Robert Cohen, Marjorie Grene, Keith Gunderson, Sigmund Koch, Alisdair MacIntyre, Charles Taylor, Marx Wartofsky, and Donald Weismann, the host.

Polanyi spent April and May as the Sara H. Schaffner Lecturer in Chicago, presenting the revised version of the series of seminars he had given in Austin. On one manuscript, the title of the lectures is "Meaning: A project by Michael Polanyi"; another manuscript calls them "Meaning, Lost and Regained."[101] "You may wonder what I had in mind in giving these lectures the title 'Meaning,'" he told his Chicago audience.

The answer is in the content of the last two lectures which will deal with Meaning Lost and Meaning Regained. This is what I shall lead up to. In the lecture on "Meaning Lost," we shall have before us a subject that is on the lips of our age in many forms. We are told every day and in a variety of ways, that meaning had got lost. The modern philosophy concerned with the existence of man arrived at the conclusion that man's existence is absurd. The most prosperous country of the world is plagued by doubts about the meaning of its natural life. Young men and women despise the prospects of their adult future, which they find meaningless, and they condemn the universities for lacking any coherent outlook which would make a use of the world.[102]

In "Acceptance of Religion," an unpublished supplement to the lectures given at the University of Texas and the University of Chicago, Polanyi examined the role of symbols in religious ritual and the Bible. In Polanyi's view the Bible had lost its authority as both a chronicle of facts and a source of information. In fact, he said, "most of what we read in the Bible has turned out to be very doubtful."[103] It cannot speak to our uneasiness about the meaning of our existence. Nonetheless, "the meaning which the Bible has in many parts and the ritual of religious service in most parts, may be deeply moving to us. It can be so, if we turn to it as an association of symbols. All our diffuse thoughts of our own unfathomable fate as human beings are given expression by these symbols" (12).

The progress of the discussion, Polanyi confided,

> made me think of the way I would wish to be buried. . . . I am reminded of the way [Dietrich Bonhoeffer], a young student of theology, who less than twenty years later was to be hanged by Hitler, opened a funeral oration on the great German theologian, Adolf von Harnack . . . with the words in German: "Wenn ein Mensch wie Harnack über die Erde geht . . ." ["When a man the likes of Harnack strides over the earth"]. This is the perspective to which the service which followed seemed to offer symbolic answers. "Corruptible puts on incorruptible," "Death, where is thy victory?" I now realize how revealing such words are of our destiny even though there is no information given by them. And I can think now of the depth of my own life being expressed by the words, spoken by the congregation on their knees, "Our Father, which art in heaven," and so on, though literally I believe none of the Lord's prayer (12).

Polanyi also told the university audiences that he did not think there was much chance of halting the decline of religious faith as long as the scientific world view continues to deny ultimate reality and the theoretical groundings of our moral nature. Although "what science says about its own subject is for the most part true and interesting . . . it does not give us an image of the world in which our position as responsible creative beings can be understood. Quite the contrary, it denies any solid foundation to our deeper beliefs and can tell us nothing about the cycle of our lives in the way we live it from our birth to our death. All this is quite meaningless to it" (11).

Polanyi added his hope that the dominance of a false view of science would not long continue. "The absurdity of the Laplacean conception of the world is being increasingly recognised and a constructive replacing of it by the more obvious features of the world's hierarchic structure may soon follow. The worst thing the reformers of religion can do, is to adapt their theology to the present world view of science and I shall suggest that attempts for making religious service more attuned to statements of fact is equally destructive" (10–11).

Polanyi concluded his remarks on "The Acceptance of Religion" by emphasizing that it was not his aim "to prove the effectiveness of religious ritual." Instead his concern was

> to explain the structure of its power, so far as it has power. And I would sum up by saying, that it is our strange capacity for integrating large, hardly coherent experiences in brief actions of ritual, and symbols in general, which is a great source of emotionally powerful meaning. And pedantically I should emphasize also that this kind of meaning is wholly different from one word or sign indicating some things on which they bear. It can be described rather as our capacity to become to some extent something else than we are, thus achieving its meaning as an expression of our own concerns. I shall call this meaning by symbolization or more generally meaning by becoming another thing of our choice. (12–13)

As usual, Polanyi enjoyed his stay at the University of Chicago. He was pleased to notice that students and professors in his seminars were well prepared by having studied his works and carried on lively discussions of his thought.[104] On his way home at the end of May, Polanyi stopped in Paris to participate in the General Assembly of the International Association for Cultural Freedom (the successor to the Congress for Cultural Freedom).[105] Before returning to Oxford, he and Magda spent a week in Sils Maria with George and Priscilla.

Polanyi felt increasingly frustrated in his desire to give more complete answers to the major questions of his time, questions which haunted his imagination: "with my ridiculously advancing age I begin to lose control over the thoughts which formed my hope for so long."[106] When the University of Chicago Press was considering a reissue of The Logic of Liberty, Polanyi proposed that Prosch or Grene serve as "supporting collaborators" for a new first half made up of The Study of Man and material not included in Knowing & Being, and that Roberts collaborate with him on economics in the second half of the book. The publisher was rather taken aback by the magnitude of the proposal,[107] so the project was dropped. Polanyi did not give up his hope that he might yet produce another work of the same scale as *Personal Knowledge* that would pull together all of the disparate strands of his work in philosophy, economics, and social theory.

At the end of July, Polanyi spent two weeks in Heidelberg advising Helmut Kuhn, professor of philosophy at the University of Munich, on his translation of *Personal Knowledge*. There he began to work on a paper tentatively entitled "Theory of Discovery" or "Grounds of Knowledge,"[108] which he was preparing for an international gathering of philosophers of science. To make more time for this research, he canceled plans for a trip to the United States in September and October. The final version, "The Grounds of Natural Science," was presented at the Colloquium of the Academie Internationale de Philosophie des Sciences in Lausanne.[109] There Polanyi met some old friends of his, including Piaget, Polya, Dockx, and Bernays.

In July 1969, Bill Scott came to Oxford for a sabbatical year to read philosophy and to engage in extended conversations with Polanyi. The focus of their meetings was generally Polanyi's current work. Polanyi's health was good and he spent most mornings at work in his study. Many times he would bring along a piece of his writing, duplicated in mimeographed form on legal-sized sheets of paper, for Scott to read and comment on. Sometimes Polanyi invited Scott to come as his guest to the high table at Merton College, where he was a Senior Fellow Emeritus. On one occasion, Scott wore a grey tweed jacket with red shirt and yellow tie instead of the traditional tuxedo. Later, as Scott was driving Polanyi home, he apologized for his costume. With exquisite courtesy, Polanyi replied, "A gentleman can wear whatever he wants, so long as he does it deliberately."

During the years in which Polanyi served as a Fellow of Merton College, Gilbert Ryle was at Magdalen, just a short walk away; however, the two men had never engaged in a serious discussion of their respective philosophies. As Lady Drusilla Scott pointed out, Polanyi was isolated from Oxford philosophers, pursuing his own lines of thought in a world apart; he either did not know how to dwell in the framework of the scholars or he was unwilling to speak their language. In the hope that a brash American might be able to help spur a dialogue, Scott invited Ryle and Polanyi to dinner at the Elizabeth. It was a pleasant evening, but without any meeting of the minds. The two men spoke only of their own work and did not find common ground between them.

On a number of other occasions Bill and Ann Scott invited Michael and Magda to join them for lunch or dinner at one of the many restaurants and inns around Oxford. Since neither of the Polanyis drove at that time, they especially enjoyed outings in the countryside, and Magda often suggested a new place that seemed worth trying. The excursions generally began over a glass of sherry at 22 Upland Park Road. In pleasant weather, the Polanyis entertained their guests on the terrace beside the garden. On colder days, the four gathered in the parlor, a darkish room dominated by the dramatic oil portrait of Michael's father, Mihály, which they had brought with them on their journeys from Budapest to Berlin, Manchester, London, and Oxford. In the hallway hung another special picture, a photograph of John and Sue's children, Margaret and Michael, running joyfully down a hillside of wild flowers.

The conversation between the Scotts and the Polanyis often turned to questions of social justice and civil rights. At that time, Magda was immersed in volunteer work with families of mentally ill persons who had recently been returned to their homes due to policy changes in the National Health Service, and the immediate problems of her clients were often on her mind. Polanyi spent most of his waking hours in his study, an orderly, book-lined room with a window looking out on the garden. Cecily Argyle, a part-time secretary, came to his office two or three days a week to assist with the typing and filing of his correspondence, but he still wrote many of his letters himself. Polanyi's bedroom was also upstairs. Magda's domain was downstairs in the section of the house that had been remodeled while Michael was lecturing at Duke. In space that had once been the dining room, she had her own bedroom and took care of the general household and the family finances. In addition to her volunteer service and work on the second edition of her *Encyclopedia of Textile Terms*, she had interests and friendships of her own in an Oxford music society and a club of professional women; she often entertained small groups of visitors and friends from the community.

As Michael's energy decreased and his alertness dimmed, Magda made more and more decisions for him. To the Scotts, Magda's attention to details was more helpful than destructive, but others saw it differently. Arthur Koestler called Magda Michael's "worst enemy." Some speculated that Magda may have unconsciously regretted her decision to give up her own career to submerge herself in her husband's work and demands. One Oxford scholar reported Magda's interrupting an interesting afternoon discussion with the abrupt announcement that it was time for Michael's nap—and Michael obediently complied by going off to his bedroom. On another occasion, however, Harry Prosch saw that Polanyi was capable of putting up effective resistance when it pleased him:

> I recall once we four: Michael and Magda and Doris and I were on our way to dine out at a restaurant when a slight rain developed. Magda pulled an umbrella from the stand and thrust it at Michael, saying, "Take this!" Michael smiled and said he didn't need it. We were going in our car. Magda said, "Take it!" and shoved it into his hand as she went out the door. We all followed her; but, as Michael came to the door, he turned, winked at us, and put the umbrella back into the stand and went out without it. He was always very kind to Magda, but his own man, I thought.[110]

In the fall of 1969, Polanyi flew to Massachusetts to take part in the Study Group Colloquium at Boston University on "Scientific Discovery" and to attend the sesquicentennial celebration of the Cambridge Philosophy Society. Upon his return to England, he received an honorary Doctor of Science at Cambridge University. Polanyi found it "pleasing" to be remembered by his old circle, but he realized that the degree "must not be thought to recognize my work in philosophy, which I think is very much more important than what I have done in science."[111] At the same time, it was his work in science that gave him the key to his philosophy: "an experience in science is by far the most important basic ground for developing philosophic ideas."[112]

Revision of "What is a Painting?" for the British aestheticians occupied much of Polanyi's time during the fall (1970c). Polanyi wanted to show that painting "possesses an artificial frame that contradicts its subject and yet is so closely fused with this subject that the union of the two acquires a quality of its own.... In this artificial estrangement of its subject lies the power of all painting to represent matters drawn from experience in terms that transcend all natural experience. And therein lies equally the power of *all* representational art" (234).

Magda suffered a severe heart attack on February 9, 1970. For several days, she lay in intensive care, then began to recover. Polanyi was deeply affected by her weakened condition; he tired more easily and began to spend hours reflecting on the past. Magda's condition delayed his next trip to the University of Chicago. Polanyi had suggested to Edward Shils that Harry Prosch should share the Willett Visiting Professorship with him. Prosch was to give a systematic course on Polanyi's thought, while Polanyi would present four public lectures. About twenty regular students signed up for Prosch's course, along with several auditors, including Polanyi's niece, Eva Zeisel. When Polanyi arrived on April 19, a full undergraduate course on his writings was in progress. Polanyi presented "What Is a Painting?", "Science and Man," "Genius in Science," and "Meaning."[113] "Genius in Science" summed up his position in the philosophy of science. In "Science and Man" he gave what he believed to be the clearest formulation of his theory of knowledge that he had yet presented.[114] He again called for a truer world view than that established by scientific objectivism so that "the grounds of man's moral being can be reestablished. For this alone can save modern man from the alternatives of blind violence and paralysing self-doubt" (1970d, 976).

A year later, in the spring of 1971, Polanyi prepared for his last lecture series. He returned to the University of Texas at Austin to give a "Seminar in Meaning," for six weeks from mid-March to the end of April. Before he delivered the lectures, he and Magda flew to Toronto to visit with John and his family. In a festive family reunion, they celebrated both Polanyi's eightieth birthday and their fiftieth wedding anniversary. "The advantage of reaching an age like 80 is, that one does at last see one's life at an end. One can look back and see what the whole thing has amounted to. In terms of a miracle life is of course astounding. I am grateful to my view of the Universe that it does let me see inklings of this unbelievable miracle."[115]

After the birthday celebration, Magda returned to England and Michael continued on to Austin. He felt very alone without her. It fell to Bill Poteat and his wife to care for him.[116] For the first time in his years of friendship with Poteat, Polanyi talked intimately about his family, reminiscing about his brothers and sisters and sharing Ilona's memoir about his brother Karl. At the same time, Polanyi was aware that his ability to marshal details in a coherent argument was fading. Poteat found conversations increasingly exhausting, since he was expected to supply what Polanyi was unable to remember. Polanyi seemed to be in a very despairing state of mind during his stay. Once he said to Poteat, "I don't believe in God, or at any rate, I don't believe in him enough for it to make any difference." Nonetheless, Polanyi carried on with the lectures.[117] He anticipated that the series would be his "last of all jobs in life."[118] He had hoped to succeed in finding and presenting a new integration of his thought, some final synthesis which he could then incorporate into a book. But his time at Austin brought no new conclusions; he did not succeed in articulating his vision of human destiny as he had hoped to—"but perhaps I have not been born to achieve this."[119]

Polanyi was so exhausted by the Austin seminars that he left for home a week early and spent four weeks recovering. John Polanyi was inducted as a Fellow of the Royal Society on July 2, 1971, joining his father as a member of the oldest scientific organization in the world. Bill Scott happened to be in England at the time, and Michael invited him to attend the induction ceremony. It was a time of profound satisfaction for Michael, who enjoyed both the recognition of his son's scholarship and the pleasure of visiting with John and Sue.

II

The Last Years: 1971–1976

By the summer of 1971, Polanyi was aware that his life was coming
to an end. Many of his friends were dying. In August, he paid a
moving visit to Gyula Hollo, the Hungarian-born physician now
living in the United States who had been his friend since they studied
medicine together in Budapest. Hollo was suffering with cancer; his
wife, Elsa, also a physician, was caring for him. Silvia Kind met
Polanyi at the New York airport, shared a meal with him, then took
him to the Hollos', leaving him to go up to the apartment alone.

For Kind, this was her last visit with Michael: "He couldn't stand
the thought of me seeing him weak and old."[1] Just a few weeks
before, Polanyi encouraged Kind to "let this take its course and remain with me in serene spirits until my death whether or not we will
be able to see each other again."[2] In confronting his own diminish-
ment, Polanyi was remarkably serene. His greatest frustration was
the feeling that he could not bring his life's work to completion.
Other than that, he was most grateful that his life seemed to be
ending peacefully. To settle his affairs, Polanyi sent a letter to his
nephew George Striker, who would be the senior member of the
family after his own death. He sought to set the record straight about
a contested will because "at the age of 80, one feels close to death
and would like to avoid leaving behind an account of actions one has
not done, particularly if these actions would have been mean and
intolerable."[3]

Melvin Lasky, the editor of *Encounter*, invited Polanyi to respond
to Jacob Bronowski's criticisms in "The Disestablishment of Science." Polanyi refused to write a reply to Bronowski's attacks in

various publications because he lacked respect for Bronowski's scientific career; furthermore, according to Polanyi, Bronowski spoke in a loose and unintelligible way. It is unfortunate that Bronowski's criticism came so late in Polanyi's life. A younger and intellectually more agile Polanyi could well have profited by taking the criticism seriously and dealing with it in detail. Bronowski was a culturally assimilated Jew who had turned from his early training in mathematics to literary analysis, cultural criticism, and evolutionary theory. He might have been an ideal sparring-partner to help Polanyi show the social implications of differing theories of science. In his old age, Polanyi did not recognize the honor Bronowski paid him by criticizing his views and was in no position to give Bronowski a fair hearing in return.

In September, Polanyi presented a paper to a colloquium on "Science, Philosophie, Foi" held in Bienne, Switzerland under the auspices of the International Academy for the Philosophy of Science. His short talk on "Discoveries of Science" called for reviving the powers of tacit ideals, for discovering a way of knowing that is not based on dissecting human nature, so that "our duty to our fellow man and to ourselves, our confidence in a sublime guidance far beyond our reach" will be able to survive (1974b). Polanyi was no longer able to lead the way, as was evident to those who heard his rather confused talk.

In 1969, the Consortium for Higher Education Religion Studies (CHERS), centered in Dayton, Ohio, under the leadership of Frederick Kirschenmann, had developed a Polanyi Studies Program. During its first year (1969–1970), the program involved an in-depth study of Polanyi's major works (*Science, Faith and Society, Tacit Dimension*, and *Personal Knowledge*) under the direction of Richard Gelwick. The following academic year (1970–1971), the Polanyi program featured a workshop series guided by Brother Bruno Manno, a student at the University of Dayton who later studied with Polanyi in Oxford and at the University of Chicago.

In October 1970, Bill Scott opened the series with two lectures on Polanyi's ontology and epistemology. The following February, Richard Gelwick examined the possibilities of a theological methodology based on Polanyi's philosophy, and in March, Harry Prosch investigated the moral and ethical aspects of Polanyi's thought. Sigmund Koch explored the implications of Polanyi's thought for the interrelationship of science, technology, and human values. Another part of the CHERS series was a seminar on the more recent development of Polanyi's thought given by Ruel Tyson, professor of religion at the University of North Carolina, in the spring semester of 1972.

In May, Polanyi attended a major CHERS conference at Dayton on "Culture and Crisis: The Social Thought of Michael Polanyi." Thirty-four participants, scholars of Polanyi's thought from the United States, Canada, and England, joined him to explore issues in literature, art, morality, and religion. Polanyi was the only formal speaker, presenting a talk entitled "From Science to Culture." He intended his lecture to be an interim summary of "the way I see things, as I shall leave them as an image of my presumably fairly last views," before completing his last book, by then a long and uncertain enterprise.[4] This was Polanyi's last scholarly presentation in public.

Even though Polanyi called the conference "a strange meeting of all the friends who have written about my work and a number of others,"[5] he very much enjoyed being the center of attention. In spite of his loss of memory and occasionally feeling tired and old, he took delight in the company of his friends and disciples. Many of those who attended the Dayton conference found it very beneficial. To continue the dialogue, the Consortium for Higher Education Religion Studies decided to launch a "Society of Explorers" (TD, 82–83); it has since been renamed "The Polanyi Society."[6]

Since first giving the lectures on "Meaning" in 1969, Polanyi had been hoping to incorporate his new material on metaphor and myth into a book. He began to plan the outlines of the book in 1970, intending to sum up the perspectives of his work as it stood then. In July 1970, he invited Bruno Manno to come to Oxford for two or three months to help him complete the projected book; at that time Polanyi thought the manuscript could be finished by February or March 1971. Manno declined Polanyi's proposal because of his teaching duties.

The manuscript was not completed in 1971, but Polanyi was filled with enthusiasm for the subject and continued to work on the text. In March 1972, Polanyi was visited by Professor Charles S. McCoy of Berkeley, who had studied Polanyi's philosophical work and directed Gelwick's dissertation on Polanyi, and his wife, Marjorie Casebier McCoy, an author and actress. They were on their way to the University of Tübingen in Germany, where McCoy had been invited to lecture during the summer of 1972. Polanyi and Margie McCoy agreed that art could express religious faith more completely than rational statements or literal interpretation. Art can carry us away into a self-giving and an indwelling that is closely akin to the indwelling and commitment of religious faith. The McCoys were impressed by Polanyi's enthusiasm for the subject. Though he was vague about some dates and people, Polanyi was, in the McCoys' view, cogent and precise in his remarks about the topic at the focus of his current work.[7]

By the time of the Dayton conference in May 1972, Polanyi had made little progress on the manuscript and was increasingly anxious to find a collaborator to help him complete his final book. He invited Harry Prosch to assist in preparing the lectures on "Meaning" for publication, scrawling a little sketch of the scheme he envisioned for the book. Prosch agreed to set aside his own work in order to assist Polanyi in the project, although his academic responsibilities precluded his coming to England to begin work until the following February.

Polanyi was by then very aware that his mind was failing. As he observed his own fading powers, he was haunted by the fear that he would not be able to complete his philosophical system. He knew that he would need help from his disciples to round out the work he had done in the preceding four years.[8] In his frustration over delays, Polanyi asked Bill Poteat to help him outline the volume before Prosch's arrival. Polanyi even suggested that he might spend six weeks at Duke, although he was happy with Poteat's alternative proposal of coming to Oxford in late December. In the end, however, Poteat could not come. Feeling old and desperate, Polanyi was forced to wait until February 1973 for Prosch to join him.

Upon his arrival in Oxford, Prosch found Polanyi ready to work. Polanyi had begun to put the lectures together; his desk was cluttered and little piles of material were stacked on a canvas cot in the order in which he planned to take them up. Prosch plunged into the lectures, which "made a great deal of sense."[9] As the two men worked together, Prosch later recalled that he himself usually made comments or raised questions rather than offering suggestions. The content of the early lectures provoked little disagreement, but Prosch "was a bit concerned about his creation myths—how anybody would receive that." Prosch thought that most people who were religious would not care much for Polanyi's "theory of incompatibles": "If they really believed, they wouldn't want to think of God as a unity of incompatibles, but rather as a person or being." However, the more Prosch considered Polanyi's views of religion, the "more fond" he became of them. Although Prosch believed that he was being influenced by Polanyi and Polanyi in turn was being influenced by him, he thought that Polanyi's influence was the greater of the two.

During this period Polanyi was having difficulty recalling names, dates, and places, a problem that was by no means new to him. He supposed that his problems were due to hardening of the arteries and sometimes told Prosch, "I am pretty bad today." Polanyi's principal frustration was his inability to put his thoughts into words. "I have always been able to write," he told Prosch sadly. In the middle of March, when Prosch was forced to return to Skidmore, the two collaborators separated the tasks ahead. Prosch would write the main body of the text and Polanyi would be responsible for the introduction.

Early in May, Magda entered the hospital for minor surgery. Although her condition was not dangerous, Polanyi went to see her twice every day, often running into George and Priscilla, who were also frequent visitors. At the end of May, Magda left the hospital; by the end of June, she had sufficiently recovered to journey to Aldeburgh, Suffolk, where she and Polanyi spent a week near the home of Sir Ian and Lady Drusilla Scott. While Magda was recuperating, Michael set aside his work on *Meaning*; he never completed the introduction that he had intended to write for it. He had also been struggling to compose a contribution to a volume in honor of Abraham Maslow, whom he knew from his year at Stanford, and an introduction to a collection of articles in honor of George S. Klein, the former editor of *Psychological Issues*. For the Maslow volume he had drafted an eight-page manuscript entitled "About Religious Faith."[10] For the Klein volume, he finally had to resign himself to submitting just three paragraphs.

To anyone familiar with the usual vigor of Polanyi's prose, the manuscript "About Religious Faith" provides a striking contrast. Although the essay draws on the material of the Chicago lectures, it lacks Polanyi's customary grasp of English idiom and smooth development of ideas; in fact, many of his numerous editorial changes serve to confuse his meaning rather than to enhance it. The reader who hopes for new insights on the theme of religious faith may read the manuscript—Polanyi's last—with disappointment. Polanyi's powers of articulation now failed him almost completely:

> Even in our shattered periods unlimited powers were guided by emotional senses. By a look on humanity at its stages through the centuries, the orders of existence were shaped and honoured by sacred histories, pointing deeply at the beginning of the world. So this is how from the origins of humanity, beyond conceivable memories, we can turn our eyes to the falls of our age, in breathless ignorance of a very next year beyond the present.

> This is briefly my account of the transcendent; namely that the progress of science is less significant for our fates and ways, since we are immersed in a system of emotional powers by which and beyond which— there lies what acts for the sake of men and their religious existence.

Even though Polanyi submitted this piece to the editors, he knew it was poorly written. In the event, there were too few contributions for the Maslow Festschrift; Polanyi wrote Berta Maslow that he was glad that his manuscript remain unpublished because it was "rash and not yet suited for publication."[11] Even if there had been enough material for the book, it is doubtful that his essay would have been included in it.

Polanyi regretfully announced to his friends that he would no longer be able to write for publication. He hoped that he could continue to revise manuscripts and read dissertations and other works on his thought. He resigned himself to living in quiet retreat. Now that Magda was well again she could keep him company and look after his needs. Friends new and old continued to comfort him by their letters and visits. He and Magda were especially grateful for the friendship of Rom Harré, a philosopher of science, and his wife, as well as a number of other members of the Oxford faculty.

Polanyi was also comforted by finding acceptance from other members of the Oxford community. Philosopher of education Robin Hodgkin, theologian

Joan Crewdson, philosopher John Brennan, and, of course, Lady Drusilla Scott were all intensely interested in Polanyi's work. Together they developed Convivium, an English organization dedicated to the exploration and promotion of Polanyian thought.

During the spring and summer of 1973, Prosch continued work on *Meaning*. When speaking with Prosch, Polanyi was generally supportive, but he sometimes told others that he doubted whether Prosch would be able to speak for him; at this remove, it is difficult to tell whether Polanyi's inability to confront Prosch directly was from a habit of avoiding direct conflict in relationships or was due to the deterioration of his mind. After thirty years of writing and lecturing in the humanities, it was hard for him to turn the task of composition over to someone else. However, he responded with enthusiasm when he received a manuscript from Prosch. "My dear Harry," he wrote on August 24, "this is just a line to tell you my delight about your section on Religion. I shall soon have more to tell you from many corners."[12]

By October, Prosch had completed a draft of the book and mailed it to Polanyi. On November 22, Polanyi cabled: "Have read your excellent manuscript and wish to be its fellow author."[13] But Polanyi later decided that he was not satisfied with the book. At that time, Polanyi was in correspondence with Richard Gelwick, who was making plans to spend a sabbatical leave with Oxford theologian and biochemist, Arthur R. Peacocke. Polanyi wrote Prosch that he would take up Gelwick's offer to work with him on a new project during the sabbatical year. In December 1973, Polanyi invited Gelwick to work with him on a synthesis of all of his manuscripts, "published or not during the last four years. Its decisive parts should be my treatment, during four years of lecturing, the structure of complex experimental judgments throughout the fields of biology up to the domains of human obligations beyond our control."[14] In this letter, Polanyi suggested that "the work of Harry Prosch should be included, but not treated at this stage." Two days later, Polanyi wrote: "There is a majority of his text which I would not sign and there is another part also which I feel to lack sufficient penetration . . . in other parts [Prosch] does rely on essential features which he can speak for with my cordial agreement."[15] Besides the work that Prosch had done on meaning, Polanyi listed four works that he wanted to include in this "decisive effort": "Logic and Psychology" (1968a), "Genius in Science" (1971), "Science and Man" (1970d), and "Life's Irreducible Structure: The Principles of Boundary Conditions" (1968d).

In the winter and spring of 1973–1974, Gelwick and Polanyi worked together under less than auspicious circumstances. Gelwick was based at Cambridge, where Arthur Peacocke had become dean of Clare College, and traveled to Oxford on a regular basis. It was his custom to spend the morning in discussion with Polanyi, then to recapitulate the substance of what they had talked about, and finally to send a written account to reinforce Polanyi's memory. The process was a frustrating experience for them both, but particularly for Polanyi, who was annoyed at himself for his inability to remember what had taken place a few hours before.

In March, Magda's heart again caused her problems, necessitating a three-week stay in the hospital, followed by a month at home in bed. Gelwick continued to visit Polanyi, whose increasing dependence on Magda was evident even while she was convalescing; she would outlive him by a decade, dying on February 17, 1986. Although Gelwick and Polanyi met together a few more times before Gelwick's departure for home in June, they were not able to produce a definite outline or make any progress on a manuscript. Polanyi's desire for a work on the same scale as *Personal Knowledge* made it difficult for him to accept the more modest project he had undertaken with Prosch.

After Gelwick had departed for the United States, Polanyi wrote to his trusted friend Lady Drusilla Scott. He had frequently proposed collaboration to her since the fall of 1969, but like his proposals to other friends, he found it difficult to bring his dreams to fruition. Now he wrote her that he wanted to develop his book "with profound reliance on the next three years with you."[16] Lady Scott answered that she did not feel competent to undertake the task. She later wrote a popular exposition of Polanyi's ideas, which she entitled *Everyman Revisited, The Common Sense of Michael Polanyi.*[17]

At the end of the summer of 1974, Harry Prosch arrived in Oxford with a contract from the University of Chicago Press for *Meaning*. Polanyi, who knew Prosch had the contract, invited him to come and talk—about everything but the book! Later they got out the manuscript and Prosch explained that he had taken most of the text word for word from Polanyi's lectures. Then they read parts of the manuscript together, Polanyi "asking if he'd said thus and so—wanting to be sure it was true."[18] After several anxious weeks, Prosch paid Polanyi a final visit. "You're looking a little depressed," Polanyi told him. "Well, I am," Prosch answered. "I've done an awful lot of work on this manuscript and I have a contract from the University of Chicago Press and you're not going to sign it." Polanyi thought for a minute. "Bring it over to me and I'll sign it." In the end, with a few very minor changes, Polanyi did sign the contract for the publication of *Meaning*. The next day, Polanyi told Gelwick he was sorry he had signed. Prosch had no inkling of Polanyi's reservations: "[It was] news to me that he regretted having signed the contract—the next day, according to Gelwick. . . . He appeared to have been genuinely happy with it, as far as I could see. He even told me, although I feel embarrassed to repeat it, that no one had understood him as well as I had."[19]

Meaning was published by the University of Chicago Press a year later, in 1975. The jacket advertises Polanyi's hope "that this view of the foundation of meaning will restore meaningfulness to the traditional human ideals that were undercut by modern science," and describes his "attempt to free men from the shackles of objectivity and skeptical criticism" as "an appropriate final achievement—a venture into the restoration of meaning toward which all his earlier efforts had pointed" (MNG, jacket). In addition to a brief preface by Prosch, the book consists of thirteen chapters, leading from discussion of the destruction of meaning through explication of the kinds of meanings manifested in metaphor, poetry, art, ritual, myth, and religion, to grounds for the eventual restoration of meaning in society at large. The central body of *Meaning* (chapters 4–10) follows for the most part Polanyi's lecture series of 1969 at the University of Texas and the University of Chicago, and much of the text is repeated word-for-word from those lectures. Prosch introduced and concluded the lectures using material drawn from Polanyi's previously published books and articles. He also took responsibility "for the division of this work into chapters; for the development of its continuity through the writing of various summary, supplementary, and bridging sections; and for the editorial work required—the final language, phrasing and footnotes" (x).

The publication of *Meaning* marked the end of Polanyi's working life. Although the book does not present a complete account of Polanyi's vision— or even a complete theory of aesthetics—it does provide a useful extension of Polanyi's theory of tacit knowing into the fields of poetry, art, and myth. The text is rich with insights, some developed through Polanyi's lifelong passion for poetry and painting, others the fruits of his later explorations into the realm of symbol and sacred myth. Frustrating as the experience of coauthorship must have been for both Polanyi and Prosch, it nonetheless resulted in a publication that accomplished Polanyi's stated purpose: the examination of the destruction of meaning through the false mythology of scientism and objectivism and the establishment of the grounds for the restoration of meaning in the whole firmament of human beliefs and values.

We can only conjecture how far the final work may be from what Polanyi hoped to accomplish in the book.[20] He was no longer able to express himself clearly in writing, and his memory was becoming quite unreliable. It is hard to decide what weight to give to Prosch and Gelwick's dramatically different accounts of what Polanyi said to them. The very weaknesses of mind and memory that necessitated collaboration also rendered Polanyi incapable of true partnership in the work. Shortly after the contract was signed, Madga wrote Gelwick that "Michael now voices objections and cannot understand my saying that it is too late for that.... Poor Michael is often bewildered and depressed, realising his condition. I try to laugh it off, but seldom get away with it."[21] Had Polanyi been able to express his criticisms of Prosch's work more directly and effectively, he might have been more satisfied with the outcome. It seems that one reason Polanyi chose Thomas Torrance as his literary executor—apart from his excellent credentials as a theologian and philosopher of science—was to avoid the kind of difficulties he experienced in working with Prosch.[22] Torrance served in that capacity until after Magda's death in 1986. Since John Polanyi then became the owner of the copyrights, Torrance persuaded him to take responsibility for his father's legacy.

During the last years of Polanyi's life, his thought received increasing attention from theologians and from others concerned with questions of faith and value in human community. Not only was he frequently invited to speak, to comment, and to provide articles on matters of interest to religious believers, but on less formal occasions many of his friends and admirers tried to find out precisely what he himself believed. Some were frustrated by the ambiguities in his writing and wanted reassurance that he believed in the reality of the existence of God, or that he was a practicing Christian.[23] Brian Gowenlok, one of Polanyi's students and colleagues at Manchester, had a long conversation with a priest of the Syrian church who had confronted Polanyi at Oxford with the question, "Can you say, Michael, 'I know whom I have believed'?" Polanyi's reply was filled with sadness: "If only I could."[24]

Paul Tillich held that religious faith is a form of "ultimate concern"; from that standpoint, Polanyi was a person of profound religious faith. Throughout his life, Polanyi was committed to truth, justice, freedom, charity, and beauty. He felt that he had been called to serve the civilization which upheld these ideals. From his roots in Hungary's liberal heritage to his endorsement of the Anglo-Saxon tradition of personal and social freedom, Polanyi strove to uphold the ideals of integrity, freedom of inquiry, mutual respect, fairness, and tolerance. Polanyi felt an ongoing responsibility as a citizen in a free society to pursue the things of the mind and to use the power of thought to seek, express, and serve the truth. He felt himself obliged to promote the social values on which civilization depends. When he wrote to his friend Karl Bonhoeffer about Dietrich Bonhoeffer's death at the hands of Hitler, he spoke of that "love of freedom which can only derive its rational justification from an obligation to the transcendental."[25] Polanyi believed in and was committed to the reality of justice and truth as a necessary condition for liberty. This reality transcends us, is inexhaustibly and unspecifiably deep, and draws us into the awareness that we cannot rid ourselves of ultimate commitment and responsibility merely by changing our minds.

In summarizing his fiduciary program, Polanyi stated "I believe that in spite of the hazards involved, I am called upon to search for the truth and state my findings" (PK, 299). Polanyi's references to God were never in the form of rational arguments. He was most explicit on this topic in his 1948 paper for the Moot in which he suggested that when a proper doctrine of encounter is once established, all references to God not in the form of prayer will seem secondary and crude. Later he said in the Gifford Lectures that any claim that God could be observed scientifically would be idolatrous. For him, the reality of God can be encountered only through the indwelling of worship rather than through observation or affirmation. "God cannot be observed, any more than truth or beauty can be observed. He exists in the sense that He is to be worshiped and obeyed, but not otherwise; not as a fact—any more than truth, beauty or justice exist as facts. All these, like God, are things which can be apprehended only in serving them. The words 'God exists' are not, therefore, a statement of fact, such as 'snow is white,' but an accreditable statement, such as ' "snow is white" is true' " (279–280). As the typescript for "Paradox in Science and Religion" shows, Polanyi continued to believe that God "can be loved but not observed."[26]

Polanyi spoke of Christian faith as a passionate heuristic impulse that is without final consummation: "The indwelling of the Christian worshiper is therefore a continued attempt at breaking out, at casting off the condition of man, even while humbly acknowledging its inescapability. Such indwelling is fulfilled most completely when it increases this effort to the utmost.... Christian worship sustains, as it were, an eternal, never to be consummated hunch: a heuristic vision which is accepted for the sake of its unresolvable tension" (PK, 198–199). Polanyi considered a sense of imperfection as essential to the Christian's faith and quoted Tillich approvingly: "Faith embraces itself and the doubt about itself" (280). For Polanyi, the proper Christian inquiry is worship. "The words of prayer and confession, the actions of the ritual, the lesson, the sermon, the church itself, are the clues of the worshiper's striving towards God. They guide his feelings of contrition and gratitude and his craving for the divine presence, while keeping him safe from distracting thoughts" (281).

In the light of his understanding of religious faith, it is not surprising to find that Christian doctrine and the study of scripture held little interest for Polanyi. Nor did he concern himself much with the historical Jesus, the events of the New Testament, or the history of the Judeo-Christian heritage, or any of the subsequent theological controversies that divided Christianity. The strongest element in his religious faith was his conviction of the truth of the Pauline scheme of redemption: we are called to carry out tasks we know to be beyond our own weak and corruptible natures in the hope of being assisted by powers beyond our own. Clearly Polanyi believed in these transcendent powers of grace opening the way to successes of scientific knowledge, art, and moral reform. He was also moved by the image and power of Christ on the Cross, embodying the great symbolism of sacrifice and redemption, and by St. Augustine's search for faith.

Although he came from a Jewish family and was baptized as a Roman Catholic in Budapest, Polanyi adopted a Protestant Christian perspective in mid-life. He noted approvingly that the Protestant tradition could be included with law and science as a third field of thought that was constantly in the process of revision and growth. He appreciated the Protestant sense of obligation to social reform and saw the openness of the various Protestant sects toward foundational questions as an expression of the ever-unfolding nature of the Christian heritage.

Polanyi consciously embraced the Christian tradition and saw himself as a member of it, but he did not consistently identify himself with any denomination. He seems never to have attended Mass regularly after his baptism as a Roman Catholic nor to have become a member or a regular participant in the parish activities of "the various Anglican, Presbyterian, and Methodist churches where he was known at times to worship."[27] On the other hand, his contacts and participation in such discussion groups as the Moot involved him closely with a part of the Christian community that shared his intellectual and cultural outlook. Outside the formal church organization, he cherished long and intimate friendships with men and women of faith. His friendships with Karl Bonhoeffer, Hugh O'Neill, and Joseph Oldham were important and long-lasting, sustained by correspondence when visiting was not possible. Through the Moot he became close to Kathleen Bliss, who shared his concern that talk of God never be trivialized. Elizabeth Sewell shared his passion for social justice. Still later he was drawn to Lady Drusilla Scott, who grasped the underlying spiritual purposes of his work, and to Richard Gelwick, Thomas Torrance, Bill Poteat, Charles McCoy, Joan Crewdson, Robin Hodgkin, and other students of his thought who valued the contribution he made to their own understanding of theology.

Polanyi consistently valued Christianity as a system of thought in respect to theology, proper life, and Christian fellowship, but he seldom spoke of his own beliefs and practices, which seem to have varied over time. Once, as we have seen, in a rare autobiographical account, he described to Karl Mannheim the religious awakening of his youth when he was moved by the silent figure of Jesus in Dostoyevsky's story of the Grand Inquisitor and by Tolstoy's interpretation of the Sermon on the Mount pointing to the individual Christian's moral imperatives: "For a time, particularly from 1915 to 1920," he reported, "I was a completely converted Christian on the lines of Tolstoy's confession of faith."[28] He added that his faith had subsequently weakened, but then to some degree returned.

In the later Manchester years, Polanyi's participation in the community of the Moot inspired a deepening of his spirituality. Here he experienced vigorous intellectual encounters and a new understanding of the centrality of prayer in the Christian community; he also began regularly attending the Sunday evening service at a neighborhood church. He told Kathleen Bliss how hard it was to enter into a life of prayer when one had not been introduced to it in childhood, drawing the analogy to learning to ride a bike in middle age. He confided that he would sometimes go to churches just to observe what people did when they prayed.[29]

Much later, when Gilbert Doan asked Polanyi for permission to say that he was a communicant member of the Anglican Church, Polanyi replied that, even though he had attended church regularly at an earlier time, he had never been a communicant.[30] He also told Doan that the concluding line of *Personal Knowledge* reflected "what I believe Christians thought when worshiping God." He continued:

> It would go too far if I tried to tell you now exactly what my religious beliefs are. Fundamental is the fact that from the beginning of my enquiries in the early years of the war, I was guided by a conviction that the Pauline scheme of redemption is the paradigm of the process of scientific discovery. It demands us to undertake a task for which our explicit faculties are clearly insufficient, trusting that our labours will be granted success by powers over which we have no command. It is this doctrine of grace which I recognised in our relations to perfection, wherever we feel charged to pursue it, well knowing that we cannot achieve this end. This conception includes an acceptance of the fact that the pursuit of our highest obligations [is] rooted in our fallen condition, which alone can enable us to make this effort and will inevitably tend to corrupt it.

Polanyi closed by saying he could tell no more "without wandering into complex and intimate matters, which I would not wish to expose at this moment."[31]

Polanyi was eager to speak—at length, with great intensity, charm, and conviviality—about the nature and needs of our world, but he was not inclined to speak in public of his emotions, his private affairs, or his personal experience of faith. Polanyi wrote Lady Scott that "I am of course aiming at the foundation of *religious faith*.... But I became increasingly restrained about this, as time went on."[32] Harry Prosch reported his frustration that he "had never been able to get out of him what he was. He seemed not to want to talk about his own religious experiences or beliefs."[33] Theologian Joan Crewdson (the second woman to obtain a Bachelor of Divinity degree from Oxford) was similarly rebuffed when she tried to determine to what extent his faith could be described as Christian.[34] Polanyi's personal reticence was consistent with his view that God is known only in worship and not in discourse.

But at the heart of the man there was "a deeper secret pivot of faith" around which his life revolved.[35] Polanyi spent his working life in scrupulous pursuit of truth. In his last philosophical effort, he was concerned to clear away false ideas of meaning so that we might once again hold our ultimate beliefs confidently and so that we might respond to "a liturgical summons should one ever come our way" (MNG, 180). Recalling St. Augustine, he reminds us conversion cannot be achieved by our deliberate efforts and choice. "It is a gift of God and may remain inexplicably denied to some of us." In his seasons of doubt, Polanyi seems to have felt "inexplicably" deprived of a gift that others enjoyed. But there were also times when the grace seemed to have been given. Richard Gelwick was with Polanyi, psychologist Carl Rogers, and Meyer Shapiro, an art historian from Columbia University, at a meeting of the Stanford Center for Advanced Studies in Behavioral Sciences in the fall of 1962:

> There was a discussion of contemporary theater of the absurd because of a play currently in San Francisco. I have forgotten which play it was. The discussion of the modern outlook led to Shapiro's asking what we thought about Rudolph Bultmann's demythologizing of the New Testament, particularly the resurrection. I did not answer immediately. But Polanyi readily said that it seemed to him that the resurrection should not be a problem for a modern person if they understood what miracles are about. Miracles, he said, are exceptional and extraordinary, which makes them miracles. We should not try to explain them away. It seemed that if God were to become a man, such a miracle as the resurrection would be expected. Then he said, "I believe that this is just the way it happened." Then he went on to talk about miracles in the way he had in *Personal Knowledge* (the discussion on religious thought in Chapter 9) stating the error of trying to reduce the supernatural to the natural. No one challenged or probed his statements. Instead, there seemed to be agreement that Bultmann's demythologizing went too far in adopting the proof standards of natural science.[36]

Polanyi was a complex and reverent person. He took God seriously. Furthermore, he was a man who saw his whole life from the perspective of a calling to faithfully pursue and articulate the truth to his utmost ability. His life bespoke the root meaning of "religious"—his science, his philosophy, his faith, his vision of the good society were all bound together. Even as his capacities declined, he was still eager to fulfill the vocation he felt that he had been given to make room in our culture for the renewal of faith.

Richard Gelwick remembers a day when he and Polanyi sat together for a few moments in the silence of Merton Chapel. As they rose to leave, Polanyi said: "When you have lived as long as I have, it is good to have a place to say 'Thank you.'"[37] Bruno Manno says that in his last years, Polanyi was "intensely concerned with the religious dimension of human life and his own death. He talked endlessly about religion and the role it plays in personal, social and cosmic reality, even while questioning his own right to talk and write on this topic."[38]

In his last days, Polanyi's mind continued to deteriorate. "Michael is no longer Michael—that's the only way I can bear witnessing his rapid decline without breaking my heart over him. He is sweet; thanking me non-stop for doing everything for him ... but is unable to fathom what is happening around him. He doesn't remember Prosch, or that a book is due to come out."[39] In a sense, Polanyi had become imprisoned in the tacit dimension: "What worries me is that Michael's brain is still over-active; he knows and understands more than he can express. 'Why have I lost my equilibrium?' he has asked me today, as he can scarcely walk. It does show that he worries over his condition and I don't know what to reply as the doctors won't tell me anything. . . . Our son George's death [on July 15, 1975, from cancer] after terrible suffering—and to have to keep it from Michael as he couldn't cope with sorrow—you and Ann will know what that has meant."[40]

Polanyi's final days were spent in a nursing home in the country town of Northampton. He appreciated the pleasant gardens and caring staff. One day before Polanyi left 22 Upland Park Road, his neighbor Angela Bolton visited him. She asked him "Michael, are you afraid of death?"

Polanyi stopped short and thought for a moment. "Yes, I am," he answered.

Then he pointed to a picture on the wall of his study. "This is what I feel," he said. He was pointing to the famous picture of Saint Augustine on the seashore, puzzling over the mystery of the Trinity.[41]

Epilogue

William T. Scott

The last time I saw Michael Polanyi was a pleasant June afternoon in
1974. Our family was visiting in Oxford. After leaving our young
children with friends, we drove to the familiar home on Upland Park
Road. There Michael and Magda entertained us on the back terrace,
where the garden was in the full bloom of summer.

In many ways, Michael was his old self, impeccably dressed,
unfailingly courteous, pleasant and kind. In other ways, we sensed
his sadness at the loss of his full powers and the consequent frustration that his work would remain incomplete. Although Michael
was not inclined to carry on a serious discussion, he was eager to
share his memories of the past. Our conversation was wide-ranging;
we spoke of friends and family, of Polanyi's impressions of first-
century art, and of his memories from Berlin. He repeated for us the
story of the day he had gathered together a group of scientists in the
hope of finding a way to oppose the alarming growth of Hitler's
power; in the conversation, Schrödinger likened the spread of
Nazism to ink spreading across a damask table cloth.

Toward the end of our visit, Michael took my wife, Ann, for
a slow walk around the border of the garden, stopping from time
to time to admire the roses. The flowers brought him joy,
reminding him of his earlier gardens in the Berlin suburb of
Dahlem and the Manchester village of Hale, and of his long-ago
wish for a small house with a large garden to delight the soul. Shortly
after our visit, the mail brought a note from Michael to me,
expressing his concern that I should have "more far reaching
employment." Although his own active days were limited—he was

then 82 years old—he had not given up the hope of furthering his ideas through his friends and disciples! He spoke of having "too much work for my restricted powers" and signed the letter "Your old man, Michael Polanyi."[1]

When the Hungarian scholar Erzsebet Vezér visited from Budapest, she found Polanyi "already very tired and weak." But sharing memories electrified and rejuvenated him. He remembered his early childhood as a time of "utmost beauty," and looked back on student debates at the Minta high school, university lectures, and warm friendships from the past. As he reminisced, "his thought continually returned to his anxiety for the survival of mankind and for the future of human culture." When Vezér took her leave, he quoted the poet Ady in impeccable Hungarian: "Tomorrow I'll have already run far / and will weep somewhere."

Polanyi died on February 22, 1976. The next day, *The London Times* reviewed the life of "the eminent chemist and philosopher," documenting his contributions in physical chemistry and his later changes of field, which were "subsequently proclaimed as a great loss to reaction kinetics, to patent-law, to economics, and to social studies." The three-column obituary ended with a personal tribute: "Those who knew Polanyi well will attest to his sweetness of character, to a pervading sadness which was none the less at every other moment illuminated by sparkling humour, gentleness tempered by a strong and courageous spirit, patent honesty and the humility which is invariably the property of the wise."

In response to *The Times'* obituary, Robin Hodgkin wrote: "Michael Polanyi's 'change of field' from physical chemistry to philosophy may have been seen as a loss by many of his colleagues. But to many others, especially to those of us who were younger, his *Personal Knowledge* offered, as it still does, an intellectual journey of profundity and moment.... It may be reasonably asked whether any philosopher has built so sure a bridge between the questioning of science and the faith of religion."

Appendix: People Interviewed by William T. Scott

Argyle, Cicely
Aron, Raymond

Baker, John R.
Baughan, Eward C.
Berg, Wolf
Blaschko, Hugh
Bliss, Kathleen
Bredig, Mrs. Max
Brill, Rudolf F.
Burkhardt, George Norman
Byers-Brown, William

Cairncross, Alec
Calvin, Melvin
Campbell, Donald
Carocci, Eva
Chambaud, Jeannette
Cooper, Sir William Mansfield
Coppock, Dennis J.
Crawford, Bryce
Cremer, Erica
Crewdson, Joan

Davies, Olive
Dearnally, John
Dentay, Greta
Dreyfus, Hubert

Eley, Daniel
Emmet, Dorothy
Erzi, Endre
Evans, Alwyn G.
Evans, Michael
Eyring, Henry

Fairbrother, Fred
Fajans, Salomea
Fellner, Valerie
Ferency, Mrs. Stephen
Forster, Peter

Gelwick, Richard
Gilson, Ralph
Gowenlock, Brian G.
Grant, Donald and Irene
Grene, Marjorie

Haberler, Gottfried
Halacsy, Andrew
Halasz, Nicholas
Hanson, Earl
Hardy, Sir Alister
Harré, Rom
Harteck, Paul
Hayek, Fritz
Heller, Wilfried

Hildebrand, Joel
Hollo, Elsa
Horner, Imre

James, Walter
Jelenski, K. A.
Jewkes, John
Josselson, Diana
Jouvenel, M. le Baron Bertrand de

Kende, Peter
Kind, Sylvia
Koestler, Arthur
Kurimoto, Shinjiro

Langford, Thomas
Laslett, Barbara
Levine, Alexander
Levitt-Polanyi, Kari
Lucas, John

Magattai, Tom
Mangold, Paul
Mark, Hermann
Martins, Leah
Mays, Wolfe
McCoy, Charles
Meier, Richard L.

Norrish, Ronald G. W.

Oliver, R. A. C., and Anna
O'Neill, Hugh

Palló, Gábor
Peacocke, Arthur
Phelps, Jim
Plesch, Peter H.
Polanyi, John
Polanyi, Kari
Polanyi, Magda
Polanyi, Priscilla
Polanyi, Thomas
Polanyi, Vera
Pols, Edward

Polya, George
Poteat, Bill
Prosch, Harry

Reiner, Erica
Robertson, John H.
Rona, Elizabeth
de Rougemont, Denis

Saboz, Andreas
Schay, Geza
Schwab, G. M.
Scott, Lady Drusilla
Sewell, Elizabeth
Shils, Edward
Skinner, Henry
Söllner, Karl
Stevenson, Ian
Stolper, Toni
Striker, George and Barbara
Szecsi-März, Maria
Szilard, Bela
Szwarc, Michael (Michael
   Schwarz)

Taylor, Alan J. P.
Taylor, Charles
Thrush, Brian
Todd, Alexander
Torrance, Thomas
Toulmin, Stephen
Tyson, Ruel

Vezér, Erzsébet
Vickers, Geoffrey
von Salis, Doris

Warhurst, Ernest
Wedgwood, Veronica
Weisskopf, Victor
West, Dame Rebecca
Wigner, Eugene

Zeisel, Eva

Notes

PREFACE

1. *The Physics of Electricity and Magnetism*, 2d ed., corrected and with a new preface (New York: Krieger Publishing, [1959, 1966] 1977).

2. *Erwin Schrödinger: An Introduction to His Writings* (Amherst: University of Massachusetts Press, 1967).

3. "Illative Sense and Tacit Knowledge: A Comparison of the Theological Implications of the Epistemologies of John Henry Newman and Michael Polanyi" (Ph.D. diss., Catholic University of America, 1991). A revised version of this dissertation, entitled *Personal Catholicism*, was published by the Catholic University of America Press in 2000.

4. "At the Wheel of the World," in *From Polanyi to the 21st Century: Proceedings of a Centennial Conference*, ed. Richard Gelwick (Biddeford, Maine: The Polanyi Society, 1997), 341–364; also in *Tradition and Discovery* 25 (1999): 10–25.

I. EARLY YEARS

1. Interview with Vera Polanyi.

2. From Eldgenossische Technische Hochschule Library, Zürich; Matriculation papers of Pollacsek, and letters by Adolf Pollacsek to the school, October 3, 1866 and May 25, 1868.

3. "Bei der Gelegenheit," sent by Erzsebet Vezér.

4. Educational and employment record from the bulletins of the Alumni Association of the ETH.

5. Interview with Barbara and Georg Striker.

6. His obituary in the German language *Pester Lloyd* (January 13, 1905) tells of 1,000 km of local lines built by him, including

Kisujszallas-Devavanya Gyoma, Szeghalom-Veszto-Kot, and Mezohegyes-Oroshaza-Szarvas.

7. Interview with Zeisel.

8. Ilona Duczynska, "Polanyi Karoly 1886–1964," *Szazadok* 105 (1971): 85–95 (in Hungarian).

9. Cecilie Pollacsek, *Die Vorgeschichte der russischen Revolution* (Verlag der Volksstimme-Buchhandlung, 1906).

10. Interviews with Polya and Chambaud; both of them were in their nineties when Scott interviewed them.

11. Karl later wrote to Michael, "My mother never understood a single life around herself" (January 8, 1925; RPC 17:3).

12. Duczynska, 86.

13. Scott interview.

14. The Hungarian philosopher and essayist George Lukács met the love of his youth, Polanyi's cousin Irma Seidler, at Cecile's literary salon on December 18, 1907.

15. S. N. Behrman, "Ferenc Molnar," *New Yorker* (May 25, 1946): 31.

16. Wohl to Laura, March 20, 1895 (EZC).

17. Polanyi to Gelwick, August 8, 1963 (RGL). Although Polanyi refers to his grandfather Wohl as "Assyrius," all other references speak of Andrej or Andreas.

18. Duczynska, 85–86.

19. Karl to Michael, June 7, 1940 (RPC 17:9).

20. Interview with Eva Carocci.

21. Interview with Maria Szesci.

22. EZC contains the agreement of the seconds to a duel with Italian swords at the Fencing Hall of the University on January 27, 1912, at 9:00 A.M. Polanyi was the offended party, and the offender was Láló Berczeller. The same document is in RPC as well.

23. Reported by Erzsebet Vezér, "Michael Polanyi," *Magyar Hirek*, Budapest, March 13, 1976.

24. Michael to Papa, June 23, 1897 (EZC).

25. Undated (EZC).

26. Karl to Michael, September 18, 1939 (RPC 17:8).

27. Michael to mother, undated (EZC).

28. Polanyi to Silvia Kind, July 30, 1962 (SKL).

29. Striker to Scott, December 26, 1985.

30. Mausi to Michael, October 7, 1930 (RPC 2:6).

31. Mihály to Cecile, November 2, 1901 (EZC).

32. Mausi to Papa, November 12, 1903 (EZC).

33. Mausi to Michael, October 7, 1930 (EZC).

34. Interview with George Striker.

35. Originally transliterated as "Stricker."

36. Paul Ignotus, "The Hungary of Michael Polanyi," in *The Logic of Personal Knowledge* (London: Routledge & Kegan Paul, 1961), 11.

37. Karl to Michael, January 11, 1952 (RPC 17:12).

38. Duczynska, 92.

39. From the Minta Gymnasium records, courtesy of Dr. Erzsebet Vezér.

40. The official name of the *Minta* was *Tanarkepzo Intezet Gyakarlo Gimnaziuma* (Practice Gymnasium of the Teacher-Training Institute). Cf. William McCagg, "Jewish Nobles and Geniuses in Modern Hungary," *East European Monographs* (New York: Columbia University Press, 1972), 210, and the *Minta* 100-year celebration volume: Gyula Fehervari, Dr. Gustav Makay, and Dr. Janos Solti, eds., *Centenariumi Emlekalbuma 1872–1972* (Budapest, 1972), 5.

41. Franz Alexander, *The Western Mind in Transition* (New York: Random House, 1960), 27. Alexander was born in Budapest on January 22, 1891—one month before Polanyi—and attended the Minta Gymnasium. He became an M.D. in 1913 and lived in Berlin from 1920 to 1930. According to Polanyi's diary, they visited each other frequently. Alexander moved to the United States in 1930 and became a noted psychoanalyst.

42. Paul Mangold, Polanyi's classmate, to Scott, April 1, 1981.

43. "Past Images," two-page manuscript, June 13, 1974 (RPC 22:17).

44. "The Fringe," only one page extant, sent by Gabor Pallo.

45. Polanyi to András Györgyey, June 14, 1972 (RPC 11:1).

46. Interview with Eva Zeisel.

47. Michael to Mama, June 29, 1907 (EZC).

48. Michael to Mausi, June 22, 1947 (EZC).

49. Gorog to Polanyi, undated (RPC 9:14).

50. George Polya recalled Cecile helpfully analyzing his habit of repeating everything he said.

51. Alexander 20–21.

52. Notebook No. 2, p. 16 (RPC 27:2).

53. Michael to mother: June 29, July 8, July 11, July 17, August 15, August 19, 1907. Michael to Mausi: July 3, August 16 (EZC).

54. Michael to Cecile, August 19, 1907 (EZC).

55. August 16, 1907.

56. Michael to Mausi, EZC.

57. Interview with Mangold.

58. Lee Congdon, "Karl Polanyi in Hungary, 1900–19," *Journal of Contemporary History*, 11 (1976): 171.

59. Karl to Michael, March 4, 1969 (RPC 17:12).

60. Ignotus, 11.

61. "Autobiographical sketch," copy from George Striker, p. 3.

62. Quoted by Congdon (172) from Karl Polanyi's essay in *Szazadok* 105 (1971): 99.

63. "Polanyi and the Treason of the Intellectuals," *Canadian–American Review of Hungarian Studies* 2 (1975): 81–82.

64. Pal Wolfner in Congdon, 169.

65. Ignotus, 12.

66. *Pesti Futar*, 1929.

67. Michael to Cecile, September 18, no year (probably 1909 or 1910; EZC).

68. The papers were 1914b, 1914c, 1919b, and 1925b. Vera Polanyi recalled from her medical school days (Italy, 1939) that more than one faculty member asked if she was related to the Michael Polanyi who had worked on colloids.

69. Reported by Polanyi in an autobiographical sketch in the Budapest personalities biweekly, *Pesti Futar*, Christmas, 1929, pp. 37–38.

70. Elizabeth Rona, *How It Came About* (Oak Ridge Associated Universities, 1978), 3.

71. Interview with Salomea Fajans.

72. Mangold to Scott, May 31, 1981. Mangold was already in Karlsruhe when Polanyi arrived.

73. Einstein to Bredig, January 30, 1913. Bredig copied the note and forwarded it to Polanyi on February 1.

74. Polanyi to Mausi, undated (EZC).

75. Polanyi to Mausi, undated (EZC).

76. Polanyi to Karl, undated (EZC).

77. Description of Curriculum and Parental Agreement (EZC).

78. This class was described, with some inaccuracies, by Arthur Koestler in the first volume of his autobiography, *Arrow in the Blue* (London: Collins with Hamish Hamilton, 1952).

79. Jeannette Chambaud to Scott, February 7, 1979.

80. The 1912/1913 second semester poster listed the teachers and courses as follows: Dénes Nagy and József Balassa, Sociology; Hugo Kentzler, Art History; József Diener-Dénes, Literature; Valéria Dienes and Cecilia Polanyi, Seminar; Vilma Glücklich, Pál Nádai, Pedagogy; Sandor Kovacs, Musical Theory; Hugo Kalmár, Technology; Hugo Rohonyi and József Madzsar, Natural Science; with lectures given by Leo Lieberman, Ferenc Tangl, Pál Ruffy, Géza Almady, Paul Ignotus, and Oszkar Jászi, among others. Jeannette Odier only served on the staff in the 1913/1914 school year, for which no poster is available.

81. Karl to Michael, February 7, 1914 (RPC 17:1).

82. Karl to Michael, March 20, 1914 (RPC 17:1).

83. Cecile to Michael, December 31, 1914 (EZC).

84. *Berichte der preussischen Akademie der Wissenschaften* (1912), 134–140.

85. The paper and the accompanying letter are not available, but Nernst's answer on August 22, 1913, a handwritten draft of Polanyi's reply, and Nernst's second letter of October 15, 1913, are in RPC 1:2.

86. Winter semester, October 1913 to February 1914: machine principles, inorganic experimental chemistry, technical drawing, organic chemistry, technical analysis, chemical laboratory. Summer semester, March–June 1914: technical drawing, machine principles, mechanical engineering, chemical-technical analysis, chemical technology II, organic chemistry II, physical chemistry II, chemical laboratory, methods of technical analysis, advanced mathematics.

2. COMING OF AGE IN THE GREAT WAR

1. The appointment to the Third Battalion of Infantry Regiment 23 was not recorded until November 16, 1914, according to an ordinance of the k.u.k. war ministry. Copies of documents referring to Polanyi were supplied by the Austrian War Archive.

2. Polanyi to Fajans, November 11, 1914, Michigan Historical Collections.

3. "Contributions to Quantum Theory," *Verhandlungen der deutschen physikalischen Gesellschaft*, 16 (1914): 820–825.

4. We are indebted to Dr. John Polanyi and Vice-President Charles E. Bloom of the American Friends of the Hebrew University for making Einstein's correspondence from 1914 to 1915 available. There were seven later exchanges in the 1920s and 1930s on other topics without any substantial exchange of views.

5. This difficulty still remains for modern discussion of the logic of the Nernst theorem.

6. Arnold Eucken, "On the Theory of Adsorption," *Verhandlungen der deutschen physikalischen Gesellschaft*, 16 (1914): 345–362.

7. A. Titoff, *Zeitschrift für physikalische Chemie* 74 (1910): 641.

8. The result was confirmed later in a number of papers by Polanyi's pupils and by other authors, and was particularly supported by Herbert Freundlich, who came to be one of Polanyi's colleagues in Berlin and published the most authoritative book on the subject, the 1922 third edition of *Kapillarchemie* (Leipzig, 1922). He offered considerable encouragement to Polanyi: "I am heavily committed now to your theory myself; I hope it is correct." Data collected much later led to greatly improved agreement of experiment with theory.

9. Interview with Magda Polanyi.

10. William M. Johnston, *The Austrian Mind: An Intellectual and Social History 1848–1938* (Berkeley: Univ. of California Press, 1972), 339–340.

11. Michael to Mausi, December 21, 1914.

12. Michael letter to Mausi, December 4, 1914.

13. Interview with Elizabeth Sewell.

14. Elizabeth Sewell recalls Michael having told her of experiences in the Carpathians.

15. Polanyi to Fajans, undated, but probably June 1915; Michigan Historical Collection.

16. Letter to Karl, probably written in November 1915.

17. Fajans to Polanyi, March 22, 1916 (RPC 1:14).

18. "The Adsorption of Gases on Glass, Mica, and Platinum," *Journal of the American Chemical Society*, 40 (1918): 1361–1403.

19. Frederick Soddy, *Nature* 92 (December 4, 1913): 399–400.

20. Kasimir Fajans, *Physikalische Zeitschrift* 15 (1914): 935–940.

21. Polanyi to Fajans, December 9, 1914; Michigan Historical Collection.

22. *Physikalische Zeitschrift* 16 (1915): 45–51.

23. Polanyi to Fajans, November 3, 1915; Michigan Historical Collection.

24. Fajans, *Physikalische Zeitschrift* 17 (1916): 1–4.

25. Paneth, *Zeitschrift für physikalische Chemie* 91 (1916): 171–198; Kasimir Fajans, *Jahrbuch der Radioactivität und Elektronik* 24 (1917): 314–352.

26. Michael to Cecile, January 29, 1915 (EZC).

27. Michael to Cecile, July 7, 1916 (EZC).

28. Congdon, "The Making of a Hungarian Revolutionary: The Unpublished Diary of Bela Balazs," *Journal of Contemporary History* 8 (1973).

29. Lee Congdon, "The Unexpected Revolutionary: Lukacs's Road to Marx," *Survey* (1974): 199.

30. Duczynska, 93.

31. Vezér Erzsebet, "Ilona Duczynska," *Elet es Irodalom*, May 6, 1978.

32. Congdon, Balazs, 58.

33. The Austrian War Archives record eight examinations, mostly followed by official reviews. The dates were August 15, 1915; December 17, reviewed January 4, 1916; February 24, in a hospital in Vienna, reviewed March 2; May 22, also in Vienna, reviewed May 24; July 6, reviewed July 14; September 29, reviewed October 6; January 4, 1917, reviewed January 14, with an inflammation of the right knee cap added to the reported ailments, and April 22, with approval on April 29.

34. Polanyi to Mausi, May 22 [1916?] (EZC).

35. Polanyi to Fajans. This evidently was the sanatorium run by Elizabeth Rona's brother-in-law, Paul Schary, where she first met Polanyi. It must also have been the place where, according to Magda, Polanyi's friend Elsa Hollo was the only woman doctor.

36. Polanyi to Fajans, April 7, 1916, Michigan Historical Collection.

37. Michael to Cecile, October 8, 1916 (EZC).

38. RPC 19:1.

39. Michael to Karl, March 26, 1917 (RPC 1:5).

40. Jeannette Odier to Scott, July 28, 1979.

41. 1929 diary (RPC 6).

42. Interview with Eva Zeisel.

43. Polanyi to Mannheim, April 19, 1944 (RPC 4:11).

44. The explanation in terms of the spirit of national policy has, of course, been often proposed.

45. Karl to Irma Pollacsek, undated, RPC 17:13.

46. Polanyi to Fajans, between March 25 and June 26, 1918; Bentley Library.

47. Ignotus, *Hungary*, 144.

48. Excerpt of Goldzieher's taped memoirs in RPC 8:5.

49. Rona, *How It Came About*, 10.

50. Polanyi to Mannheim, April 19, 1944 (RPC 4:11).

51. G. Palló, "Why Did George von Hevesy Leave Hungary?" *Periodica Technica* 30 (1985): 97–115.

52. Interview with Eva Zeisel.

3. KARLSRUHE

1. Polanyi to Mausi, October 25, 1955 (EZC).

2. Polanyi to Fajans, December 10, 1919; Bentley Library.

3. Michael to Cecile, December 21, [1919] (EZC).

4. Interview with Magda Polanyi.

5. Interview with Magda Polanyi.

6. Max Bodenstein and Samuel Colville Lind, *Zeitschrift für physikalische Chemie* 57 (1906): 168–192.

7. *Physikalische Zeitschrift*, 18 (1917): 121.

8. For a review, see K. J. Laidler and M. C. King, "The Development of Transition-State Theory," *Journal of Physical Chemistry* 87 (1983): 2657–2664.

9. Irving Langmuir, "Radiation as a Force in Chemistry," *Journal of the American Chemical Society* 42 (1920): 2190–2205.

10. *Münchner Berichte* 83 (1917).

11. László Berényi, "Tests of the Polanyi Theory of Adsorption," *Zeitschrift für physikalische Chemie* 94 (1920): 628–662, received November 20, 1919.

12. Einstein to Polanyi, March 1, 1920 (RPC 1:7). The letter from Polanyi to Einstein that initiated this discussion is not extant.

13. Announced in the *Chemiker Zeitung* for April 10 and reported in a single page of the same journal on May 4 (1920e). Polanyi did not notice that Peter Debye had just published a theory using this concept for molecular attractions in gases that approximately obey the Van der Waals equation of state (*Physikalische Zeitschrift* 21 (1920): 178–187 issue of April 1). However, Debye did not take up forces between molecules in the solid and adsorbed states.

14. Interview with Magda Polanyi.

15. Rosalie to Magda, November 5, 1920 (RPC 1:11).

4. THE FIBER INSTITUTE

1. The subjects on the certificate are 1. Inorganic, Analytical, and Introductory Organic Chemistry. 2. Physics. 3. Introduction to Machines. 4. Introduction to Higher Mathematics.

2. Herzog to Polanyi, July 27, 1920 (RPC 1:10).

3. P. Debye and Scherrer, *Physikalische Zeitschrift* 17 (1916): 277.

4. R. O. Herzog and W. Jancke, "X-Ray Spectroscopic Investigations on Cellulose," *Zeitschrift für Physik* 3 (1920): 196–198.

5. R. O. Herzog and W. Jancke, "On the Physical Structure of a Few High Molecular Organic Compounds," *Berichte der Deutschen Chemischen Gesellschaft* 53B (1920): 2162–2164.

6. Reis to Polanyi, October 14, 1920 (RPC 1:11).

7. Bredig to Polanyi, November 15, 1920 (RPC 1:11).

8. Born to Polanyi, January 12, 1921 (RPC 1:13).

9. Interview with Hermann Mark, who had been present, and Polanyi's account in "The Potential Theory of Adsorption" (KB, 87–96). The published form of the lecture did not include a report of the discussion.

10. Cecile to Mausi, undated (NZL).

11. Robert Olby interview with Polanyi, 1968 (cassette tape furnished by Olby); Olby, *The Path of the Double Helix* (London: Macmillan, 1974), 31.

12. P. T. Flory, *Principles of Polymer Chemistry* (Ithaca, New York: Cornell Univ. Press, 1953), Section I-l. Hermann Mark referred to the "small unit" idea for which there existed no real arguments except that many organic chemists felt that the idea of such enormous molecules was "outrageous" (Mark to Scott, January 3, 1979).

13. *Berichte der Deutschen Chemischen Gesellschaft* 53 (1920): 1073–1124.

14. *Berichte der Deutschen Chemischen Gesellschaft* 54 (1921): 767–774. This reference was given by Herzog in July.

15. Robert Olby interview with Michael Polanyi, 1968.

16. K. H. Meyer and H. Mark, "On the Structure of the Crystal Portion of Cellulose," *Berichte der Deutschen Chemischen Gesellschaft* 61 (1928): 593–613; H. Staudinger, "On the Constitution of High Polymers," ibid., 2427–2431.

17. 1921d. This report was omitted from Polanyi's bibliography in *The Logic of Personal Knowledge*. The copy retained in Polanyi's files was out of chronological order and was not easily recognized.

18. *Zeitschrift für angewandte Chemie* 34 (1921): 213–214.

19. Olby interview.

20. Karl Weissenberg, "A New X-ray Geometry," *Zeitschrift für Physik* 23 (1924): 229–238.

21. Born to Polanyi (RPC 1:14). In his 1962 essay "My Time with X-rays and Crystals" (KB, 100), Polanyi made the assumption more plausible by describing a crystal as a single giant molecule and the quantum jump he proposed as being like those that are well known in small molecules. Actually, modern solid-state theory does treat a crystal as a whole. However the energy jumps in the giant "molecule" never concentrate energy into a single pair of planes about to break apart.

22. Polanyi to Mausi, July 18, 1921 (EZC).

23. Magda to Cecile, October 2, 1921 (EZC).

24. Einstein Archives, Princeton, N.J.

25. The available letters are: Polanyi to Herzfeld, October 11, 20, and 29, and November 4 and 18, 1921 in the Herzfeld archives, Niels Bohr Library, Center for History of Physics (New York); Herzfeld to Polanyi, eight letters in Polanyi archives, 6 undated, two showing the dates March 25 and November 3 (RPC 14:3). Max Born to Polanyi, June 13, 1929 (RPC 1:14) and September 26, 1921 (RPC 1:15).

26. *Annalen der Physik* 59 (1919): 635–667.

27. The only publications of Born and Franck on this problem appeared in 1925, "Quantum Theory and the Formation of Molecules," *Zeitschrift für Physik* 31 (1925): 411–429 and *Annalen der Physik* 76 (1925): 225–230, by which time there was no point in referring to the supposed contradiction claimed by Polanyi or to his "magical" solution.

28. The "Deutsche Physikertag," *Physikalische Zeitschrift* 22 (1921): 320.

29. Max Born, ed., *The Born–Einstein Letters* (New York, 1971); letters 35, 36.

30. K. F. Herzfeld, *Zeitschrift für Physik* 8 (1921): 132–136.

31. Unpublished fourteen-page typescript beginning "The Private Motives of Science," RPC 26:9, pp. 3–4. See also the unpublished typescript, *Science, Ideals and Society*, 34–37 and 107–108 (handwritten pagination) in RPC 28:11.

32. Michael to Cecile, June 18, 1922 (EZC).

33. Michael to Cecile, September 4, 1921 (EZC).

34. Interview with Magda Polanyi.

35. Cecile to Polanyi, undated (RPC 19:1).

36. The articles by Schönborn and by von Gomperz appeared in *Zeitschrift für Physik* 8 (1922): 184–190 and 377–381.

37. R. O. Herzog and W. Jancke, "Verwendung von Röntgenstrahlen zur Untersuchung metamikroskopischer biologischer Strukturen," in *Festschrift der KWG zu ihrem zehnjährigem Jubiläum* (Berlin: Springer, 1921), 118–120.

38. Interview with Brill.

39. Rudolf Brill, "On Silk Fibroin I," *Justus Liebig's Annalen*, 434 (1923): 204–217.

40. Interview with Saboz.

41. Polanyi lecture to Chaos Club, Chicago, 1950 (RPC 32:15).

42. Interview with Karl Söllner.

43. Paul Harteck, "Physical Chemists in Berlin, 1919–1933," *Journal of Chemical Education* 37 (1960): 46.

44. Interview with Wolf Berg.

45. This action of Herzog was part of a formalizing of the Fiber Institute's structure. People working in different areas were designated as leaders of divisions, and Polanyi's prolific work justified setting up the new section and putting him in charge.

46. Mark to Scott, 1984.

47. Interview with Hermann Mark.

48. Mark to Scott, 1983.

49. Karl to Michael, November 12, 1922.

50. Interview with Magda Polanyi.

51. Mausi to Polanyi, May 22, 1922 (EZC).

52. Schmid to Scott, 1978.

53. The principal papers—1922h, 1922i, 1922j—were published in July and September, and some of their results were presented by Polanyi on July 7, 1922, in a talk to the Physical Society of Berlin.

54. Mark to Scott, October 29, 1984. Reference to the use of the DA was made in 1923f with more details in 1925c.

55. Polanyi–Czochralski correspondence in RPC 1:17, 1:18, 1:19, 1:20, and 2:1.

56. Jan Czochralski, *Internationale Zeitschrift für Metallographie* 6 (1914): 289 and 8 (1916): 1.

57. *Proceedings of the International Congress of Applied Mechanics*, Delft, 1924, 67–88.

58. Michael to Cecile, undated (EZC).

59. Sofie to Magda and Michael, October 12, 1921 (EZC).

60. Unpublished manuscript.

5. INSTITUTE FOR PHYSICAL CHEMISTRY

1. Polanyi to Haber, April 16, 1923 (RPC 1:19).

2. Haber to Harnack, June 9, 1923; MPG.

3. Haber and Zisch, *Zeitschrift für Physik*, 9 (1922): 302.

4. Duke Lectures 1964, Lecture 3: "Commitment to Science," pp. 21–22 and 27 (RPC 36:13–15).

5. Copy sent by Cremer, undated.

6. Interview with Heller.

7. Accounts of many of the flame experiments of Polanyi's group, in the context of the totality of work in gas reactions, are given by V. N. Kondrat'ev, *Chemical Kinetics of Gas Reactions*, trans. by J. M. Crabtree and S. N. Carruthers (Oxford: Pergamon Press 1964).

8. Hermann Mark and Eugene Wigner, *Zeitschrift für physikalische Chemie* III (1924): 398–414.

9. Neils Bohr, *Zeitschrift für Physik*, 13 (1923): 117–165.

10. Robin Hodgkin and Eugene Wigner, "Michael Polanyi: 1891–1976," *Biographical Memoirs of Fellows of the Royal Society* 23 (1977): 421–422.

11. Nine in 1920, seven in 1921, nine in 1922 (RPC 17:2).

12. Karl to Michael, March 6, 1920.

13. Karl to Michael, undated, probably fall 1923.

14. Duczynska, "Polanyi Karoly," 93.

15. May 26, 1920.

16. Toni Stolper to Bill Scott, 1979.

17. Toni Stolper, *Ein Leben in Brennpunkten unserer Zeit: Gustav Stolper 1888–1947* (Tübingen: Rainer Wunderlich Verlag, 1960), 166–188.

18. Erika Cremer to Scott, March 14, 1979.

19. Five articles during this period were patent-related: 1926e, 1926f, 1927a, 1927b, and 1927c. Of the 65 letters in the RPC for 1923–1924, 17 concern technical consulting and patent applications.

20. Notebook, Summer 1926, p. 1 (RPC 44:1).

21. RPC 43:8, undated.

22. W. Heitler and Fritz London, *Zeitschrift für Physikik*, 44 (1927): 455–472.

23. Fritz London, "Über den Mechanismus der homöopolaren Bindung," in *Probleme der modernen Physik* (Leipzig: S. Hirzel, 1928), 104–113.

24. Schay to Scott, 1979.

25. *Zeitschrift für physikalische Chemie* 1 (1928): 62–67 and 68–73.

26. *Zeitschrift für physikalische Chemie* 7 (1930): 407–421 and 422–438.

27. *Zeitschrift für physikalische Chemie* 11 (1930): 291–315.

28. *Fortschritte der Chemie, Physik, und physikalischen Chemie* 21 (1930): 1–68. Arnold Eucken, the editor of the journal, had asked Polanyi to describe the research, but Polanyi gave the task to Schay to "work out in detail the quantitative theory" (Schay to Scott, 1979).

29. A. S. Coolidge, *Journal of the American Chemical Society*, 48 (1926): 179–184; G. S. Lowry and P. S. Olmstead, *Journal of Physical Chemistry*, 31 (1972): 1601–1626. The first footnote of Coolidge's article lists fifteen theories of adsorption from 1910 to 1926, and says that only Polanyi's is promising. However, Coolidge raised an objection to Polanyi's use of the ordinary gaseous equation of state, and he made clear that there was as yet no theory of the form of the ε-φ relationship.

30. H. Zeise, *Zeitschrift für physikalische Chemie* 136A (1928): 385–410, esp. 407; later publication in *Zeitschrift für physikalische Chemie* 138A (1928): 289–299.

31. H. Zeise, *Zeitschrift für Elektrochemie* 35 (1929): 426–431; 1929f.

32. Notebook Easter 1928 (RPC 44:2).

33. Michael to Mausi, April 29, 1928.

34. Tatra Notebook August 1928 (RPC 44:3).

35. Notes, December 17, 1928, p. 1 (RPC 44:2).

36. Interview with Cremer.

37. 1929 diary, RPC 43:1; entries of January 9, 10, 13, 28, February 5, March 2, April 12, 20, and 28. Subject matter not always recorded.

38. 1929f. Leopold Frommer worked many hours with Polanyi on the text of the lecture. The two authored a paper on the effect of chlorine gas on an aluminum

surface, a non-adsorbent type of reaction that produced a blue-green luminescence in the surrounding gas (1930f) and a discussion of how to measure rapid gas reactions (1934h).

39. Interview with Erika Cremer.

40. Interview with Erika Cremer.

41. A. von Buzágh, *Colloid Systems: A Survey of the Phenomena of Modern Colloid Physics and Chemistry*, translated by Otto B. Darbishire, edited by William Clayton, foreword by Wolfgang Ostwald (London: Technical Press, 1937), 202.

42. Alfred Clark, *The Theory of Adsorption Catalysis*, number 18 in *Physical Chemistry: A Series of Monographs*, edited by Ernest M. Loebl (New York: Academic Press, 1970), ix.

43. February 26, 1929 (RPC 43:1).

44. Diary, July 1, 1929 (RPC 43:1).

45. Diary, July 6, 1929 (RPC 43:1).

46. Diary, July 12, 1929 (RPC 43:1).

47. Diary, July 2, 1929 (RPC 43:1).

48. Diary, October 5.

49. Diary, September 27.

50. Diary, September 27, sheet I.

51. October 6, 1929 (RPC 43:1).

52. *Physics Review* 34 (1929): 57–64. Morse developed a mathematically convenient model for a two-atom molecule and derived from it reasonable values for the energy levels and wave-functions of the nuclear motion. Curves of this sort approximated the result of solving the Born–Oppenheimer electron-motion problem.

53. 1930c. Further details were published by Hartel, *Zeitschrift für physikalische Chemie* 7 (1930): 316–320.

54. Interview with Schay.

55. S. Kodama, "Memories of Prof. Michael Polanyi," unpublished typescript, 1987, p. 6.

56. Kodama later trained a pupil named Kenichi Fukui, who won a Nobel Prize for the theory of reaction rates among organic substances. Fukui described himself as a "grandpupil" of Polanyi.

57. Kodama, 7.

58. Kondrat'ev, 276.

59. Michael to Karl, December 25 to 29, 1929 (RPC 2:5).

60. 1929 diary, January 15 and November 3.

61. October 1929.

62. Polanyi to Schrödinger, undated (RPC 14:9).

63. Diary, January 17, 1930.

64. Interview with Söllner.

65. Toni Stolper to Scott, 1979.

66. Diary, June 19, 1929.

67. Schmid to Scott, 1978.

68. Kodama memoir, 14.

69. The 1929 diary reports others, including visitors from out of town: Lily Brandenburg, Mr. & Mrs. Luttke, Elsa Wolfe, Fellner, Schottky, Grotman, Dr. Hauptman, Heyman, Prof. Kornhauser from Chicago, the actress Katrinka,

Klebelsberg, Kojinski, Margot Riess, Mr. and Mrs. Fuchs, Pringsheim, Rosse, C. Odier, Frau Hess, Herr and Frau Ethiers, Schur, Biberbach, Halban, Lobenstein, Kollwitz, Herr and Frau Polya, Lorand, Medi Nemes, Herr and Frau Goldschmid, Ludwig von Mises, Halban, Holitscher, Dr. Janos Plesch.

70. Among others were: Richard Becker, Frommer, the Rudolf Ladenburgs, Glum, Hartree, Hertz, Oliver Herzog, John von Neumann, Reis, von Gomperz, Ohtsuka, Paneth, Planck, Rosbaud, Schay, Volmer, Herr and Frau Jette.

71. Interview with Bela Szilard.

72. Diary, October 18, 1929.

73. Polanyi to Bonhoeffer, January 1, 1931 (MPG).

74. H. Pelzer and E. P. Wigner, "Velocity coefficient of interchange reactions," *Zeitschrift für physikalische Chemie* 15 (1932): 445–471.

75. RPC 43:1.

76. Fritz London, *Zeitschrift für Physik* 63 (1930): 245–279. More details appeared in *Zeitschrift für physikalische Chemie* 11 (1930): 222–251.

77. S. C. Wang, *Physikalische Zeitschrift* 26 (1927): 633–666.

78. From the two-molecule formula c/r^6 one can readily derive by calculus the attraction-to-a-surface formula $\varepsilon = N\ c/6d^3$ where d is the perpendicular distance from surface to molecule.

79. *Zeitschrift für angewandte Mathematik und Mechanik* 8 (1928): 85–106.

80. *Annalen der Physik* 2 (1929): 749.

81. Otto Friedrich, *Before the Deluge: A Portrait of Berlin in the 1920's* (New York: Harper and Row, 1972), 242–243.

82. Cecile to Irma Pollacsek, undated (NZL).

83. M. Storm Jameson, *Journey from the North* (New York: Harper and Row, 1969), 267.

84. Interview with Cremer.

85. Polanyi to Bonhoeffer, February 11, 1933 (MPG).

86. Interview with Cremer.

87. William Byers-Brown to Scott, November 1978.

88. Interview with Heller.

89. W. Heller, *Transactions of the Faraday Society* 33 (1937): 1516–1570.

90. Cecile to Mausi, undated (NZL).

91. Cecile to Misi (RPC 3:19).

92. Cecile to Mausi, undated (NZL).

93. Michael to Mausi, October 5 and 7, 1930 (EZC).

6. PHYSICAL CHEMISTRY AND ECONOMICS

1. Polanyi to Semenov, December 17, 1931 (RPC 2:7).

2. Willstätter to Lapworth, February 22, 1932, University of Manchester files.

3. Wigner to Polanyi, October 18, 1932 (RPC 2:9).

4. Haber to Planck, August 5, 1931 (MPG).

5. Interview with Magda Polanyi. Hugh O'Neill wrote Bill Scott that "Polanyi regretted that more of his colleagues did not resign with him in protest of Hitler becoming chancellor in January, 1933" (August 12, 1981).

6. Stolper, 300.

7. Moberly to Polanyi, November 25, 1932, Manchester University files.

8. Robinson to Moberly, November 8, 1932, Manchester University files.

9. Lapworth to Polanyi, 1932 (RPC 2:10).

10. Interview with Burkhardt.

11. Note by Sir Ernest Simon, December 7, 1932, Manchester University files.

12. Cremer to Scott, March 14, 1979 and interview.

13. Polanyi to Bonhoeffer, February 7, 1933 (MPG).

14. The same discovery was made independently and earlier by C. D. Anderson at California Institute of Technology, *Science* 78 (1932): 238.

15. Quoted by John Toland, *Adolf Hitler* (New York: Doubleday, 1976), 309.

16. Interview with Magda Polanyi.

17. Interview with Magda Polanyi.

18. The fact that the extra chair would be created only for Polanyi helped overcome the objection that Polanyi would be taking a job away from an English scientist (letter of the Earl of Crawford and Balcarres to the Vice-Chancellor, May 6, 1933, Manchester University files).

19. "Proclamation," RPC 2:11.

20. Polanyi to Haber, April 22, 1933 (RPC 2:11).

21. Polanyi to Stolper, April 25, 1933 (RPC 2:11).

22. Notice of May 3, 1933.

23. Marcovich to Jones, May 3, 1933 (RFA).

24. Polanyi to Herzog, May 6, 1933 (RPC 2:12).

25. Polanyi to Toni Stolper, April 25, 1933 (RPC 2:11).

26. Interview with Erika Cremer.

27. April 24, 25, 30; May 10, 17; June 15, 21; July 8 (RPC 2:11–12).

28. Interview with Karl Söllner.

29. Interview with Erika Cremer.

30. Schmalz to Polanyi, September 4, 1933 (RPC 2:13).

31. O'Neill to Scott, March 17, 1981 (HON).

32. Polanyi to Toni Stolper, September 17, 1933 (RPC 2:13).

33. Polanyi to George, September 29, 1933 (RPC 2:13).

34. Magda to George, September 29, 1933 (RPC 2:13).

35. Magda to George, September 25, 1933 (RPC 2:13).

36. Magda to George, October 6, 1933 (RPC 2:13).

37. Interview with Gilson and Todd.

38. Interview with Magda Polanyi.

39. Interview with Mrs. Martins.

40. Interview with Magda Polanyi.

41. Interview with Bawn.

42. Magda to George, November 12, 1933 (RPC 2:13).

43. Michael to George, November 22, 1933 (RPC 2:13).

44. Magda to George, November 22, 1933 (RPC 2:13).

45. RPC 2:13.

46. Melvin Calvin, "Memories of Michael Polanyi in Manchester," *Tradition and Discovery* 18 (1991–1992): 41.

47. 1933l and 1933m. 1934c was a reply to a criticism by J. A. V. Butler suggesting that a possible but unnoticed change in the catalyst might have occurred. Several repetitions of the experiment refuted the criticism.

48. All to be found in the *Transactions of the Faraday Society*, volumes 31 to 40 for the years 1935 to 1944; Meredith Evans contributed to three of these after his return from Princeton. Two excellent reviews that summarize all of this work are C. E. H. Bawn, "The Atomic Reactions of the Alkali Metals," *Chemical Society Annual Reports* 39 (1942): 36–49 and E. Warhurst, "The Sodium Flame Reactions," *Chemical Society Quarterly Review* 5 (1951): 44–59.

49. Interview with Bawn.

50. Gowenlock to Scott, July 13, 1981. Warhurst tells essentially the same story, but he casts Gowenlock in the role of the roving scientist rather than Perkins.

51. Interview with Bawn.

52. Interview with Fairbrother.

53. Interview with Bawn.

54. Herzog to Polanyi, December 20, 1933 (RPC 2:13).

55. Interview with Magda Polanyi.

56. May 27, 1934 (RPC 2:16).

57. Polanyi to O'Neill, June 21, 1934 (HON).

58. Hugh O'Neill as reported to Brian Gowenlock and forwarded to Scott, 1981.

59. Polanyi to O'Neill, July 5, 1934 (HON).

60. Correspondence from Karl to Michael (RPC 17:4–5).

61. Karl to Michael, September 18, 1934 (RPC 17:5).

62. Polanyi to O'Neill, October 28, 1935 (HON).

63. Cecile to Magda (RPC 18:1).

64. 1939d, 176–177, and 1964 Preface to SFS, 8.

65. John B. Polya to Scott, February 12, 1979.

66. Interview with Calvin.

67. Melvin Calvin, *Transactions of the Faraday Society* 32 (1936): 1428–1436, dated September 1936.

68. Whytlaw-Gray, Patterson, and Cawood, *Proceedings of the Royal Society* 134 (1932): 7–19.

69. 1936e, with Calvin and Eley, and 1936i, with Calvin and Cockbain.

70. Scott Interview with Eley.

71. Daniel D. Eley, *Transactions of the Faraday Society* 36 (1940): 500–505.

72. Melvin Calvin, *Transactions of the Faraday Society* 34 (1938): 1181–1191.

73. 1939b and 1939c; J. H. Baxendale and E. Warhurst, *Transactions of the Faraday Society* 36 (1940): 1181–1188. See also D. D. Eley, *Advances in Catalysis*, Volume 1, 184–187.

74. Daniel D. Eley, "Mechanisms of Hydrogen Catalysis," *Quarterly Reviews (Chemical Society)* 3 (1949): 209–225; "The Catalytic Activation of Hydrogen," *Advances in Catalysis* 1 (1948): 157–199; *Catalysis and the Chemical Bond* (Notre Dame: University of Notre Dame Press, 1954).

75. In 1962, while witnessing an experiment at the University of California at Berkeley on the $K + Br_2$ reaction, Polanyi used this picturesque and now common term, which he had used on some other unrecorded occasions, for the process

whereby an attacking alkali atom tosses out its valence electron, hooks a halogen, and hauls it in with the Coulomb force. He recalled his earlier speculation, still clear in his mind, that the reaction might proceed via an electron-stripping mechanism, where one of the bromine atoms is harpooned by the potassium and the combination K + Br- acquires a high internal excitation. Quoted by D. R. Herschbach, "Reactive Scattering in Molecular Beams," in *Advances in Chemical Physics*, Volume X, ed. John Ross (New York: John Wiley, 1966), 367. D. R. Herschbach, "Molecular Beam Studies of Internal Excitation and Reaction Products," *Applied Optics*, Supplement 2: Chemical Lasers (1965): 141 fn.

76. Professor of Social Economics 1936–1946 and of Political Economy 1946–1948.

77. Polanyi to Stolper, September 17, 1933 (RPC 2:13).

78. Hodgkin and Wigner, "Michael Polanyi," 423.

79. Interview with Jewkes.

80. Interview with A. Saboz-Bachofen.

81. Pocket notebook, Polanyi family papers, pp. 4–6.

82. Pocket notebook, Polanyi family papers, pp. 25–26.

83. Jászi to Polanyi, November 24, 1935 (RPC 3:5).

84. *The Good Society* (Boston: Little, Brown and Co., 1937).

85. Simon to Polanyi, November 6, 1935 (RPC 3:5).

86. Stolper to Polanyi, December 6, 1935 (RPC 3:5).

87. Polanyi to O'Neill, June 15, 1935 (HON).

88. See unpublished material, also called on one typescript "Attitude Toward Jews and Non-Jews" (RPC 25:8). Similar material was presented September 24, 1942 to the Manchester Branch of the Trades Advisory Council of the Board of Deputies of British Jews, under the title "Jewish Problems" and published in 1943 (1943c).

89. "Attitude Toward Jews and Non-Jews," RPC 25:8, p. 13.

90. Interview with Eva Zeisel; also Suzannah Lessard, "The Present Moment," *The New Yorker* (April 13, 1987): 36–59.

91. Koestler used elements of the story of Eva's arrest, imprisonment, and trial in his novel, *Darkness at Noon*.

92. The story of Alex Weissberg-Cybulski is told in his autobiography, *The Conspiracy of Silence* (London: Hamish Hamilton, 1952), translated by Edward Fitzgerald; published in New York under the title *The Accused* (New York: Simon and Schuster, 1951). In 1940 Alex was transferred from his Russian prison to a German concentration camp in 1940 and finally showed up in Sweden in 1946.

93. "Notes on a Film" (HON).

94. Interview with Heller.

95. Interview with Bawn.

96. Eley and Calvin interviews.

97. Polanyi to Stolper, November 4, 1935 (RPC 3:5).

98. June 1936 (RPC 25:9).

99. "Suggestion for a new research section" (RPC 25:8).

100. Stolper to Polanyi, September 1, 1935 (RPC 3:7).

101. Polanyi to Stolper, November 21, 1936 (RPC 3:7).

102. Polanyi to Stolper, September 3, 1937 (RPC 3:9).

103. "Memories of Michael Polanyi in Manchester," *Tradition and Discovery* 18 (1991–1992): 40.

104. February 22, 1937 (RPC 25:9).

105. "Historical Society Lecture" (RPC 25:12).

106. RPC 25:11. There was also a title in pencil, "Workings of Money: Booms and Slumps," at the top of the first page of introduction.

107. The society published Polanyi's lecture on that occasion together with the film commentary (1938c).

108. Memorandum on Economic Films, p. 2 (RFA).

109. Clay to Kittredge, June 2, 1938 (RFA).

110. Alwyn G. Evans, *The Reactions of Organic Halides in Solution* (Manchester: Manchester University Press, 1946), reprinted from *Memoirs and Proceedings of the Manchester Literary and Philosophical Society*, vol. 87, session 1945–1946. *Transactions of the Faraday Society* 42 (1946): 719–749 provides an abbreviated version.

111. Interview with Baughan.

7. THE PHILOSOPHY OF FREEDOM

1. Interview with Todd.

2. The library is still there but the lamp post has been replaced by a more modern one.

3. Interview with Magda Polanyi.

4. "Polanyi and the Planning of Science," Gowenlock typescript, August 18, 1981, p. 5.

5. Kittredge memorandum, May 4, 1939 (RFA).

6. Magda to Mausi, March 13, 1939, undated, and April 5, 1939 (EZC).

7. Polanyi to Wedgwood, August 5, 1947, Wedgwood papers.

8. "Memorandum on Economic Films," Polanyi to Kittredge, December 12, 1938 (RFA).

9. Polanyi to Stolper, June 17, 1939 (RPC 3:15). A later additional grant of £170 for completion and duplication was awarded in October 1940, with a remark by one of the officials that they had thought the original request was a bit too low even for one film.

10. Gary Werskey, *The Visible College: The Collective Biography of British Scientific Socialists of the 1930's* (New York: Holt, Reinhart and Winston, 1978).

11. London: Routledge, 1939.

12. Polanyi to O'Neill, October 4, 1939 (HON).

13. Interview with Magda Polanyi.

14. Imre Horner, a Hungarian physician who had met four Polanyis on four separate occasions, said in an interview that he attended Cecile on her last hospitalization. She asked for three books of current interest which he brought her to read. Two days later she returned them to him and commented on each. Laura Fermi says it was "3 or 4 books a day" (*Illustrious Immigrants* [Chicago: Chicago University Press, 1968], 113).

15. The cemetery record in Budapest records September 5. Karl Polanyi and Barbara Striker reported that September 5 was the day of Cecile's death and also the day of Mausi's departure from Southampton to New York, but Michael's telegram to Mausi after her arrival (September 15) says, "Mother died quietly in her sleep, 4 Sept., sad greeting, all our love."

16. Karl to Michael, September 8, 1939 (RPC 17:8).

17. Polanyi to O'Neill, October 4, 1939 (HON).

18. As mentioned in interviews with Andrew Saboz, Melvin Calvin, Daniel Eley, Cecil Bawn, and Ernest Warhurst.

19. "On Tolerance," December 7, 1939 (RPC 26:1).

20. "On Tolerance," p. 1.

21. "On Tolerance," p. 2.

22. RPC 26:2, dated at intervals over the period from December 30, 1939 to February 7, 1940. He outlined eight chapters on December 30, 1939, followed by about 90 pages of coherent but unedited typescript along with several short notes. After chapter 5, the outline was abandoned. The remainder of the manuscript consists of disjointed reflections on economics.

23. Notes to chapter 2, p. 5.

24. RPC 42:2.

25. "Chapters," "1929–1939," p. 9.

26. "Chapters," "1929–1939," p. 15.

27. "Chapters," "List of further points," February 18, 1940, p. 1.

28. RPC 26:4.

29. 26 pages (RPC 26:4).

30. "The Organization of Scientific Life," p. 4.

31. "The Organization of Scientific Life," p. 10.

32. "Economics by Motion Symbols," 1940f. This article and transcript of the recorded commentary were used to make up a *Handbook to the Film, 'Unemployment and Money'* (1940h). The film itself can be viewed at the Museum of Modern Art in New York City or at the National Film Archive, London. A videotape may be viewed in Special Collections at the Joseph Regenstein Library at the University of Chicago.

33. 1940h, 12.

34. "Free Trade through Full Employment," a pamphlet written in May 1942 to accompany the film, published by the Manchester Liberal Club (1946n), 2.

35. Michael to Karl, April 2, 1940 (RPC 17:9).

36. Polanyi to Mausi, April 9, 1940 (EZC).

37. Interview with Magda Polanyi.

38. For an account of the development of the Workers Education Association, see Drusilla Scott's biography of her father, *A. D. Lindsay* (Oxford: Basil Blackwell, 1971).

39. Both undated (EZC).

40. June 21, 1943, Polanyi to Mausi (EZC).

41. Mausi to Ervin Dentay [né Ervin von Gomperz], May 22, 1942.

42. Polanyi to Mausi, April 9, 1940 (EZC).

43. Michael to Mausi, July 7, 1946 (EZC).

44. Polanyi to O'Neill, June 3 and June 26, 1940 (HON).

45. Mrs. Christina Czechowsa to Hugh O'Neill, September 1, 1981; comments added by Hugh O'Neill.

46. Polanyi to Jászi, August 21, 1940, Columbia papers.

47. Michael to Mausi, August 26, 1940 (EZC).

48. Polanyi to Jászi, October 14, 1940 (RPC 4:5).

49. Notes for the second half (RPC 26:4).

50. "Planning, Culture and Freedom," p. 5.

51. "Planning, Efficiency and Liberty," p. 11 (RPC 26:4).

52. RPC 26:1; became 1944a, "Science, Its Reality and Freedom."

53. "The Social Message of Science," p. 13.

54. "Science in Modern Life," Nature 147 (May 10, 1941): 551–553. "Science and Society," Nature 147 (May 24, 1941): 637–638. RPC 26:9.

55. 1940e, which was reviewed favorably in the same journal, January 25, 1941.

56. "Science and Society," May 1941. Nachlass Born, Staatsbibliothek.

57. "Science and Society," p. 1.

58. "Science and Society," p. 2.

59. "The Society for Freedom in Science: Its Origin, Objects, and Constitution," 3rd edition, July 1953, 9.

60. According to Baker, "Bernalism is the doctrine of those who profess that the only proper objects of scientific research are to feed people and protect them from the elements, that research workers should be organized in gangs and told what to discover, and that the pursuit of knowledge for its own sake has the same value as the solution of crossword puzzles." The New Statesman 18 (July 29, 1939): 174.

61. Polanyi to Baker, November 4, 1940, Baker file.

62. Polanyi to Baker, June 4, 1962, Baker file.

63. Polanyi to Karl, June 10, 1941 (KLP).

64. "The Objects of the Society for Freedom in Science" (Oxford, 1944), 5 (quoted by Werskey, p. 282, fn. 65).

65. Henry Dale to C. Darlington, September 28, 1948; quoted by Werskey, 281.

66. Werskey, 281.

67. Interview with John Jewkes.

68. Polanyi to Mausi, August 5, 1941 (EZC).

69. Interview with Magda Polanyi.

70. Polanyi to Mausi, August 5, 1941 (EZC).

71. August 12–30, 1941 (RPC 26:9).

72. Storm Jameson to Scott, September 4, 1981.

73. EZC.

74. Polanyi to Mausi, November 19, 1944 (EZC).

75. Jameson to Scott, September 4, 1981.

76. Interview with Warhurst.

77. Notebook B, December 29, 1941 (RPC 27:2, 27 typed pages).

78. Michael to Mausi, January 17, 1942.

79. Notebook B, p. 21.

80. Notebook B, p. 16.

81. Notebook B, p. 9.

82. "Science, Welfare, and the State" (RPC 27:4).

83. This version of "City of Science" was presented to the Manchester Theological Society; Notes, September 16, 1942; outlines, September 25 and 29, 1942 (RPC 27:6).

84. Polanyi to Mausi, January 17, 1942 (EZC).

85. Polanyi to Ilona, July 30, 1941 (KLP).

86. Michael to Mausi, August 5, 1941 (EZC).

87. Polanyi to Jászi, July 29, 1941, Columbia papers.

88. Polanyi to Mausi, December 29, 1941 (EZC).

89. Ilona to Polanyi, January 27, 1942 (EZC).

90. Polanyi to Mausi, May 28, 1942 (EZC).

91. Polanyi to Mausi, February 4, 1943 (EZC).

92. Notebook #2 (RPC 27:2).

93. Notebook 2, p. 17.

94. Polanyi to Karl, October 24, 1943 (KLP).

95. Mary Roberts Fischer to Scott, transcribed by her son, January 20, 1979.

96. RPC 28:1, dated November 20, 1943, to April 15, 1944.

97. Polanyi to Mausi, November 29, 1943 (EZC).

98. Polanyi to Mausi, June 20, 1943 (EZC).

99. Polanyi to Mausi, November 29, 1943 (EZC).

100. Polanyi to Toni, October 3, 1943 (RPC 4:10).

101. RPC 28:9–12.

102. Interview with Skinner.

103. Karl to Michael, July 8, 1943 (RPC 17:10).

104. Michael to Karl, March 30, 1944 (KLP).

105. Polanyi to Mausi, May 8, 1944 (EZC).

106. Karl to Polanyi, June 12, 1944 (KLP).

107. Polanyi to Mausi, May 8, 1944 (EZC).

108. Polanyi to Mausi, February 14, 1944 (EZC).

109. Polanyi to O'Neill, April 3, 1944 (HON).

110. The members who nominated him were Eric K. Rideal, J. W. Cook, A. R. Todd, H. W. Melville, P. M. S. Blackett, C. K. Ingold, John S. B. Stopford, and H. S. Raper (from the *Candidates Book*, 1944).

111. Jászi to Polanyi, February 7 and March 23, 1941, Butler Library.

112. Polanyi wrote an essay "Three Periods of History" (RPC 29:8) for the introduction but did not get to use it for this purpose; Mannheim died in January 1947 before the arrangements for the publication were all made. The collection of essays including "Autonomy of Science" finally was published in 1951 under the title *The Logic of Liberty*.

113. Polanyi to Mannheim, April 19, 1944 (RPC 4:11).

114. Ibid., 2.

115. Mannheim to Polanyi, April 26, 1944 (RPC 4:11).

116. Polanyi to Mannheim, May 2, 1944 (RPC 4:11).

117. Polanyi to O'Neill, July 3, 1956 (HON).

118. Polanyi to Mausi, July 9, 1944; he said the book was 5/6 done. Other titles Polanyi used were: August 19, "Economics of Full Employment" (he wrote to Karl

of having finished a draft); September 15, "A Policy of Economic Expansion"; November 19, "The Principles of Economic Expansion."

119. Polanyi to Mausi, November 19, 1944 (EZC).

120. Karl to Michael, November 1, 1945 (RPC 4:13).

121. Phil Mullins has traced the eleven or twelve meetings of the Moot that Polanyi seems to have attended between 1944 and 1960 and analyzed more than one hundred letters they exchanged. Cf. "Michael Polanyi and J. H. Oldham: In Praise of Friendship," *Appraisal* 1 (1997): 179–189.

122. Kathleen Bliss, "Joseph Houldsworth Oldham," *Dictionary of National Biography*, (1901–1970): 806–808.

123. Interview with Bliss.

124. Oldham to Polanyi, May 2, 1944 (RPC 15:3). Among the "few others" were two women, Kathleen Bliss and Oldham's wife Mary; the latter attended regularly but never spoke in the discussions.

125. Oldham to Polanyi, May 2, 1944 (RPC 15:3).

126. Polanyi to Eliot, June 27, 1944 (RPC 4:11).

127. Part of "Principles of Economic Expansion," September 18, 1949 (RPC 24:8).

128. Bliss, "Joseph Houldsworth Oldham," 808.

129. *Radio Times*, January 5, 1945.

130. Polanyi to O'Neill, May 7, 1945 (HON).

131. Polanyi to Mausi, October 13, 1945 (EZC).

132. Polanyi to Mausi, undated (EZC).

133. Gowenlock to Scott, August 18, 1981.

134. Toni Stolper to Polanyi, May 20, 1946 (RPC 5:1).

135. Toni Stolper to Polanyi, December 6, 1946 (RPC 5:2).

136. Polanyi to Mausi, October 13, 1945 (EZC).

137. Koestler wrote to Scott: "I know little of Michael's youthful years—I met him for the first time in 1929 or 1930 in Paris" (November 10, 1977).

138. Polanyi to Koestler, October 20, 1945, Edinburgh University Library.

139. Polanyi to Mausi, July 7, 1946 (EZC).

140. Polanyi to Mausi, July 7, 1946 (EZC).

141. Polanyi to Mausi, November, 25, 1946 (EZC).

142. Polanyi to Mausi, June 22, 1947 (EZC).

143. Polanyi to Weaver, May 22, 1946 (RFA).

144. Polanyi to Koestler, August 28, 1946, Edinburgh University Library.

145. Mausi to Michael, April 23, 1946 (EZC).

146. *The Bicentennial Year*, 192.

147. Polanyi to Mausi, October 23, 1946 (EZC).

148. Polanyi to Mausi, March 15, 1947 (EZC).

149. Interview with Veronica Wedgwood.

150. A version edited by J. K. Woods was published in the school's new magazine, *Credere Aude*, in its first issue, December 1947 (1947l).

151. Polanyi to Wedgwood, May 6, 1947, Wedgwood letters.

152. Hodgkin and Wigner, "Michael Polanyi," 425.

153. Interview with Jewkes.

154. Gowenlock to Scott, August 18, 1981.

155. RPC 43:1, 1930 diary, continued in 1948.

156. Polanyi to Mausi, December 12, 1947 (EZC).

157. Polanyi to Mausi, January 4, 1948 (EZC).

158. Polanyi to Wedgwood, June 27, 1947, Wedgwood letters.

159. Polanyi to Karl, June 28, 1947 (KLP).

160. Polanyi to Mausi, August 2, 1947 (EZC).

161. Notebook, p. 3 (RPC 29:5).

162. Polanyi to Koestler, August 14, 1947 (RPC 5:4).

163. Polanyi to Karl Bonhoeffer, August 23, 1947 (MPG).

164. Polanyi to Wedgwood, August 5, 1947, Wedgwood letters. Wedgwood was later made a Dame of the British Empire for this book.

165. Notebook #2, p. 20.

166. Polanyi to Koestler, October 9, 1947, Edinburgh University Library letters.

167. Polanyi to Wedgwood, November 19, 1947, Wedgwood letters.

168. Polanyi to Wedgwood, January 14, 1948, Wedgwood letters.

169. Polanyi to Mausi, January 4, 1948 (EZC).

170. Polanyi to Mausi, March 16, 1948 (EZC).

171. Polanyi to Toni, December 26, 1948 (RPC 5:5).

172. January 13; Polanyi made the entry in an old diary—the previous entry is dated eighteen years previously (RPC 43:1).

173. Gowenlock to Scott, August 18, 1981.

174. Stephen Brunauer, *The Adsorption of Gases and Vapors. Volume I, Physical Adsorption* (Princeton: Princeton University Press, 1945). See especially Chapter V, 96–120.

175. *Journal of Chemical Education* 37 (1962): 167–178.

176. *Advances in Catalysis*, 26 (1977), Foreword.

177. Scott attempted in vain to determine why Polanyi did not join in the research on the atomic bomb. It is not clear whether he was not invited or whether he turned down an invitation. Sir Rudolf Peierls wrote Scott, "I am afraid I know nothing about an attempt to get Polanyi to join the atomic energy project, either in the early days of the MAUD Committee, or later under Tube Alloys [the code name for the bomb project]. . . . That Polanyi should not believe in the possibility of making a bomb is very plausible. That he should see this as a way of keeping the refugees out of the way is also very reasonable, because looked at from the outside it was remarkable that there were such strict rules against accepting refugees in all other kinds of war work, like radar, and here there were almost only refugees" (July 18, 1982).

178. Raymond Aron, *Memoirs: Fifty Years of Political Reflection*, trans. George Holoch (New York: Holmes and Meier, 1990), 176. Aron knew Polanyi from the Congress for Cultural Freedom and quotes Berlin's ironic remark only to contest its merit.

179. "Our work even today in the area of artificial photosynthesis . . . all stems from my interest in coordination chemistry which began at the University of Manchester with Polanyi. How many years ago that? Over fifty! I am still working with the same kind of stuff at a much more rarified level" (Melvin Calvin, "Memories of Michael Polanyi in Manchester," *Tradition and Discovery* 18 [1991–1992]: 42).

8. *PERSONAL KNOWLEDGE*

1. Polanyi to Karl, March 21, 1948 (KLP).
2. Polanyi to Karl, March 21, 1948 (KLP).
3. Polanyi to Karl, undated (KLP).
4. Postcard to Olive Davies, August 23, 1948, Davies letters.
5. 1948f. An expanded version of this talk was included in *The Logic of Liberty.*
6. Interview with Dennis J. Coppock, one of Polanyi's students, later a Professor of Economics at Manchester.
7. Oldham to Polanyi, May 13, 1948 (RPC 15:4).
8. Polanyi to Oldham, May 31, 1948 (RPC 15:4).
9. Phil Mullins, "Michael Polanyi and J. H. Oldham: In Praise of Friendship," *Appraisal* 1 (1997): 179–189.
10. Interview with Langford, November, 1978.
11. Niebuhr seems to have attended the Moot in person. In a report to the Rockefeller Foundation on the use of a grant, March 14, 1955, Polanyi says he brought Tillich to Manchester for a discussion of theology, but something must have interfered with that plan. According to Richard Gelwick, their first meeting in person took place in 1963. Cf. "The Polanyi–Tillich Dialogue of 1963: Polanyi's Search for a Post-Critical Logic in Science and in Theology," *Tradition and Discovery* 12 (1995–1996): 5–10.
12. Interview with Bliss.
13. Interview with Poteat.
14. Polanyi to Karl, March 29, 1949 (KLP).
15. Polanyi to Hollo, April 1, 1949 (KLP).
16. Polanyi to T. M. Taylor, September 22, 1949, Wetherick letters.
17. Polanyi to T. M. Taylor, October 4, 1949, Wetherick letters.
18. Unpublished material (RPC 32:6).
19. Polanyi to Mausi, April 11, 1950 (EZC).
20. Polanyi to Davies, January 7, 1950, Davies letters.
21. Polanyi to Wedgwood, February 23, 1950, Wedgwood letters.
22. March 24, 1950, New York Times.
23. Polanyi to Mausi, April 4, 1950 (EZC).
24. Unpublished material, from an after-dinner address to the Chaos Club (RPC 32:15), p. 3.
25. Grene to Scott, January 27, 1991.
26. Polanyi to Karl, January 3, 1950 (KLP): and Polanyi to Jászi, May 25, 1950, Butler Library.
27. Interview with Shils; Polanyi to Jászi, November 9, 1950, Butler letters.
28. Polanyi to Mausi, May 12, 1951 (EZC).
29. The Gifford Lectures, p. 185.
30. Gifford Lectures, 1, 1, p. 1.
31. Gifford Lectures 1, 7, p. 14.
32. Gifford Lectures 1, 8, p. 16.
33. Gifford Lectures 1, 9, p. 8.
34. Polanyi to Davies, August 22, 1951, Davies letters.
35. March 3, 1952.

36. Clay to Willits, January 15, 1952 (RFA).

37. Polanyi's report on expenditures of Rockefeller grant, January 22, 1953 (RFA). He also lectured on this topic to the Christian Frontier group (1953c).

38. Polanyi to Stopford, November 30, 1951 (RFA).

39. Polanyi to Karl and Ilona, January 14, 1952 (KLP).

40. Polanyi to Karl and Ilona, January 14, 1952 (KLP).

41. Although the third lecture was called "Personal Knowledge," Polanyi did not cover the wide range of topics that he later brought under this rubric.

42. Gifford Lectures 1, 7, p. 15.

43. Marjorie Grene, "Tacit Knowing: Grounds for a Revolution in Philosophy," *Journal of the British Society for Phenomenology*, 8 (1977): 164–171.

44. Gifford Lectures 2, 8, p. 2.

45. Two friends of Polanyi, Rebecca West and Valerie Fellner, interviewed by Scott, suggested that the "other data" were facts about Karl's wife Ilona who, in 1947, was banned permanently from the United States for having been a member of the Communist Party—even though she had already been expelled from it in 1922.

46. Polanyi to Wedgwood, October 29, 1953, Wedgwood letters.

47. RPC 33:8.

48. Polanyi to Mausi, March 8, 1954 (EZC).

49. Polanyi to Karl, March 4, 1954 (KLP).

50. Polanyi to Mausi, March 8, 1954 (EZC).

51. Polanyi to Toni Stolper, undated (RPC).

52. Polanyi to Bonhoeffer, September 15, 1954 (MPG).

53. Interview with Elizabeth Sewell.

54. Polanyi to Karl, October 18, 1954 (KLP).

55. Interview with Poteat, 1978.

56. June 29, 1955 (KLP).

57. Michael to Karl, November 13, 1955 (KLP).

58. Polanyi to Karl, August 27, 1955 (KLP).

59. Unpublished; microfilm from RGL.

60. Interview with Sewell.

61. At the beginning of 1957, after an extension of Sewell's Simon fellowship for another half year, she left Manchester to deliver the Christian Gauss lectures at Princeton University. Sewell continued to feel inspired and supported by Polanyi: "how broadly and intimately your thought inspires and befriends mine" (Sewell to Polanyi, September 13, 1963; RPC 6:3).

62. Polanyi to Mausi, August 27, 1956 (EZC).

63. "Committee on Science and Freedom, Application for a Grant," July 5, 1958, p. 5 (RFA).

64. Interview with Elizabeth Sewell.

65. Polanyi to O'Neill, November 6, 1956 (HON).

66. Polanyi to Mausi, March 20, 1957 (EZC).

67. Polanyi to Olive, April 10, 1957, Davies letters.

68. Polanyi to Karl, May 5, 1957 (KLP).

69. Oldham to Polanyi, May 11, 1957 (RPC 15:5).

70. Polanyi to Karl, August 13, 1957 (KLP).

71. *Philosophy of Science*, 20 (1959) 270–272.
72. 10 (1960): 377–378.
73. G. L. S. Shackle, *British Journal for the Philosophy of Science* 9 (1959): 285.
74. Alan R. White, op. cit.
75. *Hibbard Journal* 57 (1958–59): 311.
76. Polanyi to Wedgwood, August 29, 1958, Wedgwood letters.
77. Polanyi to Karl, February 5, 1958 (KLP).
78. "Here Polanyi was using understanding as a synonym for tacit knowing—a point some people misunderstand or confuse with the German sense of *verstehen* and *wissen*" (Gelwick to Moleski, January 31, 2000).
79. Polanyi to Wedgwood, April 2, 1958, Wedgwood letters.
80. Polanyi to Wedgwood, April 18, 1958, Wedgwood letters.
81. July 5, 1958, application for a grant (RFA).
82. Polanyi to Wedgwood, May 8, 1958, Wedgwood copy.
83. Interview with Ruel Tyson.
84. Polanyi to Karl, May 16, 1958 (KLP).
85. Polanyi to Wedgwood, August 29, 1958, Wedgwood letters.
86. Polanyi to O'Neill, July 3, 1958 (HON).
87. Polanyi to Karl, November 16, 1958 (KLP).
88. Polanyi to Karl, November 16, 1958 (KLP).
89. Interview with Poteat.
90. Polanyi to Karl, March 21, 1959 (KLP).
91. Polanyi to Wedgwood, April 18, 1958, Wedgwood letters.
92. Polanyi's diary entry, June 8, 1959.

9. MERTON COLLEGE, OXFORD

1. Robin Hodgkin attributed this story to R. H. C. Davis in a letter to Scott.
2. Polanyi to Karl, July 9, 1959 (KLP).
3. Polanyi to Karl, October 7, 1959 (KLP).
4. Hodgkin and Wigner, "Michael Polanyi," 435.
5. Drusilla Scott, "The Polanyis in Oxford. Memories of 1961–1976," unpublished, pp. 3–4.
6. Polanyi to Karl, December 27, 1959 (KLP).
7. Polanyi to O'Neill, January 10, 1960 (HON).
8. The archives have an outline of Lecture 2 called "Originality," which mentions Lecture 1 as being on tacit knowledge (RPC 34:1). There are no references to other lectures.
9. RPC 34:1–5.
10. Polanyi to Karl, July 9, 1959 (KLP).
11. *History and Hope: Progress in Freedom. The Berlin Conference of 1960*, edited by K. A. Jelenski (New York: A. Praeger, 1962).
12. Polanyi to Olive Davies, January 11, 1961, Davies letters.
13. Unpublished material, syllabus supplied by Vickers.
14. London: Routledge & Keegan Paul, 1961. Marjorie Grene was the collector and editor of the volume. John Polanyi contributed an "Index to Michael Polanyi's Contributions to Science."

15. Polanyi to O'Neill, March 10, 1961 (HON).

16. Kuhn to Poteat, February 28, 1967; a copy of this unpublished letter was obtained from Magda Polanyi.

17. Interview with Silvia Kind.

10. AT THE WHEEL OF THE WORLD

1. RGL microfilm.

2. Only this first lecture was published by the *Virginia Quarterly Review* (1962a).

3. Interview with Toulmin.

4. During the summer these lectures were broadcast over KPFA, a Bay Area FM station (Gelwick to Polanyi, July 16, 1962 (RGL)).

5. Polanyi to Kind, July 7, 1962 (SKL).

6. Polanyi to Koestler, November 9, 1962, Edinburgh University Library.

7. Notes, December 1962 (RPC 34:17).

8. Polanyi to Gelwick, July 20, 1963 (RGL).

9. Gelwick, "Perspectives: Polanyi, an Occasion of Thanks," *Cross Currents* 41 (1991): 381.

10. Gelwick compiled these papers (published on microfilm in 1963) with the support of a grant from the Pacific School of Religion Library. Since Polanyi had not kept a record of these publications, Gelwick had to pursue clues about where Polanyi had lectured and in which journals he had published.

11. Gelwick, "Perspectives," 381.

12. Paul Tillich, *Systematic Theology*, Volume 1 (Chicago: University of Chicago Press, 1951), 262.

13. Interview with Charles McCoy.

14. For a transcript of and commentary on these notes, see "The Polanyi–Tillich Dialogue of 1963" by Richard Gelwick, *Tradition and Discovery* 22 (1995–1996): 11–19.

15. Tillich to Polanyi, May 21, 1963 (RPC 6:3), and 1963a, 14.

16. Polanyi to Karl, September 16, 1963 (KLP).

17. Polanyi to Kind, June 25, 1963 (SKL).

18. Polanyi to Gelwick, November 14, 1963 (RGL).

19. Polanyi to Tom Polanyi, November 4, 1963, Tom Polanyi letter.

20. Polanyi to Karl, October 17, 1963 (KLP).

21. Polanyi to O'Neill, March 20, 1964 (HON).

22. This lecture, written in Oxford during November and December 1963, was revised and published under the title "Science and Reality" (1967c).

23. Magda to Gelwick, April 19, 1964 (RGL).

24. Interview with Ruel Tyson.

25. Interviews with Poteat and Gelwick.

26. Polanyi to Kind, March 13, 1964 (SKL).

27. Interview with Poteat.

28. Polanyi to Kind, May 4, 1964 (SKL).

29. Adams to Scott, May 25, 1991.

30. Adams to Scott, May 25, 1991.

31. Sewell to Polanyi, July 19, 1963 (RPC 6:3). Polanyi's answers are not extant because Sewell destroyed most letters after she had read them.

32. Interview with Sewell.

33. Polanyi to Kind, April 23, 1964 (SKL).

34. Polanyi to Kind, May 25, 1964 (SKL).

35. Polanyi made notes on Husserl earlier during his 1963 summer holiday at Sils Maria (unpublished material; RPC 23:16).

36. Polanyi to Gelwick, November 6, 1964 (RGL).

37. Cantril to Polanyi, July 28, 1964 (RPC 6:6).

38. Polanyi to Gelwick, November 6, 1964 (RGL).

39. Polanyi to Kind, October 11, 1964 (SKL).

40. Interview with Pols.

41. Polanyi to Gelwick, November 4, 1964 (RGL).

42. Polanyi to Kind, March 25, 1965 (SKL).

43. Ibid.

44. Polanyi to Kind, March 13, 1964 (SKL).

45. Polanyi to Koestler, June 22, 1964, Edinburgh University Library microfilm.

46. Polanyi to Koestler, August 9, 1964, Edinburgh University Library microfilm.

47. *The Anatomy of Knowledge: Papers Presented in the Study Group on Foundations of Cultural Unity*, Bowdoin College 1965 and 1966, Marjorie Grene, ed., (Amherst: Univ. Mass. Press, 1969), ix.

48. Polanyi to Kind, March 25, 1965 (SKL).

49. Polanyi to Kind, May 15, 1965 (SKL).

50. Polanyi delivered essentially the same paper with the title "The Body–Mind Relation" at Yale on December 10, 1965 and at a conference in San Diego, March 1966.

51. Polanyi to Kind, July 4, 1965 (SKL).

52. *New York Times* (August 29, 1965): 27.

53. Marjorie Grene, "Toward a Unity of Knowledge," *Psychological Issues*, 6, No. 2, Monograph 22 (1969), 3.

54. Since the beginning of the year Polanyi had been negotiating with Harvard concerning a professorship or guest professorship, which apparently did not work out.

55. The Regenstein Library holds copies of the five Wesleyan Lectures 37:14–16 and 38:1–3.

56. Polanyi to Kind, April 22, 1965 (SKL).

57. Unpublished material, R. E. Wilken interview with Michael Polanyi, April 5–6, 1966, p. 16.

58. Unpublished material, outline of talk delivered January 27, 1967 at 1, Canterbury Road, Oxford. RPC 38:10.

59. Polanyi to Daniel Jenkins, December 15, 1967 (RPC 6:10).

60. Wilken interview, p. 3.

61. PC 28 holds several pages of notes by Polanyi on Niebuhr dated October 1943.

62. RPC 22:6.

63. Paul Tillich, *Systematic Theology*, Volume 1 (Chicago: University of Chicago Press, 1951), 262.

64. RPC 6:8.

65. Polanyi to Kind, April 26, 1966 (SKL).

66. Polanyi to Drusilla Scott, July 23, 1966, Scott papers.

67. Polanyi to Kind, June 25, 1966 (SKL).

68. Polanyi to Kind, June 25, 1966 (SKL).

69. Polanyi to Kind, July 18, 1966 (SKL).

70. Interview with Michael Evans.

71. E.g., Heller on poetry, Eliot on seventeenth-century metaphysical poets, Wolheim's lecture on "Drawing an Object," Owen Barfield's *Saving the Appearances*, Agnes Arber's *The Mind and the Eye* (mentioned in correspondence with Angela Bolton and Marjorie Grene).

72. Polanyi to Bolton, October 16, 1966, Bolton correspondence.

73. Polanyi to Grene, October 3, 1966 (RPC 16:1).

74. Chomsky to Polanyi, November 6, 1966 (RPC 6:8).

75. Polanyi to Kind, November 16, 1966 (SKL).

76. Kind to Scott, November 4, 1980.

77. Polanyi to Kind, June 26, 1967 (SKL).

78. During the coming year, 1968, under the direction of Marjorie Grene, the Study Group had five meetings: in February on "Value Freedom," in April on "The (Ir)reducibility of Biology to Physics and Chemistry," in May on "The Programmability of Piaget," in July/August on "Art and Perception," and in November on "The Logic of Conversation," with Polanyi listed as participant in April and July/August. Marjorie Grene, ed., *Interpretations of Life and Mind* (New York: Humanities Press, 1971), xi–xiv.

79. Polanyi to Aron, May 9, 1967 (RPC 6:10).

80. "Do Life Processes Transcend Physics and Chemistry?" (1968g, includes commentary by the panel: Gerald Holton, chairman; Ernest Nagel, John R. Platt, and Barry Commoner). Published with details added at Berkeley, January 1968, as "Life's Irreducible Structures" (1968d) and in KB, 225–239.

81. 1967c, given first at Duke in 1964.

82. 1968a, an expanded version of the Washington talk to United States psychologists.

83. 1961b, given in Reno in 1961.

84. *Intellect and Hope: Essays in the Thought of Michael Polanyi*, ed. Thomas A. Langford and William H. Poteat (Durham, NC: Duke University Press, 1968).

85. Sewell to Polanyi, January 31, 1965 (RPC 6:7).

86. Polanyi to Kind, October 11, 1969 (SKL).

87. Polanyi to Harold Osborne, April 1, 1968 (RPC 7:14).

88. Polanyi to Kind, June 13, 1968 (SKL).

89. Charles Rycroft, *Imagination and Reality*; Gilbert Durand, *Symbolisme et Imagination*; I. A. Richards, *The Philosophy of Rhetoric*; Sylvia Plath, *The Bell Jar*; Earl of Listowel, *Modern Aesthetics*.

90. Polanyi to Nevill Coghill, October 22, 1963 (RPC 6:4).

91. Interview with Michael Evans.

92. Polanyi to Grene, August 22, 1968 (RPC 16:3).

93. Interview with Campbell.

94. Polanyi to Roberts, February 12, 1968 (RPC 7:15).

95. "Polanyi's Economics," *Tradition and Discovery* 25 (1999): 26.

96. Marika to Polanyi, October 6, 1968 (RPC 7:5).

97. Polanyi to Kind, January 15, 1969 (SKL).

98. I. A. Richards, *Principles of Literary Criticism*; J. Ehrlich, *Russian Formalism*; F. Nietzsche, *Werke*; L. Lévi-Bruhl, *Les fonctions mentales*; E. Cassirer, *Philosophy of Symbolic Forms*, 3 volumes; W. Listowel, *Modern Aesthetics*...; S. R. Langer, *Feeling & Form*; J. Pieper, *Leisure, the Basis of Culture*; L. R. Graham, *Soviet Academy of Sciences*...; S. Ullmann, *Style in the French Novel*.

99. Polanyi to Davies, January 3, 1969, Davies letter.

100. Polanyi to von Gomperz, March 13, 1969, Gretl von Gomperz letter.

101. RPC contains a collection of four undated lectures under the heading "Meaning" (30:6–11) with the following titles: I. "From Perception to Metaphor," II. "Works of Art," III. "Visionary Art," and IV. "Myths, Ancient and Modern," as well as a bound copy of "Meaning" (40:9) and supplemental material: Supplement #2: "Three Stages of Creative Work," Supplement #3: "Notes on the Destruction of Meaning," Supplement #4: "Acceptance of Religion" (40:1).

102. From the introductory passages of the first lecture of "Meaning: A Project" (undated; RPC 30:6).

103. RPC 30:6, 11.

104. Polanyi to Kind, April 4, 1969 (SKL).

105. Polanyi was elected honorary member of the Association the following year.

106. Polanyi to Marika, August 4, 1969 (RPC 7:14).

107. Polanyi/Philipson correspondence, June 17 and 19, 1969 (RPC 7:12).

108. Manuscript of 55 pages in RPC 39:4.

109. Polanyi later changed the title to "Tacit Foundations of Knowledge." Polanyi continued with revisions until the middle of October 1969. The paper was eventually published in 1972 as "Genius in Science" (1971).

110. Prosch to Scott, August 1, 1994.

111. Polanyi to Kind, undated (SKL).

112. Polanyi to Ruth Winters (RPC 8:2).

113. RPC 41:1–2.

114. Polanyi to Peacocke, September 16, 1970 (RPC 8:14).

115. Polanyi to Ilona, March 24, 1970 (KLP).

116. Interview with Poteat.

117. RPC has copies of five lectures given at Austin 1971: "Science and Man," "Genius in Science," "Representative Art," "Meaning," and "Expanding the Range" (41:4–9). A copy of a sixth lecture, "Honor," was supplied by Prosch; this sixth lecture was later cited in the book *Meaning* as the source of Chapter 11.

118. Polanyi to Kind, December 18, 1970 (SKL).

119. Polanyi to Dentay, May 6, 1971 (RPC 9:10).

II. THE LAST YEARS

1. Interview with Silvia Kind.
2. Polanyi to Kind, June 24, 1971 (SKL).
3. Polanyi to Striker, May 18, 1971 (RPC 9:11).
4. Polanyi to Manno, February 28, 1972 (RPC 10:10).
5. Polanyi to Gilbert, April 20, 1972 (RPC 10:11).
6. The Polanyi Society meets annually and publishes a journal entitled *Tradition and Discovery*. The current editor is Phil Mullins, Missouri Western State College, St. Joseph, MO 64507.
7. McCoy to Scott, July 20, 1994.
8. Polanyi to Horvath, September 5, 1972 (RPC 11:5).
9. Interview with Harry Prosch, April 1994.
10. Unpublished material, July 1972 (RPC 41:11).
11. Polanyi to Berta Maslow, October 2, 1972 (RPC 11:6).
12. Polanyi to Prosch, August 24, [1973], Prosch correspondence.
13. Polanyi to Prosch, cable, November 22, 1973, Prosch correspondence.
14. Polanyi to Gelwick, December 11, 1973.
15. Polanyi to Gelwick, December 13, 1973 (RPC 13:4).
16. Polanyi to Drusilla Scott, July 4, 1974 (RPC 13:12).
17. Sussex: The Book Guild Ltd., 1985.
18. Interview with Prosch.
19. Prosch to Scott, August 1, 1994.
20. Some Polanyi scholars find *Meaning* inconsistent with the earlier Polanyi. Prosch and Gelwick gave their strikingly different accounts of *Meaning* in a special issue of *Zygon* 17 (1982).
21. September 9, 1974.
22. John C. Puddefoot to Robin Hodgkin, November 2, 1994.
23. William T. Scott, "The Question of Religious Reality: Commentary on the Polanyi Papers," *Zygon* 17 (1982): 83–87.
24. Gowenlock to Scott, August 18, 1981.
25. Polanyi to Bonhoeffer, May 21, 1946 (MPG).
26. RPC 22:6.
27. McCoy to Scott, July 20, 1994.
28. Polanyi to Karl Mannheim, April 19, 1944 (RPC).
29. Interview with Bliss.
30. Doan to Polanyi, May 28, 1968 (RPC 6:14).
31. Polanyi to Doan, June 3, 1968 (RPC 7:1).
32. Polanyi to Drusilla Scott, February 9, 1968; Drusilla Scott letters.
33. Harry Prosch, "Polanyi's View of Religion in *Personal Knowledge*: A Response to Richard Gelwick," *Zygon* 17 (1982): 48.
34. Interview with Joan Crewdson.
35. Polanyi to Mannheim, May 2, 1944 (RPC 4:11).
36. Gelwick to Scott, 1994.
37. Gelwick, "Perspectives," 384.
38. "Michael Polanyi 1891–1976: A Remembrance," *Journal of Humanistic Psychology* 17 (1977): 69–70.

39. Magda Polanyi to Richard Gelwick, October 11, 1974.
40. Magda Polanyi to Bill Scott, August 9, 1975.
41. A. Bolton to Scott, April 20, 1979.

EPILOGUE

1. Polanyi to Scott, July 11, 1974.

Bibliography of Works by Michael Polanyi

Note: Titles in Hungarian and German have been translated into English. As far as possible, works have been listed in the order of their appearance.

1910

1910: "Contribution to the Chemistry of the Hydrocephalic Liquid." *Magyar ord. Archiv.* 11 (1910) 116, in Hungarian. Also in: *Biochemische Zeitschrift* 34 (1911): 205–210.

1911

1911: "Investigation of the Physical and Chemical Changes of the Blood Serum during Starvation." *Biochemische Zeitschrift* 34 (1911): 192–204.

1913

1913a: "A New Thermodynamic Consequence of the Quantum Hypothesis." *Verhandlungen der deutschen physikalischen Gesellschaft* 15 (1913): 156–161.

1913b: "New Thermodynamic Consequences of the Quantum Hypothesis." *Zeitschrift für physikalische Chemie* 83 (1913): 339–369.

1913c: With Julius Baron: "On the Application of the Second Law of Thermodynamics to Processes in the Animal Organism." *Biochemische Zeitschrift* 53 (1913): 1–20.

1914

1914a: "On the Derivation of Nernst's Theorem, I." *Verhandlungen der deutschen physikalischen Gesellschaft* 16 (1914): 333–335.
1914b: "Adsorption, Swelling and Osmotic Pressure of Colloids." *Biochemische Zeitschrift* 66 (1914): 258–268.
1914c: "Adsorption and Capillarity from the Standpoint of the Second Law of Thermodynamics." *Zeitschrift für physikalische Chemie* 88 (1914): 622–631.
1914d: "On Adsorption from the Standpoint of the Third Law of Thermodynamics." *Verhandlungen der deutschen physikalischen Gesellschaft* 16 (1914): 1012–1016.

1915

1915: "On the Derivation of Nernst's Theorem, II." *Verhandlungen der deutschen physikalischen Gesellschaft* 17 (1915): 350–353.

1916

1916a: "Adsorption of Gases by a Solid Non-Volatile Adsorbent." *Verhandlungen der deutschen physikalischen Gesellschaft* 18 (1916): 55–80. Also: *Doktori Dissertatio* (Budapest, 1917), in Hungarian.
1916b: "New Procedure to Save Washing Materials." *Vegyészeti Lapok* 12 (1916): 12–14, in Hungarian.

1917

1917a: "On the Theory of Adsorption." *Magyar Chemiai Folyóirat* 23 (1917): 3–14.
1917b: "To the Peacemakers: Some Views on the European War and the Conditions of Peace." *Huszadik Szazad* 2 (1917): 165–176, in Hungarian. Also in SEP, 15–28.

1919

1919a: With Laszlo Mandoki: "On the Causes of the Conductivity of Casein Solutions." *Magyar Chemiai Folyóirat* 25 (1919): 1–4, in Hungarian. Also in *Biochemische Zeitschrift* 104 (1920): 254–258.
1919b: "Conductivity-Lowering and Adsorption in Lyophilic Colloids." *Magyar Chemiai Folyóirat* 25 (1919): 1–11, in Hungarian. Also in *Biochemische Zeitschrift* 104 (1920): 237–253.
1919c: "Calculation of the Reaction Rates Based on Probability Theory." *Magyar Chemiai Folyóirat* 25 (1919): 136, in Hungarian.
1919d: "New Skepticism." *Szabadgondolat* (1919): 53–56, in Hungarian. Also in SEP, 29–32.

1920

1920a: "Reaction Isochore and Reaction Velocity from the Standpoint of Statistics."
    Zeitschrift für Elektrochemie 26 (1920): 49–54; corrections, 231.

1920b: "On the Absolute Saturation of Attractive Forces Acting between Atoms and
    Molecules." *Zeitschrift für Elektrochemie* 26 (1920): 161–171.

1920c: "On the Problem of Reaction Velocity." *Zeitschrift für Elektrochemie* 26
    (1920): 228–231.

1920d: "On the Nonmechanical Nature of Chemical Processes." *Zeitschrift für
    Physik* 1 (1920): 337–344.

1920e: "Advances in the Theoretical Explanation of Adsorption." *Chemiker Zeitung*
    44 (1920): 340.

1920f: "On the Theory of Reaction Velocity." *Zeitschrift für Physik* 2 (1920): 90–110.

1920g: "Adsorption from Solutions of Substances of Limited Solubility." *Zeitschrift
    für Physik* 2 (1920): 111–116.

1920h: "On the Origin of Chemical Energy." *Zeitschrift für Physik* 3 (1920): 31–35.

1920i: "On Adsorption and the Origin of Adsorption Forces." *Zeitschrift für Elek-
    trochemie* 26 (1920): 370–374.

1920j: With R. O. Herzog and W. Jancke: "X-Ray Spectroscopic Investigations on
    Cellulose." *Zeitschrift für Physik* 3 (1920): I. 196–198, II. 343–348.

1921

1921a: "On the Adsorption of Gases on Solid Substances." *Festschrift Kaiser Wilhelm
    Gesellschaft Zehnjährigens Jubiläum* (1921): 171–177.

1921b: "On the Current Resulting from the Compression of a Soldered Joint."
    Zeitschrift für physikalische Chemie 97 (1921): 459–463.

1921c: With K. Becker, R. O. Herzog, and W. Jancke: "On Methods for the Ar-
    rangement of Crystal Elements." *Zeitschrift für Physik* 5 (1921): 61–62.

1921d: "Chemical Constitution of Cellulose." *Die Naturwissenschaften,* 9 (1921): 288.
    Brief Notice.

1921e: "Fibrous Structure by X-Ray Diffraction." *Die Naturwissenschaften* 9 (1921): 337–340.

1921f: "The X-Ray Fibre Diagram." *Zeitschrift für Physik* 7 (1921): 149–180.

1921g: With M. Ettisch and K. Weissenberg: "On Fibrous Structure in Metals."
    Zeitschrift für Physik 7 (1921): 181–184.

1921h: "On Adsorption Catalysis." *Zeitschrift für Elektrochemie* 27 (1921): 142–150.

1921i: With M. Ettisch and K. Weissenberg: "X-Ray Investigation of Metals." *Phy-
    sikalische Zeitschrift* 22 (1921): 646.

1921j: "On the Nature of the Tearing Process." *Zeitschrift für Physik* 7 (1921): 323–327.

1921k: With M. Ettisch and K. Weissenberg: "Fibrous Structure of Hard-Drawn
    Metal Wires." *Zeitschrift für physikalische Chemie* 99 (1921): 332–337.

1922

1922a: "The Reinforcement of Monocrystals by Mechanical Treatment." *Zeitschrift
    für Elektrochemie* 28 (1922): 16–20.

1922b: With K. Weissenberg: "The X-Ray Fibre Diagram." *Zeitschrift für Physik* 9 (1922): 411–416.

1922c: "Reflection on Mr. A. Eucken's Work. On the Theory of Adsorption Processes." *Zeitschrift für Elektrochemie* 28 (1922): 110–111.

1922d: Review of Thermodynamics and Chemistry, by F. H. MacDougall, *Zeitschrift für Elektrochemie* 28 (1922): 111.

1922e: With K. Weissenberg: "The X-Ray Fibre Diagram." *Zeitschrift für Physik* 10 (1922): 44–53.

1922f: "Determination of Crystal Arrangement by X-Ray Diffraction." *Die Naturwissenschaften* 10 (1922): 411–416.

1922g: "Processes in the Stretching of Zinc Crystals." *Verhandlungen der deutschen physikalischen Gesellschaft* 3 (1922): 57–58.

1922h: With H. Mark and E. Schmid: "Processes in the Stretching of Zinc Crystals. I. General Description of the Phenomena and Research Methods." *Zeitschrift für Physik* 12 (1922): 58–77.

1922i: With H. Mark and E. Schmid: "Processes in the Stretching of Zinc Crystals. II. Quantitative Consideration of the Stretching Mechanism." *Zeitschrift für Physik* 12 (1922): 78–110.

1922j: With H. Mark and E. Schmid: "Processes in the Stretching of Zinc Crystals, III. Relationship between the Fibre Structure and Reinforcement." *Zeitschrift für Physik* 12 (1922): 111–116.

1923

1923a: With K. Weissenberg: "Röntgenographic Investigations on Worked Metals." *Zeitschrift für Technische Physik* 4 (1923): 199–208.

1923b: With H. Mark and E. Schmid: "Investigation of Monocrystalline Wires of Tin." *Die Naturwissenschaften* 11 (1923): 256.

1923c: "On Structural Changes in Metals through Cold Working." *Zeitschrift für Physik* 17 (1923): 42–53.

1923d: With E. Schmid: "Discussion of the Sliding Friction Dependence on Pressure Normal to the Sliding Plane." *Zietschrift für Physik* 16 (1923): 336–339.

1923e: With H. Mark: "Lattice Structure, Sliding Directions and Sliding Planes of White Tin." *Zeitschrift für Physik* 18 (1923): 75–96.

1923f: With E. Schmid: "Strengthening and Weakening of Metallic Monocrystals." *Verhandlungen der deutschen physikalischen Gesellschaft* 4 (1923): 25–27.

1923g: "Structural Analysis by Means of X-Rays." *Physikalische Zeitschrift* 24 (1923): 407–415.

1923h: With R. O. Herzog and W. Jancke: "On the Structure of the Cellulose and Silk Fibre." *Zeitschrift für Physik* 20 (1923): 413.

1923i: With G. Masing: "Cold Working and Reinforcement." *Ergebnisse der Exacten Naturwissenschaften* 2 (1923): 177–245.

1924

1924a: With H. Mark: "Correction to the Paper Lattice Structure, Sliding Directions and Sliding Planes of White Tin." *Zeitschrift für Physik* 22 (1924): 200.

1924b: With E. Schiebold and K. Weissenberg: "On the Development of the Rotating Crystal Method." *Zeitschrift für Physik* 23 (1924): 337–340.

1924c: With W. Ewald: "Plasticity and Strength of Rock Salt under Water." *Zeitschrift für Physik* 28 (1924): 29–50.

1924d: With G. Masing: "On the Increase of Tensile Strength of Zinc by Cold-Working." *Zeitschrift für Physik* 28 (1924): 169–176.

1924e: With E. Schmid: "On the Structure of Worked Meals." *Zeitschrift für Technische Physik* 5 (1924): 580–589.

1924f: With A. Schob: "Stretching Experiments with Soft Vulcanized Rubber at the Temperature of Liquid Air." *Mitteilungen aus dem Materialprüfungsamt* 42 (1924): 22–24.

1925

1925a: With W. Ewald: "On the Form Strengthening of Rock Salt in Bending Experiments." *Zeitschrift für Physik* 31 (1925): 139–144.

1925b: "Osmotic Pressure, Pressure of Swelling and Adsorption." *Zeitschrift für physikalische Chemie* 114 (1925): 387–393.

1925c: "An Elongating Apparatus for Threads and Wires." *Zeitschrift für Technische Physik* 6 (1925): 121–124.

1925d: "Deformation of Monocrystals." *Zeitschrift für Kristallographie* 61 (1925): 49–50.

1925e: With W. Ewald: "Remarks on the Work of A. Joffé and M. Levitzky, On the Limits of Strength and Elasticity of Natural Rock Salt." *Zeitschrift für Physik* 31 (1925): 746–749.

1925f: "Crystal Deformation and Strengthening." *Zeitschrift für Metallkunde* 17 (1925): 94.

1925g: With M. Fischenich: "The Origins of Conductivity in Casein Solutions." *Kolloid-Zeitschrift und Zeitschrift für Polymere* 36 (1925): 275–281.

1925h: "Moulding of Solid Bodies from the Standpoint of Crystal Structure." *Zeitschrift für Angewandte Mathematik und Mechanik* 5 (1925): 125–126.

1925i: With E. Schmid: "Strengthening and Weakening of Sn Crystals." *Zeitschrift für Physik* 32 (1925): 684–712.

1925j: With G. Sachs: "On the Release of Internal Strains by Annealing." *Zeitschrift für Metallkunde* 17 (1925): 227–228.

1925k: With G. Sachs: "On Elastic Hysteresis and Internal Strains in Bent Rock-Salt Crystals." *Zeitschrift für Physik* 33 (1925): 692–705.

1925l: With E. Wigner: "Formation and Decomposition of Molecules." *Zeitschrift für Physik* 33 (1925): 429–434.

1925m: With H. Beutler: "Chemiluminescence and Reaction Velocity." *Die Naturwissenschaften* 13 (1925): 711–712.

1926

1926a: With G. Sachs: "Elastic Hysteresis in Rock Salt." *Nature* 116 (1926): 692.

1926b: With H. Beutler and S. v. Bogdandy: "On Luminescence of Highly Dilute Flames." *Die Naturwissenschaften* 14 (1926): 164.

1926c: "Moulding of Metal Crystals and the Moulded State." *Berichte der Fachausschüsse des Vereins deutscher Eisenhüttenleute, Werkstoffausschuss Bericht* 85 (1926): 1–5.

1926d: "On Wilhelm Starlinger's Behaviour of Neutral Sodium Caseinogate in Membrane Hydrolysis." *Biochemische Zeitschrift* 171 (1926): 473.

1926e: With S. v. Bogdandy: "Ejection of Atoms from Solids by Chemical Attack on the Surface." *Die Naturwissenschaften* 14 (1926): 1205–1206.

1926f: With S. v. Bogdandy and J. Boehm: "On a Method of Producing Molecular Mixtures." *Zeitschrift für Physik* 40 (1926): 211–213.

1927

1927a: With S. v. Bogdandy: "Rapid Analysis of Brass." *Zeitschrift für Metallkunde* 19 (1927): 164–165. Also in *Metal Industry* 30 (1927): 195.

1927b: With R. L. Hasche and E. Vogt: "Spectral Intensity Distribution in the D-line of the Chemiluminescence of Sodium Vapour." *Zeitschrift für Physik* 41 (1927): 583–610.

1927c: "The Structure of Matter and X-Ray Diffraction." *Zeitschrift des Vereins Deutscher Ingenieure* 71 (1927): 565–570.

1927d: "Theory of Wall Reactions." *Chemische Rundschau für Mitteleuropa und den Balkan* 4 (1927): 16–161.

1927e: With S. v. Bogdandy: "Chemically-Induced Chain Reaction in Detonating Gas." *Die Naturwissenschaften* 15 (1927): 410.

1927f: With S. v. Bogdandy: "Chemically Induced Chain Reactions in Mixtures of Halogens, Hydrogen and Methane." *Zeitschrift für Elektrochemie* 33 (1927): 554–561.

1928

1928a: "Deformation, Rupture and Hardening of Crystals." *Die Naturwissenschaften* 16 (1928): 285–294. Also in *Transactions of the Faraday Society*, 24 (1928): 72–83.

1928b: With F. Goldmann: "Adsorption of Vapours on Carbon and the Thermal Dilation of the Interface." *Zeitschrift für physikalische Chemie* 132 (1928): 321–370.

1928c: With H. Beutler: "On Highly Dilute Flames, I." *Zeitschrift für Physik* 47 (1928): 379–406.

1928d: With K. Welke: "Adsorption, Heat of Adsorption and Character of Attachment between Small Amounts of Sulphur Dioxide and Carbon." *Zeitschrift für physikalische Chemie* 132 (1928): 371–383.

1928e: With G. Schay: "Chemiluminescence between Alkali Metal Vapours and Tin Halides." *Zeitschrift für Physik* 47 (1928): 814–818.

1928f: With W. Heyne: "Adsorption from Solutions." *Zeitschrift für physikalische Chemie*, 132 (1928): 384–398.

1928g: "Reply to the Letter of O. L. Sponsler, "Erroneous Determination of the Cellulose Space Lattice." *Die Naturwissenschaften* 16 (1928): 263–264.

1928h: With H. Beutler: "On Highly Dilute Flames, I." *Zeitschrift für physikalische Chemie* B1 (1928): 3–20.

1928i: With S. v. Bogdandy: "On Highly Dilute Flames, II, Nozzle Flames. Increase of Light Emission with Increasing Partial Pressure of Sodium Vapour." *Zeitschrift für physikalische Chemie* B1 (1928): 21–29.

1928j: With G. Schay: "On Highly Dilute Flames, III. Sodium-Chlorine Flame. Evidence for and Analysis of the Reaction and Luminescence Mechanism. Both Reaction Types. Survey of the Whole Work." *Zeitschrift für physikalische Chemie* B1 (1928): 39–61.

1928k: "The Inhibition of Chain Reactions by Bromine," *Transactions of the Faraday Society* 24 (1928): 606–611.

1928l: "On the Simplest Chemical Reaction." *Réunion Internationale Chimie Physique* (1928): 198–204.

1928m: With L. Frommer: "On Heterogeneous Elementary Reactions. 1. Action of Chlorine on Copper." *Zeitschrift für physikalische Chemie* 137 (1928): 201–208.

1928n: With E. Wigner: "On the Interference of Characteristic-Vibrations as the Cause of Energy Fluctuations and Chemical Changes." *Zeitschrift für physikalische Chemie* 139 (1928): 439–452.

1928o: "Explanation of an Intramolecular Reaction," *Transactions of the Faraday Society* 24 (1928): 733–734, a discussion note.

1928p: With G. Schay: "Correction to the Work. On Highly Dilute Flames, III." *Zeitschrift für physikalische Chemie* 1 (1928): 384.

1928q: "Theoretical and Experimental Strength." *Die Naturwissenschaften* 16 (1928): 1043.

1928r: "Application of Langmuir's Theory to the Adsorption of Gases on Charcoal." *Zeitschrift für physikalische Chemie* A138 (1928): 459–462.

1928s: "Fritz Haber." *Metallwirtschaft* 7 (1928): 1316–1317.

1929

1929a: With E. Schmid: "Problems of Plasticity. Deformation at Low Temperatures." *Die Naturwissenschaften* 17 (1929): 301–304. Also in *Mitteilungen der deutschen Materialprüfungsanstalten, Sonderhefte* 10 (1930): 101–104.

1929b: "Principles of the Potential Theory of Adsorption." *Zeitschrift für Elektrochemie* 35 (1929): 431–432.

1929c: "Consideration of Activation Processes at Surfaces." *Zietschrift für Elektrochemie* 35 (1929): 561–576.

1929d: "Atomic Reactions and Luminescence in Highly Dilute Flames." *Journal of Chemical Education* 6 (1929): 2094–2095.

1930

1930a: "On the Nature of the Solid State." *Metallwirtschaft* 9 (1930): 553–569. Also in *Mitteilungen der deutschen Materialprüfungsanstalten, Sonderhefte* 13 (1930): 113–119. *Umschau in Wissenschaft und Technik* 34 (1930): 1001.

1930b: "Förderung der Wissenschaft" ("Promotion of Science"). *Der deutsche Volkswirt* (1930): 1149–1151.

1930c: With H. v. Hartel: "On Atomic Reactions Possessing Inertia." *Zeitschrift für physikalische Chemie* B11 (1930): 97–138.

1930d: With W. Meissner and E. Schmid: "Measurements with the Aid of Liquid Helium. XII. Plasticity of Metal Crystals at Low Temperature." *Zeitschrift für Physik* 66 (1930): 477–489.

1930e: With H. Eyring: "On the Calculation of the Energy of Activation." *Die Naturwissenschaften* 18 (1930): 914–915.

1930f: With L. Frommer: "On Gas Phase Luminescence in a Heterogeneous Reaction." *Zeitschrift für physikalische Chemie* B6 (1930): 371–381.

1930g: With F. London: "The Theoretical Interpretation of Adsorption Forces." *Die Naturwissenschaften* 18 (1930): 1099–1100.

1931

1931a: With H. Eyring: "On Simple Gas Reactions." *Zeitschrift für physikalische Chemie* B12 (1931): 279–311.

1931b: "Atomic Reactions." *Zeitschrift für Angewandte Chemie* 44 (1931): 597–612.

1931c: With E. Cremer: "Decrease of Fundamental Frequency as the First Stage of Chemical Reaction." *Zeitschrift für physikalische Chemie, Bodenstein-Festband* (1931): 770–774.

1931d: With E. Cremer: "Estimation of Molecular Lattice Dimensions from Resonance Forces." *Zeitschrift für physikalische Chemie* B14 (1931): 435–442.

1931e: With P. Beck: "Recovery of Recrystallising Ability by Reformation." *Zeitschrift für Elektrochemie* 37 (1931): 521–524.

1931f: With P. Beck: "Recovery of Recrystallising Power by Reformation." *Die Naturwissenschaften* 19 (1931): 505–506.

1932

1932a: With H. Ekstein: "Note on the Mechanism of the Reaction $H_2 + I_2 \rightarrow 2HI$ and of Similar Reactions at Boundary Surfaces." *Zeitschrift für physikalische Chemie* B15 (1932): 334–341.

1932b: "Theories of the Adsorption of Gases. A General Survey and Some General Remarks." *Transactions of the Faraday Society* 28 (1932): 316–333.

1932c: With E. Horn and H. Sattler: "On Highly Dilute Flames of Sodium Vapour with Cadmium Halides and Zinc Chloride." *Zeitschrift für physikalische Chemie* B17 (1932): 220–232.

1932d: With E. Cremer: "Discussion on Ortho-Para Transformation in Solid Hydrogen." *Transactions of the Faraday Society* 28 (1932): 435.

1932e: "The Theory of Chemical Reactions." *Uspekhi Khimii* 1 (1932): 345–60. Also in *Die Naturwissenschaften* 20 (1932): 289–296.

1932f: With Hans von Hartel and N. Meer: "Investigation of the Reaction Velocity between Sodium Vapor and Alkyl Chlorides." *Zeitschrift für physikalische Chemie* B19 (1932): 139–163.

1932g: With N. Meer: "Comparison of the Reactions of Sodium Vapour with Other Organic Processes." *Zeitschrift für physikalische Chemie* B19 (1932): 164–189.

1932h: With D. W. G. Style: "On an Active Product of the Reaction between Sodium Vapour and Alkyl Halides." *Die Naturwissenschaften* 20 (1932): 401–402.

1932i: With E. Cremer: "Test of the 'Tunnel' Theory of Heterogeneous Catalysis; the Hydrogenation of Styrene." *Zeitschrift für physikalische Chemie* B19 (1932): 443–450.

1932j: *Atomic Reactions* (London: Williams & Norgate, 1932).

1933

1933a: With S. v. Bogdandy and G. Veszi: "On a Method for the Preparation of Colloids and for Hydrogenation with Atomic Hydrogen." *Zeitschrift für Angewandte Chemie* 46 (1933): 15–17. Also in *Chemische Fabrik* 6 (1933): 1–16.

1933b: With J. Curry: "On the Reaction between Sodium Vapour and Cyanogen Halides." *Zeitschrift für physikalische Chemie* B20 (1933): 276–282.

1933c: With E. Bergmann and A. Szabó: "The Mechanism of Simple Substitution Reactions and the Walden Inversion." *Zeitschrift für physikalische Chemie* B20 (1933): 161–174.

1933d: "Adsorption and Capillary Condensation." *Physikalische Zeitschrift der Sowjetunion* 4 (1933): 144–154.

1933e: With E. Cremer: "The Conversion of o- into p-Hydrogen in the Solid State." *Zeitschrift für physikalische Chemie* B21 (1933): 459–468.

1933f: "A Note on the Electrolytic Separation of Heavy Hydrogen by the Method of G. N. Lewis." *Die Naturwissenschaften* 21 (1933): 316–317.

1933g: With E. Bergmann: "Autoracemization and Velocity of Electrolytic Dissociation." *Die Naturwissenschaften* 21 (1933): 378–379.

1933h: With E. S. Gilfillan: "Micropycnometer for the Determination of Displacements of Isotopic Ratio in Water." *Zeitschrift für physikalische Chemie* A166 (1933): 254–256.

1933i: With E. Horn and D. W. G. Style: "On the Isolation of Free Methyl and Ethyl by the Reaction between Sodium Vapour and Methyl and Ethyl Bromides." *Zeitschrift für physikalische Chemie* B23 (1933): 291–304. Also in *Transactions of the Faraday Society* 30 (1934): 189–199.

1933j: With E. Cremer and J. Curry: "On a Method for the Determination of the Velocity of Gaseous Reactions of Atomic Hydrogen." *Zeitschrift für physikalische Chemie* B23 (1933): 445–468.

1933k: "A Method for the Measurement of Gaseous Reactions." *Nature* 132 (1933): 747–748.

1933l: With J. Horiuti: "A Catalysed Reaction of Hydrogen with Water." *Nature* 132 (1933): 819.

1933m: With J. Horiuti: "Catalyzed Reaction of Hydrogen with Water and the Nature of Over-voltage." *Nature* 132 (1933): 931.

1933n: "Atomic Reactions." *Uspekhi Khimii* 2 (1933): 412.

1934

1934a: With E. Horn: "On the Isolation of Free Phenyl Radicals by the Reaction of Sodium Vapour with Bromobenzene." *Zeitschrift für physikalische Chemie* B25 (1934): 151–152.

1934b: "Reaction Rates of the Hydrogen Isotopes." *Nature* 133 (1934): 26.

1934c: With J. Horiuti: "Catalytic Hydrogen Replacement and the Nature of Overvoltage." *Nature* 133 (1934): 142.

1934d: "Discussion on Heavy Hydrogen." *Proceedings of the Royal Society* A144 (London, 1934): 14–16.

1934e: With R. A. Ogg, Jr.: "The Mechanism of Ionogenic Reactions." *Memoirs and Proceedings of the Manchester Literary and Philosophical Society* 78 (1934): 41–45.

1934f: With J. Horiuti: "On the Mechanism of Ionisation of Hydrogen at a Platinum Electrode." *Memoirs and Proceedings of the Manchester Literary and Philosophical Society* 78 (1934): 47–54.

1934g: With A. L. Szabó: "On the Mechanism of Hydrolysis. The Alkaline Saponification of Amyl Acetate." *Transactions of the Faraday Society* 30 (1934): 508–511.

1934h: With L. Frommer: "A New Method for Measuring the Rate of High Velocity Gas Reactions." *Transactions of the Faraday Society* 30 (1934): 519–529.

1934i: "On a Form of Lattice Distortion that May Render a Crystal Plastic." *Zeitschrift für Physik* 89 (1934): 660–664.

1934j: "Discussion on Energy Distribution in Molecules." *Proceedings of the Royal Society* A146 (London, 1934): 253–254.

1934k: With B. Cavanagh and J. Horiuti: "Enzyme Catalysis of the Ionisation of Hydrogen." *Nature* 133 (1934): 797.

1934l: With R. A. Ogg, Jr. and L. Werner: "Optical Inversion by Negative Substitution." *Journal of the Society of Chemical Industry* 53 (1934): 614–15.

1934m: With J. Horiuti and G. Ogden: "Catalytic Replacement of Haplogen by Diplogen in Benzene." *Transactions of the Faraday Society* 30 (1934): 663–665.

1934n: With J. Horiuti: "Catalytic Interchange of Hydrogen between Water and Ethylene and between Water and Benzene." *Nature* 134 (1934): 377–78.

1934o: With J. Horiuti: "Exchange Reactions of Hydrogen on Metallic Catalysts." *Transactions of the Faraday Society* 30 (1934): 1164–1172.

1934p: With W. Heller: "Quantitative Studies of Atomic Reactions." *Comptes rendus des séances de l'Academie des Sciences* 199 (1934): 1118–1121.

1934q: With J. Horiuti: "Direct Introduction of Deuterium into Benzene." *Nature* 134 (1934): 847.

1934r: "Discussion of Methods of Measuring and Factors Determining the Speed of Chemical Reactions." *Proceedings of the Royal Society* B116 (London, 1934): 202–206.

1934s: "Heavy Water in Chemistry." *Proceedings of the Royal Society* 28 (1934): 401–424. Also in *Nature* 135 (1935): 19–26.

1935

1935a: "Heavy Water." *Journal of the Society of Dyers and Colourists* 51 (1935): 90.

1935b: With R. A. Ogg, Jr.: "Substitution of Free atoms and Walden Inversion. The Decomposition and Racemisation of Optically Active sec-Butyl Iodide in the Gaseous State." *Transactions of the Faraday Society* 31 (1935): 482–495.

1935c: With R. A. Ogg, Jr.: "Mechanism of Ionic Reactions." *Transactions of the Faraday Society* 31 (1935): 604–620.

1935d: With J. Kenner and P. Szego: "Aluminum Chloride as a Catalyst of Hydrogen Interchange." *Nature* 137 (1935): 267.

1935e: With M. G. Evans: "Some Applications of the Transition State Method to the Calculation of Reaction Velocities, Especially in Solution." *Transactions of the Faraday Society* 31 (1935): 875–894.

1935f: "Adsorption and Catalysis." *Journal of the Society of Chemical Industry* 54 (1935): 123–124.

1935g: With J. Horiuti: "Principles of a Theory of Proton Transfer." *Acta Physiocochim. URSS* 2 (1935): 505–532.

1935h: With R. A. Ogg, Jr.: "Diabatic Reactions and Primary Chemiluminescence." *Transactions of the Faraday Society* 31 (1935): 1375–1384.

1935i: With G. H. Bottomley and B. Cavanagh: "Enzyme Catalysis of the Exchange of Deuterium with Water." *Nature* 136 (1935): 103.

1935j: "USSR Economics—Fundamental Data, System and Spirit." *The Manchester School of Economics and Social Studies* 16 (1935): 67–89. Separately printed as: *USSR Economics*. Manchester: Manchester University Press, 1936.

1936

1936a: With C. Horrex: "Atomic Interchange between Water and Saturated Hydrocarbons." *Memoirs and Proceedings of the Manchester Literary and Philosophical Society* 80 (1936): 33–35.

1936b: With W. Heller: "Reactions between Sodium Vapour and Volatile Polyhalides, Velocities and Luminescence." *Transactions of the Faraday Society* 32 (1936): 633–642.

1936c: With E. Bergmann and A. L. Szabó: "Substitution and Inversion of Configuration." *Transactions of the Faraday Society* 32 (1936): 843–852.

1936d: With M. G. Evans: "Equilibrium Constants and Velocity Constants." *Nature* 137 (1936): 530–531.

1936e: "The Value of the Inexact" (letter to the editor). *Philosophy of Science* 3 (1936): 233–234. Reprinted in *Tradition and Discovery* 18 (1992): 35–36.

1936f: With M. G. Evans: "Further Considerations on the Thermodynamics of Chemical Equilibria and Reaction Rates." *Transactions of the Faraday Society* 32 (1936): 1333–1360.

1936g: With D. D. Eley: "Catalytic Interchange of Hydrogen with Water and Alcohol." *Transactions of the Faraday Society* 32 (1936): 1388–1397.

1936h: With M. Calvin and E. G. Cockbain: "Activation of Hydrogen by Phthalocyanine and Copper Phthalocynanine." *Memoirs and Proceedings of the Manchester Literary and Philosophical Society* 80 (1936): 103–104.

1936i: With M. Calvin and E. G. Cockbain: "Activation of Hydrogen by Phthalocyanine and Copper Phthalocyanine, Part I." *Transactions of the Faraday Society* 32
(1936): 1436–1443.

1936j: With M. Calvin and D. D. Eley: "Activation of Hydrogen by Phthalocyanine
and Copper Phthalocyanine, Part II." *Transactions of the Faraday Society* 32
(1936): 1443–1446.

1936k: "The Struggle between Truth and Propaganda." *The Manchester School of
Economic and Social Studies* 7 (1936): 105–118. Also in SEP, 47–60.

1937

1937a: "Catalytic Activation of Hydrogen." *Scientific Journal of the Royal College of
Science* 7 (1937): 21–31.

1937b: With M. G. Evans: "On the Introduction of Thermodynamical Variables into
Reaction Kinetics." *Transactions of the Faraday Society* 33 (1937): 448–452.

1937c: "The Transition State in Chemical Reactions." *Journal of the Chemical Society*
(1937): 629–635.

1937d: "The Transition State in Chemical Kinetics." *Nature* 139 (1937): 575–576.

1937e: "Colours as Catalysts." *Journal of the Oil and Color Chemists' Association—
Buxton Conference* 3 (1937): 3–9.

1937f: "Congrès du Palais de la Découverte: International Meeting in Paris." *Nature*
140 (1937): 710.

1938

1938a: "The Deformation of Solids." *Réunion Internationale Physique Chimie-
Biologie. Physique Générale* (1938): 47–55.

1938b: With M. G. Evans: "Inertia and Driving Force of Chemical Reactions."
Transactions of the Faraday Society 34 (1939): 11–24.

1938c: "An Outline of the Working of Money Shown by a Diagrammatic Film."
Manchester Statistical Society (1938): 1–19.

1938d: "On the Catalytic Properties of Phthalocyanine Crystals." *Transactions of the
Faraday Society* 34 (1938): 1191.

1938e: "The 'Settling Down' of Capital and the Trade Cycle." *The Manchester School
of Economic and Social Studies* 9 (November, 1938): 153–169.

1939

1939a: With M. G. Evans: "Notes on the Luminescence of Sodium Vapour in Highly
Dilute Flames." *Transactions of the Faraday Society* 35 (1939): 178–185, 195–197.

1939b: With C. Horrex and R. K. Greenhalgh: "Catalytic Exchange of Hydrogen."
Transactions of the Faraday Society 35 (1939): 511–520.

1939c: With R. K. Greenhalgh: "Hydrogenation and Atomic Exchange of Benzene."
Transactions of the Faraday Society 35 (1939): 520–542.

1939d: "The Rights and Duties of Science." *The Manchester School of Economic and
Social Studies* 10 (October, 1939): 175–193. Also in *The Contempt of Freedom.*

London: Watts, 1940. Also in *Society for Freedom in Science*, Occasional Pamphlet No. 2, June 1945. Also in SEP, 61–77.

1940

1940a: With A. R. Bennett: "Influence of Acidity on Catalytic Exchange of Hydrogen and Water." *Transactions of the Faraday Society* 36 (1940): 377–381.

1940b: "Science in USSR" *The New Statesman and Nation* 19 (February 10, 1940): 174.

1940c: With E. T. Butler: "Influence of Substitution on Organic Bond Strength." *Nature* 146 (1940): 129–130.

1940d: "Economics on the Screen." *Documentary News Letter* (August, 1940): 2.

1940e: *The Contempt of Freedom: The Russian Experiment and After*. London: Watts, 1940. Reprinted, New York: Arno Press, 1975.

1940f: "Economics by Motion Symbols." *The Review of Economic Studies* 8 (October, 1940): 1–19.

1940g: "Unemployment and Money." A diagrammatic film prepared with the assistance of Miss Mary Field, Mr. Jeffryes, and Professor John Jewkes. Videotape available in Regenstein Library.

1940h: *Unemployment and Money*, Handbook to the film. Consists of: Introduction, Recorded Commentary of the film. Reprint of "Economics by Motion Symbols."

1940i: With E. C. Baughan: "Energy of Aliphatic Carbon Links." *Nature* 146 (1940): 685–686.

1941

1941a: "Cultural Significance of Science." *Nature* 147 (January 25, 1941): 119.

1941b: With E. C. Baughan and M. G. Evans: "Covalency, Ionisation and Resonance in Carbon Bonds." *Transactions of the Faraday Society* 37 (1941): 377–393.

1941c: With E. C. Baughan: "Activation Energy of Ionic Substitution." *Transactions of the Faraday Society* 37 (1941): 648–654.

1941d: With M. G. Evans: "Effect of Negative Groups on Reactivity." *Nature* 148 (1941): 436.

1941e: "The Growth of Thought in Society." *Economica* 8 (November, 1941): 421–456.

1942

1942a: With A. G. Evans: "Calculation of Steric Hindrance." *Nature* 149 (1942): 608.

1942b: "Revaluation of Science." *The Manchester Guardian* (November 7, 1942), Letter to the Editor.

1943

1943a: With E. T. Butler: "Rates of Pyrolysis and Bond Energies of Substituted Organic Iodides, I." *Transactions of the Faraday Society* 39 (1943): 19–36.

1943b: "Resonance and Chemical Reactivity." *Nature* 151 (1943): 96.

1943c: "Jewish Problems." *The Political Quarterly* 14 (January–March 1943): 33–45. Also in SEP, 33–45.

1943d: "The Autonomy of Science." *Memoirs and Proceedings of the Manchester Literary and Philosophical Society* 85 (February 1943): 19–38. Also in *The Scientific Monthly* 60 (February 1945): 141–150, and as "Self-Government of Science" in LL, 49–68.

1943e: "Economics of Full Employment." *Manchester Guardian* (February 13, 1943).

1943f: "Research and Planning." *Nature* 152 (August 21, 1943): 217–218.

1943g: "The Hungarian Opposition." *The New Statesman and Nation* 26 (September 25, 1943): 216–217.

1943h: Review of *Reflections on the Revolution of our Time* by Harold J. Lasky, *The Manchester Guardian* (October 8, 1943).

1943i: "The English and the Continent." *The Political Quarterly* 14 (October–December, 1943): 372–381. Also in *Fortune* 29 (May 1944): 155–157.

1943j: With A. G. Evans: "Steric Hindrance and Heats of Formation." *Nature* 152 (1943): 738.

1944

1944a: "Science—Its Reality and Freedom." *The Nineteenth Century and After* 135 (February 1944): 78–83.

1944b: "The Socialist Error." Review of *The Road to Serfdom* by F. A. v. Hayek, *The Spectator*. (March 31, 1944): 293.

1944c: "Science and the Decline of Freedom." *The Listener* (June 1, 1944): 599.

1944d: "Reflections on John Dalton." *The Manchester Guardian* (July 22, 1944): 13–15. Also in *L. Farkas Memorial Volume*. Ed. Adalbert Farkas and Eugene P. Wigner. Jerusalem: Research Council of Israel, 1952.

1944e: "Patent Reform." *The Review of Economic Studies* 11 (Summer 1944): 61–76.

1945

1945a: "The Planning of Science." *The Political Quarterly* 16 (October–December, 1945): 316–326, also in *Publications of the Society for Freedom in Science*. Occasional Pamphlet 4 (February 1946) and expanded as "Science and Welfare" in LL, 68–86.

1945b: With E. T. Butler and Erna Mandel: "Rates of Pyrolysis and Bond Energies of Substituted Organic Iodides, II." *Transactions of the Faraday Society* 41 (1945): 298–306.

1945c: "Science and the Modern Crisis." *Memoirs and Proceedings of the Manchester Literary and Philosophical Society* 86 (June 1945): 7–16.

1945d: "Reform of the Patent Law in Britain." *Nature* 156 (July 14, 1945): 54.

1945e: *Full Employment and Free Trade*. Cambridge: Cambridge University Press, 1945. 2nd ed., New York: Macmillan Co., 1948.

1945f: "The Value of Pure Science." *Time and Tide* 26 (December 15, 1945): 64–65. Also in "Social Message of Pure Science" in: *The Advancement of Science*, No. 12 (April 1946): 64–65 and in LL, 3–7.

1946

1946a: With A. G. Evans, D. Holden, P. H. Plesch, H. A. Skinner, and M. A. Weinberger: "Friedel-Crafts Catalysts and Polymerization." *Nature* 157 (1946): 102.

1946b: "Activation of Catalysts in Olefine Reactions." *Nature* 157 (1946): 520.

1946c: With A. G. Evans and G. W. Meadows: "Friedel-Crafts Catalysts and Polymerization." *Nature* 158 (1946): 94–95. Also in *Rubber Chemistry and Technology* 20 (1947): 357–358.

1946d: "Soviets and Capitalism: What is the Difference?" *Time and Tide* (April 6, 1946): 317.

1946e: "Social Capitalism." *Time and Tide* (April 13, 1946): 341–342.

1946f: "Can Science Bring Peace?" *The Listener* (April 25, 1946). Also in *The Challenge of Our Time*, ed. Grace Wyndham Goldie; London: Percival Marshall, 1948.

1946g: "The Foundations of Freedom in Science." *Bulletin of Atomic Scientists* 2 (December 1, 1946): 6–7. Also in *The Nineteenth Century* 141 (April 1947): 163–167 and *Physical Science and Human Values*, ed. E. P. Wigner, 124–143; Princeton: Princeton University Press, 1947.

1946h: "Social Message of Pure Science." *The Advancement of Science* 12 (April 1946): 3–8. Also in LL, 3–7.

1946i: "Re-Dedication of Science in Germany." *Nature* 158 (July 13, 1946): 66.

1946j: "Why Profits." *The Plain View* 8 (July 1946): 197–208. Also as "Profits and Polycentricity" in *Humanitas* (Autumn 1946): 138–153. Also in LL, 138–153.

1946k: *Science, Faith and Society.* The Riddell Memorial Lectures, University of Durham. London: Oxford University Press, 1946; Chicago: Chicago University Press, 1946. Reprinted, Chicago and London: Phoenix Books, The University of Chicago Press, 1964.

1946l: "The Policy of Atomic Science." *Time and Tide* (August 10, 1946): 749.

1946m: "Science: Academic and Industrial." *Universities Quarterly* (November 1946): 71–76.

1946n: "Free Trade through Full Employment." *University Liberal* 3 (December 1946): 1–2.

1947

1947a: "Old Tasks and New Hopes." *Time and Tide* (January 4, 1947): 5–6.

1947b: "Science: Observation and Belief." *Humanitas* 1 (February 1947): 10–15. Also in SEP, 215–223.

1947c: "Countering Inflation: Problems of a Labour Government." *The Manchester Guardian* (March 3, 1947). Also in *Full Employment and Free Trade*, 2nd edition.

1947d: With A. G. Evans: "Polymerization of iso-Butene by Friedel-Crafts Catalysts." *Journal of the Chemical Society* (1947): 252–257.

1947e: With P. H. Plesch and H. A. Skinner: "The Low Temperature Polymerization of iso-Butene by Friedel-Crafts Catalysts." *Journal of the Chemical Society* (1947): 257–267.

1947f: "Organization of Universities I." *Time and Tide* (July 19, 1947): 777.

1947g: "Organization of Universities II." *Time and Tide* (July 26, 1947): 802–803.

1947h: With A. G. Evans and M. G. Evans: "Mechanism of Substitution at a Saturated Carbon Atom." *Journal of the Chemical Society* (1947): 558–559.

1947i: With A. G. Evans and G. W. Meadows: "Polymerization of Olefines by Friedel-Crafts Catalysts." *Nature* 160 (1947): 869.

1947j: "The Foundations of Academic Freedom." *Publications of the Society for Freedom in Science*, Occasional Pamphlet 6 (September 1947): 1–18. Also abbreviated in *The Lancet* (May 3, 1947): 583–586 and revised in LL, 32–48.

1947k: "What Kind of Crisis?" *Time and Tide* (October 4, 1947): 1056–1058.

1947l: "What to Believe." *Credere Aude* 1 (December 1947): 9–10.

1948

1948a: "Polymerization at Low Temperatures." *Zeitschrift für Angewandte Chemie* 60A (1948): 76–77.

1948b: "The Universities Today." *The Adelphi* 14 (January–March 1948): 98–101.

1948c: Review of *The Free Society*, by Middleton Murry, *Time and Tide* (13 March 1948): 255–256.

1948d: "The Place of Universities in the Community." Report of a discussion in *The Advancement of Science* 5 (April 1948): 13–15.

1948e: "Science in Germany." *The Manchester Guardian* (July 30, 1948).

1948f: "Ought Science to Be Planned? The Case for Individualism." *The Listener* (September 16, 1948). Also in *Bulletin of Atomic Scientists* 5 (January 1949): 17–19, 19–20. As "Planned Science," a BBC Broadcast (September 1948). Revised in LL, 86–90.

1948g: "Planning and Spontaneous Order." *The Manchester School* 16 (September 1948): 237–268. As "The Span of Central Direction" in LL, 111–137.

1948h: "Profits and Private Enterprise." In *Economic Problems in a Free Society*, 50–62. London: Central Joint Advisory Committee on Tutorial Classes, 1948. Also in SEP, 145–156.

1949

1949a: "Mechanism of Chemical Reactions." *Endeavour* 8 (1949): 3–10.

1949b: "Experimental Proofs of Hyperconjugation." *Journale de Chimie Physique* 46 (1949): 235–241.

1949c: "The Nature of Scientific Conventions." *Nineteenth Century* 146 (July 1949): 14–27. Also in *Bulletin of the Atomic Scientists* 6 (January 1950): 38–42. Expanded in LL, 8–31.

1949d: "The Authority of the Free Society." *Nineteenth Century* 146 (December 1949): 347–360.

1950

1950a: "Economic and Intellectual Liberties." *Zeitschrift für die gesamte Staatswissenschaft* 106 Heft 3 (1950): 411–447. Also as "Manageability of Social Tasks" in LL, 154–200.

1950b: "Freedom in Science." *Bulletin of Atomic Scientists* 6 (July 1950): 195–198, 224.

1950c: "Der Glaube an die Wissenschaft." *Physikalische Blätter* 6 Heft 8 (1950): 337–349.

1950d: "The Logic of Liberty: Perils of Inconsistency." *Measure* 1 (Autumn 1950): 348–362. Also in LL, 93–110.

1950e: "Scientific Beliefs." *Ethics* 61 (October 1950): 27–37.

1950f: Review of *Testament for Social Science*, by Barbara Wootton (November 15, 1950).

1951

1951a: "Salvation by Science?" Broadcast on BBC, Third Programme (January 18, 1951).

1951b: "The Hypothesis of Cybernetics." *The British Journal for the Philosophy of Science* 2 (February 1951): 312–315. Also in SEP, 309–312.

1951c: "Die Freiheit der Wissenschaft." *Physikalische Blätter* Jahrgang 7 Heft 2 (1951): 49–55.

1951d: "Autorität und Freiheit in der Wissenschaft." *Physikalische Blätter*, Jahrgang 7 Heft 3 (1951): 97–102.

1951e: "Totalitarianism," review of *Origins of Totalitarianism*, by Hannah Arendt, *Time and Tide* (August 25, 1951): 801–802.

1951f: *The Logic of Liberty*. London: Routledge and Kegan Paul, 1951; Chicago: Chicago University Press, 1951.

1952

1952a: "Why? What For?" review of *Conspiracy of Silence*, by Alex Weissberg (March 20, 1952).

1952b: "Some British Experiences. I. Michael Polanyi." *Bulletin of Atomic Scientists* 8 (October 10, 1952): 223–228.

1952c: "Science and Faith." *Question* 5 (Winter 1952): 16–36, 37–45. Also as "Science and Conscience" in *Religion in Life* 23 (Winter 1953–1954): 47–58 as and in *Uj Látáhatár* (1954): 207–214.

1952d: "The Stability of Beliefs." *The British Journal for the Philosophy of Science* 3 (November 1952): 217–232.

1952e: "Mannheim's Historicism," review of *Essays on the Sociology of Knowledge*, by Karl Mannheim, *The Manchester Guardian* (December 9, 1952).

1952f: "Skills and Connoisseurship." *Atti del Congresse di Metodologia*, Torino (December 17–20, 1952): 381–394.

1953

1953a: "Pure and Applied Science and Their Appropriate Forms of Organization," *Science and Freedom: Proceedings of a Conference Convened by the Congress for Cultural Freedom*, Hamburg (1953). Also in *Publications of the Society for Freedom in Science, Occasional Pamphlet*, 14 (December 1953), 36–46 (London: Martin

Secker and Warburg, 1955). Also in *Science and Freedom* (Boston: The Beacon Press, 1955). Revised in *Dialectica* 10 (September 1956): 231–241.

1953b: "Protests and Problems." *Bulletin of Atomic Scientists* 9 (November 1953): 322–340.

1953c: "The Power of Social Illusions." *Christian Newsletter* (November 1953). Also in *New Leader* (November 16, 1953).

1954

1954a: "On the Introduction of Science into Moral Subjects." *The Cambridge Journal* 7 (January 1954): 195–207.

1954b: "A Letter from the Chairman." *Science and Freedom: A Bulletin of the Committee on Science and Freedom* (1954): 1.

1954c: "Hide and Seek," review of *The Invisible Writing*, by Arthur Koestler, *Time and Tide* (July 3, 1954): 886–887.

1954d: "Foundations of Morality," review of *Realms of Value*, by Ralph Barton Perry, *The Manchester Guardian* (September 17, 1954).

1954e: "Sociology Surveyed," review of *Science and Social Action*, by W. J. H. Sprott, *Manchester Guardian* (November 3, 1954).

1954f: Review of *Science and the Common Understanding*, by J. Robert Oppenheimer, *Manchester Guardian* (September 1954).

1955

1955a: "On Liberalism and Liberty." *Encounter* 4 (March, 1955): 29–34. Also in SEP, 199–209.

1955b: "From Copernicus to Einstein." *Encounter* 5 (September 1955): 54–63.

1955c: "Words, Conceptions and Science." *The Twentieth Century* 158 (September 1955): 256–267.

1955d: "Preface." *Science and Freedom: Proceedings of a Conference Convened by the Congress for Cultural Freedom, Hamburg, 1953*, ed. George Polanyi, 9–11. London: Martin Secker and Warburg, 1955.

1956

1956a: "This Age of Discovery." *The Twentieth Century* 159 (March 1956): 227–234.

1956b: "Passion and Controversy in Science." *The Lancet* (June 16, 1956): 921–924. Also in *Bulletin of Atomic Scientists* 13 (April 1957): 114–119. Also in Alexander Vavoulis and A. Wayne Colver, eds., *Science and Society: Selected Essays*, 95–103. San Francisco: Holden-Day, 1966.

1956c: "Ethics and the Scientist." *The Bulletin of the Institute of Physics* (July 1956): 1–21.

1956d: " 'The Magic of Marxism' and 'The Next Stage of History.' " Special Supplement to *The Bulletin of the Committee on Science and Freedom* (November 1956).

1956e: "The Magic of Marxism." *Bulletin of Atomic Scientists* 12 (June 1956): 211–214, 232. Also in *Encounter* 7 (December, 1956): 5–17. Translated as "Die Magie des Marxismus." *Der Monat* 11 (December 1958): 3–15.

1956f: "What is Truth?" review of *Society and Knowledge*, in *Society and Knowledge*, 1956.

1957

1957a: "Scientific Outlook: Its Sickness and Cure." *Science* 125 (March 15, 1957): 480–484.

1957b: "Oscar Jászi and Hungarian Liberalism." *Science and Freedom* 8 (April 1957).

1957c: "Problem Solving." *The British Journal for the Philosophy of Science* 8 (August 1957): 89–103.

1957d: "Beauty, Elegance and Reality in Science." *Symposium on Observation and Interpretation, Bristol, April 1, 1957*, ed. S. Körner, 102–106. London: Butterworths Scientific Publications, Autumn 1957.

1957e: "The Foolishness of History: November 1917–November 1957." *Encounter* 9 (November 1957): 33–37. Also in SEP, 157–163.

1957f: "Science and Morality." *Uj Látóhatár* (1957): 337–342.

1958

1958a: "Apartheid and the World's Universities." *A Bulletin of the Committee on Science and Freedom* 10 (February 10, 1958).

1958b: "On Biassed Coins and Related Problems." *Zeitschrift für physikalische Chemie, Neue Folge, Bonhoeffer-Gedenkband* 15 (1958): 290–296.

1958c: *Personal Knowledge*. London: Routledge and Kegan Paul, 1958; Chicago: Chicago University Press, 1958. London: Torch Books, 1964.

1958d: "The Impact of Science." (Text of a BBC broadcast, June 27, 1958) *Quest* (Bombay, 1958): 32–35.

1958e: "Editorial." *A Bulletin of the Committee on Science and Freedom*, 11.

1958f: "Tyranny and Freedom, Ancient and Modern." *Quest* (Bombay, 1958): 9–18.

1959

1959a: Review of *Darwin and The Darwininan Revolution*, by G. Himmelfarb, *The New Leader* (August 31, 1959): 24.

1959b: "The Two Cultures." *Encounter* 13 (September 1959): 1–4. Also in KB, 40–46.

1959c: *The Study of Man: The Lindsay Memorial Lectures 1958*. University College of North Staffordshire, 1959. London: Routledge and Kegan Paul, 1959. Chicago: Chicago University Press, 1959. Chicago: Phoenix Books, 1964.

1959d: "A Philosophy of Perception," review of *The Nature of Experience*, by Sir Russell. *Brain* 82 (1959).

1959e: "The Organization of Science and the Claim to Academic Freedom." *Science and Freedom*, 13 (November 1959): 1–9. Also in *The Scholar and Society* (1959).

1959f: "Commentary on 'The Genesis of the Special Theory of Relativity' " by Adolph Grünbaum, *Current Issues in the Philosophy of Science: Symposia of Scientists and Philosophers*, ed. Herbert Feigl and Grover Maxwell, 53–55. New York: Holt, Rinehart and Winston, 1959 [1961].

1960

1960a: "An Epic Theory of Evolution," review of *The Phenomenon of Man*, by Pierre
    Teilhard de Chardin, *Saturday Review* 43 (January 30, 1960): 21.
1960b: *Beyond Nihilism. The Eddington Lecture, February 16, 1960.* London: Cam-
    bridge University Press, 1960. Also in *Encounter* 14 (March 1960): 34–43. Also
    in *History and Hope: Progress in Freedom. The Berlin Conference of 1960,* ed.
    K. A. Jelenski, New York: A. Praeger, 1962, 17–35. Also in *Crisis and Continuity
    in World Politics,* ed. George A. Lanyi and Wilson C. McWilliams, Random
    House, 1966, 214–227. Also as *Jenseits des Nihilismus,* translated by Irmela Nitz,
    Dordrecht and Stuttgart: Reidel, 1961. Also in KB, 3–23.
1960c: "Lecomte du Noüy Foundation Award to Michael Polanyi," acceptance
    speech. *The Christian Scholar* 43 (March 1960): 57–58.
1960d: "Freedom and Responsibility." *Science and Freedom* 11 (April 12, 1960).
1960e: "Congress for Cultural Freedom." Closing address of the Tenth Anniversary
    Session of the General Assembly of the Congress held at Berlin on June 22,
    1960. *Congress for Cultural Freedom* (1960): 1–6.
1960f: "Der Sinn des Ungarnaufstandes." *Der Monat* (October 1960). Translated as
    "The Message of the Hungarian Revolution," *Christianity and Crisis* 26 (Oc-
    tober 1966): 240–243. Also in *The American Scholar* 35 (Autumn 1966): 661–
    676. Also in *Anatomy of Knowledge,* ed. Marjorie Grene (London: Routledge and
    Kegan Paul, 1969; 149–165). Also in KB, 24–39.
1960g: "Towards a Theory of Conspicuous Producton." *Soviet Survey* 34 (October–
    December 1960): 90–99. Also as "Conspicuous Production." *Quest* (Bombay)
    41 (April–June 1964): 16–21. Also in SEP, 165–181.
1960h: "Morals—A Product of Evolution," review of *The Ethical Animal,* by
    C. H. Waddington. *The New Scientist* (December 1960): 1666–1667.

1961

1961a: "The Study of Man." *Quest* 29 (1961): 26–34.
1961b: "Science: Academic and Industrial." *Journal of the Institute of Metallurgy* 89
    (1961): 401–406.
1961c: "Faith and Reason." *Journal of Religion* 41, No. 4 (October 1961): 237–247.
    Also as "Scientific Revolution." *The Student World* 54, No. 3 (1961): 287–302.
    Also in *Christians in a Technological Era,* ed. Hugh C. White, Jr. New York:
    Seabury Press, 1964. Also in SEP, 329–343.
1961d: "Knowing and Being." *Mind* 70 (October 1961): 458–470. Also in KB, 123–137.
1961e: "The Unaccountable Element in Science." *Transactions of the Bose Research
    Institute* (Calcutta) 24, No. 4 (December 1961): 175–184. Also in *Philosophy* 37,
    No. 139 (January 1962): 1–14. Also in *Philosophy Today* 6 (Autumn 1962): 171–
    182. Also in KB, 105–120.

1962

1962a: "History and Hope: An Analysis of Our Age." *The Virginia Quarterly Review*
    38, 2 (Spring 1962): 177–195. Also in SEP, 79–93.

1962b: "The Republic of Science. Its Political and Economic Theory." *Minerva* 1 (October 1962): 54–73. Also in 1968e. Also in KB, 49–72.

1962c: "Tacit Knowing: Its Bearing on Some Problems of Philosophy." *Reviews of Modern Physics*, 34 (October 1962): 601–616. Also in *Philosophy Today* 6 (Winter 1962): 239–262. Also in KB, 159–180.

1962d: "Clues to an Understanding of Mind and Body." In *The Scientist Speculates*, ed. I. J. Good, 71–78. New York: Basic Books, London: Heinemann, 1962.

1962e: "Commentary on the 'The Uses of Dogmatism in Science'" by Thomas Kuhn. In *The Structure of Scientific Change*, ed. A. G. Crombie, 375–380. London: Heinemann, 1962.

1962f: "My Time with X-Rays and Crystals." In *Fifty Years of X-Ray Diffraction*, ed. P. P. Ewald, 629–636. Utrecht: A. Oosthoek, 1962. Also in KB, 97–104.

1962g: "The Terry Lectures." Yale University, 1962. Mimeographed for private circulation.

1962h: "A Postscript," in *History and Hope: Progress in Freedom. The Berlin Conference of 1960*, ed. K. A. Jelenski. New York: A. Praeger, 1962; 185–196. Also in SEP, 95–106.

1963

1963a: "Science and Religion: Separate Dimensions or Common Ground?" *Philosophy Today* 7 (Spring 1963): 4–14.

1963b: "The Potential Theory of Adsorption: Authority in Science Has Its Uses and Dangers." *Science* 141 (September 1963): 1010–1013. Also in KB, 87–96.

1963c: "Experience and Perception of Pattern." In *The Modeling of Mind*, ed. K. M. Sayre and F. J. Crosson, 207–220. Notre Dame, Indiana: Notre Dame Press, 1963. Same as 1961e, "The Unaccountable Element in Science."

1964

1964a: "The Feelings of Machines." *Encounter* 22 (January 1964): 85–86.

1964b: "Background and Prospect." Preface to new edition of *Science, Faith and Society*, 7–19. Chicago: Phoenix Books, 1964.

1964c: Preface to *Personal Knowledge*. Oxford: Torch Book Edition, 1964.

1964d: "Science and Man's Place in the Universe." In *Science as a Cultural Force*, ed. Harry Woolf, 54–76. Baltimore: Johns Hopkins Press, 1964. London: Oxford University Press, 1965.

1965

1965a: "On the Modern Mind." *Encounter* 24 (May 1965): 12–20.

1965b: "The Structure of Consciousness." *Brain* 88 (September 1965): 12–20. Also as "The Body–Mind Relation," as delivered at Yale, December 10, 1965. Mimeographed. Also in *Man and the Science of Man*, ed. William R. Coulson and C. R. Rogers, 85–102. Columbus, Ohio: Charles Merrill Pub. Co., 1968. Also in KB, 211–224. Also in *Anatomy of Knowledge*, ed. Marjorie Grene (London: Routledge and Kegan Paul, 1969), 315–328. Also in SEP, 313–328.

1966

1966a: "The Logic of Tacit Inference: Address to the International Congress for the Philosophy of Science in Jerusalem on August 25, 1964." *Philosophy* 41 (January 1966): 369–386. Also in KB, 138–158.

1966b: "The Creative Imagination." *Chemical and Engineering News* 44 (April 1966): 85–93. Also in *Tri-Quarterly* (Winter 1967): 11–124. Also in *Toward a Unity of Knowledge*, ed. Marjorie Grene, *Psychological Issues*, Monograph 22, 6, no. 2 (1969): 53–71. Also as "Schöpferische Einbildungskraft," *Zeitschrift für philosophische Forschung*, 1968. Also in SEP, 249–265.

1966c: *Michael Polanyi and Carl Rogers: A Dialogue.* Transcript of televised dialogue, San Diego: San Diego State Profile, 1966.

1966d: " 'Polanyi's Logic' by Gwynn Nettler—Answer by M. Polanyi." *Encounter* 27 (September 1966): 92. Also in SEP, 345–346.

1966e: *The Tacit Dimension. The Terry Lectures, Yale University, 1962.* London: Routledge and Kegan Paul; Garden City, NY: Doubleday, 1966.

1966f: "On Reading *The Edge of Objectivity* by Charles Gillespie." *Forum for Correspondence and Contact* (1966): 23–27.

1967

1967a: "The Growth of Science in Society." *Minerva* (Summer 1967): 533–545. Also in 1968e and 1968f. Also in KB, 73–86.

1967b: "Life Transcending Physics and Chemistry." *Chemical and Engineering News* 45 (August 1967): 54–66. Also in SEP, 283–303.

1967c: "Science and Reality." *British Journal for the Philosophy of Science* 18 (1967): 177–196. Also in SEP, 225–247.

1967d: "Sense-Giving and Sense-Reading." *Philosophy* 42 (October 1967): 301–325. Also as *Sinngebung und Sinndeutung* in *Das Problem der Sprache*, 1967. Also in *Intellect and Hope*, ed. T. A. Langford and W. H. Poteat. Durham, NC: Duke University Press, 1968. Also in KB, 181–207.

1967e: "The Society of Explorers." *Encounter*, 1967.

1968

1968a: "Logic and Psychology." *The American Psychologist* 12 (January 1968): 27–43.

1968b: "Wider die Skepsis des Modernen Denkens." *Gehört gelesen* (January 1968): 28–40.

1968c: "A Conversation with Michael Polanyi." Interview by Mary Harrington Hall. *Psychology Today* 1 (May 1968): 20–25, 65–67.

1968d: "Life's Irreducible Structures." *Science* 160 (June 1968): 1309–1312. Also in KB, 225–239.

1968e: "The Growth of Science in Society" and "The Republic of Science." In *Criteria for Scientific Development, Public Policy and National Goals*, ed. E. Shils. Cambridge, MA: Massachusetts Institute of Technology, 1968.

1968f: "The Growth of Science in Society" and "The Body–Mind Relation," with discussion. Contributing authors: Michael Polanyi, Jacob Bronowski, and Carl

Rogers. In *Man and the Science of Man*, ed. William R. Coulson and
C. R. Rogers. Columbus, Ohio: Charles Merrill Pub. Co., 1968.

1968g: "Symposium: Do Life Processes Transcend Physics and Chemistry?" *Zygon*
3–4 (December 1968): 442–472.

1969

1969a: "On Body and Mind." *The New Scholasticism* 43 (1969): 195–204.

1969b: "The Determinants of Social Action." In *Roads to Freedom: Festschrift for*
F. A. von Hayek, ed. Erich Streissler, 165–179. London: Routledge and Kegan Paul,
1969. New York: Augustus M. Kelly Publishers, 1969. Also in SEP, 183–197.

1969c: *Knowing and Being: Essays by Michael Polanyi*, ed. Marjorie Grene. London:
Routledge and Kegan Paul, 1969; Chicago: University of Chicago Press, 1969.

1969d: "Objectivity in Science—a Dangerous Illusion." *Scientific Research*. April 28, 1969.

1970

1970a: "Reflections on Viewing a Painting." Foreword to *Optics, Painting and*
Photography, by M. H. Pirenne. Cambridge: Cambridge University Press, 1970.

1970b: "Transcendence and Self-Transcendence." *Soundings*, 53, no. 1 (Spring
1970): 88–94. Also in *Science et conscience de la société*, ed. J. C. Casanova.
France: Calmann-Levy, 1971.

1970c: "What is a Painting?" *British Journal of Aesthetics*, 10, no. 3 (July 1970): 225–
236. Also in *The American Scholar*, 39, no. 4 (Autumn 1970): 655–669. Also in
SEP, 347–359.

1970d: "Science and Man." *Proceedings of the Royal Society of Medicine* 58 (September
1970): 969–976.

1970e: "Why Did We Destroy Europe?" *Studium Generale*, 23, no. 20 (October
1970): 909–916. Also in *Knowledge in Search of Understanding: The Frensham*
Pond Papers, ed. Paul Weiss (Mount Kisco, New York: Futura Publishing, 1975).
Also in SEP, 107–115.

1971

1971: "Genius in Science." *Archives de Philosphie, Colloque de L'Academie Inter-*
nationale de Philosophie des Sciences. Lausanne, Septembre 2–9, 1969, 34, no. 4
(Octobre–Décembre 1971): 593–607. Also in *De La Méthode: Méthodologie*
Particulières et Méthodologique en Général. Archives de l'Institut International des
Sciences Théoriques. Office International de Librairie (1972), 11–25. Also in
Boston Studies in the Philosophy of Science, 14: 57–71. Also in *Encounter* 38
(January 1972): 43–50. Also in SEP, 267–281.

1974

1974a: *Scientific Thought and Social Reality: Essays by Michael Polanyi*. Ed. Fred
Schwartz. *Psychological Issues*, Monograph 32, 8, no. 4. New York: International
Universities Press, 1974.

1974b: "Discoveries of Science." *Science Philosophie Foi: Colloque de l'Académie Internationale de Philosophie des Sciences*, 71–76. Beauchesne, Paris, 1974.

1975

1975a: "Polanyi, Michael (March 11, 1891–)." *World Authors, 1950–1970*, ed. John Wakeman, 1151–1153. Wilson: New York, 1975.
1975b: With Harry Prosch: *Meaning*. Chicago: University of Chicago Press, 1975.
1975c: With Harry Prosch: "Truth in Myths." In *Cross Currents*, 25, no. 2 (1975): 149–162.

1981

1981: "Forms of Atheism." *Convivium* 13 (1981): 5–13.

Index

academic community
  atomic warfare opposed by, 232
  attracted to Marxism, 227–228
  autonomy in, 268
  and cafeteria attitude, 115
  continuum of humanities and
    sciences in, 231–233, 245, 249, 251,
    257–259, 262
  conviviality in, 159, 229, 249–250,
    260, 290
  freedom in, 202–203, 228, 244, 287
  and the idea of a university, 232,
    245, 273
  and obligations of intelligence, 166,
    232–233, 236
  reality greater than disciplines in,
    245, 258–260
  research first priority in, 138
  serves civilization, 166, 197, 206,
    208, 271, 273
  specialization in, 249
  and spiritual realities, 203
  vision needed in, 273
Adams, Douglas, 255
Adler, Alfred, 18
adsorption, 24–25
  and activation energy, 111
  attractive potential of, 107–108,
    111–112, 125–126
  and catalysis, 72, 111, 146–147
  chemisorption vs. physisorption,
    37, 112
  and dispersion forces, 125–126

  and electron mobility, 62–64, 111,
    125, 157
  genesis of theory of, 24–25, 31–32,
    34–36
  Ph.D. thesis on, 42–43
  vindication of theory of, 125–126, 207
  See also dipoles; kinetics; Langmuir
Ady, Endre, 17, 22, 294
aesthetics, 258
  and creativity, 260–261
  of metaphor, 270
  of music, 127, 266, 272
  of myth, 270, 272, 281–282, 291
  of painting, 18, 267, 270, 277
  of poetry, 17, 29
  and reality of art, 261, 270
  of symbols, 273–274, 281, 287–288
  See also imagination
Alexander, Franz, 16 n. 41, 18, 24, 122
Allen, J. H., 192
Allmand, Arthur John, 133–134, 137
Anderson, C. D., 137 n. 14
Antal, Frederick, 41
apprenticeship, 75–76, 241
Arendt, Hannah, 219
Argyle, Cecily, 276
Arnheim, Rudolf, 270
Aron, Raymond, 208 n. 178, 219, 270
Askenazy, Paul, 26
atheism, 212–214. *See also* Christianity;
  civilization; God
atomic reaction. *See* kinetics
Atomic Reactions, 124

Minta Gymnasium, 15–16, 24, 294
Moberly, Sir Walter, 135, 137–139, 197
Moelwyn-Hughes, E. A., 145
Monnerat, Jules, 224
Moore, Edward C., 231
Moot. *See* Oldham, Joseph H.
moral inversion
  a denial of values, 41, 198,
    227–228
  a destructive consciousness, 161
  a prophetic passion, 175, 177, 242
  See also Communism; knowledge;
    Marxism; nihilism; philosophy;
    socialism; social studies
morality, 104
  elevated by understanding, 162, 227,
    273–274
  independent of technology, 109, 234
  and meaning, 128, 218, 221
  and the moral person, 257
  personal judgments in, 224
  science as a model for, 22, 247, 262
  tradition of, 232, 249, 287
  universal obligations in, 232, 247
  See also civilization; economics; history;
    knowledge; moral inversion;
    philosophy; science; social studies
Morse, P. M., 117
Müller, H. J., 222
Mullins, Phil, 281 n. 6
Mure, G. E., 239
Murray, Henry, 260

Nabokov, Nicolas, 222
Nagel, Ernst, 222, 225
Namier, Lewis, 152, 165
nationalism, 23, 45–47, 234. *See also*
  civilization; history; social studies
Nernst, Walter, 21, 25, 64, 84–85
  heat theorem, 25–28, 30–31,
    35, 37
Newman, M., 215
Niebuhr, Reinhold, 202, 213, 262
nihilism
  a denial of meaning, 273–274
  a denial of values, 41–42, 242
  and doubt, 218
  of intellectuals, 127–128
  and models of science,
    285–286
  rationalistic, 18, 262
  See also civilization; doubt; knowledge;
    meaning; moral inversion; morality;
    objectivism; philosophy; rationalism
Novotny, Anna. *See* Polanyi, Ilona

objectivism
  dehumanizing, 244, 277, 280
  a self-defeating ideal, 218, 224, 227–228,
    230, 231, 236, 241, 251, 262,
    277, 285–286
Odier, Jeannette. *See* Chambaud, Jeannette
  Odier
Ogg, Richard A., Jr., 158
Oldham, Joseph H., 242, 289
  and the Moot, 196–197, 212, 289
  and *Personal Knowledge*, 229
  and *The Study of Man*, 232
Oliphant, Marcus L. E., 149
Oliver, Anna, 180
Olmsted, P. S., 107
Oman, John, 213
O'Neill, Hugh
  and economics film, 163
  friendship with, 143, 197–198,
    242, 289
  and Night of the Long Knives,
    152–153
  in wartime, 180
Ootuka, Haruo, 107
Oppenheimer, Robert, 225
Orowan, Egon, 127
Orr, John, 135
Osborne, Harold, 270

Paneth, Fritz, 39–40, 64, 123
Pantin, C. F. A., 260
Parker, L. K., 148
Pauli, Wolfgang, 63, 80
Pauling, Linus, 202
patents, 103, 115, 185. *See also* economics;
  science; technology
Peacocke, Arthur R., 284
Peierls, Sir Rudolf, 208 n. 177
Peirce, Charles S., 231
Pelzer, H., 123
Perelman, Chaim, 253
Perkins, Frank, 151
Perrin, Francis, 115
Personal Knowledge
  composition of, 196, 221, 224–230
  conclusion of, 290
  on conflicting visions, 38
  essays related to, 269
  honored, 249
  reviews of, 231, 257, 265
  and tacit knowledge, 187, 249
  See also Gifford Lectures
Peters, J., 82–83
Petöfi Circle, 228
Pfeifer, Ignatz, 25, 87